I0214766

THE

Compleat Housewife:

OR,

Accomplished Gentlewoman's COMPANION.

BEING

A COLLECTION of upwards of Six Hundred of the most approved RECEIPTS in

COOKERY,	CAKES,
PASTRY,	CREAMS,
CONFECTIONARY,	JELLIES,
PRESERVING,	MADE WINES,
PICKLES,	CORDIALS.

With COPPER PLATES, curiously engraven, for the regular Disposition or Placing of the various DISHES and COURSES.

AND ALSO

BILLS of FARE for every Month in the Year.

To which is added,

A COLLECTION of above Three Hundred Family RECEIPTS of MEDICINES; *viz. Drinks, Syrups, Salves, Ointments,* and various other Things of sovereign and approved Efficacy in most Distempers, Pains, Aches, Wounds, Sores, *&c.* particularly Mrs. *Stephens*'s Medicine for the Cure of the Stone and Gravel, and Dr. *Mead*'s famous Receipt for the Cure of a Bite of a mad Dog; with several other excellent Receipts for the same, which have cured when the Persons were disordered, and the salt Water fail'd; never before made publick; fit either for private Families, or such publick-spirited Gentlewomen as would be beneficent to their poor Neighbours.

WITH

DIRECTIONS for MARKETING

By *E. SMITH.*

The SIXTEENTH EDITION, with ADDITIONS.

LONDON:

Printed for C. HITCH and L. HAWES, JOHN RIVINGTON, JAMES RIVINGTON and J. FLETCHER, J. WARD, W. JOHNSTON, S. CROWDER, P. DAVEY and B. LAW, T. LONGMAN, C. WARE, and M. COOPER. MDCCLVIII.

Price FIVE SHILLINGS.

The COMPLEAT HOUSEWIFE. *frontespiece*

Printed for R. Ware, T. Longman, S. Birt, C. Hitch, J. Hodges, J. & J. Rivington, J. Ward, W. Johnston, & M. Cooper.

PREFACE.

IT *being grown as unfashionable for a Book now to appear to People without a Preface, as for a Lady to appear at a Ball without a Hoop-Petticoat; I shall conform to Custom for Fashion sake, and not through any Necessity: The Subject being both common and universal, needs no Arguments to introduce it, and being so necessary for the Gratification of the Appetite, stands in need of no Encomiums to allure Persons to the Practice of it, since there are but few now-a-days who love not good Eating and Drinking; therefore I intirely quit those two Topics; but having three or four Pages to be filled up previous to the Subject itself, I shall employ them on a Subject I think new, and not yet handled by any of the Pretenders to the Art of Cookery; and that is, the Antiquity of it; which, if it either instruct or divert, I shall be satisfied if you are so.*

COOKERY, Confectionary, *&c. like all other Arts, had their Infancy, and did not arrive at a State of Maturity but by slow Degrees, various Experiments, and a long Track of Time; for in the Infant Age of the World, when the new Inhabitants contented themselves with the simple Provision of Nature,* viz. *the Vegetable Diet, the Fruits and Productions of the Earth, as they* *succeeded one another in their several peculiar Seasons the Art of Cookery was unknown: Apples, Nuts, and Herbs, were both Meat and Sauce, and Mankind stood in no need of additional Sauces, Ragoos,* &c. *to procure a good Appetite; for a healthful and vigorous Constitution, a clear, wholesome, odoriferous Air, moderate Exercise, and an Exemption from anxious Cares, always supplied them with it.*

WE read of no palled Appetites, but such as proceeded from the Decays of Nature by reason of an advanced Old-Age; but on the contrary, a craving Stomach even upon a Death-bed, as in Isaac; *nor no Sicknesses, but those that were both the first and the last, which proceeded from the Struggles of Nature, which abhorred the Separation of Soul and Body; no Physicians to prescribe for the Sick, nor Apothecaries to compound Medicines, for two thousand Years and upwards; Food and Physic were one and the same Thing.*

BUT when Man began to pass from a Vegetable to an Animal Diet, and feed on Flesh, Fowls and Fish, then Seasonings grew necessary, both to render it more palatable and savoury, and also to preserve that Part which was not immediately spent from Stinking and Corruption; and probably Salt was the first Seasoning discovered; for of Salt we read, Gen. xiv.

AND this seems to be necessary, especially for those who are advanced in Age, whose Palates, with their Bodies, had lost their Vigor as to Taste; whose digestive Faculty grew weak and impotent; and thence proceeded the Use of Soops and savoury Messes; so that COOKERY *then began to be in use, tho'* LUXURY *had not brought it to the Height of an ART. Thus we read, that* Jacob *made such palatable Pottage, that* Esau *purchased a Mess of it at the extravagant Price of his Birth-right. And* Isaac, *before, by his last Will and Testament, he bequeathed his Blessing to his Son* Esau, *required him to make some*

ſome ſavoury Meat, ſuch as his Soul loved; i. e. *ſuch as was reliſhable to his blunted Appetite.*

SO that Seaſonings of ſome ſort were then in uſe; though, whether they were Salt, ſavoury Herbs, or Roots only, or Spices, the Fruits of Trees, ſuch as Pepper, Cloves, Nutmegs; Bark, as Cinnamon; Roots, as Ginger, &c. *I ſhall not determine.*

AS for the Methods of the Cookery of thoſe Times, Boiling or Stewing ſeems to have been the principal; Broiling or Roaſting the next; beſides which, I preſume ſcarce any other were uſed for two thouſand Years and more; for I remember no other in the Hiſtory of Geneſis.

THAT Eſau *was the firſt Cook, I ſhall not preſume to aſſert; for* Abraham *gave Orders to dreſs a fatted Calf; but* Eſau *is the firſt Perſon mentioned that made any Advances beyond plain Dreſſing, as Boiling, Roaſting,* &c. *For tho' we find, indeed, that* Rebecca, *his Mother, was accompliſhed with the Skill of making ſavoury Meat as well as he, yet whether he learned it from her, or ſhe from him, is a Queſtion too knotty for me to determine.*

BUT Cookery *did not long remain a bare Piece of Houſewifery, or Family Oeconomy; but in Proceſs of Time, when Luxury entered the World, it grew to an Art, nay a Trade: For in* 1 Sam. viii. 13. *when the* Iſraelites *grew Faſhioniſts, and would have a King, that they might be like the reſt of their Neighbours, we read of Cooks, Confectioners,* &c.

THIS Art being of univerſal Uſe, and in conſtant Practice, has been ever ſince upon the Improvement; and we may, I think, with good Reaſon believe it is arrived at its greateſt Height and Perfection, if it is not got beyond it, even to its Declenſion; for whatſoever new, upſtart, out-of-the-way Meſſes ſome Humouriſts have invented, ſuch as ſtuffing a roaſted Leg of Mutton with pickled Herring, and the like, are only the Sallies of a capricious

Appetite, and debauching rather than improving the Art itſelf.

THE Art of Cookery, &c. *is indeed diverſified, according to the Diverſity of Nations or Countries, and to treat of it in that Latitude, would fill an unportable Volume, and rather confound than improve thoſe who would accompliſh themſelves with it: I ſhall therefore confine what I have to communicate within the Limits of Practicalneſs and Uſefulneſs; and ſo within the Compaſs of a Manual, that ſhall neither burthen the Hands to hold, the Eyes in reading, nor the Mind in conceiving.*

WHAT you will find in the following Sheets, are Directions generally for dreſſing after the beſt, moſt natural and wholeſome Manner, ſuch Proviſions as are the Product of our own Country; and in ſuch a Manner as is moſt agreeable to Engliſh *Palates; ſaving that I have ſo far temporized, as, ſince we have, to our Diſgrace, ſo fondly admired the* French *Tongue,* French *Modes, and alſo* French *Meſſes, to preſent you now and then with ſuch Receipts of the* French *Cookery as I think may not be diſagreeable to* Engliſh *Palates.*

THERE are indeed already in the World various Books that treat on this Subject, and which bear great Names, as Cooks to Kings, Princes, and Noblemen, and from which one might juſtly expect ſomething more than many, if not moſt of thoſe I have read, perform; but found myſelf deceived in my Expectations; for many of them to us are impracticable, others whimſical, others unpalatable, unleſs to depraved Palates; ſome unwholeſome; many Things copied from old Authors, and recommended, without (as I am perſuaded) the Copiers ever having had any Experience of the Palatableneſs, or had any Regard to the Wholeſomeneſs of them; which two Things ought to be the ſtanding Rules, that no Pretenders to Cookery ought to deviate from. And I cannot

not but believe, that these celebrated Performers, notwithstanding all their Professions of having ingenuously communicated their Art, industriously concealed their best Receipts from the Public.

BUT what I here present the World with, is the Product of my own Experience, and that for the Space of Thirty Years and upwards; during which Time I have been constantly employed in fashionable and noble Families, in which the Provisions ordered according to the following Directions, have had the general Approbation of such as have been at many noble Entertainments.

THESE Receipts are all suitable to English *Constitutions, and* English *Palates, wholesome, toothsome, all practicable and easy to be performed; here are those proper for a frugal, and also for a sumptuous Table; and if rightly observed, will prevent the spoiling of many a good Dish of Meat, the Waste of many good Materials, the Vexation that frequently attends such Mismanagements, and the Curses not unfrequently bestowed on Cooks, with the usual Reflection, that whereas* God sends good Meat, the Devil sends Cooks.

AS to those Parts that treat of Confectionary, Pickles, Cordials, English *Wines,* &c. *what I have said in relation to Cookery, is equally applicable to them also.*

IT is true, I have not been so numerous in Receipts, as some who have gone before me; but I think I have made Amends, in giving none but what are approved and practicable, and fit either for a genteel or a noble Table; and although I have omitted odd and fantastical Messes, yet I have set down a considerable Number of Receipts.

PREFACE.

THE Treatise is divided into ten Parts: Cookery contains above an hundred Receipts; Pickles, fifty; Puddings above fifty; Pastry, above forty; Cakes, forty; Creams and Jellies, above forty; Preserving, an hundred; made Wines, forty; cordial Waters and Powders, above seventy; Medicines and Salves, above three hundred; in all near eight hundred.

I HAVE likewise presented you with Schemes, engraven on Copper-plates, for the regular Disposition or Placing of the Dishes of Provision on the Table, according to the best Manner, both for Summer and Winter, first and second Courses, &c.

AS for the Receipts for Medicines, Salves, Ointments, good in several Diseases, Wounds, Hurts, Bruises, Aches, Pains, &c. *which amount to above three hundred, they are generally Family Receipts, that have never been made public, excellent in their Kind, and approved Remedies, which have not been obtained by me without much Difficulty, and of such Efficacy in Distempers,* &c. *to which they are appropriated, that they have cured when all other Means have failed; and a few of them, which I have communicated to a Friend, have procured a very handsome Livelihood.*

THEY are very proper for those generous, charitable, and christian Gentlewomen, who have a Disposition to be serviceable to their poor Country Neighbours, labouring under any of the afflicting Circumstances mentioned; who by making the Medicines, and generously contributing as Occasions offer, may help the Poor in their Afflictions, gain their Good-Will and Wishes, entitle themselves to their Blessings and Prayers, and also have the Pleasure of seeing the Good they do in this World, and have good Reason to hope for a Reward (though not by way of Merit) in the World to come.

AS

PREFACE.

AS the Whole of this Collection has cost me much Pains, and a thirty Years diligent Application, and as I have had Experience of their Use and Efficacy, I hope they will be as kindly accepted, as by me they are generously offered to the Public; and if they prove to the Advantage of many, the End will be answered that is proposed by her that is ready to serve the Public in what she may.

IT may be necessary to observe, that the Proprietors, being desirous of rendering this Edition as complete and useful as possible, have (besides many new Receipts) added Directions for Marketing, or the best Method of chusing Butcher's Meat, Fish, Fowl, &c. *also Directions for Boiling, Roasting, Broiling,* &c. *which were wanting in the former Impressions. And, as these Additions have rendered the Work more beneficial and useful, it is to be hoped that this Edition will meet with as favourable a Reception from the Public as any of the former.*

A BILL

A Bill *of* Fare *for every Season of the Year.*

For January.

First Course.

COllar of Brawn
Bisque of Fish
Soop with Vermicelly
Orange Pudding with Patties
Chine and Turkey
Lamb Pasty
Roasted Pullets with Eggs
Oyster Pye
Roasted Lamb in Joints
Grand Sallad with Pickles.

Second Course.

Wild Fowl of all Sorts
Chine of Salmon boiled with Smelts
Fruit of all Sorts
Jole of Sturgeon
Collared Pig
Dried Tongues, with salt Sallads
Marinated Fish.

Another first Course.

Soop à-la-royal
Carp Blovon
Tench stewed, with pitch-cocked Eels
Rump of Beef à-la-braise
Turkeys à-la-daube
Wild Ducks comporté
Fricando of Veal, with Veal Olives.

Another Second Course.

Woodcocks
Pheasants
Salmigondin
Patridge Poults
Bisque of Lamb
Oyster Loaves
Cutlets
Turkeys Livers forced
Pippins stewed.

For February.

First Course.

SOOP Lorain
Turbot boiled, with Oysters and Shrimps
Grand Patty
Hen Turkeys with Eggs
Marrow Puddings
Stewed Carps and broiled Eels
Spring Pye
Chine of Mutton with Pickles
Dish of Scotch Collops
Dish of Salmigondin.

Second Course.

Fat Chickens and tame Pigeons
Asparagus and Lupins
Tansy and Fritters
Dish of Fruit of Sorts
Dish of fried Soles
Dish of Tarts, Custards, and Cheesecakes.

Another first Course.

Soop à-la-Princesse
Fish, the best you can get
Calf's-head hashed
Pullets à-la-royal
Kettle Drums
Beef Collops
French Patties
Pupton of Veal.

Another Second Course.

Ducklings
Quails
Roasted Lobsters
Potted Lampreys
Blamange
Orange Loaves
Morels and Truffles ragooed
Green Custard.

For MARCH.

First Course.

DISH of Fish of all Sorts
Soop de Santé
Westphalia Ham and Pigeons
Battalia Pye
Pole of Ling
Dish of roasted Tongues and Udders
Peas Soop
Almond Pudding of Sorts
Olives of Veal à-la-mode
Dish of Mullets boiled.

Second Course.

Broiled Pike
Dish of Notts, Ruffs, and Quails
Skerret Pye
Dish of Jellies of Sorts
Dish of Fruit of Sorts
Dish of cream'd Tarts.

Another first Course.

Green Puery Soop
Fish of Sorts
Tongue Pye
Chine of Mutton, or Fillet of Beef stuffed, larded and roasted
Pigeons comporté
Beef à-la-mode
Roasted Ham and Peepers.

Another second Course.

Green Geese
Sweetbreads roasted
Chickens à-la-Crême
Cocks-combs and Stones comporté
Crocande of Pippins
Custard Pudding
Fried Oysters
Butter'd Cray-fish

For APRIL.

First Course.

WEstphalia Ham and Chickens
Dish of hashed Carps
Bisque of Pigeons
Lumber Pye
Chine of Veal
Grand Sallad
Beef à-la-mode
Almond Florentines
Fricassee of Chickens
Dish of Custards.

Second Course.

Green Geese and Ducklings
Butter'd Crab, with Smelts fried
Dish of sucking Rabbits
Rock of Snow and Syllabubs
Dish of souced Mullets
Buttered Apple Pye
March-pain.

Another first Course.

Soop Lorain
Salmon Blovon
Breast of Veal ragooed
Cutlets à-la-Maintenon
Pupton of Pigeons
Bisque of Sheeps Tongues
Saddle of Mutton
Almond Pudding.

Another second Course.

Turkey Poults
Leverets
Green Peas
Bisque of Mushrooms
Tarts creamed
Ragoo of Green Morels
Lobsters serene
Fried Smelts.

For MAY.

First Course.

JOLE of Salmon, &c.
Craw-fish Soop

Diſh of ſweet Puddings of Colours
Chicken Pye
Calf's-head haſhed
Chine of Mutton
Grand Sallad
Roaſted Fowls à-la-daube
Roaſted Tongues and Udders
Ragoo of Veal, *&c.*

Second Courſe.

Diſh of young Turkeys larded, and Quails
Diſh of Peas
Biſque of Shell-fiſh
Roaſted Lobſters
Green Geeſe
Diſh of Sweetmeats
Orangeado Pye
Diſh of Lemon and Chocolate Creams
Diſh of collared Eels with Cray-fiſh.

Another firſt Courſe.

Soop à-la-Sante
Calvert Salmon
Haunch of Veniſon
Veniſon Paſty
Roaſted Geeſe
Chine of Veal, with Fillets ragooed
Beef à-la-braiſe.

Another ſecond Courſe.

Pheaſants
Peas à-la-Crème
Peepers roaſted
Stewed Aſparagus
Codling Tart
Fruit of all Sorts
Fried Lamb-ſtones.

For June.

Firſt Courſe.

ROaſted Pike and Smelts
Weſtphalia Ham and young Fowls
Marrow Puddings
Haunch of Veniſon roaſted
Ragoo of Lamb-ſtones and Sweetbreads
Fricaſſee of young Rabbits, *&c.*
Umble Pyes
Diſh of Mullets
Roaſted Fowls
Diſh of Cuſtards.

Second Courſe.

Diſh of young Pheaſants
Diſh of fried Soles and Eels
Potatoe Pye
Jole of Sturgeon
Diſh of Tarts and Cheeſecakes
Diſh of Fruit of Sorts
Syllabubs.

Another firſt Courſe.

Soops
Fiſh of Sorts
Comporté of Fowls
Pupton of Sheeps Trotters
Collared Veniſon with Ragoo
Chickens boiled, with Lemon Sauce
Mackrel
Leg of Lamb forced, with the Loin fricaſſeed in the Diſh.

Another ſecond Courſe.

Roaſted Lobſters
Piſtachio Pudding
White Fricaſſee of Rabbits
Gooſeberry Tarts
Cray-fiſh
Salmigondin
Fiſh in Jelly
Fried Artichokes.

For July.

Firſt Courſe.

COCK Salmon with buttered Lobſters

Dish of Scotch Collops
Chine of Veal
Venison Pasty
Grand Sallad
Roasted Geese and Ducklings
Patty Royal
Roasted Pig larded
Stewed Carps
Dish of Chickens boiled, with Bacon, &c.

Second Course.

Dish of Partridges and Quails
Dish of Lobsters and Prawns
Dish of Ducks and tame Pigeons
Dish of Jellies
Dish of Fruit
Dish of marinated Fish
Dish of Tarts of Sorts.

Another first Course.

Rice Soop with Veal
A Dish of Trouts
A brown Fricassee of Fowls
A Calf's Head boned, cleared, and stewed, with a Ragoo of Mushrooms
Mutton Maintenon
Rabbits with Onions
Lumber Pye
Ham Pye.

Another second Course.

A Hare larded
Neck of Venison
Partridges
Ragoo of Artichokes
Cocks-combs à-la-Crême
Fruit of Sorts
Currant Tart
Apple Puffs.

For AUGUST.

First Course.

WEstphalia Ham and Chickens
Bisque of Fish
Haunch of Venison roasted
Venison Pasty
Roasted Fowls à-la-daube
Umble Pyes
White Fricassee of Chickens
Roasted Turkeys larded
Almond Florendines
Beef à-lamode.

Second Course.

Dish of Pheasants and Partridges
Roasted Lobsters
Broiled Pike
Creamed Tart
Rock of Snow and Syllabubs
Dish of Sweetmeats
Salmigondin.

Another first Course.

Stewed Venison in Soop
Haddock and Soles
Leg of Mutton à-la-daube
Rabbit Patty
Chine of Lamb
Beams and Ham
Neck of Mutton boned and roasted with a Ragoo of Cucumbers.

Another second Course.

Bisque of Lamb white
Turkeys roasted and larded
Sweet-breads and Lamb-stones
Fruit of Sorts
Morello Cherry Tarts
Strawberries or Raspberries
Artichokes.

For SEPTEMBER.

First Course.

BOiled Pullets with Oysters, Bacon, &c.
Bisque of Fish
Battalia Pye,
Chine of Mutton

Dish

Diſh of Pickles
Roaſted Geeſe
Lumber Pye
Olives of Veal with Ragoo
Diſh of boiled Pigeons with Bacon.

Second Courſe.

Diſh of Ducks and Teal
Diſh of fried Soles
Butter'd Apple-pye
Jole of Sturgeon
Diſh of Fruit
March-pane.

Another firſt Courſe.

Green Peas Soop
Fiſh of Sorts
Geeſe à-la-daube
Stewed Hare
Biſque of Pigeons
Breaſt of Veal à-la-Crême
Biſque of Rabbits
Leg of Veal, with Sorrel Sauce.

Another ſecond Courſe.

Pheaſant larded, with Celery Sauce
Potted Wheat-ears
Scolloped Lobſters
Butter'd Crabs
Stewed Muſhrooms
Collared Eels
Crocande of Sweetmeats.

For OCTOBER.

Firſt Courſe.

WEſtphalia Ham and Fowls
Cod's-head with Shrimps and Oyſters
Haunch of Doe with Udder à-la-force
Minced Pyes
Chine and Turkey
Biſque of Pigeons
Roaſted Tongues and Udders
Scotch Collops
Lumber Pye.

Second Courſe.

Wild Fowl of Sorts
Chine of Salmon broiled
Artichoke Pye
Broiled Eels and Smelts
Salmigondin
Diſh of Fruit
Diſh of Tarts and Cuſtards,

Another firſt Courſe.

Soop of Beef Bollin
Crimped Cod and Sentry
Pullets with Oyſters
Calf's Head à-la-Crême
Veniſon Paſty
Beef à-la-mode
Ox-cheek, with Ragoo of Herbs
Lemon Torte.

Another ſecond Courſe.

Teals and Larks
Turkeys roaſted
Tanſy and Black-caps
Florendines
Scolloped Oyſters
Fried Smelts
Cocks-combs comporté
Fruit, of Sorts.

For NOVEMBER.

Firſt Courſe.

BOiled Fowls with Savoys, Bacon, *&c.*
Diſh of ſtew'd Carps and ſcolloped Oyſters
Chine of Veal and Ragoo
Sallad and Pickles
Veniſon Paſty
Roaſted Geeſe
Calf's Head haſhed
Diſh of Gurnets
Grand Patty
Roaſted Hen Turkey with Oyſters.

Second Course.

Chine of Salmon and Smelts

Wild Fowl of Sorts

Potatoe Pye

Sliced Tongues with Pickles

Dish of Jellies

Dish of Fruit

Quince Pye.

Another first Course.

Harrico of Mutton

Fish of Sorts

Haunch of Venison

Fillet of Veal à-la-braise

Chine of Mutton, with stewed Celery

A Pupton, with Maintenon Cutlets.

Another second Course.

Roasted Woodcocks

Roasted Lobsters

Buttered Crabs

Larks with brown Crumbs

Fried Oysters round two Sweetbreads, larded and roasted

A Pear Tart

Crocande of Sweetmeats.

For DECEMBER.

First Course.

WEstphalia Ham and Fowls

Soop with Teal

Turbot, with Shrimps and Oysters

Marrow Pudding

Chine of Bacon and Turkey

Battalia Pye

Roasted Tongue and Udder, and Hare

Pullets and Oysters, Sausages, *&c.*

Minced Pyes

Cod's-head with Shrimps

Second Course.

Roasted Pheasants and Partridges

Bisque of Shell-fish

Tansy

Dish of roasted Ducks and Teals

Jole of Sturgeon

Pear Tart creamed

Dish of Sweetmeats

Dish of Fruit of Sorts.

Another first Course.

Vermicelly Soop

Fish of Sorts

Jugged Hare

Beef à-la-royal

Scotch Collops

French Patty, with Teal, *&c.*

Rice Pudding.

Another second Course.

Snipes, with a Duck in the Middle

Broiled Chickens with Mushrooms

Pickles of Sorts

White Fricassee of Tripe

Pulled Chickens

Stewed Oysters

Stewed Calves-feet

Curdoons.

THE

THE

Compleat Houſewife:

OR,

Accompliſh'd Gentlewoman's COMPANION.

DIRECTIONS *for* MARKETING.

To chuſe Beef.

F it be true ox-beef it will have an open grain, and the fat, if young, of a crumbling, or oily ſmoothneſs, except it be the briſket and neck pieces, with ſuch others as are very fibrous. The colour of the lean ſhould be of a pleaſant carnation red, the fat rather inclining to white than yellow, and the ſuet of a curious white colour.

Cow-beef is of a cloſer grain, the fat whiter, the bones leſs, and the lean of a paler colour. If it be young and tender the dent you make with your finger by preſſing it, will in a little time, riſe again.

Bull-beef is of a more dusky red, a closer grain, and firmer than either of the former; harder to be indented with your finger, and rising again sooner. The fat is very gross and fibrous, and of a strong rank scent. If it be old it will be so very tough, that if you pinch it you will scarce make any impression in it. If it be fresh it will be of a lively fresh colour, but if stale of a dark dusky colour, and very clammy. If it be bruised, the part affected will look of a more dusky or blackish colour than the rest.

To chuse Pork.

PINCH the lean between your fingers; if it break, and feel soft and oily, or if you can easily nip the skin with your nails, or if the fat be soft and oily, it is young; but if the lean be rough, the fat very spungy, and the skin stubborn it is old. If it be a boar, or a hog gelded at full growth, the flesh will feel harder and rougher than usual, the skin thicker, the fat hard and fibrous, the lean of a dusky red, and of a rank scent. To know if it be fresh or stale, try the legs and hands at the bone, which comes out in the middle of the fleshy part, but putting in your finger, for as it first taints in those places, you may easily discover it by smelling to your finger; also the skin will be clammy and sweaty when stale, but smooth and cool when fresh.

To chuse Brawn.

THE best method of knowing whether brawn be young or old, is by the extraordinary or moderate thickness of the rind, and the hardness and softness of it; for the thick and hard is old, the moderate and soft is young. If the rind and fat be remarkably tender it is not boar brawn, but barrow or sow.

To chuse dried Hams and Bacon.

TAKE a sharp-pointed knife, run it into the middle of the ham on the inside under the bone, draw it out quickly and smell to it; if its flavour be fine and relishing, and the knife little daubed, the ham is sweet and good; but if, on the contrary, the knife be greatly daubed, has a rank smell, and a hogoo issues from the vent it is tainted. Or you may cut off a piece at one end to look on the meat, if it appear white and be well scented, it is good; but if yellowish, or of a rusty colour, and not well scented, it is either tainted or rusty, or at least, will soon be so. A gammon of bacon may be tried in the same manner, and be sure to observe that the flesh stick close to the bones, and the fat and lean to each other; for if it does not, the hog was not sound. Take care also that the extreme part of the fat near the rind be white, for if that be of a darkish or dirty colour, and the lean pale and soft, it is rusty.

To chuse Venison.

TRY the haunches, shoulders, and fleshy parts of the sides with your knife, in the same manner as before directed for ham, and in proportion to the sweet or rank smell it is new or stale. With relation to the other parts, observe the colour of the meat; for if it be stale or tainted it will be of a black colour intermixed with yellowish or greenish specks. If it be old the flesh will be tough and hard, the fat contracted, the hoofs large and broad, and the heel horny and much worn.

To chuse Mutton.

TAKE some of the flesh between your fingers and pinch it; if it feels tender, and soon returns to its former place it is young; but if it wrinkles, and remain ſo, it is old. The fat will, alſo, eaſily ſeparate from the lean if it be young; but if old it will adhere more firmly, and be very clammy and fibrous. If it be ram mutton the fat will be ſpungy, the Grain cloſe, the lean rough and of a deep red, and when dented by your finger will not riſe again. If the ſheep had the rot, the fleſh will be paliſh, the fat a faint white, inclining to yellow; the meat will be looſe at the bone, and, if you ſqueeze it hard, ſome drops of water reſembling a dew or ſweat, will appear on the ſurface. If it be a fore quarter, obſerve the vein in the neck, for if it look ruddy, or of an azure colour it is freſh; but if yellowiſh, it is near tainting, and if green, it is already ſo. As for the hind-quarter ſmell under the kidney, and feel whether the knuckle be ſtiff or limber; for if you find a faint or ill ſcent in the former, or an unuſual limberneſs in the latter, it is ſtale.

To chuſe Veal.

OBSERVE the vein in the ſhoulder; for if it be of a bright red it is newly killed; but if greeniſh, yellowiſh, or blackiſh, or be more clammy, ſoft, and limber than uſual, it is ſtale. Alſo if it has any green ſpots about it, it is either tainting or already tainted. If it be wrapped in wet cloths it is apt to be muſty; therefore always obſerve to ſmell to it. The loin taints firſt under the kidney, and the fleſh, when ſtale, will be ſoft and ſlimy. The neck and breaſt are firſt tainted at the upper end, and when ſo will have a duſky, yellowiſh, or greeniſh appearance, and the ſweet-bread on the breaſt will be clammy. The leg, if newly killed, will be ſtiff in the Joint; but if ſtale, limber and the fleſh clammy, intermixed with green or yellowiſh ſpecks. The fleſh of a bull-calf is firmer grained and redder than that of a cow-calf, and the fat more curdled.

To chuſe Butter and Eggs.

WHEN you buy butter taſte it yourſelf at a venture, and do not truſt to the taſte they give you, leaſt you be deceived by a well taſted and ſcented piece artfully placed in the lump. Salt butter is better ſcented than taſted, by putting a knife into it, and putting it immediately to your noſe; but if it be a caſk it may be purpoſely packed, therefore truſt not to the top alone, but unhoop it to the middle, thruſting your knife between the ſtaves of the caſk, and then you cannot be deceived.

When you buy eggs put the great end to your tongue; if it feels warm, it is new; but if cold it is ſtale; and according to the heat or coldneſs of it, the egg is newer or ſtaler. Or take the egg, hold it up againſt the ſun or a candle, if the white appears clear and fair, and the yolk round, it is good; but if muddy or cloudy, and the yolk broken, it is nought. Or take the egg and put it into a pan of cold water; the freſher it is the ſooner it will ſink to the bottom; but if it be rotten, or addled, it will ſwim on the ſurface of the water. The beſt way to keep them is in bran or meal; though ſome place their ſmall ends downwards in fine wood-aſhes.

To chuſe Cheeſe.

WHEN you buy cheeſe obſerve the coat; for if the cheeſe be old, and its coat be rough, rugged, or dry at top, it indicates mites, or little worms. If it be ſpungy, moiſt, or full of holes, it is ſubject to maggots. If you perceive on the outſide any periſhed place, be ſure to examine its deepneſs.

To chuse Poultry.

To know if a Capon be a true one or not, or whether it be young, or old, new or stale.

IF a capon be young his spurs will be short and blunt, and his legs smooth: If a true capon, it will have a fat vein on the side of the breast, a thick belly and rump, and its comb will be short and pale. If it be new it will have a close hard vent; but if stale an open loose vent.

To chuse a Cock or Hen Turkey, Turkey Poults, &c.

IF the spurs of a turkey cock are short, and his legs black and smooth, he is young; but if his spurs be long, and his legs pale and rough, he is old. If long killed, his eyes will be sunk into his head, and his feet feel very dry; but if fresh his feet will be limber, and his eyes lively. For the hen, observe the same signs. If she be with egg she will have an open vent; but if not, a close hard vent. The same signs will serve to discover the newness or staleness of turkey poults; and, with respect to their age, you cannot be deceived.

To chuse a Cock, Hen, &c.

IF a cock be young his spurs will be short and dubbed; (but be sure to observe that they are not pared or scraped to deceive you) but if sharp and standing out he is old. If his vent be hard and close, it is a sign of his being newly killed; but if he be stale his vent will be open. The same signs will discover whether a hen be new or stale; and if old her legs and comb will be rough; but if young, smooth.

To know if Chickens are new or stale.

IF they are pulled dry, they will be stiff when new; but when stale they will be limber and their vents green. If they are scalded, or pulled wet, rub the breast with your thumb or finger, and if they are rough and stiff they are new; but if smooth and slippery, stale.

To chuse a Goose, wild Goose, and Bran-Goose.

IF the bill and foot be red, and the body full of hairs, she is old; but if the bill be yellowish, and the body has but few hairs, she is young. If new, her feet will be limber, but if stale, dry. Understand the same of a wild goose, and bran goose.

To chuse wild and tame Ducks.

THESE fowls are hard and thick on the belly, when fat, but thin and lean, when poor; limber footed when new; but dry footed when stale. A wild duck may be distinguished from a tame one by its foot being smaller and reddish.

To chuse the Bustard.

OBSERVE the same rules in chusing this curious fowl, as those already given for the turkey.

To chuse the Shuffler, Godwitz, Marrel Knots, Gulls, Dotters, and Wheat-Ears.

THESE birds, when new, are limber footed; when stale, dry footed: When fat, they have a fat rump; when lean, a close and hard one: When young their legs are smooth; when old, rough.

To chuse the Pheasant Cock and Hen.

THE spurs of the pheasant cock, when young, are short and dubbed; but long and sharp when old; when new he has a firm vent, when stale an open and flabby one. The pheasant hen, when young, has smooth legs, and her flesh is of a fine and curious grain; but when old her legs are rough, and her flesh hairy when pulled. If she be with egg her vent will be open, if not close. The same signs, as to newness or staleness, are to be observed as were before given for the cock.

To chuse Heath and Pheasant Poults.

THE feet of these, when new, are limber, and their vents white and stiff; but when stale, are dry footed, their vents green, and if you touch it hard, will peel.

To chuse the Heath-Cock and Hen.

THE newness or staleness of these are known by the same signs as the foregoing; but when young their legs and bills are smooth; when old both are rough.

To chuse the Woodcock and Snipe.

THESE fowls are limber-footed when new; but stale, dry-footed: If fat thick and hard; but if their noses are snotty, and their throats moorish and muddy they are bad.

To chuse the Partridge Cock or Hen.

THESE fowls, when young, have black bills, and yellowish legs; when old, white bills and bluish legs; when new, a fast vent; when stale a green and open one, which will peel with a touch: If they have fed lately on green wheat, and their crops be full, smell to their Mouths, lest their crops be tainted.

To chuse Doves or Pigeons, Plovers, &c.

THE turtle-dove is distinguished by a bluish ring round its neck, the other parts being almost white. The stock-dove exceeds both the wood-pigeon and ring-dove in bigness. The dove-house pigeons are red-leged when old: If new and fat, limber-footed, and feel full in the vent; but when stale, their vents are green and flabby.

After the same manner you may chuse the gray and green plover, thrush, mavis, lark, blackbird, *&c.*

To chuse Teal and Widgeon.

THESE, when new, are limber-footed; when stale, dry footed. Thick and hard on the belly, if fat, but thin and soft, if lean.

To chuse a Hare.

IF the claws of a hare are blunt and rugged, her ears dry and tough, and the clift in her lip spread much, she is old; but the opposite if young: if new and fresh killed, the flesh will be white and stiff; if stale, limber and blackish in many places.

To chuse a Leveret.

THE newness or staleness may be known by the same signs as the hare: but in order to discover if it be a real leveret, feel near the foot on its fore leg, if you find there a knob or small bone, it is a true leveret; but if not a hare.

To chuse a Rabit or Coney.

IF a rabbit or coney be old, the claws will be very long and rough, and grey hairs intermixed with the wool; but if young, the claws and wool smooth;

ſmooth; if ſtale, it will be limber, and the fleſh will look blueiſh, having a kind of ſlime upon it; but if freſh it will be ſtiff, and the fleſh white and dry.

Of F I S H.

To chuſe Salmon, Trout, Carp, Tench, Pike, Graylings, Barbel, Chub, Whiting, Smelt, Ruff, Eel, Shad, &c.

THE newneſs or ſtaleneſs of theſe fiſh, are known by the colour of their gills, their being hard or eaſy to be opened, the ſtanding out or ſinking of their eyes, their fins being ſtiff or limber, and by ſmelling to their gills.

To chuſe the Turbutt.

IF this fiſh be plump and thick, and its belly of a cream colour, it is good; but if thin, and of a blueiſh white on the belly, not ſo.

To chuſe Soals.

IF theſe are thick and ſtiff, and of a cream colour on the belly, they will ſpend well; but if thin, limber, and their bellies of a blueiſh white, they will eat very looſe.

To chuſe Plaiſe and Flounders.

WHEN theſe fiſh are new they are ſtiff, and the eyes look lively, and ſtand out; but when ſtale, the contrary. The beſt plaiſe are blueiſh on the belly; but flounders of a cream colour.

To chuſe Cod and Codling.

CHUSE thoſe which are thick towards the head, and their fleſh, when cut very white.

To

To chuse fresh Herrings and Mackerel.

IF these are new, their gills will be of a lively shining redness, their eyes sharp and full, and the fish stiff; but if stale, their gills will look dusky and faded, their eyes dull and sunk down, and their tails limber.

To chuse pickled Salmon.

THE scales of this fish, when new and good, are stiff and shining, the flesh oily to the touch, and parts in fleaks without crumbling; but the opposite when bad.

To chuse pickled and Red Herrings.

TAKE the former and open the back to the bone, if it be white, or of bright red, and the flesh white, oily, and fleaky, they are good. If the latter smell well, be of a good gloss, and part well from the bone, they are also good.

To chuse dried Ling.

THE best sort of dried ling is that which is thickest in the pole, and the flesh of the brightest yellow.

To chuse pickled Sturgeon.

THE veins and gristle of the fish, when good, are of a blue colour, the flesh white, the skin limber, the fat underneath of a pleasant scent, and you may cut it without its crumbling.

To chuse Lobsters.

IF a lobster be new, it has a pleasant scent at that part of the tail which joins to the body, and the tail will, when opened, fall smart like a spring; but when stale it has a rank scent, and the tail limber and flagging If it be spent, a white scurf will issue from the

the mouth and roots of the small legs. If it be full, the tail about the middle will be full of hard reddish skin'd meat, which you may discover by thrusting a knife between the Joints, on the bend of the tail. The heaviest are best if there be no water in them. The cock is generally smaller than the hen, of a deeper red when boiled, has no spawn or seed under its tail, and the uppermost fins within its tail, are stiff and hard.

To chuse Crab-fish, great and small.

WHEN they are stale their shells will be of a dusky red colour, the joints of their claws limber; they are loose and may be turned any way with the finger, and from under their throat will issue an ill smell; but if otherwise they are good.

To chuse Prawns and Shrimps.

IF they are hard and stiff, of a pleasant scent, and their tails turn strongly inward, they are new; but if they are limber, their colour faded, of a faint smell, and feel slimy, they are stale.

COOKERY, *&c.*

General Directions for Boiling.

LET your pot be very clean; and as a scum will arise from every thing, be sure to shake a small handful of flour into it, which will take all the scum up, and prevent any from falling down to make the meat black. All salt meat must be put in when the water is cold; but fresh meat, not till it boils; and as many pounds as your piece weighs, so many quarters of an hour it will require in boiling.

To

To boil a Tongue.

IF it be a dry tongue it muſt be laid in warm water for ſix hours, then change your water, and let it lay three hours more ; the ſecond water muſt be cold. Then take it out and boil it three hours, which will be ſufficient. If your tongue be juſt out of pickle it muſt lay three hours in cold water, and boil it till it will peel.

To boil a Ham.

LAY your ham in cold water for two hours, waſh it clean, and tie it up in clean hay ; put it into freſh water, boil it very ſlow for one hour, and then very briſkly an hour and an half more. Take it up in the hay and let it lie in it till cold, then rub the rind with a clean piece of flannel.

To boil Houſe-Lamb, or Fowls.

THESE are the beſt boiled in milk and water, being tied up in a clean cloth well floured. An hour will boil it if large, and ſo in proportion if ſmaller.

To boil pickled Pork.

WASH your pork, and ſcrape it clean ; then put it in when the water is cold, and boil it till the rind be tender.

To dreſs Greens, Roots, &c.

WHEN you have nicely picked and waſhed your greens, lay them in a cullender to drain, for if any cold water hang to them they will be tough ; then boil them alone in a copper ſauce-pan, with a large quantity of water, for if any meat be boiled with them it will diſcolour them. Be ſure not to put them in till the water boils.

To

To dress Spinach.

WASH it in several waters, put it into a sauce-pan with no more water than what hangs to it; when it boils up pour the liquor from it, and put in a piece of butter and some salt; then boil it till the spinach falls to the bottom; take it up, press it very dry, and serve it up with melted butter.

To dress Carrots.

SCRAPE them very clean, and when the water boils, put them into your pot or sauce-pan; if they are young spring carrots, they will be boiled in half an hour, but if large they will require an hour. Then take them out, slice them into a plate, and pour over them some melted butter.

To dress Parsnips.

BOIL them in a large quantity of water, after they are cleanly scraped, and when they are enough, which may be known by their being soft, take them up, and separate from them all the sticky parts; then put them in a sauce-pan with some milk, a proper quantity of butter, and some salt; set them over the fire, stir them till they are thick, taking great care that they do not burn, and when the butter is melted send them to table.

To dress Potatoes.

PUT your potatoes into the sauce-pan with a proper quantity of water; and when they are enough, which may be known by their skins beginning to crack, drain all the water from them, and let them stand close covered up for two or three minutes; then peel them, place them in a plate, and pour over them a proper quantity of melted butter: Or after you have peeled them, lay them on a gridiron,

gridiron, and, when they are of a fine brown, send them to table. Or you may cut them into slices, fry them in butter, and season them with pepper and salt.

To dress Turneps.

THEY are best boiled in the pot; when they are enough put them into a pan with some butter and salt, and after you have mashed them send them to table. Or, after your turneps are pared, you may cut them into small pieces, and boil them in a sauce-pan with as much water as will just cover them; when they are enough, put them into a sieve to drain; then put them into a sauce-pan with a proper quantity of butter, and, after stirring them five or six minutes over the fire, send them to table.

To dress Broccoli.

AFTER you have separated the small branches from the large ones, and taken off the hard outside skin, throw them into water; then place your stew-pan, containing a sufficient quantity of water mixed with some salt, on the fire, and when the water boils put in your broccoli; when they are enough, which may be known by the stalks being tender, send them to table with melted butter in a cup.

To dress Asparagus.

LET all the stalks be carefully scraped till they look white, cut them of an equal length, and throw them into water; set your stew-pan with a proper quantity of water, having some salt in it, on the fire, and when the water boils put in your asparagus, after being tied up in small bundles. When they are enough, which may be known by their being somewhat tender, take them up, for if they boil too long, they will lose both their colour and taste.

Then cut a round off a small loaf, and having toasted it brown on both sides, dip it in the liquor of the asparagus, laying it in your dish. Melt some butter, and pour it on the toast, laying the asparagus on it round the dish, with the bottom part of the stalks outward. Put the remaining part of the butter in a bason, because pouring it over the asparagus makes them greasy, and send them to table.

To dress French Beans.

TAKE your beans, string them, cut them in two, and then a-cross, or else into four, and then a-cross, put them into water with some salt; set your sauce-pan full of water over the fire, cover them close, and when it boils put in your beans, with a little salt. They will be soon done, which you may know by their being tender; then take them up before they lose their fine green, and having put them in a plate, send them to table with butter in a cup.

To dress Artichokes.

AFTER you have twisted the heads from the stalks, put them into the sauce pan with the water cold, placing their tops downwards, by which means all the dust and sand contained between the leaves will boil out. When they have boiled about an hour and a half they will be enough; then take them up, and send them to table with melted butter in a bason.

To dress Cauliflowers.

CUT off all the green part from your flowers, and divide them into four parts, laying them in water for an hour. Put some milk and water into your sauce-pan, and set it over the fire, when i boils put in your cauliflowers, observing to skim your sauce-pan well. When they are enough, which you may know by the ſtalks being tender, take them up into a colander to drain. Take a quarter of a pound of butter, a ſpoonful of water, a little flour, and a little pepper and ſalt; put them into a ſtew-pan, place it on the fire, ſhaking it often till the butter is melted; then take half of the cauliflower, divide it into ſmall pieces, and put them into the ſtew-pan, ſhaking it often for ten minutes; place the boiled round the ſides of the plate, and the ſtewed in the middle; pour the butter you ſtewed it in over it, and ſend it to table.

Rules to be obſerved in Roaſting.

LET your fire be made in proportion to the piece you are to dreſs; that is, if it be a little or thin piece, make a little briſk fire that it may be done quick and nice; but if a large joint obſerve to lay a good fire to cake, and let it be always clear at the bottom.

When your meat is about half done, move it, and the dripping-pan a little diſtance from the fire, which ſtir up and make it burn briſk; for the quicker your fire is, the ſooner and better will your meat be done.

To roaſt Beef.

IF the rib, ſprinkle it with ſalt for half an hour, dry and flour it; then butter a piece of paper very thick, faſten it on the beef, with the buttered ſide next it. If a rump or ſir-loin, do not ſalt it, but lay it a good diſtance from the fire; baſte it once or twice with ſalt and water, then with butter, flour it, and keep it baſting with what drops from it. Take three ſpoonfuls of vinegar, a pint of water, a ſhallot, a ſmall piece of horſe-radiſh, two ſpoonfuls of catchup, and one glaſs of claret, baſte it with this once or twice, then ſtrain it and put it under your beef; garniſh with horſe-radiſh and red-cabbage.

To roast Pork.

ALL pork must be flour'd thick, and laid at first a good distance from the fire; and when the flour begins to dry, wipe it clean. Then with a sharp knife cut the skin a-cross. Heighten the fire, and put your meat near it, baste, and roast it as quick as you can. If a leg, you must cut it very deep. When almost done, fill the cuts with grated bread, sage, parsley, a small piece of lemon-peel cut small, a piece of butter, two eggs, a little pepper, salt and nutmeg, mixed together: when it is enough send it to table with gravy and apple-sauce. If you roast a spare-rib baste it with a little butter, flour, and sage shred small. When it is ready send it to table with apple-sauce.

To roast a Pig.

LAY your pig in warm milk for a quarter of an hour, and wipe it very dry. Take of butter and crumbs of bread, of each a quarter of a pound, a little sage, thyme, parsley, sweet marjoram, pepper, salt, and nutmeg, the yolks of two eggs, mix these together, and sew it up in the belly. Flour it very thick; then spit it, and lay it to the fire, taking care that your fire burns well at both ends, or till it does, hang a flat iron in the middle of the grate. When you find the crackling grows hard, wipe it clean with a cloth wet in salt and water, and baste it with butter. As soon as the gravy begins to run, put basons in the dripping-pan to receive it. When the pig is enough, take about a quarter of a pound of butter, put it into a coarse cloth, and, having made a brisk fire, rub the pig all over with it, till the crackling is quite crisp, and then take it from the fire. Cut off the head, and cut the pig in two, before you take it from the spit. Then having cut the ears off and placed one at each end, and, also, the under-

under-jaw in two, and placed one part on each ſide, take ſome good butter, melt it, mix it with the gravy, the brains bruiſed, and ſome ſage ſhred ſmall, and ſend it to table.

To roaſt Mutton and Lamb.

BEFORE you lay the mutton down, take care to have a clear quick fire; baſte it often, and when it is almoſt done, drudge it with a little flour. If it be a breaſt, ſkin it before you lay it down.

To roaſt Veal.

IF a ſhoulder baſte it with milk till half done, then flour it and baſte it with butter. A fillet muſt be ſtuffed with thyme, marjoram, parſley, a ſmall onion, a ſprig of ſavory, a bit of lemon-peel cut very ſmall, nutmeg, pepper, mace, ſalt, crumbs of bread, four eggs, a quarter of a pound of butter or marrow, mixed with a little flour to make it ſtiff. Half of the above muſt be put into the udder, and the other into holes made in the fleſhy part.

If it be a loin paper the Fat, that as little of it may be loſt as poſſible. If it be the breaſt you muſt cover it with the caul, and faſten the ſweetbread on the backſide of it with a ſkewer. When it is almoſt done, take off the caul, baſte and drudge it with a little flour. Send it up with melted butter, and garniſh'd with Lemon.

To roaſt a Hare.

TAKE crumbs of bread, and ſuet cut ſmall, of each half a pound; ſome parſley and thyme ſhred ſmall; ſome ſalt, pepper, cloves, mace, and nutmegs pounded; three dried muſh-rooms cut ſmall, two eggs, a glaſs of claret, two ſpoonfuls of catchup; mix all theſe together, and ſew it up in the belly of the hare; lay it down to a very slow fire, baste it with milk, till it becomes very thick; then make a brisk fire, roast it for half an hour, baste it with butter, and drudge it with a little flour.

To roast Venison.

WASH your venison in vinegar and water, dry it with a cloth, and cover it with the caul, or, instead of that a buttered paper. Make a brisk fire, lay it down, and baste it with butter till it is almost done. Then take a pint of claret, boil it in a sauce-pan with some whole pepper, nutmeg, cloves and mace. Pour this liquor twice over your venison. Have your dish on a chafing-dish of coals to keep it hot. Then take it up, strain the liquor you poured over the venison, and serve it in the same dish with the venison, with good gravy in one bason and sweet sauce in another.

To roast Rabbits.

WHEN you have lain your rabbits down to the fire, baste them with good butter, and then drudge them with flour. If they are small, and your fire quick and clear, half an hour will do them, but if large they will require three quarters of an hour. Melt some good butter, and having boiled the liver with a bunch of parsley, and chop'd them small, put half into the butter, and pour it into the dish, garnishing it with the other half.

To roast a Tongue, or Udder.

TAKE your Tongue or udder and parboil it; then stick into it ten or twelve cloves, and while it is roasting baste it with butter. When it is ready take it up, and send it to table with some gravy and sweet sauce.

To

To roaſt Mutton like Veniſon.

TAKE a fat hind quarter of mutton, and cut the leg like a haunch of veniſon, rub it well with ſalt petre, hang it in a moiſt place for two days, wiping it two or three times a day with a clean cloth. Then put it into a pan, and having boiled a quarter of an ounce of all-ſpice in a quart of red wine, pour it boiling hot over your mutton, cover it cloſe for two hours; take it out, ſpit it, lay it down to the fire and conſtantly baſte it with the ſame liquor and butter. If you have a good quick fire, and your mutton not prodigious large, it will be ready in an hour and a half. Then take it up and ſend it to table with ſome good gravy in one cup, and ſweet ſauce in another.

To roaſt Woodcocks and Snipes.

PUT them on the ſpit without taking any thing out of them; baſte them with butter, and when the tail begins to drop, put into the diſh to receive it a round of a three-penny loaf toaſted brown. When they are done put the toaſt into the diſh, with about a quarter of a pint of good gravy, put the woodcocks on it, and ſet it over a lamp or chaſing-diſh of coals for about three minutes, and ſend them to table.

To roaſt the hind quarter of a Pig Lamb faſhion.

TAKE the hind quarter of a large pig, ſkin it, and when it is roaſted, which will be in three quarters of an hour, ſend it to table with mint ſauce, a ſallad, or a *Seville* orange.

To roaſt Pigeons.

TAKE a little pepper and ſalt, a ſmall piece of butter, and ſome parſley cut ſmall; mix thefe together, put them into the bellies of your pigeons, tying the neck ends tight; take another ftring, faften one end of it to their legs and rumps, and the other to the mantle-piece. Keep them conftantly turning round, and bafte them with butter. When they are done, take them up, lay them in a difh, and they will fwim with gravy.

To roaft a Goofe.

TAKE a little fage, and a fmall onion chopt fmall, fome pepper and falt, and a bit of butter; mix thefe together, and put it into the belly of the goofe. Then fpit it, finge it with a bit of white paper, drudge it with a little flour, and bafte it with butter. When it is done, which may be known by the leg being tender, take it up, and pour thro' it two glaffes of red wine, and ferve it up in the fame difh, and apple fauce in a bafon.

To roaft a Turkey.

TAKE a quarter of a pound of lean veal, a little thyme, parfley, fweet marjoram, a fprig of winter favory, a bit of lemon peel, one onion, a nutmeg grated, a dram of mace, a little falt, and half a pound of butter; cut your herbs very fmall, pound your meat as fmall as poffible, and mix all together with three eggs, and as much flour or bread, as will make it of a proper confiftence. Then fill the crop of your turkey with it, paper the breaft and lay it down at a good diftance from the fire. An hour and a quarter will roaft it if not very large.

General Directions for Broiling.

Firft, TAKE care that your fire be very clear before you lay your meat on the gridiron.

Secondly, Turn your meat, when it is down, quick, having, at the fame time, a difh placed on a cha-

fing-

fing-dish of hot coals to put your meat in as fast as it is ready, and carry it to the table covered hot.

Thirdly, Observe never to baste any thing on the gridiron, for that causes it to be both smoked and burnt.

To broil Stakes.

WHEN you have made a clear brisk fire, make your gridiron very clean, put some hot coals from the fire into a chafing-dish, and place a dish over them, in order to receive your stakes when ready; take rump-stakes, which should be about half an inch thick; after you have thrown over them a little pepper and salt, place them on the gridiron, and do not turn them till that side be done; when you have turned them you will soon perceive a fine gravy laying on the upper part of the stake, which you must carefully preserve by taking the stakes when ready, warily from your gridiron, and placing them in your dish: Then covering your dish, send them hot to table with the cover on. Some before they take the stake from the gridiron, cut into the dish a shalot or two, or a fine onion, and a little vinegar.

To broil a Pigeon.

YOU may either split and broil them with a little pepper and salt; or you may take a small piece of butter, a little pepper and salt, and having put it into their bellies, tie both ends close. Then lay them on your gridiron, taking care to place it high, that they may not burn, and when they are ready send them to table with a little melted butter in a cup.

To bake a Pig.

TAKE your pig, flour it well, and having butter'd your dish, lay your pig into it, and put it into the oven. When it is ready and you have drawn it out of the oven, rub it all over with a buttery cloth; then put it again into the oven, and when it is dry take it out, lay it in your dish, and cut it up. Take the gravy which remains in the dish you baked it in, after you have skimmed off the fat; mix it with some good gravy, a sufficient quantity of butter rolled in flour, and a glass of white-wine; set it on the fire, and as soon as it boils, pour it into the dish with the brains and the sage which was roasted in its belly.

To bake a Leg of Beef.

TAKE a leg of beef, cut it and break the bones; put it into an earthen pan with a spoonful of whole pepper, a few cloves and blades of mace, two onions, and a bundle of sweet herbs; cover it with water, and, having tied the pot down close with brown paper, put it into the oven to bake. When it is enough strain it through a sieve, and pick out all the fat and sinews, putting them into a sauce-pan with a little gravy, and a piece of butter rolled in flour. Set the sauce-pan on the fire, shaking it often, and when it is thoroughly hot pour it into the dish, and send it to table.

To bake an Ox's Cheek.

OBSERVE the same directions as those given for baking a leg of beef.

Sauce for boiled Ducks or Rabbits.

TAKE a sufficient quantity of onions, peel them, and boil them in a large quantity of water: When they are about half boiled, throw that water away and fill your sauce-pan with half milk and half water, in which let them boil till they are enough; then take them up into a colander, and when they are drained, chop them with a knife; put them into a sauce-pan with a piece of butter

ter rolled in flour; set the sauce-pan over the fire, shaking it often till the butter is melted, then pour it over your boiled ducks or rabbits, and send them to table.

Sauce for a boiled Turkey.

TAKE a piece of white bread, put it into a quart of water, with a blade of mace, a little pepper and salt, and a bit of onion. Boil it to a pint; strain it, and add to it the yolk of an egg beat, a piece of butter rolled in flour, and a glass of white wine. Garnish with forc'd-meat balls and oysters.

Sauce for a boiled Goose.

YOU may either make onion sauce as directed for boiled ducks, *&c.* or you may boil some cabbage, and then stew it a small time in butter.

Sauce for roast Venison.

TAKE a pound of lean beef, and a quarter of a pound of lean bacon, cut into small pieces; put it into a stew-pan with three pints of water, a bunch of sweet herbs, and an onion; boil it till half is consumed. Strain it, and add to it two spoonfuls of catchup, as much oyster-liquor, and thicken it with brown-butter. Or,

Take half the crumb of a half-penny loaf, a large stick of cinnamon, some mace and nutmeg, and a race of ginger, put these into a sauce-pan with a pint of water; boil it; beat it very fine, and strain it through a sieve, adding to it half a pint of red wine, and sweeten it to your taste.

Different Sauces for a Hare.

TAKE some good gravy, and a proper quantity of butter rolled in flour; when it is melted pour it into your dish. Or take half a pound of butter

butter, put it into a sauce-pan, set it over the fire, keeping it continually stirred till the butter is melted, and the sauce thick; then take it from the fire and pour it into the dish. Or take a pint of red wine and half a pound of sugar, and after it has simmer'd about a quarter of an hour over the fire, pour it into the dish.

Different Sauces for a Pig.

TAKE a good piece of crumb of bread, a little whole pepper, and a blade of mace, boil these about six minutes in a pint of water; then pour off the water, take out the spice, and beat up the bread with a proper quantity of butter. Some add a few currants, a glass of wine, and a little sugar. Or take the gravy which dropped from the pig, half a pint of good gravy, three spoonfuls of catchup, and a piece of butter rolled in flour; boil these together, and mix it with the brains of the pig. If you have not gravy enough from the pig you may supply its place by stewing the petty-toes.

Sauce for Larks.

TAKE for every dozen of larks a quarter of a pound of butter, the crumb of a half-penny loaf rubbed small; when the butter is melted put in your bread, keeping it constantly stirring till it becomes brown; then drain it through a sieve, and place it round your larks.

To make a Soup.

TAKE a leg of beef, and boil it down with some salt, a bundle of sweet-herbs, an onion, a few cloves, a bit of nutmeg; boil three gallons of water to one; then take two or three pounds of lean beef cut in thin slices; then put in your stew-pan a piece of butter as big as an egg, and flour it, and let the pan be hot, and shake it till the butter be brown; then lay your beef in your pan over a pretty quick fire,

fire, cover it cloſe, give it a turn now and then, and ſtrain in your ſtrong broth, with an anchovy or two, a handful of ſpinach and endive boiled green, and drained and ſhred groſs; then have pallets ready boiled and cut in pieces, and toaſts fry'd and cut like dice, and forc'd-meat-balls fry'd: take out the fry'd beef, and put all the reſt together with a little pepper, and let it boil a quarter of an hour, and ſerve it up with a knuckle of veal, or a fowl boiled in the middle.

Another Gravy Soup.

TAKE a leg of beef, and a piece of the neck, boil it till you have all the goodneſs out of it; then ſtrain it from the meat; take half a pound of freſh butter, and put it in a ſtew-pan, and brown it; adding an onion ſtuck with cloves, ſome endive, celery and ſpinach, and your ſtrong broth, ſeaſoning it to your palate with ſalt, pepper, and ſpices; let it boil together, and put in chips of *French* bread dry'd by the fire, and ſerve it with a *French* roll toaſted in the middle.

To make Craw-fiſh or Lobſter-Soup.

TAKE whitings, flounders, and grigs, put them in a gallon of water, with pepper, ſalt, cloves, mace, a bunch of ſweet herbs, a little onion, and boil them to pieces, and ſtrain them out of the liquor; then take a large carp, and cut off the fiſh of one ſide of it, and put ſome eel to it; and make forc'd-meat of it, and lay it on the carp as before; dredge grated bread over it, butter a diſh well, put it in an oven, and bake it; take an hundred of craw-fiſh, break all the ſhells of the claws and tails, and take out the meat as whole as you can; then break all the ſhells ſmall, and the ſpawn of a lobſter, putting them to the ſoup, and if you pleaſe, ſome gravy; and give them a boil together, and

and ſtrain the liquor out into another ſauce-pan, with the tops of *French* rolls dried, beat, and ſifted, and give it a boil up to thicken; then brown ſome butter, and put in the tails and claws of your craw-fiſh, and ſome of your forc'd-meat made into balls, putting your baked carp into the middle of the diſh, and pour your ſoup on boiling hot, and your craw-fiſh or lobſter in it; garniſh the diſh with lemon and ſcalded greens.

A Faſting-Day Soup.

TAKE ſpinach, ſorrel, chervil, and lettuce, and chop them a little; then brown ſome butter, and put in your herbs, keep them ſtirring that they don't burn; then, having boiling water over the fire, put to it a very little pepper, and ſome ſalt, a whole onion ſtuck with cloves, a *French* roll cut in ſlices and dried very hard, ſome Piſtachia kernels, blanched and ſhred fine, and let all boil together; then beat up the yolks of eight eggs with a little whitewine and the juice of a lemon; mix it with your broth, toaſt a whole *French* roll, and put it in the middle of your diſh, pouring your ſoup over it; garniſh your diſh with ten or twelve poach'd eggs and ſcalded ſpinach.

Savoury Balls.

TAKE part of a leg of lamb or veal, and ſcrape it fine, with the ſame quantity of minc'd beef-ſuet, a little lean bacon, ſweet herbs, a ſhallot, and anchovies; beat it in a mortar till it is as ſmooth as wax: ſeaſon it with ſavoury ſpice, and make it into little balls.

Another Way.

TAKE the fleſh of fowl, beef-ſuet, and marrow, the ſame quantity; ſix or eight oyſters, lean bacon, ſweet herbs and ſavoury ſpices; pound it, and make it into little balls.

A Caudle

A Caudle for fweet Pyes.

TAKE fack and whitewine alike in quantity, a little verjuice and fugar, boil it, and brew it with two or three eggs, as butter'd ale; when the pyes are baked, pour it in with a funnel, and fhake it together.

A Lear for favoury Pyes.

TAKE claret, gravy, oyfter-liquor, two or three anchovies, a faggot of fweet-herbs and an onion; boil it up and thicken it with brown butter, then pour it into your favoury pyes when called for.

A Ragoo for made Difhes.

TAKE claret, gravy, fweet-herbs, and favoury fpice, tofs up in it lamb-ftones, cock's-combs, boiled, blanched, and fliced, with fliced fweet-meats, oyfters, mufhrooms, truffles, and murrels; thicken thefe with brown butter; ufe it when called for.

To make Plumb Porridge.

TAKE a leg and fhin of beef to ten gallons of water, boil it very tender, and when the broth is ftrong, ftrain it out; wipe the pot, and put in the broth again; flice fix penny loaves thin, cutting off the top and bottom: put fome of the liquor to it, cover it up, and let it ftand a quarter of an hour, and then put it in your pot; let it boil a quarter of an hour, then put in five pounds of currants; let them boil a little, and put in five pounds of raifins, and two pounds of prunes, and let them boil till they fwell, then put in three quarters of an ounce of mace, half an ounce of cloves, two nutmegs, all of them beat fine, and mix it with a little liquor cold, and put them in a very little while; then take off the pot, and put in three pounds of fugar, a little falt, a quart of fack, a quart of claret, and the juice of two or three lemons; you may thicken with fago inftead instead of bread, if you please; pour them into earthen pans, and keep them for use.

A Soup or Pottage.

TAKE several knuckles of mutton, a knuckle of veal, a shin of beef, and put to these twelve quarts of water, cover the pot close, and set it on the fire; let it not boil too fast; scum it well, and let it stand on the fire twenty-four hours; then strain it through a colander, and when it is cold take off the fat, and set it on the fire again, and season it with salt, a few cloves, pepper, a blade of mace, a nutmeg quarter'd, a bunch of sweet-herbs, and a pint of gravy; let all these boil up for half an hour, and then strain it; put spinach, sorrel, green peas, asparagus, or artichoke-bottoms, according to the time of the year; then thicken it up with the yolks of three or four eggs; have in readiness some sheeps tongues, cock's-combs and sweet-breads, sliced thin and fry'd, and put them in, some mushrooms, and *French* bread dry'd and cut in little bits, some forc'd-meat-balls, and some very thin slices of bacon; make all these very hot, and garnish the dish with coleworts and spinach scalded green.

To make Peas Pottage.

TAKE a quart of white peas, a piece of neck-beef, and four quarts of fair water; boil them till they are all to pieces, and strain them thro' a colander; then take a handful or two of spinach, a top or two of young coleworts, and a very small leek; shred the herbs a little, and put them into a frying-pan, or stew-pan, with three quarters of a pound of fresh butter, but the butter must be very hot before you put in your herbs; let them fry a little while, then put in your liquor, and two or three anchovies, some salt and pepper to your taste, a sprig of mint rubb'd in small, and let it all boil together till you think it is thick enough; then have in readineſs ſome forc'd meat, and make three or fourſcore balls, about the bigneſs of large peas, fry them brown, and put them in the diſh you ſerve it in, and fry ſome thin ſlices of bacon, put ſome in the diſh, and ſome on the rim of the diſh, with ſcalded ſpinach : fry ſome toaſts after the balls are brown and hard, and break them into the diſh; then pour your pottage over all, and ſerve to the table.

To burn Butter.

SHAKE ſome flour upon two or three ounces of butter, put it into a hot frying-pan that it may hiſs ; let it boil, and do not ſtir it ; when it turns brown, put in the liquor you intend to thicken, and keep it quick ſtirring ; boil it well, or it will taſte raw.

To make ſtrong Broth to keep for Uſe.

TAKE part of a leg of beef, the ſcrag end of a neck of mutton, break the bones in pieces, put to it as much water as will cover it, and a little ſalt ; when it boils ſcum it clean, and put into it a whole onion ſtuck with cloves, a bunch of ſweet-herbs, ſome pepper, a nutmeg quartered ; let theſe boil till the meat is boiled in pieces, and the ſtrength boiled out of it ; then put to it two or three anchovies ; when they are diſſolved, ſtrain it out, and keep it for any ſort of haſh or fricaſee.

To make forc'd Meat.

TAKE part of a leg of mutton, veal, or beef, and pick off the ſkins and fat, and to every pound of meat put two pounds of beef-ſuet ; ſhred them together very fine, then ſeaſon it with pepper, ſalt, cloves, mace, nutmeg, and ſage ; put all into a ſtone mortar, and to every two pounds of meat put half a pint of oyſters, and ſix eggs well beaten, then mix them all together, beat it very well, and keep it in an earthen pot for your uſe ; put a little

flour

flour on the top, and when you roll them up flour your hands.

To stew a Rump of Beef.

STUFF the under part of the beef with forc'd meat made of grated bread, beef-suet, sweet-herbs, spice, anchovy, a little salt, fresh oysters or mushrooms, and two or three eggs beaten fine to mix up mith the stuffing; then put it into a pot to stew, with as much water as will near cover it, some whole pepper, three or four cloves, and a little shred-nutmeg, or a few blades of mace; take up the beef, and separate all the fat, putting in a pint of stale beer, with a good quantity of strong gravy, and let it stew in a small quantity of liquor; it must be turned once or twice: fry some crumbs of bread brown, strain the Liquor, and put in these crumbs to thicken it; then put in your gravy and not before; let it just simmer a little; you may put in some oysters, mushrooms, and ox's palate: this requires six or seven hours stewing. Make some sauce of the liquor.

To roast a Rump of Beef.

LET your beef lie two days in salt, then wash it, and lay it one hour in a quart of red wine and a pint of elder vinegar, with which baste the beef very well while it is roasting; then take two pallets well boiled, and sliced thin; make your sauce with burnt butter, gravy, mushrooms, oysters; to which add the palates, and serve it up.

To roast a loin of Mutton.

FLEE off the skin, and when it drips, drudge it with grated bread and mole-hill-thyme powder'd; do so till it is enough: you may run a long case-knife into the flesh on the inside, and stuff the whole full of forc'd meat, with bread, herbs, lemon-peel, and an egg beat up; make savoury sauce.

To roast a Breast of Mutton.

A Breast of mutton dress'd thus is very good; the forc'd-meat must be put under the skin at the end, and then the skin pinn'd down with thorns; before you dredge it, wash it over with a bunch of feathers dipt in eggs.

To roast a Shoulder of Mutton in Blood.

CUT the shoulder as you do venison, take off the skin, let it lie in the blood all night; then take as much powder of sweet-herbs as will lie on a sixpence, a little grated bread, some pepper, nutmeg and ginger, a little lemon-peel, the yolks of two eggs boil'd hard, and about twenty oysters and salt; temper all together with some of the blood, and stuff the meat thick with it, and lay some of it about the mutton; then wrap the caul of the sheep round the shoulder; roast it, and baste it with blood till it is near roasted; then take off the caul, dredge it, and baste it with butter and serve it to the table with venison-sauce in a bason. If you do not cut it venison-fashion, yet take off the skin, because it eats tough; let the caul be spread while it is warm, or it will not do well; and next day when you are to use it, wrap it up in a cloth that has been dipt into hot water: for sauce, take some of the bones of the breast, chop them, and put to them a whole onion. a bay-leaf, a piece of lemon peel, two or three anchovies, with spice that please; stew these, then add some red wine, oysters and mushrooms.

To stew a Head, Chine, and Neck of Venison.

FIRST take off all the fat, then cut it in pieces to your liking, and season it with your compound seasoning, an onion or two quartered, and two or three bay-leaves; put them in a stew-pan, with water near enough to cover them; let it ſtew till it is almoſt enough, and then put in a bottle of ſtale beer, or half red wine and half beer; it may ſtew two hours before this is in, and one after; burn a quarter of a pound of butter pretty thick with the liquor of the veniſon, and mix it with it when you ſerve it: the fat taken off muſt be put in ſome time before the veniſon has done ſtewing. If you put in beer inſtead of red wine, boil it and ſcum it before you put it in.

A Lamb Pye.

CUT a hind quarter of lamb into thin ſlices, ſeaſon it with ſweet ſpices, and lay it in the pye, mix'd with half a pound of raiſins of the ſun ſtoned, half a pound of currants, two or three *Spaniſh* potatoes boil'd, blanched, and ſliced; or an artichoke bottom or two, with prunella's, damſons, gooſberries, and cloſe the pye; when 'tis baked make a caudle for it.

A Chicken Pye.

TAKE ſix ſmall chickens; roll up a piece of butter in ſweet ſpice, and put it into them; then ſeaſon them, and lay them in the pye, with the marrow of two bones, with fruit and preſerves, as the lamb pye, with a caudle.

A Lumber Pye.

TAKE a pound and a half of fillet of veal, and mince it with the ſame quantity of beefſuet; ſeaſon it with ſweet ſpice, five pippins, an handful of ſpinach, and a hard lettuce, thyme and parſley: mix it with a penny white loaf grated, the yolks of eggs, ſack and orange-flower water, a pound and a half of currants and preſerves, as the lamb pye, with a caudle. An umble pye is made the ſame way.

A Lamb Pye.

CUT a hind quarter of lamb into thin ſlices; ſeaſon it with ſavoury ſpice, and lay them in the pye with a hard lettuce and artichoke bottoms, the tops of an hundred of aſparagus: Lay on butter, and cloſe the pye. When it is baked, pour into it a lear.

A Mutton Pye.

SEASON your mutton-ſtakes with ſavoury ſpice; fill the pye, lay on the butter, and cloſe the pye: when it is baked, toſs up a handful of chop'd capers, cucumbers and oyſters, in gravy, anchovy, and drawn butter.

A Pigeon Pye.

TRUSS and ſeaſon your pigeons with ſavoury ſpice, lard them with bacon, ſtuff them with forc'd meat, and lay them in the pye with the ingredients for ſavoury pyes, with butter, and cloſe the pye. A Lear. A chicken or capon pye is made the ſame way.

A Battalia Pye.

TAKE four ſmall chickens, four ſquab pigeons, four ſucking rabbits; cut them in pieces, ſeaſon them with ſavoury ſpice; and lay them in the pye, with four ſweet-breads ſliced, and as many ſheep's-tongues, two ſhiver'd pallates, two pair of lamb-ſtones, twenty or thirty cock's-combs, with ſavoury balls and oyſters. Lay on butter, and cloſe the pye. A Lear.

A Neats-Tongue Pye.

HALF boil the tongues, blanch and ſlice them; ſeaſon them with ſavoury ſpice, with balls, ſliced lemon and butter, and cloſe the pye. When it is baked pour into it a ragoo.

To pickle Oysters.

TAKE a quart of oysters, and wash them in their own liquor very well, till all the grittiness is out; put them in a sauce-pan or stew-pan, and strain the liquor over them, set them on the fire, and scum them; then put in three or four blades of mace, a spoonful of whole pepper-corns; when you think they are boiled enough, throw in a glass of white-wine; let them have a thorough scald; then take them up, and when they are cold, put them in a pot, and pour the liquor over them, and keep them for use. Take them out with a spoon.

To collar Eels.

TAKE your eel, and cut it open; take out the bones, cut off the head and tail, and lay the eel flat on a dresser; shred sage as fine as possible, and mix it with black pepper beat, nutmeg grated, and salt, and lay it all over the eel, and roll it up hard in little cloths, and tie it up tight at each end: then set over some water with pepper and salt, five or six cloves, three or four blades of mace, a bay-leaf or two; boil it and the bones and head and tail together; then take out the head and tail, and put it away, and put in your eels, and let them boil till they are tender; then take them out of the liquor and boil the liquor longer; then take it off, and when it is cold put it to your eels, but do not take off the little cloths till you use them.

To pot Lobsters.

TAKE a dozen of large lobsters; take out all the meat of their tails and claws after they are boiled; then season them with beaten pepper, salt, cloves, mace, and nutmeg, all finely beaten and mixed together; then take a pot, put therein a layer of fresh butter, upon which put a layer of lobsters, and then strew over some seasoning, and repeat

peat the same till your pot is full, and your lobster all in; bake it about an hour and a half, then set it by two or three days, and it will be fit to eat. It will keep a month or more, if you pour from it the liquor when it comes out of the oven, and fill it up with clarified butter. Eat it with vinegar.

Hung Beef.

MAKE a strong brine with bay-salt, peter-salt, and pump water, and steep therein a rib of beef for nine days; then hang it up a chimney where wood or saw-dust is burnt; when it is a little dry, wash the outside with blood two or three times to make it look black, and when it is dryed enough, boil it for use.

To roast a Cod's Head.

TAKE the head, wash and scour it very clean, then scotch it with a knife, strew a little salt on it, and lay it on a stew-pan before the fire, with something behind it; throw away the water that runs from it the first half hour, then strew on it some nutmeg, cloves, mace, and salt, and baste it often with butter, turning it till it is enough. If it be a large head it will take four or five hours roasting; then take all the gravy of the fish, as much white-wine, and more meat gravy, some horse-radish, one or two eschalots, a little slic'd ginger, some whole pepper, cloves, mace, and nutmeg, a bay-leaf or two; beat this liquor up with butter and the liver of the fish boiled, broke, and strained into it with the yolks of two or three eggs, some oysters and shrimps, balls made of fish and fried fish round it. Garnish with lemon and horse-radish.

To pickle Ox Palates.

TAKE your palates and wash them well with salt in the water, and put them in a pipkin, with water and ſome ſalt, and when they are ready to boil ſcum them very well, and put into them whole pepper, cloves and mace, as much as will give them a quick taſte: when they are boiled tender (which will require four or five hours) peel them and cut them into ſmall pieces, and let them cool; then make the pickle of white-wine vinegar, and as much white wine; boil the pickle, and put in the ſpice as was boil'd in the palates, adding a little freſh ſpice: put in ſix or ſeven bay-leaves, and let both pickle and palates be cold before you put them together; then keep them for uſe.

To make a Ragoo of Pigs-Ears.

TAKE a quantity of pigs-ears. and boil them in one half wine and the other water; cut them in ſmall pieces, then brown a little butter, and put them in, and a pretty deal of gravy, two anchovies, an eſchalot or two, a little muſtard, and ſome ſlices of lemon, ſome ſalt and nutmeg: ſtew all theſe together, and ſhake it up thick. Garniſh the diſh with barberries.

Beef to collar.

TAKE beef and ſeaſon it with ſalt, pepper, and ſpice, and put in a pound with a pint of claret, then roll it up with tape, and bake it in this liquor with brown bread.

To make collar'd Beef.

TAKE a flank of beef, ſalt it with white ſalt, and let it lie forty-eight hours; then waſh it, and hang it in the wind to dry twenty-four hours; then take pepper, ſalt, cloves, mace, nutmegs, and ſalt-petre, all beaten fine; mix them together, and rub it all over the inſide; roll it up hard, and tie it faſt with tape; put it in a pan with a few bay-leaves, and four pounds of butter, covering the pot with rye-paſte; bake it with houſhold bread.

Oyster Loaves.

TAKE a quart of middling oysters, and wash them in their own liquor; then strain them thro' a flannel, and put them on the fire to warm; then take three quarters of a pint of gravy and put to the oysters, with a blade of mace, a little white pepper, a little horse-radish, a piece of lean bacon, and half a lemon; then strew them leisurely. Take three penny loaves, and pick out the crumb clean; then take a pound of butter, and set on the fire in a sauce-pan that will hold the loaves, and when it is melted, take it off the fire, and let it settle; then pour off the clear, and set it on the fire again with the loaves in it, turning them about till you find them crisp; then put a pound of butter in a frying-pan, and with a dredging-box dust in flour till you find it of a reasonable thickness, then mix that and the oysters together; when they are stewed enough take out the bacon, and put the oysters into the loaves; then put them into a dish, and garnish the loaves with the oysters you cannot get in, and with slices of lemon; and when you have thickened the liquor, squeeze in lemon to your taste; or you may fry the oysters with batter to garnish the loaves.

To stew Oysters in French *Rolls.*

TAKE a quart of large oysters; wash them in their own liquor, strain it, and put them in it with a little salt, some pepper, mace, and sliced nutmeg; let the oysters stew a little with all these things, and thicken them up with a great deal of butter; then take six *French* rolls, cut a piece off the top, and take out the crumbs; take your oysters boiling hot, and fill the rolls full, set them near the fire on a chafing-dish of coals, and let them be hot through; as the liquor soaks in, fill them up with more, if you have it, or some hot gravy: So serve them up instead of a pudding.

A Veal Pye.

RAISE an high pye, then cut a fillet of veal into three or four ſlices, ſeaſon it with ſavoury ſpice, a little minced ſage and ſweet herbs; lay it in the pye, with ſlices of bacon at the bottom, and betwixt each piece lay on butter, and cloſe the pye.

A Turkey Pye.

BONE the turkey, ſeaſon it with ſavoury ſpice and lay it in the pye with two capons, or two wild-ducks cut in pieces to fill up the corners; lay on butter, and cloſe the pye.

A Florendine of a Kidney of Veal.

SHRED the kidney, fat and all, with a little ſpinach, parſley and lettuce, three pippins and orange-peel; ſeaſon it with ſweet-ſpice, ſugar, a good handful of currants, two or three grated biſkets, ſack, orange-flower-water, and two or three eggs; mix it into a body, and put it into a diſh, being cover'd with puff-paſte; lay on a cut-lid, and garniſh the brim.

A Marrow Pudding.

BOIL a quart of cream or milk, with a ſtick of cinnamon, a quarter'd nutmeg and a large blade of mace; then mix it with eight eggs well beat, a little ſalt, ſugar, ſack, and orange-flower-water; ſtrain it; then put to it three grated biſkets, an handful of currants, as many raiſins of the ſun, the marrow of two bones. all in four large pieces; put it into a diſh, having the brim thereof garniſh'd with puff-paſte, and raiſed in the oven; then lay on the four pieces of marrow, knots and paſtes, ſliced citron and lemon-peel.

A Calves-Foot Pudding.

TAKE calves-feet, ſhred them very fine, and mix them with a penny-loaf grated and ſcalded with a pint of cream; put to it half a pound of ſhred beef-ſuet, eight eggs, and a handful of plump'd currants; ſeaſon it with ſweet ſpice and ſugar, a little ſack, orange-flower-water, and the marrow of two bones; then put it in a veal caul, being waſhed over with batter of eggs; then wet a cloth and put it therein; tie it cloſe up; when the pot boils, put it in; boil it about two hours, and turn it in a diſh, ſticking in it ſliced almonds and citron; let the ſauce be ſack and orange-flower-water, with lemon-juice, ſugar and drawn butter.

To ſtuff a Shoulder or Leg of Mutton with Oyſters.

TAKE a little grated bread, ſome beef-ſuet, yolks of hard eggs, three anchovies, a bit of an onion, ſalt, pepper, thyme, winter-ſavoury, twelve oyſters, and ſome nutmeg grated: Mix all theſe together, ſhred them very fine, and work them up with raw eggs, like a paſte; ſtuff your mutton under the ſkin in the thickeſt place, or where you pleaſe, and roaſt it; for ſauce take ſome of the oyſter liquor, ſome claret, two or three anchovies, a little nutmeg, a bit of onion, and the reſt of the oyſters: ſtew all theſe together, then take out the onion, and put it under the mutton.

Sauce for boil'd Mutton.

TAKE a piece of liver as big as a pigeon's egg, and boil it tender, with half a handful of parſley and a few ſprigs of pot thyme, with the yolks of three or four eggs boiled hard; bray them with a ſpoon till they are diſſolved; then add one anchovy waſhed and ſtripped from the bone, thyme, beaten

pepper

pepper and grated nutmeg, with a little ſalt; put all theſe together in a ſauce-pan, with a glaſs of white wine, and the gravy that has drained from your leg of mutton after it is taken out of the pot, or a quarter of a pint of the liquor the mutton is boiled in: mix it all together, and give it a boil, then beat it up with three ounces of butter: you may add a tea ſpoonful of vinegar, which takes off a ſweetneſs it's apt to have: it's beſt to make the ſauce thick, or it will be too thin when the mutton is cut.

To boil a Pike.

CUT open the pike, gut it, and ſcour the outſide and inſide very well with ſalt, then waſh it clean, and have in readineſs the following pickle to boil it in; water, vinegar, mace, whole pepper, a bunch of ſweet herbs, and a ſmall onion; there muſt be liquor enough to cover it; when the liquor boils put in the pike, and make it boil ſoon, (half an hour will boil a very large pike;) make your ſauce with white wine, a little of the liquor, two anchovies, ſome ſhrimps, lobſter, or crab; beat and mix with it grated nutmeg, and butter floured to thicken it; pour your ſauce over the fiſh, garniſh with horſe-radiſh and ſliced lemon.

Soles to ſtew.

WHEN your ſoles are waſh'd, and the fins cut off, put them into a ſtew-pan, with no liquor but a quarter of a pint of white wine, ſome mace, whole pepper, and ſalt; when they are half ſtew'd, put in ſome thick cream, and a little piece of butter dipp'd in flour; when that is melted, put in ſome oyſters with their liquor; keep them often ſhaking, till the fiſh and oyſters are enough, or that the oyſters will break; ſqueeze in a little piece of lemon, give them a ſcald, and pour it into the diſh.

To

To roaſt a Pike.

TAKE a large pike, gut it, clean it, and lard it with eel and bacon, as you lard a fowl; then take thyme, ſavoury, ſalt, mace, nutmeg, ſome crumbs of bread, beef-ſuet, and parſley; ſhred all very fine, and mix it up with raw eggs; make it in a long pudding, and put it in the belly of your pike; ſew up the belly, and diſſolve the anchovies in butter, baſting it with it; put two ſplints on each ſide the pike, and tie it to the ſpit; melt butter thick for the ſauce, or if you pleaſe, oyſter-ſauce, and bruiſe the pudding in it. Garniſh with lemon.

To roaſt a Pike in Embers.

WHEN your fiſh is ſcal'd, and well dry'd in a cloth, make a pudding with ſweet-herbs, grated bread, and onion, wrapt up in butter; put it into the belly, and ſew it up, turn the tail into the mouth, and roll it up in white paper, and then in brown, wet them both, and tie them round with packthread; then rake it up in the embers, and let it lie two or three hours; then take it up, and take the pudding out of the belly; mix it with ſauce, ſuch as is uſually made for fiſh, and ſerve it up.

A Ragoo of Sweet-breads.

TAKE your ſweet-breads and ſkin them; put ſome butter in the frying-pan, brown it with flour, and put the ſweet-breads in; ſtir them a little, and turn them; then put in ſome ſtrong broth and muſhrooms, ſome pepper, ſalt, cloves and mace; let them ſtew half an hour; then put in ſome forc'd-meat balls, ſome artichoke bottoms cut ſmall and thin; make it thick, and ſerve it up with ſlic'd lemon.

A Ragoo of Oyſters.

PUT into your ſtew-pan a quarter of a pound of butter, and let it boil; then take a quart of oy-ſters, ſtrain them from their liquor, and put them to the butter; let them ſtew with a bit of eſchalot ſhred very fine, ſome grated nutmeg, and a little ſalt; then beat the yolks of three or four eggs with the oyſter liquor and half a pound of butter; ſhake all very well together till 'tis thick, and ſerve it up with ſippets, and garniſh with ſliced lemon.

To mumble Rabbits and Chickens.

PUT into the bellies of your rabbits, or chickens, ſome parſley, an onion, and the liver; ſet it over the fire in the ſtew-pan with as much water mixed with a little ſalt as will cover them; when they are half boiled take them out, and ſhred the parſley, liver, and onion; tear the fleſh from the bones of the rabbit in ſmall flakes, and put it into the ſtew-pan again with a very little of the liquor it was boiled in, a pint of white-wine, ſome gravy, half a pound or more of butter, and ſome grated nutmeg; when 'tis enough, ſhake in a little flour, and thicken it up with butter. Serve it on ſippets.

To ſtew Muſhrooms.

TAKE ſome ſtrong broth, ſeaſon it with a bunch of ſweet herbs, ſome ſpice and anchovies, ſetting it over the fire till 'tis hot; then put in the muſhrooms, and juſt let them boil up; then take the yolks of eggs, with a little minced thyme, parſley, and ſome grated nutmeg; and ſtir it over the fire till 'tis thick. Serve it up with ſliced lemon.

To collar a Calf's Head.

TAKE a calf's head with the ſkin and hair upon it; ſcald it to fetch off the hair; parboil it, but not too much; then get it clean from the bones while it is hot; you muſt ſlit it in the fore-part; ſeaſon it with pepper, ſalt, cloves, mace, nutmeg, and ſweet-herbs, ſhred ſmall, and mix'd together with the yolks of three or four eggs; ſpread it over the head, and roll it up hard. Boil it gently for

for three hours, in just as much water as will cover it; when it is tender it is boiled enough. If you do the tongue, first boil it and peel it, and slice it in thin slices, and likewise the palate, putting them and the eyes in the inside of the head before you roll it up. When the head is taken out, season the pickle with salt, pepper, and spice, and give it a boil, adding to it a pint of white wine, and as much vinegar. When it is cold, put in the collar; and when you use it, cut it in slices.

To collar Cow-Heels.

TAKE five or six cow-heels or feet, and bone them while they are hot; lay them one upon another, strewing some salt between; then roll them up in a coarse cloth, and squeeze in both ends, and tie them up very hard; boil it an hour and half; then take it out, and when it is cold put it in common souce-drink for brawn. Cut off a little at each end, it looks better. Serve it in slices, or in the collar, as you please.

A Tansy.

BOIL a quart of cream or milk with a stick of cinnamon, quarter'd nutmeg, and a large blade of mace; when half cold, mix it with twenty yolks of eggs, and ten whites; strain it, then put to it four grated biskets, half a pound of butter, a pint of spinach-juice, a little tansy, sack, orange-flower-water, sugar, and a little salt; then gather it to a body over the fire, and pour it into your dish, being well butter'd: When it is baked turn it on a pye-plate; squeeze on it an orange, grate on sugar, and garnish it with slic'd orange and a little tansy. Made in a dish; cut as you please.

Scotch Collops.

CUT your collops off a fillet of veal; cut them thin, hack them and fry them in fresh butter; then

then take them out and brown your pan with butter and flour, as you do for a ſoup. Do not make it too thick; put in your collops and ſome bacon cut thin and fry'd, and ſome forc'd-meat balls fry'd, ſome muſhrooms, oyſters, artichoke bottoms, ſliced lemon, and ſweet-breads, or lamb-ſtones; ſome ſtrong broth, gravy, and thick butter; toſs up all together. Garniſh the diſh with ſliced lemon.

To ſtew a Rump of Beef.

SEASON your rump of beef with two nutmegs, ſome pepper and ſalt, and lay the fat ſide downward in your ſtew-pan; put to it a quarter of a pint of vinegar, a pint of claret, three pints of water, three whole onions ſtuck with a few cloves, and a bunch of ſweet-herbs; cover it cloſe, and let it ſtew over a gentle fire four or five hours; ſcum off the fat from the liquor. Lay your meat on ſippets, and pour your liquor over it. Garniſh your diſh with ſcalded greens.

To roaſt an Eel.

TAKE a large eel, and ſcour him well with ſalt; ſkin him almoſt to the tail; then gut, and waſh, and dry him; take a quarter of a pound of ſuet, ſhred as fine as poſſible; put to it ſweet-herbs, an eſchalot likewiſe, ſhred very fine, and mix it together with ſome ſalt, pepper, and grated nutmeg; ſcotch your eel on both ſides, the breadth of a finger's diſtance, and waſh it with yolks of eggs, and ſtrew ſome ſeaſoning over it, and ſtuff the belly with it; then draw the ſkin over it, put a long ſkewer thro' it, and tie it to the ſpit, baſte it with butter, and make the ſauce anchovy and butter melted.

To make a pale Fricaſee.

TAKE lamb, chicken, or rabbits, cut in pieces, waſh it well from the blood, then put it in a broad pan or ſtew-pan; put in as much fair

water

water as will cover it ; add ſalt, a bunch of ſweet-herbs, ſome pepper, an onion, two anchovies, and ſtew it till it is enough ; then mix in a porringer ſix yolks of eggs, a glaſs of white wine, a nutmeg grated, a little chop'd parſley, a piece of freſh butter, and three or four ſpoonfuls of cream ; beat all theſe together, and put it in a ſtew-pan, ſhaking it together till it is thick. Diſh it on ſippets, and garniſh with ſliced lemon.

To pickle Oyſters.

OPEN your oyſters, get the grit from them, and ſtew them in their own liquor in an earthen pipkin till they are tender ; then take up the oyſters, and cover them, that they may not be diſcoloured ; then increaſe the liquor with as much more water, and let it boil till one third is conſumed ; then put your oyſters into your pot or barrel, laying between the rows ſome whole pepper and ſpice, and a few bay-leaves ; and when the pickle is cold, put it to your oyſters, and keep them very cloſe covered.

To haſh a Calf's Head.

BOIL your calf's head almoſt enough, and when it is cold, cut the meat in thin ſlices clean from the bones ; put it into a ſtew-pan, with ſome ſtrong broth, a glaſs of white wine, ſome oyſters and their liquor, a bunch of ſweet-herbs, two or three eſchalots, a nutmeg quarter'd, and let theſe ſtew over a ſlow fire till they are enough ; then put in two or three anchovies, the yolks of four eggs well beaten and a piece of butter, and thicken it up ; then have ready fry'd ſome thin ſlips of bacon, ſome forc'd-meat balls, ſome large oyſters dipp'd in butter ; the brains firſt boiled and then fried, ſome ſweet-herbs cut in ſlices, ſome lamb-ſtones cut in rounds ; then put your haſh in your diſh, and the other things, ſome round and ſome on it. Garniſh the diſh with ſliced lemon.

To make Scotch Collops.

CUT thin flices out of a leg of veal, as many as you think will ferve for a difh, hack them, and lard fome with bacon, and fry them in butter; then take them out of the pan, and keep them warm; clean the pan, and put into it half a pint of oyfters, with their liquor, fome ftrong broth, one or two efchalots, a glafs of white wine, two or three anchovies minced, fome grated nutmeg; let thefe have a boil up, and thicken it with four or five eggs and a piece of butter; then put in your collops, and fhake them together till it is thick; put dried fippets on the bottom of the difh, and put your collops in, and fo many as you pleafe of the things in your hafh.

A Fricafee of Veal.

CUT a fillet of veal in thin flices, a little broader than a crown-piece, beat them with a rolling-pin to make them tender; then fteep them in milk three hours, take a blade or two of mace, a few corns of pepper, a fmall fprig of thyme, a little piece of lemon-peel, a bone of mutton and the veal-bones; ftew them gently all together for fauce; if you have no mutton, a little piece of beef, if no beef, a fpoonful of gravy at leaft; then drain the milk from the veal, and put frefh milk into a ftew-pan, and ftew the veal in it without falt, for that curdles the milk; ftew it till it is enough, or you may half ftew it, and fry it as pale as poffible; then drain it, and ftrain the fauce, which beat up with fome falt, flour, and butter, a pretty deal of cream, and fome white wine: juft at the laft you may fhred a little parfley, and fcalding it, ftrew it upon the veal, and fqueeze a little lemon, which will thicken the fauce. You may make the fame fauce for this as you do for the boiled turkey, if you like it better.

Pulled Chickens.

BOIL six chickens near enough; flea them and pull the white flesh all off from the bones; put it in a stew-pan with half a pint of cream, made scalding hot, the gravy that runs from the chickens, a few spoonfuls of that liquor they were boil'd in; to this add some raw parsley shred fine, give them a toss or two over the fire, and dust a little flour upon some butter, and shake up with them. Chicks done this way must be killed the night before, and a little more than half boiled, and pulled in pieces as broad as your finger, and half as long; you may add a spoonful of white wine.

A Fricasee of Chickens.

AFTER you have drawn and washed your chickens, half boil them; then take them up, cut them in pieces, put them into a frying-pan, and fry them in butter; then take them out of the pan, clean it, and put in some strong broth, some white wine, some grated nutmeg, a little pepper, salt, a bunch of sweet herbs, and an eschalot or two; let these, with two or three anchovies, stew on a slow fire and boil up; then beat it up with butter and eggs till it is thick; put your chickens in, and toss them well together; lay sippets in the dish, and serve it up with sliced lemon and fried parsley.

A fine Side-Dish.

TAKE veal, chicken, or rabbit, with as much marrow, or beef-suet, as meat; a little thyme, lemon-peel, marjoram, two anchovies, washed and boned; a little pepper, salt, mace, and cloves; bruise the yolks of hard eggs, some oysters, or mushrooms; mix all these together, chop them, and beat them in a mortar very fine;

 then

then spread the caul of a breast of veal on a table, and lay a layer of this, and a layer of middling bacon, cut in thin small pieces, rolling it up hard in the caul; roast or bake it, as you like; cut it into thin slices, and lay it in your dish, with a rich gravy sauce.

Gravy to keep for Use.

TAKE a piece of coarse beef, cover it with water; when it has boiled some time, take out the meat; beat it very well, and cut it in pieces to let out the gravy; then put it in again, with a bunch of sweet herbs, an onion stuck with cloves, a little salt, and some whole pepper; let it stew, but not boil; when it is of a brown colour it is enough; take it up; put it in an earthen pot, and let it stand to cool; when it is cold skim off the fat: it will keep a week unless the weather be very hot. If for a brown fricasee, put some butter in your frying pan, and shake in it a little flour as it boils, and put in some gravy, with a glass of claret, and shake up the fricasee in it. If for a white fricasee, then melt your butter in the gravy, with a little white wine, a spoonful or two of cream, and the yolks of eggs.

An Amulet of Eggs the savoury Way.

TAKE a dozen of eggs, beat them very well, season them with salt, and a little pepper, then have your frying-pan ready with a good deal of fresh butter in it, and let it be thoroughly hot; then put in your eggs, with four spoonfuls of strong gravy, and have ready parsley, and a few chives cut, and throw them over it, and when it is enough turn it; and when done, dish it, and squeeze orange or lemon over it.

A Fricasee of Rabbits.

CUT and wash your rabbits very well; put them in a frying-pan, with a pound of butter, an onion stuck with cloves, a bunch of sweet herbs, and some salt; let it stew till it is enough; then beat up the yolks of six eggs, with a glass of white wine, a little parsley shred, a nutmeg grated, and mix it by degrees with the liquor in your pan; shake it till it is thick, and serve it up on sippets. Garnish the dish with sliced lemon.

A Fricasee of Tripe.

TAKE lean tripes, cut and scrape them from all the loose stuff; cut them in pieces two inches square, and then cut them a-cross from corner to corner, or in what shape you please; put them into a stew-pan, with half as much white wine as will cover them, sliced ginger, whole pepper, a blade of mace, a little sprig of rosemary, a bay-leaf, an onion, or a small clove of garlick; when it begins to stew, a quarter of an hour will do it; then take out the herbs and onion, and put in a little shred parsley, the juice of a lemon, and a little piece of anchovy shred small, a few spoonfuls of cream, the yolk of an egg, or a piece of butter: salt it to your taste; when it is in the dish, you may lay on a little boiled spinach and sliced lemon.

A Fricasee of double Tripe.

CUT your tripe in slices two inches long, and put it into a stew-pan; put to it a quarter of a pound of capers, as much samphire shred, half a pint of strong broth, as much white wine, a bunch of sweet herbs, a lemon shred small; stew all these together till it is tender; then take it off the fire, and thicken up the liquor with the yolks of three or four eggs, a little parsley boiled green and chopt, some grated nutmeg and salt; shake it well together; serve it on sippets; garnish with lemon.

A Fricasee of Ox-Palates.

MAKE the gravy thus: Take two pounds of beef, cut it in little bits, and put it in a sauce-pan, with a quart of water, some salt, some whole pepper, an onion, an eschalot or two, two or three anchovies, a bit of horse-radish; let all these stew till it is strong gravy; then strain it out, and set it by; then have ten or twelve ox-palates, boil them till they are tender, peel them, and cut them in square pieces; then flay and draw two or three chickens, cut them between every joint, season them with a little nutmeg, salt, and shred thyme, put them in a pan, and fry them with butter; when they are half fry'd, put in half your gravy, and all your palates, and let them stew together; put the rest of your gravy into a sauce-pan, and when it boils, thicken it up with the yolks of three or four eggs, beaten with a glass of white wine, a piece of butter, and three or four spoonfuls of thick cream; then pour all into your pan, shake it well together, and dish it up; garnish with pickled grapes.

A Fricasee of great Plaice or Flounders.

RUN your knife all along upon the bone on the back-side of your plaice, then raise the flesh on both sides from the head to the tail, and take out the bone clear; then cut your plaice in six collops, dry it very well from the water, sprinkle it with salt, flour it well, and fry it in a very hot pan of beef-dripping, so that it may be crisp; take it out of the pan, and keep it warm before the fire; then make clean the pan, and put into it oysters and their liquor, some white wine, the meat of the shell of a crab or two: mince half the oysters, some grated nutmeg, three anchovies; let all these stew up together;

together; then put in half a pound of butter, and put in your plaice; toſs them well together, diſh them on ſippets, and pour the ſauce over them; garniſh the diſh with yolks of hard eggs minced, and ſliced lemon. After this manner do ſalmon, or any firm fiſh.

To fricaſee Fiſh.

MELT butter according to the quantity of fiſh you have, melt it thick, cut your fiſh in pieces in length and breadth three fingers, then put them and your butter into a frying or ſtew-pan; it muſt not boil too faſt, for fear of breaking the fiſh, and turning the butter into oil; turn them often till they are enough; put in a bunch of ſweet herbs at firſt, an onion, two or three anchovies cut ſmall, a little pepper, nutmeg, mace, lemon-peel, two or three cloves; when all theſe are in, put in ſome claret, and let them ſtew all together; beat up ſix yolks of eggs and put them in, with ſuch pickles as you pleaſe, as oyſters, muſhrooms, and capers; ſhake them well together that they do not curdle; if you put the ſpice in whole, take it out when it is done; the ſeaſoning ought to be ſtewed firſt in a little water, and then the butter melted in that and wine before you put the fiſh in. Jacks do beſt this way.

A Craw-fiſh Soup.

CLEANSE your craw fiſh, and boil them in water, ſalt and ſpice, pull off their feet and tails, and fry them; break the reſt of them in a ſtone-mortar, ſeaſon them with ſavoury ſpice and an onion, hard eggs, grated bread, and ſweet herbs boiled in ſtrong broth; ſtrain it; put to it ſcalded chopt parſley and *French* rolls, then put them therein with a few dry'd muſhrooms: garniſh the diſh with ſliced lemon, and the feet and tails of the craw-fiſh. A lobſter-ſoup is done the ſame way.

To boil Mullet, or any sort of Fish.

SCALE your fish, and wash them, saving their liver, or tripes, rows or spawn; boil them in water seasoned with salt, white wine vinegar, white wine, a bunch of sweet herbs, a sliced lemon, one or two onions, some horse-radish; and when it boils up put in your fish; and for sauce, a pint of oysters with their liquor, a lobster bruised or minced, or shrimps, some white wine, two or three anchovies, some large mace, a quartered nutmeg, a whole onion; let these have a boil up, and thicken it with butter and the yolks of two or three eggs: serve it on sippets, and garnish with lemon.

To butter Shrimps.

STEW a quart of shrimps in half a pint of white wine, a nutmeg grated, and a good piece of butter; when the butter is melted, and they are hot through, beat the yolks of four eggs, with a little white wine, and pour it in; shake it well, till it is of the thickness you like; then dish it on sippets, and garnish with sliced lemon.

To butter Crabs or Lobsters.

YOUR crabs and lobsters being boiled and cold, take all the meat out of the shells and body, break the claws, and take out all their meat, mince it small, and put it altogether, adding to it two or three spoonfuls of claret, a very little vinegar, a nutmeg grated; let it boil up till it is thorough hot; then put in some butter melted, with some anchovies and gravy, and thicken up with the yolks of an egg or two; when it is very hot put it in the large shell, and stick it with toasts.

Another.

TAKE the meat out of the ſhells, and mix it well together with ſome white wine, grated nutmeg, ſalt, and the juice of a lemon, or a little vinegar, put it into a ſauce-pan and ſtir it over a ſlow fire, with a piece of butter. If they are crabs, warm the ſhells and put the meat in again; if lobſters, in a china diſh; ſome beaten pepper does well.

To roaſt Lobſters.

TIE your lobſters to the ſpit alive, baſte them with water and ſalt till they look very red, and are enough; then baſte them with butter and ſalt, take them up, and ſet little diſhes round with the ſauce, ſome plain melted butter, ſome oyſter-ſauce.

To ſtew Carp.

TAKE a live carp, cut him in the neck and tail, and ſave the blood; then open him in the belly; take care you do not break the gall; put a little vinegar in the belly, to waſh out the blood; ſtir all the blood with your hand; then put your carp into a ſtew-pan; if you have two carps, you may cut off one of their heads an inch below the gills, and ſlit the body in two, and put it into your ſtew-pan after you have rubbed them with ſalt; but before you put them in, your liquor muſt boil, a quart of claret, or as much as will cover them, the blood you ſaved, an onion ſtuck with cloves, a bunch of ſweet-herbs, ſome gravy, three anchovies. When this liquor boils up, put in your fiſh, cover it cloſe, and let it ſtew up for about a quarter of an hour; then turn it, and let it ſtew a little longer; then put your carp into a diſh, and beat up the ſauce with butter melted in oyſter-liquor, and pour your ſauce over it. Your milt, ſpawn, and rivets muſt be laid on the top: garniſh the diſh with fry'd ſmelts, oyſters, or pitchcock-eel, lemon and fry'd parſley.

Another Way to ſtew Carp.

TAKE two carps, ſcale and rub them well with ſalt; cut them in the nape of the neck and round the tail, to make them bleed; cut up the belly, take out the liver and guts, and if you pleaſe to cut each carp in three pieces, they will eat the firmer; then put them in a ſtew-pan, with their blood, a quart of claret, a bunch of ſweet herbs, an onion, one or two eſchalots, a nutmeg, a few cloves, mace, whole pepper; cover them cloſe and let them ſtew till they are half enough, then turn them, and put half a pound of freſh butter, four anchovies, the liver and guts taking out the gall, and let them ſtew till they are enough; then beat the yolks of five or ſix eggs wih a little verjuice, and by degrees mix it with the liquor the carp was ſtewed in: juſt give it a ſcald to thicken it; then put your carp in a diſh, and pour this over it; garniſh the diſh with a ſliced lemon.

To collar Salmon.

TAKE a ſide of ſalmon, and cut off about a handful of the tail; waſh your large piece very well, and dry it with a cloth; waſh it over with the yolks of eggs; then make ſome forc'd-meat with that you cut off the tail; but take off the ſkin, and put to it a handful of parboil'd oyſters, a tail or two of lobſter, the yolks of three or four eggs boil'd hard, ſix anchovies, a good handful of ſweet herbs chopt ſmall, a little ſalt, cloves, mace, nutmeg, pepper, and grated bread; work all theſe together into a body with the yolks of eggs, and lay it all over the fleſhy part, and a little more pepper and ſalt over the ſalmon; ſo roll it up in a collar, and bind it with broad tape; then boil it in water and ſalt, and vinegar; but let the liquor boil firſt;

then

then put in your collars, and a bunch of sweet herbs, sliced ginger and nutmeg; let it boil, but not too fast; it will require near two hours boiling; when it is near enough, take it up; put it in your sousing-pan, and when the pickle is cold, put it to your salmon, and let it stand in it till used; otherwise you may pot it after it is boiled, and fill it up with clarified butter, as you pot fowls; that way will keep longest and best.

Eels to collar.

SPLIT them down the belly, and take the bones out clean, make a seasoning with spice powder'd, and herbs chopt fine; strew it in, and roll them up, and sew a cloth over each eel, so boil them in a pickle made as for tench, and when they are boiled enough, lay them out and keep them in it; the cloths must be taken off when the eels are cold.

To collar Venison.

TAKE a side of venison, bone it, and take away all the sinews, and cut it into square collars, of what bigness you please; it will make two or three collars; lard it with fat clear bacon, cut your lards as big as the top of your finger, and as long as your little finger, then season your venison with pepper, salt, cloves, mace, and nutmeg; roll up your collars, and tie them close with coarse tape; them put them into deep pots; put seasoning at the bottom of the pot, with fresh butter, and three or four bay-leaves; then put in your venison, some seasoning, and butter on the top, and over that some beef-suet finely shred and beaten; then cover up your pot with coarse paste; they will take four or five hours baking; then take them out of the oven, and let it stand a little; then take out your venison, and let it drain well from the gravy: take off all the fat from the gravy, and add more butter to that fat, and set it over a gentle fire to clarify; then

then take it off, and let it ſtand a little, and ſkim it well; then make your pots clean, or have pots fit for each collar: put a little ſeaſoning at the bottom, and ſome of your clarified butter; then put in your veniſon, and fill up your pots with clarified butter; and be ſure your butter be an inch above the meat; and when it is thorough cold, tie it down with double paper, and lay a tile on the top; they will keep ſix or eight months: you may, if you pleaſe, when you uſe a pot, put it in boiling water a minute, and it will come whole out: Let it ſtand till it is cold, and ſtick it round with bay-leaves, and one ſprig on the top.

To pot Neats-Tongues.

TAKE neats-tongues, and rub them very well with ſalt and water (bay ſalt is beſt;) then take pump-water, with a good deal of ſalt-petre, ſome white ſalt, and ſome cloves and mace; boil it well and ſkim it; when it is cold put your tongues in, and let them lie in it ſix days; then waſh them out of the liquor, put them in a pot, and bake them with bread till they are very tender; when they are taken out of the oven, pull off their ſkins, put them in the pot you intend to keep them in, and cover them over with clarified butter: they will keep four or five months.

To collar a Breaſt of Veal.

TAKE a breaſt of veal, bone it, waſh it, and dry it in a clean cloth; then ſhred thyme, winter-ſavoury, and parſley, very ſmall, and mix it with ſalt, pepper, cloves, mace, and nutmeg; then ſtrew it on the inſide of your meat, and roll it up hard, beginning at the neck end; tie it up with tape, and put it in a pot fit to boil it in, ſtanding upright: you muſt boil it in water and ſalt, and a bunch of ſweet herbs; when it is boiled enough take it off the fire, put it in an earthen pot, and when the

the liquor is cold pour it over, or else boil salt and water strong enough to bear an egg; and when that is cold, pour it on your veal: when you serve it to the table, cut it in round slices. Garnish with laurel and fennel.

To collar a Pig.

CUT off the head of your pig, and the body asunder; bone it, and cut two collars off each side; lay it in water to take out the blood; then take sage and parsley, shred them very small, mix them with pepper, salt, and nutmeg, strewing some on every side, or collar, and roll it up, and tie it with coarse tape; boil them in fair water and salt, till they are very tender: put two or three blades of mace in the kettle, and when they are enough, take them up and lay them in something to cool; strain out some of the liquor, and add to it some vinegar and salt, a little white wine, and three or four bay-leaves; give it a boil up, and when it is cold put it to the collars, and keep them for use.

To pot Beef.

TAKE a good buttock of beef, cut out the bone, lay it flat, and slash it in several places; salt it well, and let it lie in the salt three days; then take it out, and let it lie in running water with a handful of salt three days longer; then take it out, dry it with a cloth, and season it with pepper, salt, nutmeg, cloves, mace, and two ounces of salt-petre finely beaten; then shred two or three pounds of beef-suet, and one pound in lumps, and three pounds of butter, put some in the bottom of the pot you bake it in; then put in your beef and the rest of the butter and suet on the top; cover your pot over with coarse paste, and set it in all night with houshold-bread; in the morning draw it, and pour off all the fat into a pot, and drain out all the gravy; pull the meat all to pieces, fat and lean,

lean, and work it into your pots that you keep it in while it is hot, or it will not close so well; then cover it with the clear fat you poured off; paper it when it is cold; it will keep good a month or six weeks.

To make artificial Venison.

BONE a rump of beef, or a large shoulder of mutton; then beat it with a rolling-pin; season it with pepper and nutmeg; lay it twenty-four hours in sheep's-blood; then dry it with a cloth, and season it again with pepper, salt, and spice. Put your meat in the form of a paste, and bake it as a venison-pasty, and make a gravy with the bones, to put in when it is drawn out of the oven.

Scotch-Collops.

TAKE the skin from a fillet of veal, and cut it in thin collops, hack and scotch them with the back of a knife, lard half of them with bacon, and fry them with a little brown butter; then take them out and put them into another tossing-pan; then set the pan they were fry'd in over the fire again, and wash it out with a little strong broth, rubbing it with your ladle, then pour it to the collops, do this every pan full till all are fried; then stew and toss them up with a pint of oysters, two anchovies, two shiver'd palates, cock's-combs, lamb-stones, and sweet-breads, blanch'd and sliced, savoury balls, onions, a faggot of sweet herbs; thicken it with brown butter, and garnish it with lemons.

Chickens forced with Oysters.

LARD and truss them; make a forcing with oysters, sweet-breads, parsley, truffles, mushrooms, and onions; chop these together, and season it; mix it with a piece of butter and the yolk of an egg; then tie them at both ends and roast them; then make for them a ragoo, and garnish them with sliced lemon.

A Calf's

A Calf's-Head haſh'd.

YOUR calf's-head being ſlit and cleanſed, half boiled and cold, cut one ſide into thin pieces and fry it in butter; then having a toſſing-pan on the ſtove with a ragoo for made-diſhes, toſs it up and ſtew it together, and ſcotch the other ſide croſs and croſs, flour, baſte, and boil it. The haſh being thickened with brown butter, put it in the diſh; lay over and about it fried balls, and the tongue ſliced and larded with bacon, lemon-peel, and beet-root; then fry the batter of eggs, ſliced ſweet-breads, carv'd ſippets and oyſters; lay in the head, and place theſe on and about the head; and garniſh it with ſliced orange and lemon.

A Ragoo of a Breaſt of Veal.

BONE a breaſt of veal, cut a handſome ſquare piece, and the other part into ſmall pieces, brown it in butter; then ſtew and toſs it up in your ragoo for made-diſhes; thicken it with brown butter; put then the ragoo in the diſh, lay on the ſquare piece dic'd, with lemon, ſweet-breads, ſippets, and bacon fry'd in the batter of eggs, and garniſh it with ſliced orange.

To recover Veniſon when it ſtinks.

TAKE as much cold water in a tub as will cover it a handful over, and put in good ſtore of ſalt, and let it lie three or four hours; then take your veniſon out, and let it lie in as much hot water and ſalt; and let it lie as long as before; then have your cruſt in readineſs, and take it out, and dry it very well, and ſeaſon it with pepper and ſalt pretty high, and put it in your paſty. Do not uſe the bones of your veniſon for gravy, but get freſh beef or other bones.

How to force a Fowl.

TAKE a good fowl, kill, pull and draw it; slit the skin down the back, take off the flesh from the bones; mince it very small, and mix it with one pound of beef-suet shred, and a pint of large oysters chop'd, two anchovies, an eschalot, a little grated bread, some sweet herbs; shred all these very well, mix them, and make it up with yolks of eggs, put all these ingredients on the bones again, and draw the skin over again; sew up the back, and put the fowl in a bladder; boil it an hour and a quarter; then stew some more oysters in gravy, bruise in a little of your forc'd-meat, and beat it up with fresh butter; put the fowl in the middle; pour on the sauce and garnish with sliced lemon.

To boil Fowls and Cabbage.

TAKE a well-shap'd cabbage, peel off some of the out-side leaves, and cut a piece out of the top; then scoop out the inside, and fill the hole with savoury forc'd-meat beat up with two eggs; let it be tied up as a pudding in a cloth, but first put on the top of the cabbage. When the out-side is tender, lay it between two bon'd fowls, and on them all some melted butter and slices of fried bacon.

To marinade a Leg of Lamb.

TAKE a leg of lamb, cut it in pieces the bigness of a half crown; hack them with the back of a knife; then take an eschalot, three or four anchovies, some cloves, mace, nutmeg, all beaten; put your meat in a dish, strew the seasoning over it, put it in a stew-pan, with as much white wine, as will cover it, and let it lie two hours; then put it all together in a frying-pan, and let it be half enough; then take it out, drain it through a colander, saving the liquor, and put to it a little pepper and salt, and half

half a pint of gravy; dip your meat in yolks of eggs, and fry it brown in butter; thicken up your sauce with yolks of eggs and butter, and pour it in the dish with your meat: lay sweet-breads and forc'd-meat balls over your meat; dip them in eggs, and fry them. Garnish with lemon.

To force a Leg of Veal, Mutton, or Lamb.

TAKE out all the meat, and leave the skin whole; then take the lean of it and make it into forc'd-meat thus: to two pounds of your lean meat, three pounds of beef-suet; take away all skins from the meat and suet; then shred both very fine, and beat it with a rolling-pin, till you know not the meat from the suet; then mix with it four spoonfuls of grated bread, half an ounce of cloves and mace beaten, as much pepper, some salt, a few sweet-herbs shred small; mix all these together with six raw eggs, and put into the skin again, and sew it up. If you roast it, serve it with anchovy-sauce; if you boil it, lay cauliflower or *French*-beans under it. Garnish with pickles, or stew oysters and put under it, with forc'd-meat balls, or sausages fry'd in butter.

To ragoo a Breast of Veal.

LARD your breast of veal with bacon; then half boil it in water and salt, whole pepper, and a bunch of sweet herbs; take it out, and dust it with some grated bread, sweet herbs shred small, and grated nutmeg and salt, all mixed together; then broil it on both sides, and make a sauce of anchovies and gravy thicken'd up with butter. Garnish with pickles.

To fry Oysters.

BEAT eggs with a little salt, grated nutmeg, and thicken it like thick batter, with grated white

white bread and fine flour; then dip the oysters in it, and fry them brown with beef-dripping.

Beef A-la-mode.

TAKE a good buttock of beef interlarded with great lard, roll'd up in savoury spice and sweet herbs; put it in a great sauce-pan, and cover it close, and set it in the oven all night. This is fit to eat cold.

A Goose, Turkey, or Leg of Mutton, A-la-daube.

LARD it with bacon, and half roast it; take it off the spit, and put it in as small a pot as will boil it, put to it a quart of white wine, strong broth, a pint of vinegar, whole spice, bay-leaves, sweet-marjoram, winter-savoury, and green onions. When it is ready, lay it in the dish, make sauce with some of the liquor, mushrooms, dic'd lemon, two or three anchovies, thicken it with brown butter, and garnish it with sliced lemon.

A Leg of Mutton A-la-royal.

LARD your mutton and slices of veal with bacon roll'd in spice and sweet herbs; bring them to a brown with melted lard; boil the leg of mutton in strong broth, with all sorts of sweet-herbs, and an onion stuck with cloves; when it is ready lay it on the dish, lay round the collops, then pour on it a ragoo; garnish with lemon and orange.

A brown Fricasee of Chickens or Rabbits.

CUT them in pieces, and fry them in butter; then having ready hot a pint of gravy, a little claret, white wine, strong broth, two anchovies, two shiver'd palates, a faggot of sweet herbs, savoury balls and spice, thicken it with brown butter, and squeeze on it a lemon.

A white

A white Fricaſee of the ſame.

CUT them in pieces, waſh them from the blood, and fry them on a ſlow fire; then put them in a toſſing pan, with a little ſtrong broth; ſeaſon them, and toſs them up with muſhrooms, and oyſters; when almoſt enough, put to them a pint of cream, thicken it with a bit of butter rolled up in flour.

A Fricaſee of Lamb.

CUT an hind quarter of lamb into thin ſlices, ſeaſon it with ſavoury ſpice, ſweet-herbs, and a ſhallot; then fry then, and toſs them up in ſtrong broth, white wine, oyſters, balls and palates, a little brown butter tc thicken it, or a bit of butter roll'd up in flour.

Sauce for a Woodcock.

TAKE a very little claret, ſome good gravy. a blade of mace, ſome whole pepper, an eſchalot; let theſe ſtew a little, then thicken it up with butter; roaſt the guts in the woodcock, and let them run on ſippets, or a toaſt of white bread, and lay it under your woodcock, and pour the ſauce into the diſh.

White Cucumber Sauce.

TAKE ſix or eight cucumbers for ſix chickens, according as they are in bigneſs; pare and ſlice them with a piece of onion, ſome pepper, and ſalt, and as much water as will ſtew them till they are tender; then toſs them up in ſome butter roll'd in flour; it muſt be as thick as you can well make it, without burning it, which it is ſubject to; you may ſtrain it through a thin colander into another ſauce-pan, to take out the ſeeds, then heat it, and you may pour it upon the chickens, rabbets, or neck of veal.

Brown Cucumber Sauce.

PARE and slice them with a piece of onion, then put a piece of butter in the frying-pan, and when it is hot put in your cucumbers with flour on them, and stew them till they are brown; then take them out of the pan with a slice, and put them into a sauce-pan, with a little sauce made of broth or gravy, that is savoury; when you have so done, burn a piece of butter in a pan, and when it is sufficiently burnt, put your cucumber sauce in by degrees, and season it with salt to your taste.

To fry Cucumbers for Mutton Sauce.

YOU must brown some butter in a pan, and cut the cucumbers in thin slices; drain them from the water, then fling them into the pan, and when they are fry'd brown, put in a little pepper and salt, a bit of onion and gravy, and let them stew together, and squeeze in some juice of lemon; shake them well, and put them under your mutton.

To hash roasted Mutton.

TAKE your mutton half roasted, and cut it in pieces as big as a half-crown; then put into your sauce-pan half a pint of claret, as much strong broth or gravy (or water, if you have not the other) one anchovy, an eschalot, a little whole pepper, some nutmeg sliced, salt to your taste, some oyster-liquor, a pint of oysters; let these stew a little, then put in the meat, and a few capers and samphire shred; when it is hot through, thicken it up with a piece of fresh butter roll'd in flour; toast sippets, and lay in your dish, and pour your meat on them. Garnish with lemon.

To hash a Lamb's Pumice.

BOIL the head and neck at most a quarter of an hour, the heart five minutes, and the lights

lights half an hour, the liver boil'd or fry'd in ſlices (but not haſh'd) ſlice all the reſt very thin, put in the gravy that runs from it, and a quarter of a pint of the liquor they are boiled in, a few ſpoonfuls of walnut liquor, or a little elder vinegar, a little catchup, pepper, ſalt, and nutmeg, the brains a little boil'd and chopt, with half a ſpoonful of flour and a piece of butter as big, as a walnut mixed up with them; but before you put in the butter, put in four middling cucumbers ſlic'd thin and ſtew'd a little time, or you may fry them in butter before you put them into the haſh, and ſhake them up together; but they are excellent good if only ſtew'd: at the time of the year, green gooſberries ſcalded, and in grape time, green grapes, to ſtew on the top.

To make a ſavoury Diſh of Veal.

CUT large collops out of a leg of veal, ſpread them abroad on a dreſſer, hack them with the back of a knife, dip them in the yolks of eggs, and ſeaſon them with cloves, mace, nutmeg, ſalt, pepper; then make forc'd-meat with ſome of your veal, beef-ſuet, oyſters chopt, ſweet herbs ſhred fine, and the aforeſaid ſpice, and ſtrew all theſe over your collops; roll and tie them up, put them on ſkewers, tie them to a ſpit, and roaſt them; to the reſt of your forc'd-meat add the yolk of an egg or two, make it up in balls, and fry them; put them in the diſh with your meat when roaſted, and make the ſauce with ſtrong broth, or anchovy, an eſchalot, and a little white wine and ſpice; let it ſtew, and thicken it up with butter.

Mutton Cutlets.

CUT a neck of mutton bone by bone, and beat it flat with your cleaver; have ready ſeaſoning, with grated bread, a little thyme rubb'd to powder, ſhred parſley, with grated nutmeg, and ſome lemon-peels minced; then beat up two eggs, flour your cutlets on both ſides; dip them in the eggs beat up with a little ſalt, and roll them in the grated bread and ſeaſoning; put ſome butter in your frying-pan, and when it is hot lay in your cutlets, and fry them brown on both ſides; for ſauce, take gravy or ſtrong broth, an onion, ſome ſpice, a bit of bacon and a bay-leaf, and boil them well together; then beat it up with an anchovy, or ſome oyſters, and a quarter of a pint of red wine; ſtrew upon your cutlets pickled walnuts in quarters, barberries, ſamphire or cucumbers and a little ſliced lemon.

To ſtew a Knuckle of Veal.

CUT your veal in proper pieces, ſeaſon it with ſalt, whole pepper, and large mace, and put the bone chopt amongſt the meat; fill it a little more than half full with water; ſtew it ſlowly near an hour; then take up the meat, and cover it up warm, ſtrain out the ſpice and bones, bray the mace with a little of the liquor, and put in a quarter of a pint of thick cream and the yolk of an egg; if you have no cream, ſome butter dipt in flour; ſcald it in well over the fire with the reſt of the liquor, then pour upon the veal, and ſerve it.

To dreſs a Neck of Mutton.

TAKE the beſt end of a neck of mutton, cut it into ſtakes, and beat them with a rolling-pin; then ſtrew ſome ſalt on them, and lay them in a frying-pan; hold the pan over a ſlow fire, that may not burn them; turn them as they heat, and there will be gravy enough to fry them in till they are half enough; then put to them broth made thus: take the ſcrag end of the mutton, break it in pieces, and put it in a pipkin with three pints of water, an onion, and ſome ſalt; when it firſt boils ſkim it very well, cover it, and let it boil an hour; then put to it half a pint of white wine, a ſpoonful of vinegar, a nutmeg quarter'd, a little pepper,

per, a bunch of ſweet herbs; cover it again, and let it boil till it comes to a pint; then ſtrain it thro' a hair ſieve, and put this liquor in the frying-pan, and let it fry together till it is enough; then put in a good piece of butter, ſhake it together, and ſerve it up. Garniſh with pickles.

Collar'd Mutton to eat hot.

TAKE two loins of mutton, or a neck and breaſt, bone them, and take off all the ſkin; then take ſome of the fat off from the loins, and make ſavoury forc'd-meat to ſpread on them, and clap the two inſides together, and where the fleſh is thick, cut it, and put in ſome of the forc'd-meat, (firſt beating it with a rolling-pin) and ſeaſon it well with pepper and ſalt, beſides the ſpice that is in the forc'd-meat; roll this up as cloſe as you can, and then bind a cloth over it, and ſew it up cloſe: boil it in broth, or ſalt and water; and when it is more than half boiled, ſtraiten the cloth; when enough, cut the collar into three pieces, lay upon them heaps of boiled ſpinach, ſliced lemon, and pickled barberries: before you divide your collar, cut a little ſlice off from each end, that they may ſtand well in the diſh; make ſauce with the bones of the mutton boiled in ſome of the broth, an onion, ſome whole ſpice, a piece of bacon, a bay-leaf, an anchovy, a little piece of lemon-peel, and ſome red wine; beat it up with butter, and ſome oyſters, if you have them; this will require near four hours boiling: your collar may be made over night; you may boil a little brown toaſt in your ſauce with walnut pickle; you ought to make forc'd-meat enough for balls, to fry and put into the ſauce.

To collar a Breaſt of Mutton.

TAKE a large breaſt of mutton, cut off the red ſkin, the bones and griſtles, then grate white bread, a little cloves, mace, ſalt, and pepper,

 the

the yolks of three hard eggs bruiſed ſmall, and a little lemon-peel ſhred fine; make your meat even and flat, and ſtrew your ſeaſoning over it, with four or five anchovies waſh'd and bon'd; then roll your meat like a collar, and bind it with coarſe tape, and bake, boil, or roaſt it; cut it into three or four pieces, and diſh it with ſtrong gravy ſauce thickened with butter; you may fry oyſters and forc'd-meat balls on it if you pleaſe; it is very good cold: cut it in ſlices like collar'd beef.

To collar Beef.

TAKE a flank and cut the ſkin off, lay it in pump-water, with three handfuls of bay-ſalt and an ounce of ſalt-petre; let it lie in the brine three days; then take ſome pepper, two nutmegs, and a good handful of green ſweet-marjoram, half a handful of ſage, ſome roſemary and thyme, all green, with a good handful of parſley; chop the herbs ſmall, then lay the beef on the table; cut the lean piece, and put in the thick fat part, ſtrew it all over with the herbs and ſpice; roll it up as cloſe as you can, tie it very well with tape bound about it; then put it into a long pot, and fill it up with the brine it was laid in, tie a wet paper over it, put it in an oven when your bread is drawn, let it ſtand all night; next day heat your oven hot, and let your beef ſtand four hours, then draw it out, and let it ſtand in the liquor till it is half cold, then take it out, and ſtrain your tape and bind it up cloſer: you muſt put two middling handfuls of ſalt into the herbs when you roll it up, beſides the brine; the roſemary ought to be chopt fine by itſelf; and then with the reſt of the herbs.

Another.

LAY your flank of beef in ham-brine eight or ten days, then dry it in a cloth, and take out all the leather and the ſkin; ſcotch it croſs and croſs, ſeaſon it with ſavoury ſpice, two or three anchovies, an handful or two of thyme, ſweet-marjoram, winter-ſavoury, and onions; ſtrew it on the meat, and roll it in a hard collar in a cloth; ſew it cloſe, and tie it at both ends; put it in a long pan, with a pint of claret, and cochineal, and two quarts of pump-water, and bake it all night; then take it out hot, and tie it cloſe at both ends; then ſet it upon one end, put a weight upon it, and let it ſtand till it is cold; then take it out of the cloth, and keep it dry.

To keep collared Beef.

YOU may keep a collar of beef two months in a liquor made of one quart of cyder and two of ſtale ſmall beer, boil'd with a handful of ſalt; if it mothers, take it off, and boil it again, and when cold put in your beef; firſt keep it as long as you can dry, which is to be done by rolling it up in a cloth when it is firſt baked, tying it up at both ends, hanging it up to dry till cold, and taking off the cloths, wrap it up in white paper and keep it in a dry place, but not near the fire; when you have kept it dry as long as you can, put it into the pickle as before.

To collar Pig.

SLIT the pig down the back, take out all the bones, waſh it from the blood in three or four waters, wipe it dry, and ſeaſon it with ſavoury ſpice, thyme, parſley, and ſalt, and roll it in a hard collar; tie it cloſe in a dry cloth, and boil it with the bones in three pints of water, a handful of ſalt, a quart of vinegar, a faggot of ſweet herbs, whole ſpice; when it is boiled tender take it off, and when cold take it out of the cloth, and keep it in the pickle.

To pot Ducks or any Fowls, or ſmall Birds.

BREAK all the bones of your ducks with a rolling-pin, take out the thigh-bones, and as many others as you can; keeping the ducks whole; ſeaſon it with pepper, ſalt, nutmeg, and cloves; lay them cloſe in a pot with their breaſt down, put in a little red wine, a good deal of butter, and lay a ſmall weight upon them; when they are bak'd, let them ſtand in the pot till they are near cold, to ſuck up the ſeaſoning the better; then put them in another pot, and pour clarified butter on them; if they are to keep long, put away the gravy; if to ſpend ſoon, put it in. Take care to ſeaſon them well.

To pot a Swan.

BONE and ſkin your ſwan, and beat the fleſh in a mortar, taking out the ſtrings as you beat it; then take ſome clear fat bacon and beat with the ſwan, and when it is of a light fleſh-colour there is bacon enough in it; when it is beaten till it is like dough, it is enough; then ſeaſon it with pepper, ſalt, cloves, mace, and nutmeg, all beaten fine; mix it well with your fleſh, and give it a beat or two all together; then put it in an earthen pot, with a little claret and fair water, and at the top two pounds of freſh butter ſpread over it; cover it with coarſe paſte, and bake it with bread; then turn it out into a diſh; ſqueeze it gently to get out the moiſture; then put it in a pot fit for it; and when it is cold cover it with clarified butter, and next day paper it up; in this manner you may do gooſe, duck, or beef, or hare's fleſh.

To dreſs a Hare.

FLEA your hare, and lard it with bacon; take the liver, give it one boil; then bruiſe it ſmall, and mix it with ſome marrow, or a quarter of a pound of beef-ſuet ſhred very fine, two anchovies chopt ſmall, ſome ſweet herbs ſhred very ſmall, ſome grated bread, a nutmeg grated, ſome ſalt, a little bit of eſchalot cut fine; mix theſe together with the yolks of two or three eggs; then work it up in a good piece of butter; flour it, and when your hare is ſpitted, put this pudding in the belly, and ſew it up, and lay it to the fire; put a diſh under to receive what comes from the hare; baſte it well with butter, and when it is enough, put in the diſh with it a ſauce made with ſtrong broth, the gravy of your hare, the fat being taken off, and ſome claret; boil theſe up, and thicken it up with butter: when the hare is cut up, mix ſome of the pudding with your ſauce. Garniſh the diſh with ſliced lemon.

Some, inſtead of the pudding in the belly, roaſt a piece of bacon, with ſome thyme; and for ſauce, have melted butter and thyme mixed with what comes from the hare.

To make Weſtphalia *Bacon.*

MAKE a pickle as follows: take a gallon of pump-water, a quarter of a peck of bay-ſalt, as much of white ſalt, a pound of petre-ſalt, and a quarter of a pound of ſalt-petre, a pound of coarſe ſugar, and an ounce of ſocho tied up in a rag; boil all theſe together very well, and let it ſtand till it is cold; then put in the pork, and let it lie in this pickle a fortnight; then take it out, and dry it over ſaw-duſt: this pickle will do tongues, but you muſt firſt let the tongues lie ſix or eight hours in pump-water, to take out the ſlimineſs: and when you have laid them in the pickle, dry them as your pork.

To ſalt and dry a Ham of Bacon.

TAKE bay-ſalt; and put it in a veſſel of water ſuitable to the quantity of hams you do; make your pickle ſtrong enough to bear an egg with your bay-ſalt; then boil and ſcum it very well; then let the pickle be thoroughly cold, and put into it ſo much red ſaunders as will make it of the colour of claret; then let your pickle ſtand three days before you put your hams into it; the hams muſt lie

lie in the pickle three weeks; then carefully dry them where wood is burnt.

To dry Tongues.

TAKE to every two ounces of salt-petre, a pint of petre-salt, and rub it well, after it is finely beaten, strew it over your tongue, and then beat a pint of bay-salt, and rub that on over it, and every three days turn it; when it has lain nine or ten days, hang it in wood-smoke to dry. Do a hog's-head this way. For a ham of pork or mutton, have a quart of bay-salt, half a pound of petre-salt, a quarter of a pound of salt-petre, a quarter of a pound of brown sugar, all beaten very fine, mix'd together, and rubb'd well over it; let it lie a fortnight; turn it often, and then hang it up a day to drain, and dry it in wood-smoke.

To salt Hams, or Tongues, &c.

TAKE of bay-salt a peck, of salt-petre four ounces; three pounds of very brown sugar: put to all these water till it will but just bear an egg; after it is well stirred lay in the hams so that they are covered with the pickle; let them lie three weeks, if middling hams, if large a month; when you take them out, dry them well in a cloth and rub them with bay-salt, then hang them up to dry, and smoke them with saw-dust every day for a fortnight together; the chimney you hang them in must be of a moderate heat, the pickle must be raw, and not boil'd. This quantity is enough to salt six hams at a time. When you take them out, you may boil the pickle, and skim it clean, putting in some fresh salt. If you keep your hams till they are dry and old, lay them in hot grains, and let them lie till cold, then wrap them up in hay, and boil them tender; set them on in cold water when they are dry, the houghs being before stop'd with salt, and tied up close in brown paper, to keep out the flies.

Neats

Neats Hearts, Tongues, or Hogs Cheeks, do well in the same pickle; the best way is to rub hams with bay-salt and sugar three or four days before you put them in this pickle.

Another.

TAKE three or four gallons of water, put to it four pounds of bay-salt, four pounds of white-salt, a pound of petre-salt, a quarter of a pound of salt-petre, two ounces of prunella-salt, a pound of brown sugar; let it boil a quarter of an hour; scum it well, and when it is cold sever it from the bottom into the vessel you keep it in.

Let hams lie in this pickle four or five weeks.

A clod of *Dutch* beef as long.

Tongues a fortnight.

Collared beef eight or ten days.

Dry them in a stove, or with wood in a chimney.

To make Dutch *Beef.*

TAKE the lean part of a buttock of beef raw; rub it well with brown sugar all over, and let it lie in a pan or tray two or three hours; turning it three or four times; then salt it well with common salt and salt-petre, and let it lie a fortnight, turning it every day; then roll it very strait in a coarse cloth, and put it in a cheese-press a day and a night, and hang it to dry in a chimney. When you boil it, you must put it in a cloth: when it is cold, it will cut out into shivers as *Dutch* beef.

To dry Mutton to cut out in Shivers as Dutch *Beef.*

TAKE a middling leg of mutton, then take half a pound of brown sugar, rub it hard all over your mutton, and let it lie twenty-four hours; then take an ounce and half of salt-petre, and mix it with a pound of common salt, and rub that all over the mutton every other day, till it is all on, and let it lie nine days longer; keep the

place

place free from brine, and hang it up to dry three days; then smoak it in a chimney where wood is burnt; the fire must not be too hot; a fortnight will dry it: boil it like other hams, and when it is cold cut it out in shivers like *Dutch* Beef.

To dry a Leg of Mutton like Pork.

TAKE a large leg of mutton, and beat it down flattish with a cleaver, to make it like *Westphalia* ham; then take two ounces of salt-petre, beat it fine, rub it all over your mutton, and let it lie all night; then make a pickle with bay-salt and pump-water, strong enough to bear an egg, put your mutton into it, and let it lie ten days; then take it out and hang it in a chimney where wood is burnt, till it is thorough dry, which will be about three weeks. Boil it with hay, till it is very tender; do it in cool weather, or it will not keep well.

To salt Bacon.

CUT your flitches of bacon very smooth, make no holes in it: to about threescore pounds of bacon, ten pounds of salt; dry your salt very well, and make it hot, then rub it hard over the outside, or skinny part, but on the inside lay it all over, without rubbing, only lightly on, about half an inch thick. Let it lie on a flat board, that the brine may run from it nine days; then mix with a quart of hot salt, two ounces of salt-petre, and strew it all over your bacon; then heat the rest of your salt, put over it, and let it lie nine days longer; then hang it up a day, and put it in a chimney, where wood is burnt, and there let it hang three weeks or more, as you see occasion.

To pot Salmon.

SCALE and chine your salmon down the back, and dry it well; cut it as near the shape of your pot as you can; take two nutmegs, near an ounce of of cloves and mace, half an ounce of white pepper, about an ounce of ſalt; take out all the bones, and cut off the joll below the fins; cut off the tail; ſeaſon the ſcaly ſide firſt, and lay that at the bottom of the pot; then rub the ſeaſoning on the other ſide; cover it with a diſh, and let it ſtand all night. It muſt be put double, and the ſcaly ſide top and bottom. Put butter on the bottom and top; cover the pot with ſome ſtiff coarſe paſte; three hours if it is a large fiſh, if not, two hours will bake it. When it comes out of the oven, let it ſtand half an hour; then uncover it, and raiſe it up at one end that the gravy may run out; then put a trencher and a weight on it, to preſs out the gravy, melt the butter that came from it, but let no gravy be in it, let the butter boil up, and add more butter to it, if there be occaſion. Scum it, and fill the pot with the clear butter; when 'tis cold, paper it up.

Salmon or Mackrel to pot.

AFTER you have waſhed and cleans'd them, dry them in a cloth, cut off the heads, tails and fins, cut them down the bellies, take out the rows, and wipe the black that lies under the rows; take out the bones as clean as you can; ſeaſon twelve or thirteen with four ounces of ſalt, half an ounce of nutmegs, as much pepper, a quarter of an ounce of cloves, as much ginger beat very fine; mix with the ſalt and ſeaſon them; lay them into a long pot with a few bay-leaves and lemon-peel on the top, a good quantity of freſh butter, and bake them with houſhold bread at leaſt three hours: lay on a double brown paper wetted and tied cloſe. When they are baked, take them out of the pot while hot, and pull them in ſmall pieces with your fingers; place them cloſe in your potting-pots, and pour clarified butter on the top.

To pot Beef.

TAKE six pounds of the buttock of beef, cut it in pieces as big as your fist, season it with a large spoonful of mace, a spoonful of pepper, with twenty-five or thirty cloves, and a good race of ginger; beat them all very fine, mix them with salt, and put them to the beef; lay it in a pot, and upon it two pounds of butter: bake it three or four hours, well cover'd up with paste; before it is cold take out the beef, beat it fine, putting in the warm butter as you do it, and put it down close in pots; if you keep it long, keep back the gravy, and if it wants seasoning, add some in the beating; pour on clarified butter.

To stew Pigeons.

SEASON your pigeons with pepper, salt, cloves and mace, with some sweet herbs; wrap a seasoning up in a bit of butter, and put it in their bellies, then tie up the neck and vent, and half roast them; then put them in a stew-pan, with a quart of good gravy, a little white wine, some pickled mushrooms, a few pepper-corns, three or four blades of mace, a bit of lemon-peel, a bunch of sweet herbs, a bit of onion, some oyster-pickle: let them stew till they are enough; then thicken it up with butter and yolks of eggs. Garnish with lemon. Do ducks the same way. You may put forc'd-meat in their bellies, or shred thyme wrap'd up in butter. Put forc'd-meat balls in both.

To fricasee a Pig.

HALF roast your pig, then take it up, and take off the coat, pull the meat in flakes from the bones, and put it in a stew-pan, with some strong broth, some white wine, a little vinegar, an onion stuck with cloves, some mace, a bunch of sweet herbs, and some salt, and lemon-peel; when it is almost done, take out the onions, herbs, and lemon-mon-peel, and put in ſome muſhrooms, and thicken it with cream and eggs. The head muſt be roaſted whole, and ſet in the middle, and the fricaſee round it. Garniſh with lemon.

To ſtew Cod.

CUT your cod in thin ſlices, and lay them one by one in the bottom of a diſh; put in a pint of white wine, half a pound of butter, ſome oyſters and their liquor, two or three blades of mace, a few crumbs of bread, ſome pepper and ſalt, and let it ſtew till it is enough. Garniſh the diſh with lemon.

To make Skuets.

TAKE fine, long and ſlender ſkewers; then cut veal ſweet-breads into pieces like dice, and ſome fine bacon in thin ſquare bits; ſeaſon them with forc'd-meat, and then ſpit them on the ſkewers, a bit of ſweet-bread, a bit of bacon, till all is on; roaſt them, and lay them round a fricaſee of ſheeps-tongues.

To pot a Hare.

TAKE three pounds of the pure fleſh of hare, and a pound and half of the clear fat of pork or bacon, and beat them in a mortar, till you cannot diſtinguiſh each from the other; then ſeaſon it with pepper, ſalt, a large nutmeg, a large handful of ſweet herbs, ſweet-marjoram, thyme, and a double quantity of parſley; ſhred all very fine, mix it with the ſeaſoning, and beat it all together, till all is very well mingled; then put it into a pot, laying it lower in the middle than the ſides, and paſte it up; two hours will bake it: when it comes out of the oven, have clarified butter ready; fill the pot an inch above the meat while it is hot; when it is cold, paper it up, and keep it; which you may do three or four months before it is cut: the fat of pork is much better than the fat of bacon.

To make a Bisk of Pigeons.

TAKE twelve pigeons, fill the bellies with forc'd-meat, and half roast them, or half boil them in strong broth; then have slices of *French* bread, toasted hard and stew'd in strong broth, and have in readiness some lamb-stones, and sweet-breads, and palates, they being first boiled tender; then stew them with your pigeons in your strong broth; add balls of forc'd meat first stewed or fry'd; lay your pigeons in a dish; lay on them thin slices of broiled bacon, and your other ingredients, and pour in your strong broth, and garnish with lemon. You may leave out the sweet-breads, palates, and lamb-stones, and put in scalded herbs; as for soops, and turneps half boil'd, cut like dice, and fry'd brown, and so serve it like a soop, and but six pigeons.

To do Pigeons in Jelly.

TAKE a knuckle of veal, and a good piece of ising-glass, and make a strong jelly; season it with mace, white-pepper, salt, bay-leaves, and lemon-peel; then truss your pigeons as for boiling, and boil them in the jelly; when they are cold, put them in the dish you serve them in; then add the juice of a lemon to your jelly, clarify it with the the whites of eggs, run it through a jelly-bag into a pan, and keep it till 'tis cold: with a spoon lay it in heaps, on and between your pigeons. Garnish with sliced lemon and bay-leaves.

To make a Poloe.

TAKE a pint of rice, boil it in as much water as will cover it; when your rice is half boiled put in your fowl, with a small onion, a blade or two of mace, some whole pepper, and some salt; when 'tis enough, put the fowl in the dish, and pour the rice over it.

To stew Cucumbers.

PARE twelve cucumbers, slice them as for eating, put them to drain, and lay them in a coarse cloth till they are dry; flour them, and fry them brown in butter; then put to them some gravy, a little claret, some pepper, cloves and mace, and let them stew a little; then roll a bit of butter in flour, and toss them up; put them under mutton or lamb roasted.

To pot Goose and Turkey.

TAKE a fat goose, and a fat turkey; cut them down the rump, and take out all the bones; lay them flat open, and season them very well with white pepper, nutmeg and salt, allowing three nutmegs, with the like proportion of pepper, and as much salt as both the spices; when you have season'd them all over, let your turkey be within the goose, and keep them in season two nights and a day; then roll them up as collared beef, very tight, and as short as you can, and bind it very fast with strong tape. Bake it in a long pot, with good store of butter, till it is very tender, as you may feel by the end; let it lie in the hot liquor an hour, then take it out, and let it stand till next day; then unbind it, place it in your pot, and melt butter, and pour over it. Keep it for use, and slice it out thin.

To make a Fricasee of Eggs.

BOIL your eggs hard, and take out a good many of the yolks whole, then cut the rest in quarters, yolks and whites together. Set on some gravy, with a little shred thyme and parsley in it, give it a boil or two; then put in your eggs, with a little grated nutmeg; shake it up with a bit of butter, till it be as thick as another fricasee: then fry artichoke bottoms in thin slices, and serve it up. Garnish with eggs shred small.

Another Fricasee of Eggs.

BOIL six eggs hard, slice them in round slices, then stew some morels in white wine, with an eschalot, two anchovies, a little thyme, a few oysters or cockles, and salt to your taste; when they have stew'd well together, put in your eggs and a bit of butter; toss them up together till it is thick, and then serve it up.

To fricasee Artichoke-bottoms for a Side-dish.

BOIL your artichokes tender, take off the leaves and choke; when cold split every bottom, dredging them with flour, and then dip them in beaten eggs, with some salt and grated nutmeg; then roll them up in grated bread, fry them in butter; make gravy sauce thicken'd with butter, and pour under them.

To make forc'd-meat.

TAKE a piece of a leg of veal, the lean part and some lean bacon; mince them very fine, and add a double quantity of suet: put it all in a marble mortar, beat it well, sprinkle it with a little water in the beating; season it with pepper, salt, and a little cloves and mace, to your taste; shred spinach very fine if you would have it look green, or else without; make it up as you use it, with an egg or two, and roll it in long or round balls.

To keep Smelts in Jelly.

TAKE smelts alive, if you can get them; chuse out the firmest without spawn, set them a boiling in a gallon of water, a pint of wine vinegar, two handfuls of salt, and a bunch of sweet herbs, and lemon-peel; let them boil three or four walms, and take them up before they break. The jelly make thus: take a quart of the liquor, a quart of vinegar, a quart of white wine, one ounce of ising-glass, some cloves, mace, sliced ginger, whole pepper, and salt; boil these over a gentle fire till a third part be consumed, and the ising-glass be melted; then set it by till almost cold: lay your smelts in a china plate one by one, then pour it on your smelts; set it in a cool place; it will jelly by next day.

To stew a Turkey.

TAKE a fine young turkey, kill'd, pull'd, and drawn, fill the skin on the breast with forc'd-meat, and lard it on the sides with bacon; put into the belly half an eschalot, two anchovies, and a little thyme shred small; brown it in a pan with a little butter; when it is very brown put it in a stew-pan, with strong gravy, some white wine, or claret, two or three anchovies, some mace, sweet herbs, and a little pepper; let it stew till it is thoroughly enough, then thicken the liquor with butter and eggs: fry some *French* loaves dipt in cream, after the top and the crumb is taken out; then fill them with stewed oysters, or shrimps, or cockles, and with them garnish the dish, or with slic'd lemon. A hen, goose, or duck, does well this way.

To bake a Rump of Beef.

BONE a rump of beef, beat it very well with a rolling-pin, cut off the sinew, and lard it with large pieces of bacon; roll your lards in seasoning, which is pepper, salt, and cloves; lard athwart the meat, that it may cut handsomely; then season it all over the meat with pepper and salt pretty thick, tie it with packthread cross and cross, and put the top under the bottom, and tie it up tight; put it in an earthen pot, break all the bones, and put in the sides and over, to keep it fast that it cannot stir; then put in half a pound of butter, some bay-leaves, whole pepper, an eschalot or two, and some sweet herbs; cover the top of the pot with coarse paste; put it in the oven, and let it stand eight hours. Serve it up with its own liquor, and ſome dry'd ſippets.

To make Veal Cutlets.

CUT your veal ſteaks thin, hack them, and ſeaſon them with pepper and ſalt, and ſweet herbs; waſh them over with eggs, and ſtrew over them ſome forc'd-meat; put two ſteaks together, and lard them with bacon; waſh them over with melted butter, and wrap them in white papers butter'd; roaſt them on a lark ſpit, or bake them; when they are enough, unpaper them, and ſerve them with good gravy and ſliced lemon.

To dreſs a Calf's Head.

SCALD the hair off, and take out the bones, then have in readineſs palates boiled tender, yolks of hard eggs, oyſters ſcalded, and forc'd-meat; ſtuff all this into your head, and ſew it up cloſe in a cloth; boil it three hours; make a ſtrong gravy for ſauce, and garniſh with fry'd bacon.

To make a Pulpatoon of Pigeons.

TAKE muſhrooms, palates, oyſters, ſweet-breads, and fry them in butter; then put all theſe into a ſtrong gravy; give them a heat over the fire, and thicken up with an egg and a bit of butter; then half roaſt ſix or eight pigeons, and lay them in a cruſt of forc'd-meat, as follows: ſcrape a pound of veal and two pounds of marrow, and beat it together in a ſtone mortar, after it is ſhred very fine; then ſeaſon it with ſalt, pepper, ſpice, and put in hard eggs, anchovies, and oyſters; beat all together, and make the lid and ſides of your pye of it; firſt, lay a thin cruſt in your pattipan, then put in your forc'd-meat, then lay an exceeding thin cruſt over them, then put in your pigeons and other ingredients, with a little butter on the top; bake it two hours.

To

To pot Mushrooms.

TAKE of the best mushrooms, and rub them with a woollen cloth; those that will not rub, peel, and take out the gills, and throw them into water, as you do them; when they are all done, wipe them dry, and put them in a sauce-pan, with a handful of salt and a piece of butter; stew them till they are enough, shaking them often for fear of burning; then drain them from their liquor, and when they are cold wipe them dry, and lay them in a pot one by one as close as you can, till your pot be full; then clarify butter; let it stand till it is almost cold, and pour it into your mushrooms; when cold, cover them close in your pot; when you use them, wipe them clean from the butter, and stew them in gravy thicken'd, as when fresh.

To pot Herrings.

CUT off their heads, and put them in an earthen pot, lay them close, and between every layer of herrings strew some salt, not too much; put in cloves, mace, whole pepper, and nutmeg cut in bits; fill up the pot with vinegar, water and a quarter of a pint of white wine; cover it with brown paper, tie it down, and bake it with brown bread. When cold it is fit to eat.

To bake Herrings.

TAKE thirty herrings, scale them, cut off their heads, pull out their roes, wash them very clean, and lay them to drain four or five hours; roll them in a dry cloth, season them with pepper and salt, and lay them in a long venison pot at full length; when you have laid one row, shred a large onion very small, and mix it with a little cloves, mace and ginger cut small, and strew it all over the herrings; and then another row of herrings, and seasoning; and so do till all is in the pot, let it stand season'd an hour before it is put in the oven: then put in a quart of claret, and tie it over with paper, and bake it with houſhold bread.

To make a Soup.

TAKE twelve pounds of beef, a ſcrag of mutton, and knuckle of veal: it muſt be neck-beef, and the ſticking-piece, put your beef in a ſauce-pan, and half fry it with a bit of butter; then put all in a pot, with nine quarts of water, a good handful of ſalt, a piece of bacon, boil and ſkim it, then ſeaſon it with three onions ſtuck with cloves, whole pepper, *Jamaica*-pepper, and a bunch of ſweet herbs; let it boil five or ſix hours cloſe covered; then ſtrain it out, and put it in your diſh, with ſtew'd herbs and toaſted bread.

To make Muſhroom Liquor and Powder.

TAKE a peck of muſhrooms, waſh and rub them clean with a piece of flannel, cutting out all the gills, but not peeling off the ſkins; put to them ſixteen blades of mace, four cloves, ſix bay-leaves, twice as much beaten pepper as will lie on a half crown, a handful of ſalt, a dozen onions, a piece of butter as big as an egg, and half a pint of vinegar; ſtew them up as faſt as you can, keeping them ſtirring till the liquor is out of your muſhrooms; drain them thro' a colander, ſave the liquor and ſpice, and when cold bottle it up for uſe; dry the muſhrooms firſt on a broad pan in the oven, afterwards put them on ſieves, till they are dry enough to pound to powder. This quantity uſually makes about half a pound.

Peas Soup.

TAKE the broth of a leg of beef, and boil in it a piece of of bacon and a ſheep's-head, to maſh with a good quantity of peas; ſtrain the broth from the huſks, then take half a nutmeg, four cloves, and a race of ginger, ſome pepper, a pretty deal of mint, ſome ſweet-marjoram and thyme; bruiſe the ſpice,

ſpice, powder the herbs, and put them into the ſoup; boil leeks in two or three waters till they are tender, and the rankneſs out of them; put in what other herbs you pleaſe, as ſpinach, lettuce, beets, *&c.* forget not to boil an onion or two in the broth at firſt; ſome will burn butter in a ſtew-pan, and when it is boiling put in a large plate of ſliced onions; let them boil till they are tender, keeping them ſtirring all the time, and boil them in a ſoup; others will ſcrape a little cheſhire cheeſe, and ſtrew in the butter and onions; it ought to be old cheſhire-cheeſe; if you put in the onions mentioned laſt, they muſt be fry'd in butter, brown, before they are put into the ſoup; when you put them into the frying-pan flour them well, put in celery and turneps, if you like the taſte, but ſtrain the turneps out: to throw an old pigeon in with the meat at firſt, gives a high taſte, or a piece of lean bacon dry'd.

Oyſter Soup.

TAKE a quart of ſmall oyſters, put them into a colander to drain; then ſtrain the liquor through a muſlin rag, and put to it half a pint of water, and a quarter of a pint of white wine; let them ſtew with a few ſprigs of parſley, and a little thyme, a little eſchalot or onion, a little lemon-peel, a few cloves, a blade of mace, and a little whole pepper; let them ſtew gently a pretty while; take a quarter of a pound of butter and put into a pan, but flour it well firſt, then fry it till it has done hiſſing; dry the oyſters in a cloth, and flour them; put them into the butter, and fry them till they are plump; then take one anchovy and diſſolve in the liquor; add ſome freſh wine, the yolks of two eggs, well beaten; put all into the pan together, and give it a ſcald; keeping it ſtirring all the time it is on the fire; before you put the ſoup into the diſh, lay the cruſt of a *French* loaf, or a toaſt, at the bottom, which muſt ſoak with ſome of the liquor over coals.

Before you put in the whole, you may add ſtrong broth or fried gravy, if not in *Lent*. This ſoup muſt be thick with butter'd crumbs: you may add burnt butter or ſago, but that you muſt boil in ſeveral waters, the more, the whiter it looks. Vermicelly is good in this, but that muſt boil but little time. Crawfiſh and ſhrimps do well in this ſoup; if you have ſhrimps, the ſewer oyſters will do.

To make green Peas Soup.

TAKE half a buſhel of the youngeſt peas, divide the great from the ſmall; boil the ſmalleſt in two quarts of water, and the biggeſt in one quart; when they are well boil'd, bruiſe the biggeſt, and when the thin is drain'd from it, boil the thick in as much cold water as will cover it; then rub away the ſkins, and take a little ſpinach, mint, ſorrel, lettuce, parſley, and a good quantity of marigolds; waſh, ſhred, and boil theſe in half a pound of butter, and drain the ſmall peas; ſave the water, and mingle all together, with a ſpoonful of whole pepper; then melt a quarter of a pound of butter, ſhake a little flour into it, and let it boil; put the liquor to the butter, and mingle all well together, and let them boil up; ſo ſerve it with dry'd bread.

To keep green Peas till Chriſtmas.

SHELL what quantity you pleaſe of young peas, put them in the pot when the water boils, let them have four or five walms: then firſt pour them into a colander, and then ſpread a cloth on a table, and put them on that, and dry them well in it; have bottles ready dried, and fill them to the necks, and pour over them melted mutton fat, and cork them down very cloſe, that no air come to them; ſet them in your cellar, and when you uſe them, put them into boiling water, with a ſpoonful of fine ſugar, and a good piece of butter; and when they are enough, drain and butter them.

To make Asparagus Soup.

TAKE twelve pounds of lean beef, cut in thin slices; then put a quarter of a pound of butter in a stew-pan over the fire, and put your beef in; let it boil up thick till it begins to brown; then put in a pint of brown ale, and a gallon of water; cover it close, and let it stew gently for an hour and half; put in what spice you like in the stewing, and strain out the liquor, and skim off all the fat; then put in some vermicelly, some celery wash'd and cut small, half a hundred of asparagus cut small, and palates boiled tender and cut; put all these in, and let them boil gently till tender; just as it is going up fry a handful of spinach in butter, and throw in a *French* roll.

Asparagus Soup, or green Peas.

TAKE some strong broth of beef, mutton, or both, boil in it a large brown toast, a little flour sifted from oatmeal, and three or four handfuls of asparagus cut small, so far as they are green (or green peas) some spinach, white beets, and what herbs you like, a little celery, and a few sprigs of parsley; toast little white toasts, butter them, and pour your soup upon them; the brown bread ought to be strain'd off before your asparagus goes in; season it with salt to your taste.

White Soup.

TAKE some liquor that has had a leg of mutton boil'd in it, in which you may stew a knuckle of veal, an onion, and a bay-leaf; strain it off and put it again into your stew-pan, with a handful of shred celery, and a good quantity of oysters; let them boil till they will break, then put in such a quantity of butter'd crumbs as will make it thick; you may boil in this some vermicelly; grate in half a nutmeg, salt it to your taste; some celery if you please.

To

To make Scotch Collops.

CUT thin ſlices of a fillet of veal, and hack them; then take the yolks of four eggs; beat a little melted butter, a little ſalt, and ſome nutmeg, or lemon-peel grated in it; then dip in each collop, lay them in a pewter diſh, flour them and let them lie till you want them. Put a bit of butter in the frying-pan, and your collops, and fry them quick, ſhaking them all the while to keep the butter from oiling; then pour it into a ſtew-pan cover'd cloſe, and keep it warm; then put to them ſome good gravy, ſome muſhrooms, or what elſe you like, a bit of butter, toſs it up thick, and ſqueeze an orange over it.

A brown Fricaſee.

TAKE lamb or rabbet cut in ſmall pieces; grate on it a little nutmeg, or lemon-peel; fry it quick and brown with butter, then have ſome ſtrong broth, in which put your morels and muſhrooms, a few cock's-combs boil'd tender, and artichoke-bottoms; a little walnut-liquor, and a bay-leaf; then roll a bit of butter in flour, ſhake it well, and ſerve it up, you may ſqueeze an orange or lemon over it.

To make Hams of Pork like Weſtphalia.

TO two large hams, or three ſmall ones, take three pounds of common ſalt, and two pounds and a half of brown coarſe ſugar; mix both together, rub it well into the hams, let them lie ſeven days, turning them every day, and rub the ſalt in them, when you turn them; then take four ounces of ſalt-petre beat ſmall, and mix with two handfuls of common ſalt, and rub that well in your hams, and let them lie a fortnight longer; then hang them up high in a chimney to ſmoke.

To make a Pickle for Tongues.

MAKE your pickle with bay-salt, some salt-petre, coarse sugar, and spring-water; make it strong, boil and skim it, and when 'tis cold put in your tongues; turn them often; let them lie three weeks, then dry them.

To make Sausages.

TAKE three pounds of fat, and three pounds of lean pork; cut the lean into thin slices; and scrape every slice, and throw away the skin; have the fat cut as small as can be; mix fat and lean together, shred and mix them well; two ounces and a half of salt, half an ounce of pepper, thirty cloves, and three or four large blades of mace, six spoonfuls of sage, two spoonfuls of rosemary cut exceeding fine, with three nutmegs grated; beat six eggs, and work them well together with a pint of water that has been boil'd, and is perfectly cold: If you put in no herbs, slice a penny white loaf in cream, steep it all night, and work it in well with sausage-meat, with as much cream as will infuse the bread. If you put in raw water, the sausages are said not to keep so well as when it is boiled.

Very fine Sausages.

TAKE a leg of pork or veal; pick it clean from skin or fat, and to every pound of lean meat put two pounds of beef-suet pick'd from the skins; shred the meat and suet severally very fine; then mix them well together, and add a large handful of green sage shred very small, season it with grated nutmeg, salt and pepper; mix it well, and press it down hard in an earthen pot, and keep it for use. When you use them roll them up with as much egg as will make them roll smooth, but use no flour: in rolling them up, make them the length of your finger, and as thick as two fingers: fry them in clarified suet, which must be boiling hot before you put

put them in. Keep them rolling about in the pan; when they are fried through, they are enough.

To ſtew Pigeons with Aſparagus.

DRAW your pigeons, and wrap up a little ſhred parſley, with a very few blades of thyme, ſome ſalt and pepper in a piece of butter; put ſome in the belly, ſome in the neck, and tie up the vent and the neck, and half roaſt them; then have ſome ſtrong broth and gravy, put them together in a ſtew-pan; ſtew the pigeons till they are full enough; then have tops of aſparagus boil'd tender, and put them in, and let them have a walm or two in the gravy, and diſh it up.

A Pickle for either Tongues or Hams.

TAKE what quantity of water you pleaſe, and with bay ſalt and common ſalt make it ſtrong enough to bear an egg; then to every gallon of this pickle add half a pound of petre-ſalt, a pound of coarſe ſugar, and two or three ounces of ſalt-petre beat fine; boil it and ſkim it,and when it is thorough cold put in your hams or tongues; turn them often; the hams may lie in pickle about a month, the tongues three weeks; then hang them up to dry.

To ſtew Pigeons.

SEASON eight pigeons with pepper and ſalt only; take a middling cabbage cut a-croſs the middle, and lay the bottom with the thick pieces in the ſtew-pan; then lay on your pigeons, and cover 'em with the top of your cabbage; pour in a pint of red wine, and a pint of water; let it ſtew ſlowly an hour or more.

Another.

STUFF your pigeons with ſweet herbs chopp'd ſmall, ſome bacon minced ſmall, grated bread, ſpice, butter, and yolk of egg; ſew them up top and

and bottom, and stew them in strong broth, with half a pint of white wine to six pigeons, and as much broth as will cover them well, with nutmeg, whole pepper, mace, salt, a little bundle of sweet herbs, a bit of lemon-peel, and an onion; when they are almost done, put in some artichoke bottoms ready boiled, and fried in brown butter, or asparagus-tops ready boiled, thicken up the liquor with the stuffing out of the pigeons, and a bit of butter roll'd in flour: take out the lemon-peel, bunch of herbs, and onion. Garnish the dish with sliced lemon, and very thin bits of bacon toasted before the fire.

To pickle Hams or Ribs of Beef.

TAKE six gallons of your bloody beef-brine, or from pork, and put to it two pounds of brown sugar, and a pound of salt-petre; boil 'em together, and skim it well; when 'tis cold put it into the thing you design to pickle in, and put in your hams; large ones must lie in the pickle three weeks; small ones but a fortnight, sometimes turning them; the pickle must be strong enough to bear an egg; this way is only for great families, that kill or use a great deal of beef.

To stew green Peas.

TAKE five pints of young green peas, put them into a dish with a little spring-water, savoury, some sweet marjoram, thyme, and onion, a few cloves, and a little whole pepper; melt half a pound of sweet butter, with a piece of dried fat bacon the bigness of an egg, in a stew-pan, and let it boil till it is brown; take the white part of three hard lettuces cut very small, and put them into the butter; set it again on the fire for half a minute, stirring the lettuces four or five times; then put in the peas, and after you have given them five or six tosses, put in as much strong broth as will stew them; then add half a pint of cream, and let them boil till the

the liquor is almoſt waſted; bruiſe them a little with a ſpoon, and put a quarter of a pint of more cream to them; toſs them five or ſix times, and diſh them. Any good gravy may be added.

To make Green Peas Soup.

MAKE ſtrong broth of a leg of beef, a knuckle or ſcrag end of veal, and ſcrag of mutton; clear it off; then chop ſome cabbage lettuce, ſpinach, and a little ſorrel; then put half a pound of butter in a flat ſauce-pan, dredge in ſome flour, put it over the fire until 'tis brown: then put in your herbs and toſs them up a little over the fire; then put in a pint and half of green peaſe half boiled before, adding your ſtrong broth, and let it juſt ſimmer over the fire half an hour; then cut ſome *French* bread very thin; dry it well before the fire, put it in, and let it ſtew half an hour longer; ſeaſon your broth with pepper, ſalt, and a few cloves and mace. Garniſh the diſh with ſpinach ſcalded green, and ſome very thin bits of bacon toaſted before the fire.

Strong Broth.

TAKE twelve quarts of water, two knuckles of veal, a leg, or two ſhins of beef,two pair of calf's-feet, a chicken, a rabbet, two onions, cloves, mace, pepper, ſalt, a bunch of ſweet herbs; cover it cloſe, and let it boil till ſix quarts are conſumed: ſtrain it out, and keep it for uſe.

To make Craw-fiſh Soop.

TAKE a gallon of water, and ſet it a boiling; put in it a bunch of ſweet herbs, three or four blades of mace, an onion ſtuck with cloves, pepper, and ſalt; then have about two hundred of craw fiſh, ſave out about twenty; pick the reſt from their ſhells; ſave the tails whole, the bodies and ſhells beat in a mortar, with a pint of peaſe green or dry, that have been boiled tender; put your boiling

water

water to it, and ſtrain it boiling hot through a cloth, till you have got all the goodneſs out, and ſome good gravy; then ſlice *French* bread very thin, and ſet it to dry very hard: ſet your ſoop over a ſtew in a diſh, and the *French* bread in it; cover it, and let it ſtew till it is ſerved up; then brown a piece of butter in a broad ſauce-pan, and put into it your tails, a ladleful of broth, and an onion: cover that, and ſet it over a ſtew, and when you are ready to uſe it, take out the onion, and put all together in the diſh you ſerve it in, with a whole *French* roll toaſted and put in the middle of the diſh, and the twenty craw-fiſh you ſaved out, fried, and laid round the diſh to garniſh it.

If you have a carp, ſcale and flea it, take the fiſh from the bones, and mince the fiſh ſmall, with a very little bit of eſchalot, an anchovy, ſome parſley and thyme, ſome ſpice, ſalt, a little grated bread, and the yolks of two eggs; make it up, and ſew it in the ſkin of the carp; then boil it, but not long, and put it in the middle of your ſoop, inſtead of your *French* roll.

To ſtew a Neck of Veal.

CUT your neck of veal in ſteaks; beat them flat and ſeaſon them with ſalt, grated nutmeg, thyme and lemon-peel, ſhred very fine; when you put it into your pan, put to it ſome thick cream, according to the quantity you do, and let it ſtew ſoftly till enough; then put into your pan two or three anchovies, a little gravy, or ſtrong broth, a bit of butter, and ſome flour duſted in, and toſs it up till 'tis thick, then diſh it. Garniſh with lemon.

To ſtew Carps.

SCALE and gut your carp, and waſh the blood out of their bellies with vinegar; then flour them well, and fry them in butter till they are thorough hot, then put them into your ſtew-pan, with a pint of claret, two anchovies, an onion ſtuck with three

three or four cloves, two or three blades of mace, a bunch of sweet herbs, and a pound of fresh butter; put them over a soft fire, three quarters of an hour will do them; then take your fish up, and put them in the dish you serve them in; if your sauce is not thick enough, boil it a little longer; then strain it over your carp. This is a very good way to stew eels, only cut them in pieces, and not fry them. Garnish with horse radish and lemon.

To pot Eels.

CASE your eels and gut them, wash them, and dry them, slit them down the back, and take out the bones; cut them in pieces to fit your pot; then rub every piece on both sides with pepper, salt, and grated nutmeg; then lay them close in the pot till 'tis full; cover the pot with close paste, and bake them. A pot that holds eight pound weight must have two hours baking; when they come out of the oven open the pot and pour out all the liquor, then cover them with clarified butter.

Mackrel to caveack.

CUT your mackrel in pieces; season them as for potting, and rub it in well; fry them in oil or clarified butter, then lay them on straw by the fire to drain; when cold put them in vinegar, and cover them with oil, dry them before you season them: They will keep. and are extremely good.

To pickle Mackrel.

SLIT your mackrel in halves, take out the roes, gut and clean them, strew salt over them, and lay one on another, the back of one to the inside of the other; let them lie two or three hours, then wipe every piece clean from the salt, and strew them over with pepper beaten, and grated nutmeg, let them lie two or three hours longer; then fry them well, take them out of the pan, and lay them on coarse cloths to drain; when cold put them in a

pan,

pan, and cover them over with a pickle of vinegar boiled with ſpice, when it is cold.

To haſh a Calf's Head.

BOIL the head almoſt enough, then cut it in half, the faireſt half ſcotch and ſtrew it over with grated bread, and a little ſhred parſley; ſet it before the fire to broil, and baſte it with butter.

Cut the other half and the tongue in thin ſlices as big as a crown piece: have ſome ſtrong gravy ready, and put it in a ſtew-pan with your haſh, an anchovy waſhed, boned, the head and tail off; a bit of onion, two or three cloves, and two blades of mace, juſt bruiſed and put into a rag; then ſtrew in a little flour, and ſet it to ſtew: when it is enough have in readineſs the yolks of four eggs well beaten, with two or three ſpoonfuls of white wine, and ſome grated nutmeg, and ſtir it in your haſh till it is thick enough; then lay your broiled head in the middle, and your haſh round. Garniſh with lemon and little ſlices of bacon; always have forc'd-meat balls. You may add ſweet-breads, lamb-ſtones, *&c.*

To jug a Hare.

CUT a hare in pieces, but do not waſh it; ſeaſon it with half an onion ſhred very fine, a ſprig of thyme, a little parſley all ſhred, beaten pepper and ſalt, as much as will lie on a ſhilling, half a nutmeg, and a little lemon peel; ſtrew all theſe over your hare, and cut half a pound of fat bacon into thin ſlices; then put your hare into a jug, a layer of hare, and the ſlices of bacon on it; ſo do till all is in the jug; ſtop the jug cloſe that not any ſteam can go out; then put it in a pot of cold water, lay a tile on the top, and let it boil three hours; take the jug out of the kettle, put half a pound of butter in it, and ſhake it together till the butter is melted; then pour it in your diſh. Garniſh with lemon.

To jug Pigeons.

PULL, crop, and draw your pigeons, but not wash them; save the livers, put them in scalding water, and set them on the fire for a minute or two; then take them out, and bruise them small with the back of a spoon; mix them with a little pepper, salt, grated nutmeg, lemon-peel shred very fine, chopt parsley, two yolks of eggs very hard, and bruised as you did the liver, suet shaved exceeding fine, and some grated bread; work these together with raw eggs, roll it in butter, putting a bit into the crop and belly of your pigeon, and sew up the neck and vent; then dip your pigeons in water, seasoning them with pepper and salt, as for a pye; then put them into your jug, with a piece of celery; stop them up close, set them in a kettle of cold water, with a tile on the top, and let it boil three hours; then take them out of the jug, and put them in your dish; take out the celery, and put in a piece of butter roll'd in flour; shake it till it is thick, and put it on your pigeons. Garnish with lemon.

To make Pockets.

CUT three slices out of a leg of veal, the length of a finger, the breadth of three fingers, the thickness of a thumb, with a sharp penknife; give it a slit thro' the middle, leaving the bottom and each side whole, the thickness of a straw, then lard the top with small fine lards of bacon; then make a forc'd-meat of marrow, sweet-breads and lamb-stones just boiled; make it up after it is seasoned and beaten together with the yolks of two eggs, and put it into your pockets, as if you were filling a pin-cushion; then sew up the top with fine thread, flour them, put melted butter on them, and bake them; roast three sweet-breads to put between, and serve them with gravy sauce.

To make Runnet.

TAKE a calf's bag, ſkewer it up, and let it lie a night in cold water, then turn out the curd into freſh water, waſh and pick it very clean, and ſcour the bag inſide and outſide; then put a handful of ſalt to the curd, put it into a bag, ſkewer it up, and let it lie in a clean pot a year; then put half a pint of ſack into the bag, and as much into the pot, and prick the bag, then bruiſe one nutmeg, four cloves, a little mace, and tie them up in a bit of thin cloth; put it into the pot, and now and then ſqueeze the ſpice cloth; in a few days you may uſe it; put a ſpoonful, or at moſt a ſpoonful and half, to twenty quarts of milk.

To make a Summer Cream-Cheeſe.

TAKE three pints of milk juſt from the cow, and five pints of good ſweet cream, which you muſt boil free from ſmoke; then put it to your milk, cool it till it is but blood-warm, and then put in a ſpoonful of runnet: when it is well come, take a large ſtrainer, lay it in a great cheeſe-fat, then put the curd in gently upon the ſtrainer, and when all the curd is in, lay on the cheeſe-board, and a weight of two pound; let it ſo drain three hours, till the whey be well drained from it: then lay a cheeſe-cloth in your leſſer cheeſe-fat, and put in the curd, laying the cloth ſmooth over it as before, the board on the top of that, and a four pound weight on it; turn it every two hours into dry cloths before night, and be careful not to break it next morning; ſalt it, and keep it in the fat till next day; then put it into a wet cloth, which you muſt ſhift every day till it is ripe.

To make a New-market *Cheeſe to cut at two years old.*

ANY morning in *September* take twenty quarts of new milk warm from the cow, and colour it it with marigolds; when this is done, and the milk not cold; get ready a quart of cream and a quart of fair water, which must be kept stirring over the fire till it is scalding hot, then stir it well into the milk and runnet, as you do other cheese; when it is come, lay cheese-cloths over it, and settle it with your hands; the more hands the better; as the whey rises, take it away, and when it is clean gone, put your curd into your fat, breaking it as little as you can: then put it in the press, and press it gently an hour; take it out again, and cut it in thin slices, and lay them singly on a cloth, and wipe them dry; then put it in a tub, and break it with your hands as small as you can, and mix it with a good handful of salt, and a quart of cold cream; put it in the fat, and lay a pound weight on it till next day; then press and order it as others.

To make a Runnet-Bag.

LET the calf suck as much as he will just before he is kill'd, then take the bag out of the calf, and let it lie twelve hours, cover'd over in stinging nettles till it is very red; then take out your curd, wash your bag clean, salt it within-side and without, letting it lie sprinkled with salt twenty-four hours; then wash your curd in warm new milk, pick it, and put away all that is yellow and hollow, keep what is white and close; then wash it well, and sprinkle it with salt; when the bag has lain twenty-four hours, put it into the bag again, and put to it three spoonfuls of the stroakings of a cow, beat up with the yolk of an egg or two, twelve cloves, and two blades of mace; put a skewer thro' it, and hang it in a pot; then make the runnet-water thus:

Take half a pint of fair water, a little salt, and six tops of the red buds of black-thorn, as many sprigs of burnet, and two of sweet-marjoram; boil these in the water, and strain it out; when it is cold put one half in the bag, and let the bag lie in the other half, taking it out as you uſe it; when you want, make more runnet, which you may do ſix or ſeven times; three ſpoonfuls of this runnet will make a large cheſhire or chedder-cheeſe, and half as much to a common cheeſe.

To make a Chedder-*Cheeſe.*

TAKE the new milk of twelve cows in the morning, and the evening cream of twelve cows, putting to it three ſpoonfuls of runnet: when it is come, break it, and whey it; that being done, break it again, work into the curd three pounds of freſh butter, put it in your preſs; turn it very often for an hour or more, and change the cloths, waſhing them every time you change them; you may put wet cloths at firſt to them, but towards the laſt put two or three fine dry cloths; let it lie thirty or forty hours in the preſs, according to the thickneſs of the cheeſe: then take it out, waſh it in whey, and lay it in a dry cloth till it is dry; then lay it on your ſhelf, and turn it often.

French *Butter.*

TAKE the yolks of four hard eggs, half a pound of loaf-ſugar beat and ſifted, and half a pound of ſweet butter; bray them in a marble mortar, or ſome other convenient thing, with a ſpoonful or two of orange flower water; when it is well mix'd force it thro' the corner of a coarſe cloth, in little heaps on a china-plate, or through the top of a dredging-box.

To make Butter.

AS ſoon as you have milked, ſtrain your milk into a pot, and ſtir it often for half an hour, then put it in your pans or trays; when it is cream'd, ſkim it exceeding clean from the milk, and put your cream into an earthen pot; if you do not churn immediately for butter, ſhift your cream once in twelve hours into another clean ſcalded pot, and if you find any milk at the bottom of the pot, put it away; when you have churned, waſh your butter in three or four waters, and then ſalt it to your taſte, and beat it well, but not waſh it after it is ſalted: let it ſtand in a wedge, if it be to pot, till the next morning, and beat it again, and make your layers the thickneſs of three fingers, and then ſtrew a little ſalt on it, and ſo do till your pot is full.

The Queen's Cheeſe.

TAKE ſix quarts of the beſt ſtroakings, and let them ſtand till they are cold, then ſet two quarts of cream on the fire till it is ready to boil, take it off, and boil a quart of fair water, and take the yolks of two eggs, one ſpoonful of ſugar, and two ſpoonfuls of runnet; mingle all theſe together, and ſtir it till it is but blood warm; when the cheeſe is come, uſe it as other cheeſe; ſet it at night, and the third day lay the leaves of nettles under and over it; it muſt be turn'd and wip'd, and the nettles ſhifted every day, and in three weeks it will be fit to eat. This cheeſe is made between *Michaelmas* and *Allhallowtide.*

To make a thick Cream-Cheeſe.

TAKE the morning's milk from the cow, and the cream of the night's milk and runnet, pretty cool together, and when it is come, make it pretty much in the cheeſe-fat, and put in a little ſalt, and make the cheeſe thick in a deep mould, or a melon-mould, if you have one; keep it a year and half, or two years before you cut it; it muſt be well ſalted on the outſide.

To make Slip-Coat Cheeſe.

TAKE new milk and runnet, quite cold, and when it is come, break it as little as you can in putting it into the cheeſe-fat; let it ſtand and whey

whey itſelf for ſome time; then cover it, and ſet about two pound weight on it; when it will hold together, turn it out of that cheeſe-fat, and keep it turning upon clean cheeſe-fats for two or three days, till it has done wetting, and then lay it on ſharp-pointed dock-leaves till it is ripe; ſhift the leaves often.

A Cream Cheeſe.

TAKE ſix quarts of new milk warm from the cow, and put it to three quarts of good cream, and runnet it; when it comes, put a cloth in the cheeſe-mould, and with your ſlitting diſh take it out in thin ſlices, and lay on your mould by degrees till it is all in; then let it ſtand with a cheeſe-board upon it till it is enough to turn, which will be at night: then ſalt it on both ſides a little, and let it ſtand with a two pound weight on it all night; then take it out, and put it into a dry cloth; and ſo do till it is dry; ripen it with laying it on nettles; ſhift the nettles every day.

All Sorts of PICKLES.

To pickle Muſhrooms.

GATHER your muſhrooms in the morning, as ſoon as poſſible after they are out of the ground; for one of them that are round and unopened, is worth five that are open; if you gather any that are open, let them be ſuch as are reddiſh in the gills, for thoſe that have white gills are not good: having gathered them, peel them into water; when they are all done, take them out and put them into a ſauce-pan; then put to them a good quantity of ſalt, whole pepper, cloves, mace, and nutmeg quartered; let them boil in their own liquor a quarter of an hour with a quick fire; then take them off the fire, and drain them thro' a colander, and let them ſtand till they are cold; then put all the ſpice that was uſed in the boiling them, to one half white wine, and the other half white wine vinegar, ſome ſalt, and a few bay-leaves; then give them a boil or two; there muſt be liquor enough to cover them; when they are cold, put a ſpoonful or two of oil on the top to keep them: you muſt change the liquor once a month.

To make Melon Mangoes.

TAKE ſmall melons not quite ripe, cut a ſlip down the ſide, and take out the inſide very clean; beat muſtard-ſeeds, and ſhred garlick, which mix with the ſeeds, and put in your mangoes; put the pieces you cut out into their places again, tie them up, and put them into your pot; then boil ſome vinegar (as much as you think will cover them) with whole pepper, ſome ſalt, and *Jamaica* pepper, which pour in ſcalding hot over your mangoes, and cover them cloſe to keep in the ſteam; repeat this nine days, and when they are cold cover them with leather.

To pickle Walnuts.

TAKE walnuts about midſummer, when a pin will paſs through them, put them in a deep pot, and cover them over with ordinary vinegar; change them into freſh vinegar once in fourteen days, for ſix weeks; then take two gallons of the beſt vinegar, and put into it coriander-ſeeds, carraway-ſeeds, and dill-ſeeds, of each an ounce groſly bruiſed, ginger ſliced three ounces, whole mace one ounce, nutmeg and pepper bruiſed, of each two ounces; give all a boil or two over the fire, and have your nuts ready in a pot, and pour the liquor boiling hot over them; repeat this nine times.

To pickle Cucumbers in slices.

SLICE your cucumbers pretty thick, and to a dozen of cucumbers cut in two or three good onions, strew on them a large large handful of salt, and let them lie in their liquor twenty-four-hours: then drain them, and put them between two coarse cloths; then boil the best white wine vinegar, with some cloves, mace and *Jamaica* pepper in it, and pour it scalding hot over them, as much as will cover them all over; when they are cold, cover them up with leather, and keep them for use.

To pickle Sprats for Anchovies.

TAKE an anchovy-barrel, or a deep glazed pot, put a few bay-leaves at the bottom, a layer of bay-salt, and some petre-salt mixed together; then a layer of sprats, crouded close, then bay-leaves, and the same salt and sprats and so till your barrel or pot be full; then put in the head of your barrel close, and once a week turn the other end upwards; in three months they will be fit to eat as anchovies raw, but they will not dissolve.

To pickle Sparrows, or Squab-Pigeons.

TAKE your sparrows, pigeons, or larks, draw them, and cut off their legs; then make a pickle of water, a quarter of a pint of white wine, a bunch of sweet herbs, salt, pepper, cloves and mace; when it boils put in your sparrows, and when they are enough take them up, and when they are cold put them in the pot you keep them in; then make a strong pickle of rhenish wine and white wine vinegar; put in an onion, a sprig of thyme and savoury, some lemon peel, some cloves, mace, and whole pepper; season it pretty high with salt; boil all these together very well; then set it by till it is cold, and put it to your sparrows; once in a month new boil the pickle, and when the bones are dissolv'd they are fit to eat; put them in china saucers and mix with your pickles.

To pickle Naſturtium Buds.

GATHER your little knobs quickly after your bloſſoms are off; put them in cold water and ſalt for three days, ſhifting them once a day; then make a pickle (but do not boil it at all) of ſome white wine, ſome white wine vinegar, eſchalot, horſe-radiſh, pepper, ſalt, cloves and mace whole, and nutmeg quartered; then put in your ſeeds and ſtop them cloſe; they are to be eaten as capers.

To keep Quinces in pickle.

CUT five or ſix quinces all to pieces, and put them in an earthen pot or pan, with a gallon of water, and two pounds of honey; mix all theſe together well, and then put them in a kettle to boil leiſurely half an hour, and then ſtrain your liquor into an earthen pot; and when 'tis cold, wipe your quinces clean, and put them into it: They muſt be vered very cloſe, and they will keep all the year.

To pickle Aſparagus.

GATHER your aſparagus, and lay them in an earthen pot; make a brine of water and ſalt ſtrong enough to bear an egg, pour it hot on them, and keep it cloſe covered: when you uſe them hot, lay them in cold water for two hours, then boil and butter them for the table; if you uſe them as a pickle, boil them and lay them in vinegar.

To pickle Aſhen-keys.

TAKE aſhen-keys as young as you can get them, and put them in a pot with ſalt and water; then take green whey, when 'tis hot, and pour over them; let them ſtand till they are cold before you cover them; when you uſe them, boil them in fair water till they are tender; then take them out, and put them in ſalt and water.

To

To pickle Samphire.

PICK your ſamphire from dead or withered branches; lay it in a bell metal or braſs pot; then put in a pint of water and a pint of vinegar; ſo do till your pickle is an inch above your ſamphire; have a lid for the pot, and paſte it cloſe down, that no ſteam may go out; keep it boiling an hour, take it off, and cover the pot cloſe with old ſacks, *&c.* when 'tis cold, put it up in tubs or pots; the beſt by itſelf; the great ſtalks lay uppermoſt in boiling; it will keep the cooler and better. The vinegar you uſe muſt be the beſt.

To mango Cucumbers.

CUT a little ſlip out of the ſide of the cucumber, and take out the ſeeds, but as little of the meat as you can; then fill the inſide with muſtard-ſeed bruiſed, a clove of garlick, ſome ſlices of ginger, and ſome bits of horſe-radiſh; tie the piece in again, and make a pickle of vinegar, ſalt, whole pepper, cloves, mace, and boil it, and pour it on the mangoes, and do ſo for nine days together; when cold, cover them with leather.

Another Way to pickle Walnuts.

TAKE walnuts about *Midſummer*, when a pin will paſs through them; and put them in a deep pot, and cover them over with ordinary vinegar: change them into freſh vinegar, once in fourteen days, repeat this four times; then take ſix quarts of the beſt vinegar, and put into it an ounce of dill-ſeeds groſly bruiſed, ginger ſliced three ounces, mace whole one ounce, nutmegs quartered two ounces, whole pepper two ounces; give all a boil or two over the fire; then put your nuts into a crock, and pour your pickle boiling hot over them; cover them up cloſe till 'tis cold, to keep in the ſteam; then have gallipots ready, and place your nuts

nuts in them till your pots are full; put in the middle of each pot a large clove of garlick ſtuck full of cloves; ſtrew over the tops of the pots muſtard-ſeed finely beaten, a ſpoonful, more or leſs, according to the bigneſs of your pot; then put the ſpice on, lay vine-leaves, and pour on the liquor, laying a ſlate on the top to keep them under the liquor. Be careful not to touch them with your fingers, leaſt they turn black; but take them out with a wooden ſpoon; put a handful of ſalt in with the ſpice. When you firſt boil the pickle, you muſt likewiſe remember to keep them under the pickle they are firſt ſteeped in, or they will looſe their colour. Tie down the pots with leather. A ſpoonful of this liquor will reliſh ſauce for fiſh, fowl, or fricaſee.

To pickle Lobſters.

BOIL your lobſters in ſalt and water, till they will eaſily ſlip out of the ſhell; take the tails out whole, juſt crack the claws, and take the meat out as whole as poſſible; then make the pickle half white wine and half water; put in whole cloves, whole pepper, whole mace, two or three bay-leaves; then put in the lobſters, and let them have a boil or two in the pickle; then take them out, and ſet them by to be cold, boil the pickle longer, and when both are cold put them together, and keep them for uſe. Tie the pot down cloſe; eat them with oil, vinegar, and lemon.

Tench to pickle.

WHEN your tench are cleanſed, have a pickle ready boil'd, half white wine and half vinegar, a few blades of mace, ſome ſlic'd ginger, whole pepper, and a bay-leaf, with a piece of lemon-peel and ſome ſalt; boil your tench in it, and when it is enough, lay them out to cool, and when the liquor is cold, put them in; it will keep but few days.

An

An excellent way to pickle Mushrooms.

PUT your mushrooms into water, and wash 'em clean with a spunge, throw them into water as you do them; then put in water and a little salt, and when it boils put in your mushrooms; when they boil up scum them clean, and put them into cold water, and a little salt: let them stand twenty four hours, and put them into white wine vinegar, and let them stand a week; then take your pickle from them, and boil it very well with pepper, cloves, mace, and a little all spice; when your pickle is cold, put it to your mushrooms in the glass or pot you keep them in; keep them close tied down with a bladder; the air will hurt them: if your pickle mothers, boil it again: you may make your pickle half white wine, and half white wine vinegar.

Another.

AFTER your mushrooms are well cleansed with a woollen cloth in salt and water, boil milk and water and put them in; let them boil eight or ten minutes; drain them in a sieve; put them immediately into cold water that has been boiled and made cold; take them out of it, and put them into boil'd vinegar that is cold also; let them stand twenty-four hours, and in that time get ready a pickle with white wine vinegar, a few large blades of mace, a good quantity of whole pepper and ginger sliced; boil this, and when cold put in your mushrooms from the other vinegar. Put them into wide-mouth glasses, and oil upon them; they will keep a great while, if you put them thus in two pickles.

To pickle Oysters.

WASH your oysters in their own liquor, squeezing them between your fingers, that there be no gravel in them; strain the liquor, and wash

wash the oysters in it again; put as much water, as the liquor, set it on the fire, and as it boils skim it clean; then put a pretty deal of whole pepper, boil it a little, then put in some blades of mace, and your oysters, stirring them apace, and when they are firm in the middle-part, take them off, pour them quick into an earthen pot, and cover them very close; put in a few bay-leaves; be sure your oysters are all under the liquor; the next day put them up for use, cover them very close: When you dish them to eat, put a little white wine or vinegar on the plate with them.

To pickle Pods of Radishes.

GAther the youngest pods, and put them in water and salt twenty four hours; then make a pickle for them of vinegar, cloves, mace, and whole pepper; boil this, drain the pods from the salt and water, and pour the liquor on them boiling hot: put to them a clove of garlick a little bruised.

To pickle Cucumbers.

WIPE your cucumbers very clean with a cloth, then get so many quarts of vinegar as you have hundreds of cucumbers, and take dill and fennel, cut it small, put to it vinegar, set it over the fire in a copper kettle, and let it boil; then put in your cucumbers till they are warm through, but not boil while they are in; when they are warm thro', pour all out into a deep earthen pot, and cover it up very close till the next day; then do the same again; but the third day season the liquor before you set it over the fire; put in salt till 'tis brackish, some sliced ginger, whole pepper, and whole mace; then set it over the fire again, and when it boils put in your cucumbers: when they are hot through, pour them into the pot, cover it close; when they are cold, put them in glasses, and strain the liquor over them; pick out the spice, and put to them; cover them with leather.

To

To pickle French *Beans.*

TAKE young slender *French* beans; cut off top and tail; then make a brine with cold water and salt, strong enough to bear an egg; put your beans into that brine, and let them lie fourteen days; then take them out, wash them in fair water, set them over the fire in cold water, without salt, and let them boil till they are so tender as to eat; when they are cold, drain them from their water, and make a pickle for them: To a peck of *French* beans, you must have a gallon of white wine vinegar; boil it with some cloves, mace, whole pepper, and sliced ginger; when 'tis cold put it and your beans into a glass, and keep them for use.

Another Way to pickle French *Beans.*

PICK the small slender beans from the stalks, and let them lie fourteen days in salt and water, then wash them clean from the brine, and put them in a kettle of water over a slow fire, covered over with vine-leaves; let them stew, but not boil, till they are almost as tender as for eating; then strain them off, laying them on a coarse cloth to dry; then put them in your pots: Boil alegar, skim it and pour it over them, covering them close; boil it so three or four days together, till they be green: Put spice, as to other pickles; and when cold cover with leather.

French *Beans to keep.*

TAKE a peck of *French* beans, break them every one in the middle; to them put two pounds of beaten salt; ram them well together, and when the brine arises put them in a narrow-mouth'd jar; press them down close, and lay somewhat that will keep them down with a weight, and tie them up close, that no air comes to them; the night before you use them, lay them in water.

To

To pickle Currants for present Use.

TAKE either red or white, being not thorough ripe; give them a warm in white wine vinegar, with as much sugar as will indifferently sweeten them; keep them well covered with liquor.

To pickle Asparagus.

TAKE of the largest asparagus, cut off the white at the ends, and scrape them lightly to the head, till they look green; wipe them with a cloth, and lay them in a broad gallipot very even; throw over them whole cloves, mace, and a little salt; put over them as much white wine vinegar as will cover them very well: Let them lie in the cold pickle nine days; then pour the pickle out into a brass kettle, and let them boil; then put them in, stove them down close, and set them by a little; then set them over again, till they are very green; but take care they don't boil to be soft; then put them in a large gallipot, place them even, and pour the liquor over them; when cold tie them down with leather: 'Tis a good pickle, and looks well in a savoury made dish or pye.

To pickle Broom-Buds.

PUT your broom-buds into little linnen-bags, tie them up; make a pickle of bay-salt and water boiled, and strong enough to bear an egg; put your bags in a pot, and when your pickle is cold, put it to them; keep them close. and let them lie till they burn black: then shift them two or three times, till they change green; then take them out, and boil them as you have occasion for them: When they are boiled, put them out of the bag; in vinegar they will keep a month after they are boiled.

To pickle Purslane Stalks.

WASH your stalks, and cut them in pieces six inches long; give them in water and salt a dozen walms; take them up, drain them, and when they cool make a pickle of ſtale beer, white wine vinegar, and ſalt; put them in, and cover them cloſe.

Cabbage Lettuce to keep.

ABOUT the latter end of the ſeaſon take very dry ſand, and cover the bottom of a well ſeaſon'd barrel; then ſet your lettuce in ſo as not to touch one another: you muſt not lay above two rows one upon another; cover them well with ſand, and ſet them in a dry place, and be careful that the froſt come not at them. The lettuce muſt not be cut, but be pull'd up by the roots.

To pickle Red Cabbage.

TAKE your cloſe-leav'd red cabbage, and cut it in quarters; when your liquor boils put in your cabbage, and give it a dozen walms; then make the pickle of white wine vinegar and claret: you may put to it beet-root, boil them firſt, and turneps half boiled; it is very good for the garniſhing diſhes, or to garniſh a ſalad.

To pickle Barberries.

TAKE of white wine vinegar, and fair water an equal quantity, and to every pint of this liquor put a pound of ſix-penny ſugar; ſet it over the fire, and bruiſe ſome of the barberries and put in it a little ſalt; let it boil near half an hour; then take it off the fire, and ſtrain it, and when it is pretty cold pour it into a glaſs over your barberries; boil a piece of flannel in the liquor and put over them, and cover the glaſs with leather.

Another Way to pickle Barberries.

TAKE water, and colour it red with ſome of the worſt of your barberries, and put ſalt to it, and make it ſtrong enough to bear an egg; then ſet it over the fire, and let it boil half an hour;

ſkim it, and when it is cold ſtrain it over your barberries; lay ſomething on them to keep them in the liquor, and cover the pot or glaſs with leather.

To pickle Salmon.

TAKE two quarts of good vinegar, half an ounce of black pepper, and as much *Jamaica* pepper; cloves and mace, of each a quarter of an ounce, near a pound of ſalt; bruiſe the ſpice groſly, and put all theſe to a ſmall quantity of water, put juſt enough to cover your fiſh; cut the fiſh round, three or four pieces, according to the ſize of the ſalmon, and when the liquor boils put in your fiſh, boil it well; then take the fiſh out of the pickle, and let it cool; and when it is cold put your fiſh into the barrel or ſtein you keep it in, ſtrewing ſome ſpice and bay-leaves between every piece of fiſh; let the pickle cool, and ſkim off the fat, and when the pickle is quite cold pour it on your fiſh, and cover it very cloſe.

To pickle Oyſters.

TAKE a hundred and half of large oyſters, waſh them and ſcald them in their own liquor; then take them out, and lay them on a clean cloth to cool; ſtrain their liquor, and boil and ſkim it clean, adding to it one pint of white wine, half a pint of white wine vinegar, one nutmeg beat groſly, one onion ſlit, an ounce of white pepper, half whole the other half juſt bruiſed, ſix or eight blades of mace, a quarter of an ounce of cloves, and five or ſix bay-leaves; boil up this pickle till it is of a good taſte, then cool it in broad diſhes, and put your oyſters in a deep pot or barrel, and when the pickle is cold put it to them; in five or ſix days they will be ready to eat, and will keep three weeks or a month, if you take them out with a ſpoon, and not touch them with your fingers.

The

The Lemon Salad.

TAKE lemons and cut them into halves, and when you have taken out the meat, lay the rinds in water twelve hours; then take them out, and cut the rinds thus ⅁; boil them in water till they are tender; take them out and dry them; then take a pound of loaf fugar, putting to it a quarter of a pint of white wine, and twice as much white wine vinegar, and boil it a little; then take it off, and when it is cold put it in the pot to your peels; they will be ready to eat in five or fix days; it is a pretty falad.

To pickle Pigeons.

TAKE your pigeons and bone them, beginning at the rump; take cloves, mace, nutmegs, pepper, falt, thyme, and lemon-peel; beat the fpice, fhred the herbs and lemon-peel very fmall, and feafon the infide of your pigeons; then few them up, and place the legs and wings in order; then feafon the outfide, and make a pickle for them: to a dozen of pigeons two quarts of water, one quart of white wine, a few blades of mace, fome falt, fome whole pepper; and when it boils put in your pigeons, and let them boil till they are tender; then take them out, and ftrain out the liquor, and put your pigeons in a pot, and when the liquor is cold pour it on them; when you ferve them to table, dry them out of the pickle, and garnifh the difh with fennel or flowers; eat them with vinegar and oil.

To pickle Purflane Stalks.

TAKE the largeft and greeneft purflane-ftalks, gather them dry, and ftrip off all the leaves; lay the ftalks clofe in an earthen pot; you may lay kidney-beans among them, for you may do them the fame way; then lay a ftick or two a-crofs to ceep them under the pickle, which muft be made

 thus:

thus: take whey, and ſet it on the fire, with as much ſalt as will make it almoſt as ſalt as brine; ſkim off all the curd, and let it boil a quarter of an hour longer, with *Jamaica* pepper in it; next day, when it is cold, pour the clear thro' a clean cloth upon the pickles, and tie it down cloſe, and ſet it in a cool cellar; in winter, take a few out as you uſe them; waſh them till the water runs clean; then put your beans or ſtalks into cold water, and ſet them over the fire, very cloſe cover'd, and let them ſcald two hours; and tho' they be as black as ink, or ſtink before you put them in, they will be very green and good when done; then boil vinegar, ſalt, pepper, *Jamaica* pepper, ginger, for half a quarter of an hour; and when your ſtalks are well drain'd from the water thro' a colander, then put your pickle to them, and when theſe are uſed, green more, but do not do many at a time.

To make English *Katchup.*

TAKE a wide-mouth'd bottle, put therein a pint of the beſt white wine vinegar, putting in ten or twelve cloves of eſchalot peeled and juſt bruiſed; then take a quarter of a pint of the beſt langoon white wine, boil it a little, and put to it twelve or fourteen anchovies waſhed and ſhred, and diſſolve them in the wine, and when cold, put them in the bottle; then take a quarter of a pint more of white wine, and put in it mace, ginger ſliced, a few cloves, a ſpoonful of whole pepper juſt bruiſed, and let them boil all a little; when near cold, ſlice in almoſt a whole nutmeg, and ſome lemon peel, and likewiſe put in two or three ſpoonfuls of horſe-radiſh; then ſtop it cloſe, and for a week ſhake it once or twice a day; then uſe it; it is good to put into fiſh ſauce, or any ſavoury diſh of meat; you may add to it the clear liquor that comes from muſhrooms.

To pickle Cucumbers in Slices.

TAKE your cucumbers at the full bigness, but not yellow, and slice them half an inch thick; cut an onion or two with them, and strew a pretty deal of salt on them; and let them stand to drain all night; then pour the liquor clear from them; dry them in a coarse cloth, and boil as much vinegar as will cover them, with whole pepper, mace, and a quarter'd nutmeg; pour it scalding hot on your cucumbers, keeping them very close stopt; in two or three days heat your liquor again, and pour over them; so do two or three times more; then tie them up with leather.

To pickle small Onions.

TAKE young white unset onions, as big as the tip of your finger; lay them in water and salt two days; shift them once, then drain them in a cloth; boil the best vinegar with spice according to your taste, and when it is cold, keep them in it, covered with a wet bladder.

Another Way to pickle Walnuts.

TAKE your nuts fit to preserve, prick them full of holes, and cut the slit in the crease half through; put them as you do them into brine; let them lie three weeks, changing the brine every four days; take them out with a cloth, and wipe them dry; put them in a pot, with a good deal of bruised mustard-seed; then have your pickle ready, which must be wine vinegar, as much as will cover them; put in cloves, mace, ginger, pepper, salt, three or four cloves of garlick stuck with cloves, and pour the liquor boiling hot upon them, and keep them close tied for a fortnight; boil the pickle again, so do three times; put oil on the top.

To distil Vinegar for Mushrooms.

TO a gallon of vinegar put an ounce and half of ginger sliced, one ounce of nutmegs, bruised, half an ounce of mace, half an ounce of white pepper, as much *Jamaica* pepper, both bruised, a few cloves; distil this: take care it does not burn in the still.

To pickle Mushrooms.

TAKE only the buttons, wash them in milk and water with a flannel; put milk on the fire, and when it boils put in your mushrooms, and give them four or five boils; have in readiness a brine made with milk and salt, and take them out of the boiling brine, and put them into the milk-brine, covering them up all night; then have a brine with water and salt; boil it, and let it stand to be cold, and put in your buttons, and wash them in it. When you first boil your mushrooms, you must put with them an onion and spice; then have in readiness a pickle made with half white wine, and half white wine vinegar; boil it in ginger, mace, nutmegs, and whole white pepper; when it is quite cold put your mushrooms into the bottle, and some bay-leaves on the sides; and strew between some of your boiled spice; then put in the liquor, and a little oil on the top; cork and rosin the top; set them cool and dry, and the bottom upwards.

To marinate Smelts.

TAKE your smelts, gut them neatly, wash and dry them, and fry them in oil; lay them to drain and cool, and have in readiness a pickle made with vinegar, salt, pepper, cloves, mace, onion, horse-radish; let it boil together half an hour; when it is cold put in your smelts.

To pickle Lemons.

TAKE twelve lemons, ſcrape them with a piece of broken glaſs, then cut them croſs into four parts downright, but not quite through, but that they will hang together; then put in as much ſalt as they will hold, rub them well, and ſtrew them over with ſalt: let them lie in an earthen diſh, and turn them every day for three days; then ſlice an ounce of ginger very thin, and ſalted for three days, twelve cloves of garlick parboil'd and ſalted three days, a ſmall handful of muſtard-ſeed bruiſed, and ſearced thro' a hair ſieve, ſome red *Indian* pepper, one to every lemon; take your lemons out of the ſalt, and ſqueeze them gently, and put them into a jar with the ſpice, and cover them with the beſt white wine vinegar; ſtop them up very cloſe, and in a month's time they will be fit to eat.

To keep Artichokes in pickle, to boil all Winter.

THROW your artichokes into ſalt and water half a day, then make a pot of water boil, and put in your artichokes, and let them boil till you can juſt draw off the leaves from the bottom; then cut off the bottom very ſmooth and clean, and put them into a pot with pepper, ſalt, cloves, mace, two bay-leaves, and as much vinegar as will cover them; then pour as much melted butter over them as will cover them inch thick; tie it down cloſe, and keep them for uſe; when you uſe them put them into boiling water, with a piece of butter in the water to plump them; then uſe them for what you pleaſe.

To pickle Muſhrooms.

RUB your muſhrooms with a piece of flannel in a little water, and as you clean them, put others

others into your pot you design to use them in; then set them into a pot of hot water, as if you were going to infuse them; let them be covered close, and boil them till they be settled about half from what they were at first; take them out into a sieve to let the liquor run off; and immediately spread them on a clean coarse cloth, and smother them up close; when cold put them in the best white wine vinegar and salt, and let them lie nine or ten days in it; then make your pickle with fresh white wine vinegar, white pepper whole, and a little salt.

To pickle Walnuts.

IN *July* gather the largest walnuts, and let them lie nine days in salt and water, shifting them every third day; let the salt and water be strong enough to bear an egg, then put two pots of water on the fire; when the water is hot put in your walnuts; shift them out of one pot into the other for the more clean water they have the better; when some of them begin to rise in the water they are enough; then pour them into a colander, and with a woollen cloth wipe them clean, and put them in the jar you keep them in; then boil as much vinegar as will cover them, with beaten pepper, cloves, mace, and nutmeg, just bruised, and put some cloves of garlick into the pot to them, with whole spice, and *Jamaica* pepper; when they are cold put into every half hundred of nuts three spoonfuls of mustard seed; tie a bladder over them and leather.

Another way to pickle Mushrooms.

SCRAPE the buttons carefully with a penknife, and throw them into cold water, as you scrape them; and put them into fresh water, and set them close cover'd over a quick clear fire; blow under

under it, to make it boil as fast as possible half a quarter of an hour; strain them off, and turn the hollow end down upon a wooden board as quick as you can, whilst they remain hot, and then sprinkle them over with a little salt; when they are cold put them into bottles or glasses, with a little mace, and sliced ginger, and cover them with cold white wine-vinegar; tie bladders or leather over them.

To make Gooseberry Vinegar.

TAKE gooseberries full ripe, bruise them in a mortar, then measure them, and to every quart of gooseberries put three quarts of water, first boiled, and let it stand till cold; let it stand twenty-four hours; then strain it thro' a canvas, then a flannel; and to every gallon of this liquor put one pound of feeding brown sugar; stir it well, and barrel it up; at three quarters of a year old it is fit for use; but if it stands longer it is the better: this vinegar is likewise good for pickles.

To make the Mushroom Powder.

TAKE the large mushrooms, wash them clean from grit; cut off the stalks, but do not peel or grill them; so put them into a kettle over the fire, but no water; put a good quantity of spice of all sorts, two onions stuck with cloves, a handful of salt, some beaten pepper, and a quarter of a pound of butter; let all these stew, till the liquor is dried up in them; then take them out, and lay them on sieves to dry, till they will beat to powder; press the powder hard down in a pot, and keep it for use, what quantity you please at a time in sauce.

To pickle Muſhrooms.

TAKE your muſhrooms freſh gathered, peel or rub them, and put them in milk, with water and ſalt; when they are all peeled, take them out of that, and put them into freſh milk, water, and ſalt to boil, adding an onion ſtuck with cloves; when they have boiled a little, take them off, and take them out of that, and ſmother them between two flannels; then take as much good alegar as you think will cover them, and boil it with ginger, mace, nutmeg, and whole pepper; when it is cold, let it be put on your muſhrooms, and cover them cloſe.

To pickle Muſcles or Cockles.

TAKE your freſh muſcles or cockles; waſh them very clean, and put them in a pot over the fire till they open; then take them out of their ſhells, pick them clean, and lay them to cool; then put their liquor to ſome vinegar, whole pepper, ginger ſliced thin, and mace, ſetting it over the fire; when it is ſcalding hot, put in your muſcles, and let them ſtew a little; then pour out the pickle from them, and when both are cold put them in an earthen jug, and cork it up cloſe: in two or three days they will be fit to eat.

To make Hung Beef.

TO a pound of beef, put a pound of bay-ſalt, two ounces of ſalt-petre, and a pound of ſugar mix'd with the common ſalt; let it lie ſix weeks in this brine, turning it every day, then dry it and boil it.

To do the fine hanged Beef.

THE piece that is fit to do, is the navel-piece, and let it hang in your cellar, as long as you dare for stinking, and till it begins to be a little sappy; take it down, and wash it in sugar and water; wash it with a clean rag very well, one piece after another: for you may cut that piece in three; then take six penny worth of salt petre, and two pounds of bay-salt; dry it, and pound it small, and mix with it two or three spoonfuls of brown sugar, and rub your beef in every place very well with it; then take of common salt, and strew all over it as much as you think will make it salt enough; let it lie close, till the salt be dissolved, which will be in six or seven days; then turn it every other day, the undermost uppermost, and so for a fortnight; then hang it where it may have a little warmth of the fire; not too hot to roast it. It may hang in the kitchen a fortnight; when you use it, boil it in hay and pump-water, very tender: it will keep boiled two or three months, rubbing it with a greasy cloth, or putting it two or three minutes into boiling water to take off the mouldiness,

To distil Verjuice for Pickles.

TAKE three quarts of the sharpest verjuice, and put in a cold still, and distil it off very softly; the sooner it is distill'd in the spring, the better for use.

To pickle Mushrooms.

TAKE your mushrooms as soon as they come in; cut the stalks off, and throw your mushrooms into water and salt as you do them; then rub them with a piece of flannel, and as you do them, throw them into another vessel of salt and water, and when all is done, put some salt and water on the fire,

fire, and when 'tis ſcalding hot, put in your muſhrooms, and let them ſtay in as long as you think will boil an egg: throw them into cold water as ſoon as they come off the fire; but firſt put them in a ſieve, and let them drain from the hot water, and be ſure to take them out of the hot water immediately, or they will wrinkle and look yellow. Let them ſtand in the cold water till next morning. then take them out, and put them into freſh water and ſalt, and change them every day for three or four days together; then wipe them very dry, and put them into diſtill'd vinegar: the ſpice muſt be diſtilled in the vinegar.

Sauce for boiled Turkey or Chickens.

BOIL a ſpoonful of the beſt mace very tender, and the liver of the turkey, but not too much, for then it will be hard; bray the mace with a few drops of liquor to a very fine pulp, then bray the liver and put about half of it to the mace with a little pepper, and ſome ſalt, if you pleaſe you may put the yolk of an egg boil'd hard and diſſolved; to this add by degrees a little of the liquor that drains from the turkey, or ſome other gravy; put theſe liquors to the pulp, and boil them ſome time; then take half a pint of oyſters and boil them no longer than till they will break; and laſt put in white wine and butter wrapt in flour: let it boil but a little, leſt the wine make the oyſters hard, and juſt at the laſt ſcald four or five ſpoonfuls of thick new cream, with a few drops of lemon or vinegar; muſhrooms pickled do well, but then leave out the other acids; ſome like this ſauce beſt thicken'd with yolks of eggs and no butter.

Sauce for Fiſh or Fleſh.

TAKE a quart of verjuice, and put it into a jug; then take *Jamaica* pepper whole, ſome ſliced

sliced ginger, some mace, a few cloves, some lemon-peel, horse-radish root sliced, some sweet herbs, six eschalots peeled, and eight anchovies; two or three spoonfuls of shred capers; put all these into a linen bag, and put the bag into your verjuice; stop the jug close, and keep it for use; a spoonful cold or mixed in sauce for fish or flesh.

All Sorts of PUDDINGS.

To make an Orange-Pudding.

TAKE two large *Seville* oranges, and grate off the rind, as far as they are yellow; then put your oranges in fair water, and let them boil till they are tender, shift the water three or four times to take out the bitterness; when they are tender cut them open, take away the seeds and strings, and beat the other part in a mortar, with half a pound of sugar, till 'tis a paste; then put in the yolks of six eggs, three or four spoonfuls of thick cream, half a *Naples* bisket grated; mix these together, and melt a pound of very good fresh butter, and stir it well in; when 'tis cold, put a bit of fine puff paste about the brim and bottom of your dish; put it in and bake it about three quarters of an hour.

Another Sort of Orange-Pudding.

TAKE the outside rind of three *Seville* oranges, boil them in several waters till they are tender; then pound them in a mortar with three quarters of a pound of sugar; then blanch and beat half a pound a pound of almonds very fine, with rose-water to keep them from oiling; then beat sixteen eggs, but six whites, and a pound of fresh butter; beat all these tog•ther very well till it is light and hollow; then put it in a dish with a sheet of puff-paste at the bottom, and bake it with tarts; scrape sugar on it, and serve it up hot.

To make a Carrot Pudding.

TAKE raw carrots, and scrape them clean, grate them with a grater without a back. To half a pound of carrots, take a pound of grated bread, a nutmeg, a little cinnamon, a very little salt, half a pound of sugar, half a pint of sack, eight eggs, a pound of butter melted, and as much cream as will mix it well together; stir it and beat it well up, and put it in a dish to bake; put puff-paste at the bottom of your dish.

To make an Almond Pudding.

TAKE a pound of the best *Jordan* almonds blanched in cold water, and beat very fine with a little rose-water; then take a quart of cream, boiled with whole spice, and taken out again, and when it is cold, mix it with the almonds, and put to it three spoonfuls of grated bread, one spoonful of flour, nine eggs, but three whites, half a pound of sugar, and a nutmeg grated; mix and beat these well together, put some puff-paste at the bottom of a dish: put your stuff in, and here and there stick a piece of marrow in it. It must bake an hour, and when it is drawn, scrape sugar on it, and serve it up.

To make a Marrow Pudding.

TAKE out the marrow of three or four bones, and slice it in thin pieces; and take a penny loaf, cut off the crust, and slice it in as thin slices as you

you can, and ſtone half a pound of raiſins of the ſun; then lay a ſheet of thin paſte in the bottom of a diſh; ſo lay a row of marrow, or bread, and of raiſins, till the diſh is full; then have in readineſs a quart of cream boiled, and beat five eggs, and mix with it; put to it nutmeg grated, and half a pound of ſugar. When 'tis juſt going into the oven, pour in your cream and eggs; bake it half an hour, ſcrape ſugar on it when it is drawn, and ſerve it up.

A Bread and Butter Pudding for Faſting-Days.

TAKE a two penny loaf, and a pound of freſh butter; ſpread it in very thin ſlices, as to eat; cut them off as you ſpread them, and ſtone half a pound of raiſins, and waſh a pound of currants; then put puff-paſte at the bottom of a diſh, and lay a row of your bread and butter, and ſtrew a handful of currants, a few raiſins, and ſome little bits of butter, and ſo do till your diſh is full; then boil three pints of cream and thicken it when cold with the yolks of ten eggs, a grated nutmeg, a little ſalt, near half a pound of ſugar, and ſome orange flower-water; pour this in juſt as the pudding is going into the oven.

Another baked Bread Pudding.

TAKE a penny loaf, cut it in thin ſlices, then boil a quart of cream or new milk, and put in your bread, and break it very fine; put five eggs to it, a nutmeg grated, a quarter of a pound of ſugar, and half a pound of butter; ſtir all theſe well together; butter your diſh, and bake it an hour.

A Lemon Pudding.

TAKE two clear lemons, grate off the outſide rinds; then grate two *Naples*-biſkets, and mix with

with your grated peel, adding to it three quarters of a pound of fine ſugar, twelve yolks and ſix whites of eggs, well beat, three quarters of a pound of butter melted, and half a pint of thick cream; mix theſe well together put in a ſheet of paſte at the bottom of the diſh, and juſt as the oven is ready put your ſtuff in the diſh; ſift a little double-refined ſugar over it before you put it in the oven; an hour will bake it.

To make a Calf's-Foot-Pudding.

TAKE two calf's-feet finely ſhred; then take of biſkets grated, and ſtale mackaroons broken ſmall, the quantity of a penny loaf; then add a pound of beef-ſuet, very finely ſhred, half a pound of currants, a quarter of a pound of ſugar; ſome cloves, mace, and nutmeg, beat fine; a very little ſalt, ſome ſack and orange-flower water, ſome citron and candied orange peel; work all theſe well together with yolks of eggs; if you boil it, put it in the caul of a breaſt of veal, and tie it over with a cloth, it muſt boil four hours. For ſauce, melt butter, with a little ſack and ſugar; if you bake it, put ſome paſte in the bottom of the diſh, but none on the brim, then melt half a pound of butter, which mix with your ſtuff,and put it in your diſh, ſticking lumps of marrow in it: bake it three or four hours; ſcrape ſugar over it, and ſerve it hot.

A Rice Pudding.

SET a pint of thick cream over the fire, and put into it three ſpoonfuls of the flour of rice, ſtir it, and when 'tis pretty thick, pour it into a pan, adding to it a pound of freſh butter; ſtir it till 'tis almoſt cold; then add to it a grated nutmeg, a little ſalt, ſome ſugar, a little ſack, the yolks of ſix eggs; ſtir it well together; put ſome puff paſte in the

the bottom of the diſh, pour it in; an hour or leſs will bake it.

An Apple Pudding.

PEEL and quarter eight golden runnets, or twelve golden pippins; put them into water, in which boil them as you do apple-ſauce; ſweeten them with loaf ſugar, ſqueeze in two lemons, and grate in their peels; break eight eggs, and beat them all well together; pour it into a diſh covered with puff-paſte, and bake it an hour in a ſlow oven.

To make an Oatmeal Pudding.

TAKE three pints of thick cream, and three quarters of a pound of beef-ſuet ſhred very fine; when the cream boils, put into it the ſuet, a pound of butter, half a pound of ſugar, a nutmeg grated, and a little ſalt; then thicken all with a pint of fine oatmeal; ſtir all together; pour it into a pan, and cover it up cloſe till 'tis almoſt cold; then put in the yolks of ſix eggs; mix it all well together, and put a very thin paſte at the bottom of the diſh, and ſtick lumps of marrow in it; bake it two hours.

To make a French *Barley Pudding.*

TAKE a quart of cream, and put to it ſix eggs well beaten, but three of the whites; then ſeaſon it with ſugar, nutmeg, a little ſalt, orange-flower water, and a pound of melted butter; then put to it ſix handfuls of *French* barley that has been boiled tender in milk: Butter a diſh, and put it in, and bake it. It muſt ſtand as long as a veniſon-paſty, and it will be good.

A colouring liquor for Puddings.

BEAT an ounce of cochineal very fine, put it in a pint of water in a ſkillet, and a quarter of an ounce of roach allum, boil it till the goodneſs is out; ſtrain it into a phial, with two ounces of fine ſugar; it will keep ſix months.

A good boiled Pudding.

TAKE a pound and a quarter of beef-ſuet, after it is ſkin'd, and ſhred very fine; then ſtone three quarters of a pound of raiſins, and mix with it, as alſo a grated nutmeg, a quarter of a pound of ſugar, a little ſalt, a little ſack, four eggs, four ſpoonfuls of cream, and about half a pound of fine flour; mix theſe well together pretty ſtiff, tie it in a cloth, and let it boil four hours; melt butter thick for ſauce.

Orange Pudding.

TAKE half a pound of loaf-ſugar, beat half a pound of freſh butter, the yolks of ſix eggs beaten, half a candied orange cut as ſmall as you can; melt the butter, and put in the ſugar and eggs, ſtir it over the fire a pretty while, then put in your orange, keep it ſtirring over the fire till it be pretty thick, then take it off the fire, and let it ſtand till cold, then put it into a diſh with puff-paſte under and over it; half an hour will bake it; then make them into little pats like cheeſecakes; it is good cold.

To make a Quaking Pudding.

TAKE a pint of cream, and boil it with nutmeg, cinnamon and mace; take out the ſpice, when it is boiled; then take the yolks of eight eggs, and four of the whites, beat them very well with ſome ſack; then mix your eggs and cream, with a little ſalt and ſugar, and a ſtale half penny white-loaf, one ſpoonful of flour, and a quarter of a pound of almonds blanch'd and beat fine, with ſome roſe-water; beat all theſe well together; then wet a thick cloth, flour it, and put it in when the pot boils; it muſt boil an hour at leaſt; melt butter, ſack and ſugar for the ſauce; ſtick'd blanch'd almonds and candied orange-peel on the top.

To make a Cow-Heel Pudding.

TAKE a large cow-heel, and cut off all the meat but the black toes; put them away, but mince the reſt very ſmall, and ſhred it over again, with three quarters of a pound of beef-ſuet; put to it a penny loaf grated, cloves, mace, nutmeg, ſugar, a little ſalt, ſome ſack, and roſe-water; mix theſe well together with ſix raw eggs well beaten; butter a cloth, put it in, and boil it two hours; for ſauce, melt butter, ſack and ſugar.

To make a Curd Pudding.

TAKE the curd of a gallon of milk, whey it well, and rub it thro' a ſieve; then take ſix eggs, a little thick cream, three ſpoonfuls of orange-flower water, one nutmeg grated, grated bread and flour, of each three ſpoonfuls, a pound of currants and ſtoned raiſins; mix all theſe together; butter a thick cloth, and tie it up in it; boil it an hour; for ſauce, melt butter with orange-flower water and ſugar.

To make a Pith Pudding.

TAKE a quantity of the pith of an ox, and let it lie all night in water to ſoak out the blood; the next morning ſtrip it out of the ſkins, and beat it with the back of a ſpoon in orange-flower water till it is as fine as pap; then take three blades of mace, a nutmeg quartered, a ſtick of cinnamon; then take half a pound of the beſt *Jordan* almonds, blanch'd in cold water, beat them with a little of the cream, and as they dry put in more cream, and when they are all beaten, ſtrain the cream from them to the pith; then take the yolks of ten eggs, the whites of but two, beat them very well, and put them to the Ingredients, then take a ſpoonful of grated bread, or *Naples* biſket; mingle all theſe to-

 gether,

gether, with half a pound of fine sugar, the marrow of four large bones, and a little salt; fill them in small ox or hogs guts, or bake it with puff-crust.

A Rice Pudding.

TAKE two large handfuls of rice well beaten and searced: then take two quarts of milk or cream, set it over the fire with the rice, put in cinnamon and mace, let it boil a quarter of an hour; it must be as thick as hasty pudding; then stir in half a pound of butter while it is over the fire; then take it off to cool, and put in sugar, and a little salt; when it is almost cold put in ten or twelve eggs, take out four of the whites; butter the dish; an hour will bake it; searce sugar over it.

Butter'd Crumbs.

PUT a piece of butter into a sauce-pan, and let it run to oil; then skim it clean, and pour it off from the settlement; to this clear oil put grated crumbs of bread, and keep them stirring till they are crisp.

Orange-Custard or Pudding.

TAKE *Seville* oranges, and rub the outside with a little salt very well, pare them, and take half a pound of the peel, and lay them in several waters till the bitterness is abated; beat them small in a stone or wooden mortar, then put in ten yolks of eggs and a quart of thick cream, mix them well, and sweeten them to your taste; melt half a pound of butter and stir it well in, if you design it for a pudding, and pour it into a dish covered with paste; if for custards, leave out the butter, and pour it into *China* cups, and bake it to eat cold.

A Pudding for little Dishes.

TAKE a pint of cream, boil it, and slice a half-penny loaf, and pour your cream over it hot,

hot, and cover it close till it is cold; then put in half a nutmeg grated, a quarter of a pound of sugar, the yolks of four eggs, the whites of but two; butter your dish and put it in, and let it boil an hour; melt butter, sack and sugar for sauce.

A Hasty Pudding to butter itself.

SET a quart of thick cream upon the fire, put into it the crumb of a penny white loaf grated, boil it pretty thick together, with often stirring it; a little before you take it up, put in the yolks of four eggs, with a spoonful of sack, or orange-flower water and some sugar; boil it very slow, keeping it stirring; some make it with grated *Naples* bisket, and put no eggs in; you may know when it is enough by an oil round the edge of the skillet, and soon all over it; then pour it out; it will require half an hour or more before it is enough; some put a few almonds blanched, and beat very fine, with a spoonful of wine, to keep them from oiling.

Another Hasty Pudding.

BREAK an egg into fine flour, and with your hand work up as much as you can into as stiff a paste as possible; then mince it as small as if it were to be sifted; then set a quart of milk a boiling, and put in your paste, so cut as before mentioned; put in a little salt, some beaten cinnamon and sugar, a piece of butter as big as a walnut, and keep it stirring all one way, till it is as thick as you would have it; and then stir in such another piece of butter; and when it is in the dish stick it all over with little bits of butter.

To make stew'd Pudding.

GRATE a two penny loaf, and mix it with half a pound of beef-suet finely shred, and three quarters of a pound of currants, and a quarter of a pound of sugar, a little cloves, mace, and nutmeg; then beat five or six eggs, with three or four

 spoonfuls

spoonfuls of rose-water, beat all together, and make them up in little round balls the bigness of an egg, some round and some long, in the fashion of an egg; then put a pound of butter in a pewter dish, when it is melted and thorough hot, put in your puddings, and let them stew till they are brown; turn them, and when they are enough, serve them up with sack, butter, and sugar for sauce.

To make a Cabbage Pudding.

TAKE two pounds of the lean part of a leg of veal, of beef-suet, the like quantity, chop them together, then beat them together in a stone mortar, adding to it half a little cabbage scalded, and beat that with your meat; then season it with mace and nutmeg, a little pepper and salt, some green gooseberries, grapes, or barberries in the time of the year; in the winter put in a little verjuice, then mix all well together, with the yolks of four or five eggs well beaten; wrap it up in green cabbage leaves, tie a cloth over it, boil it an hour: melt butter for sauce.

A Venison Pasty.

BONE your venison, take out the gristles, skin and films; to a side of doe venison three ounces of salt, and three quarters of an ounce of pepper: or to seven pounds of lean venison, without the bones, put in two ounces and a half of salt, and half an ounce of pepper.

Very fine Hogs Puddings.

SHRED four pounds of beef-suet very fine, mix with it two pounds of fine sugar powder'd, two grated nutmegs, some mace beat, a little salt, and three pounds of currants wash'd and pick'd; beat twenty four yolks, twelve whites of eggs, with a little sack; mix all well together, and fill your guts, being clean, and steep'd in orange-flower water; cut your guts quarter and half long, fill them half full;

tie

tie at each end, and again thus oooo; boil them as others, and cut them in balls when sent to the table.

To make Almond Hogs Puddings.

TAKE two pounds of beef-suet, or marrow shred very small, a pound and half of almonds blanched, and beaten very small with rose-water, one pound of grated bread, a pound and a quarter of fine sugar, a little salt, one ounce of mace, nutmeg and cinnamon, twelve yolks of eggs, four whites, a pint of sack, a pint and half of thick cream, some rose or orange-flower water; boil the cream, tie a little saffron in a rag, and dip it in the cream, to colour it; first beat your eggs very well, then stir in your almonds, then the spice, salt, and suet; then mix all your ingredients together; fill your guts but half full, put some bits of citron in the guts as you fill them; tie them up, and boil them about a quarter of an hour.

To make Hogs Puddings with Currants.

TAKE three pounds of grated bread to four pounds of beef-suet finely shred, two pounds of currants, cloves, mace, and cinnamon, of each half an ounce beaten fine, a little salt, a pound and half of sugar, a pint of sack, a quart of cream, a little rose-water, twenty eggs well beaten, but half the whites; mix all these well together, and fill the guts half full; boil them a little, and prick them as they boil, to keep them from breaking the guts; take them up on clean cloths.

Another Sort of Hogs Puddings.

TO half a pound of grated bread put half a pound of hogs liver boil'd, cold, and grated, a pound and half of suet finely shred, a handful of salt, a handful of sweet herbs, chopt small, some spice; mix all these together, with six eggs well beaten, and a little thick cream; fill your guts and boil them; when cold, cut them in round slices an inch thick; fry them in butter, and garniſh your diſh of fowls, haſh, or fricaſee.

To make Rice Pancakes.

TAKE a quart of cream and three ſpoonfuls of the flour of rice, boil it till it is as thick as pap, and as it boils ſtir in half a pound of butter, a nutmeg grated; then pour it out into an earthen pan, and when it is cold put in three or four ſpoonfuls of flour, a little ſalt, ſome ſugar, nine eggs well beaten; mix all well together, and fry them in a little pan, with a ſmall piece of butter; ſerve them up four or five in a diſh.

To make black Hogs Puddings.

BOIL all the hog's harſlet in about four or five gallons of water till it is very tender, then take out all the meat, and in that liquor ſteep near a peck of groats; put in the groats as it boils, and let them boil a quarter of an hour; then take the pot off the fire, and cover it up very cloſe, and let it ſtand five or ſix hours; chop two or three handfuls of thyme, a little ſavory, ſome parſley, and pennyroyal, ſome cloves and mace beaten, a handful of ſalt; mix all theſe with half the groats and two quarts of blood; put in moſt part of the leaf of the hog; cut it in ſquare bits like dice, and ſome in long bits; fill your guts, and put in the fat as you like it; fill the guts three quarters full, put your puddings into a kettle of boiling water, let them boil an hour, and prick them with a pin, to keep them from breaking; lay them on clean ſtraw when you take them up.

The other half of the groats you may make into white puddings for the family; chop all the meat very ſmall, and ſhred two handfuls of ſage very fine, an ounce of cloves and mace finely beaten, and ſome ſalt; work all together very well with a little flour, and put into the large guts; boil them about an hour, and keep them and the black near the fire till uſed.

To make a Chesnut Pudding.

TAKE a dozen and half of chesnuts, put them in a skillet of water, and set them on the fire till they will blanch; then blanch them, and when cold put them in cold water, then stamp them in a mortar, with orange-flower water and sack till they are very small; mix them in two quarts of cream, and eighteen yolks of eggs, the whites of three or four; beat the eggs with sack, rose-water, and sugar, put it in a dish with puff-paste; stick in some lumps of marrow or fresh butter, and bake it.

To make a brown Bread Pudding.

TAKE half a pound of brown bread, and double the weight of it in beef-suet, a quarter of a pint of cream, the blood of a fowl, a whole nutmeg, some cinnamon, a spoonful of sugar, six yolks of eggs, three whites; mix it all well together, and boil it in a wooden dish two hours; serve it with sack and sugar, and butter melted.

To make a baked Sack Pudding.

TAKE a pint of cream, and turn it to a curd with sack; bruise the curd very small with a spoon, and grate in two *Naples* biskets, or the inside of a stale penny loaf, mix it well with the curd, and half a nutmeg grated, some fine sugar, and the yolks of four eggs, the whites of two, beaten with two spoonfuls of sack; then melt half a pound of fresh butter, and stir all together till the oven is hot; butter a dish, put it in, and sift some sugar over it just as it is going into the oven; half an hour will bake it.

To make a Marjoram Pudding.

TAKE the curd of a quart of milk finely broken, a good handful or more of sweet-marjoram chopt as small as dust, and mingle with the curd five eggs, but three whites, beaten with rose-water, some

ſome nutmeg and ſugar, and half a pint of cream; beat all theſe well together, and put in three quarters of a pound of melted butter; put a thin ſheet of paſte at the bottom of your diſh; then pour in your pudding, and with a ſpur cut out little ſlips of paſte the breadth of a little finger, and lay them over croſs and croſs in large diamonds; put ſome ſmall bits of butter on the top, and bake it. *This is old faſhioned, and not good.*

To make Pancakes.

TAKE a pint of cream, and eight eggs, whites and all, a whole nutmeg grated, and a little ſalt; then melt a pound of rare diſh butter, and a little ſack; before you fry them, ſtir it in: it muſt be made as thick with three ſpoonfuls of flour, as ordinary batter, and fried with butter in the pan, the firſt pancake, but no more: ſtrew ſugar, garniſh with orange, turn it on the backſide of a plate.

To make a Tanſy to bake.

TAKE twenty eggs, but eight whites, beat the eggs very well, and ſtrain them into a quart of thick cream, one nutmeg, and three *Naples*-biſkets grated, as much juice of ſpinach, with a ſprig or two of tanſy, as will make it as green as graſs; ſweeten it to your taſte; then butter your diſh very well, and ſet it into an oven, no hotter than for cuſtards; watch it, and as ſoon as it is done, take it out of the oven, and turn it on a pye-plate; ſcrape ſugar, and ſqueeze orange upon it. Garniſh the diſh with orange and lemon, and ſerve up.

To make a Gooſberry Tanſy.

PUT ſome freſh butter in a frying-pan; when it is melted put into it a quart of gooſberries, fry them till they are tender, and break them all to maſh; then beat ſeven eggs, but four whites, a pound of ſugar, three ſpoonfuls of ſack, as much cream, a penny loaf grated, and three ſpoonfuls of flour;

flour; mix all these together, then put the gooseberries out of the pan to them, and stir all well together, and put them into a sauce-pan to thicken; then put butter into the frying-pan, and fry them brown: strew sugar on the top.

To make Curd Fritters.

TAKE a handful of curds, a handful of flour, ten eggs well beaten and strained, some sugar, some cloves, mace, nutmeg, and a little saffron; stir all well together, and fry them in very hot beef-dripping; drop them in the pan by spoonfuls; stir them about till they are of a fine yellow brown; drain them from the suet, and scrape sugar on them, when you serve them up.

To make fried Toasts.

CHIP a manchet very well, and cut it round-ways into toasts; then take cream and eight eggs, season'd with sack, sugar, and nutmeg; and let these toasts steep in it about an hour; then fry them in sweet butter, serve them up with plain melted butter, or with butter, sack and sugar, as you please.

To make Parsnep Fritters.

BOIL your parsneps very tender, peel them and beat them in a mortar; rub them through a hair sieve, and mix a good handful of them with some fine flour, six eggs, some cream, and new milk, salt, sugar, a little nutmeg, a small quantity of sack and rose-water; mix all well together a little thicker than pancake batter; have a frying-pan ready with good store of hog's-lard very hot over the fire, and put in a spoonful in a place, till the pan be so full as you can fry them conveniently; fry them a light brown on both sides. For sauce, take sack and sugar, with a little rose-water or verjuice, strew sugar on them when in the dish.

To

To make Apple Fritters.

TAKE the yolks of eight eggs, the whites of four, beat them well together, and ſtrain them into a pan; then take a quart of cream, warm it as hot as you can endure your finger in it; then put to it a quarter of a pint of ſack, three quarters of a pint of ale, and make a poſſet of it; when your poſſet is cool, put to it your eggs, beating them well together; then put in the nutmeg, ginger, ſalt, and flour to your liking: your batter ſhould be pretty thick; then put in pippins ſliced or ſcraped; fry them in good ſtore of hot lard with a quick fire.

To make an Apple Tanſey.

TAKE three pippins, ſlice them round in thin ſlices, and fry them with butter; then beat four eggs, with ſix ſpoonfuls of cream, a little roſe-water, nutmeg, and ſugar; ſtir them together, and pour it over the apples: let it fry a little, and turn it with a pye-plate. Garniſh with lemon and ſugar ſtrew'd over it.

To make a Lemon Tart.

TAKE three clear lemons, and grate off the outſide rinds; take the yolks of twelve eggs, and ſix whites; beat them very well, ſqueeze in the juice of a lemon; then put in three quarters of a pound of fine powdered ſugar, and three quarters of a pound of freſh butter melted; ſtir all well together, put a ſheet of paſte at the bottom, and ſift ſugar on the top; put it in a briſk oven, three quarters of an hour will bake it: ſo ſerve it to the table.

A Rye-bread Pudding.

TAKE half a pound of four rye-bread grated, half a pound of beef-ſuet finely ſhred, half a pound of currants clean waſhed, half a pound of ſugar, a whole nutmeg grated; mix all well together,

ther, with five or six eggs: butter a dish, boil it an hour and a quarter, and serve it up with melted butter,

A baked Pudding.

BLANCH half a pound of almonds, and beat them fine with sweet water, ambergrease dissolv'd in orange-flower water, or in some cream; then warm a pint of thick cream. and melt in it half a pound of butter, then mix it with your beaten almonds, a little salt, a grated nutmeg, and sugar, and the yolks of six eggs; beat it up together, and put it in a dish with puff-paste, the oven not too hot; scrape sugar on it just before it goes into the oven.

To make a Custard Pudding.

TAKE a pint of cream, and mix with it six eggs well beat, two spoonfuls of flour, half a nutmeg grated, a little salt, and sugar to your taste; butter a cloth, put it in when the pot boils: boil it just half an hour; melt butter for sauce.

Boil'd Custards.

TAKE a pint of cream, and put into it two ounces of almonds, blanch'd and beaten very fine with rose or orange-flower water, or a little cream; let them boil till the cream is a little thickened, then sweeten your eggs, and keep it stirring over the fire till it is as thick as you would have it; then put into it a little orange-flower water, stir it well together, and put it into *China* cups.

N. B. You may make them without almonds.

Rice Custards.

TAKE a quart of cream, and boil it with a blade of mace, and a quarter'd nutmeg; put into it boiled rice, well beat with your cream; mix them together, and stir them all the while it boils on the fire; when 'tis enough take it off, and sweeten

to

to your taste; put in a little orange-flower water pour it in your dishes; when cold serve it.

To make Almond Tourt.

BLANCH and beat half a pound of *Jordan* almonds very fine; use orange-flower water, in the beating your almonds; pare the yellow rind of a lemon pretty thick; boil it in water till 'tis very tender: beat it with half a pound of sugar, and mix it with the almonds, and eight eggs, but four whites, half a pound of butter melted, almost cold, and a little thick cream; mix all together, and bake it, in a dish with paste at bottom. This may be made the day before 'tis used.

To make Hasty Puddings, to boil in Custard Dishes.

TAKE a large pint of milk, put to it four spoonfuls of flour; mix it well together, set it over the fire, and boil it into a smooth hasty pudding; sweeten it to your taste, grate nutmeg in it, and when 'tis almost cold, beat five eggs very well, and stir into it; then butter your custard-cups, put in your stuff, and tie them over with a cloth, put them in the pot when the water boils, and let them boil something more than half an hour; pour on them melted butter.

To make a Sweet-meat Pudding.

PUT a thin puff paste at the bottom of your dish, then have of candied orange, lemon, and citron peel, of each an ounce; slice them thin, and put them in the bottom on your paste; then beat eight yolks of eggs, and two whites, near half a pound of sugar, and half a pound of butter melted; mix and beat all well together, and when the oven is ready, pour it on your sweet-meats in the dish. An hour or less will bake it.

To

To make Carrot, or Parsnep Puffs.

SCRAPE and boil your carrots and parsnips tender; then scrape or mash them very fine, add to it a pint of pulp, the crumb of a penny loaf grated, or some stale bisket, if you have it, some eggs, but four whites, a nutmeg grated, some orange-flower water, sugar to your taste, a little sack, and mix it up with thick cream; they must be fried in rendered suet, the liquor very hot when you put them in: put in a good spoonful in a place.

To make New College *Puddings.*

GRATE a penny stale loaf, put to it a like quantity of beef-suet finely shred, a nutmeg grated, a little salt, and some currants; then beat some eggs in a little sack, and some sugar; mix all together, knead it as stiff as for manchet, and make it up in the form and size of a turkey egg, but a little flatter; then take a pound of butter, put it in a dish, set the dish over a clear fire in a chafing dish, and rub your butter about the dish till 'tis melted; put your puddings in, and cover the dish, but often turn your puddings, untill they are all brown alike, and when they are enough, scrape sugar over them, and serve them up hot for a side-dish.

You must let the paste lie a quarter of an hour before you make up your puddings.

To make an Oatmeal Pudding.

TAKE a pint of great oatmeal, beat it very small, then sift it fine; take a quart of cream, boil it and your oatmeal together, stirring it all the while until 'tis pretty thick; then put it in a dish, cover it close, and let it stand a little; then put into it a pound and half of fresh butter, and let it stand two hours before you stir it; put to it twelve eggs, a nutmeg grated, a little salt, sweeten it to your taste; a little sack, or orange-flower water;

ter; ſtir all very well together, put paſte at the bottom of your diſh, and put in your pudding-ſtuff, the oven not too hot; an hour will bake it.

To make fine Fritters.

TAKE half a pint of thick ſweet cream, put to it four eggs well beaten, a little brandy, ſome nutmeg and ginger; make this into a thick batter with flour: your apples muſt be golden pippins pared and cut in thin ſlices, dip them in batter, and fry them in lard. It will take up two pounds of lard to fry this quantity.

To make a Marrow Pudding.

TAKE a quart of cream, and three *Naples* biſkets grated, a nutmeg grated, the yolks of ten eggs, the whites of five well beaten, and ſugar to your taſte; mix all well together, and put a little bit of butter in the bottom of your ſauce-pan; then put in your ſtuff, and ſet it over the fire, and ſtir it till it is pretty thick; then put it into your pan, with a quarter of a pound of currants that have been plump'd in hot water; ſtir it together, and let it ſtand all night. The next day put ſome fine paſte rolled very thin at the bottom of your diſh, and when the oven is ready, pour in your ſtuff, and on the top lay large pieces of marrow. Half an hour will bake it.

Lemon Pudding.

GRATE the peels of three large lemons, only the yellow, then take two lemons more, and the three you have grated, and roll them under your hand on a table till they are very ſoft; but be careful not to break them; then cut and ſqueeze them, and ſtrain the juice from the ſeeds to the grated peels, then grate the crumb of three half-penny loaves, (or ten ounces of crumb, white loaves) into a baſon, and make a pint of white wine ſcalding hot,

hot, pour it to your bread, and ſtir it well together to ſoak, then put to it the grated peel and juice; beat the yolks of eight eggs and four whites together, and mingle with the reſt three quarters of a pound of butter that is freſh and melted, and almoſt a pound of white ſugar, beat it well together till it be thoroughly mixt, then lay a ſheet of puff-paſte at the bottom and brim, cutting it into what form you pleaſe; the paſte that is left roll out, and with a jagging iron cut them out in little ſtripes, neither ſo broad or long as your little finger, and bake them on a floured paper; let the pudding bake almoſt an hour, when it comes out of the oven ſtick the pieces of paſte on the top of it to ſerve it to table. It eats well either hot or cold.

The Ipſwich *Almond Pudding.*

STEEP ſomewhat above three ounces of the crumb of white bread ſliced, in a pint and half of cream, or grate the bread; then beat half a pound of blanched almonds very fine till they do not gliſter, with a ſmall quantity of perfumed water, beat up the yolks of eight eggs and the whites of four; mix all well together, put in a quarter of a pound of white ſugar; then ſet it into the oven, but ſtir in a little melted butter before you ſet it in; let it bake but half an hour.

Oatmeal Pudding.

A Wine pint of oatmeal pick'd from the blacks, a pint and a quarter of milk warmed; let it ſteep one night; three quarters of a pound of beef-ſuet ſhred, one nutmeg, three ſpoonfuls of ſugar, a ſmall handful of flour, four eggs, and ſalt to your taſte; make two puddings, and boil them three hours; if the oatmeal be too large, beat it, and if you make it into but one pudding, boil it four hours.

To make a fine Bread Pudding.

TAKE three pints of milk and boil it; when it is boiled, ſweeten it with half a pound of ſugar, a ſmall nutmeg grated, and put in half a pound of butter; when it is melted, pour it in a pan, over eleven ounces of grated bread, cover it up; the next day put to it ten eggs well beaten, ſtir all together, and when the oven is hot, put it in your diſh, three quarters of an hour will bake it; boil a bit of lemon-peel in the milk, take it out before you put your other things in.

To make a Spread Eagle Pudding.

CUT off the cruſt of three half-penny rolls, and ſlice them into your pan; then ſet three pints of milk over the fire, make it ſcalding hot, but not boil, put it over your bread, cover it cloſe, and let it ſtand an hour; then put in a good ſpoonful of ſugar, a very little ſalt, a nutmeg grated, a pound of ſuet after it is ſhred, half a pound of currants waſh'd and pick'd, four ſpoonfuls of cold milk, ten eggs, but five of the whites; and when all is in ſtir it, but not till all is in; then mix it well, butter a diſh; leſs than an hour will bake it.

To make a very fine plain Pudding.

TAKE a quart of milk, and put ſix laurel leaves into it; when it has boil'd a little, take out your leaves, and with fine flour make that milk into haſty pudding, pretty thick; then ſtir in half a pound of butter, a quarter of a pound of ſugar, a ſmall nutmeg grated, twelve yolks, ſix whites of eggs well beaten; mix and ſtir all well together, butter a diſh, and put in your ſtuff; a little more than half an hour will bake it.

A fine Rice Pudding.

TAKE of the flour of rice ſix ounces, put it in a quart of milk, and let it boil till it is

pretty

pretty thick, ſtirring it all the while; then pour it into a pan, and ſtir in it half a pound of freſh butter, and a quarter of a pound of ſugar, or ſweeten it to your taſte; when it is cold grate in a nutmeg, and beat ſix eggs, with a ſpoonful or two of ſack, and beat and ſtir all well together; put a little fine paſte at the bottom of your diſh, and bake it.

To make a Ratafia Pudding.

TAKE a quart of cream, boil it with four or five laurel leaves; then take them out, and break in half a pound of *Naples* biſket, half a pound of butter, ſome ſack, nutmeg, and ſalt; take it off the fire, cover it up; when it is almoſt cold put in two ounces of almonds blanched, and beaten fine, with the yolks of five eggs; mix all well together, and bake it in a moderate oven half an hour; ſcrape ſugar on it as it goes into the oven.

Vermicelly Pudding.

BOIL five ounces of vermicelly in a quart of milk till it is tender, with a blade of mace, and a rind of lemon or *Seville* orange, ſweeten it to your taſte, the yolks of ſix eggs, and four whites; have a diſh ready cover'd with paſte, and juſt before you ſet it into the oven, ſtir in half a pound of melted butter, a very little ſalt does well; if you have no peels, put in a little orange-flower water.

All Sorts of PASTRY.

To make a Tureiner.

TAKE a china pot or bowl, and fill it as follows: at the bottom lay ſome freſh butter, then put in three or four beef-ſteaks larded with bacon, then cut ſome veal-ſteaks from the leg, hack them, and waſh them over with the yolk of an egg, and afterwards lay it over with forc'd-meat, and roll it up, and lay it in with young chickens, pigeons and rabbits, ſome in quarters, ſome in halves, ſweet-breads, lamb-ſtones, cocks-combs, palates after they are boiled, peeled and cut in ſlices; tongues, either hogs or calf's, ſlic'd, and ſome larded with bacon, whole yolks of hard eggs, piſtachia-nuts peel'd, forc'd balls, ſome round, ſome like an olive, lemon ſliced, ſome with the rind on, barberries and oyſters; ſeaſon all theſe with pepper, ſalt, nutmeg, and ſweet herbs, mix'd together after they are cut very ſmall, and ſtrew it on every thing as you put it in your pot; then put in a quart of gravy, and ſome butter on the top; cover it cloſe with a lid of puff-paſte pretty thick; eight hours will bake it.

A Battalia Pye, or Bride Pye.

TAKE young chickens as big as black-birds, quails, young partridges, larks, and ſquab-pigeons, truſs them, and put them in your pye; then have ox-palates boiled, blanched, and cut in pieces, lamb-ſtones, ſweet-breads, cut in halves or quarters, cocks-combs blanched, a quart of oyſters dipt in eggs, and dredged over with grated bread and marrow: ſheeps-tongues boiled, peeled, and cut in ſlices; ſeaſon all with ſalt, pepper, cloves, mace, and nutmegs, beaten and mix'd together; put butter at the bottom of the pye, and place the reſt in with the yolks of hard eggs, knots of eggs, forc'd-meat balls; cover all with butter, and cloſe up the pye; put in five or ſix ſpoonfuls of water when it goes into the oven, and when it is drawn pour it out and put in gravy.

To make an Oyſter Pye.

MAKE good puff-paſte, and lay a thin ſheet in the bottom of your pattipan; then take two quarts of large oyſters, waſh them well in their own liquor, take them out of it, dry them, and ſeaſon them with ſalt, ſpice, and a little pepper, all beaten fine; lay ſome butter in the bottom of your pattipan, then lay in your oyſters and the yolks of twelve hard eggs whole, two or three ſweet-breads cut in ſlices, or lamb-ſtones, or for want of theſe a dozen of larks, two marrow-bones, the marrow taken out in lumps, dipt in the yolks of eggs, and ſeaſoned as you did your oyſters, with ſome grated bread duſted on it, and a few forc'd-meat balls; when all theſe are in put ſome butter on the top, and cover it over with a ſheet of puff-paſte, and bake it; when it is drawn out of the oven, take the liquor of the oyſters, boil it, ſkim it, and beat it up thick with butter, and the yolks of two or three eggs; pour it hot into your pye, ſhake it well together, and ſerve it hot.

To make a Salmon Pye.

MAKE a good puff-paſte, and lay it in your pattipan, then take the middle piece of ſalmon, ſeaſon it pretty high with pepper, ſalt, cloves and mace, cut it in three pieces, then lay a layer of butter and a layer of ſalmon, till all is in; make forc'd-meat balls of an eel, chop it fine with the yolks of hard eggs, two or three anchovies, marrow, (or, if for a faſting-day, butter) ſweet herbs, ſome grated bread, and a a few oyſters and grated nutmeg, ſome ſmall pepper, and a little ſalt; make it up with raw eggs into balls, ſome long, ſome round, and lay them about your ſalmon; put butter over all, and lid your pye; an hour will bake it.

To make Egg Pyes.

TAKE the yolks of two dozen of eggs boiled hard, and chopt with double the quantity of beef-ſuet, and half a pound of pippins pared, cored, and ſliced; then add to it one pound of currants wash'd and dried, half a pound of sugar, a little salt, some spice beaten fine, the juice of a lemon, and half a pint of sack, candied orange and citron cut in pieces, of each three ounces, some lumps of marrow on the top, fill them full; the oven must not be too hot; three quarters of an hour will bake them; put the marrow only on them that are to be eaten hot.

To make a Sweetbread Pasty to fry or bake.

PARBOIL your sweet-breads, and shred them very fine, with an equal quantity of marrow; mix with them a little grated bread, some nutmeg, salt, the yolks of two hard eggs bruised small, and sugar; then mix up with a little cream and the yolk of an egg: make paste with half a pound of the finest flour, an ounce of double-refined sugar beat and sifted, the yolks of two eggs, and white of one, and fair water; then roll in half a pound of butter, and roll it out in little pasties the breadth of your hand; put your meat in, close them up well, and fry or bake them; a very pretty side-dish.

To make a Lumber Pye.

TAKE a pound and half of veal, parboil it, and when it is cold chop it very small, with two pounds of beef-suet, and some candied orange-peel, some sweet herbs, as thyme, sweet marjoram, and an handful of spinach; mince the herbs small before you put them to the other; chop all together, and a pippin or two, then add a handful or two of grated bread, a pound and half of currants wash'd and dried, some cloves, mace, nutmeg, a little salt, sugar and sack, adding to all these as many yolks of raw eggs, and whites of two, as will make it a moist forc'd-meat; work it with your hands into a body, and make it into balls as big as a turkey's egg, then having your coffin made, put in your balls; take the marrow out of three or four bones as whole as you can; let your marrow lie a little in water, to take out the blood and splinters; then dry it, and dip

dip it in yolks of eggs; season it with a little salt, nutmeg grated, and grated bread; lay it on and between your forc'd-meat balls, and over that sliced citron, candied orange and lemon, eringo-roots, and preserved barberries; then lay on sliced lemon, and thin slices of butter over all; then lid your pye, and bake it; and when it is drawn, have in readiness a caudle made of white wine and sugar, and thickened with butter and eggs, and pour it hot into your pye.

To make little Pasties to fry.

TAKE the kidney of a loin of veal or lamb, fat and all, shred it very small, season it with a little salt, cloves, mace, nutmeg, all beaten small, some sugar, and the yolks of two or three hard eggs minc'd very fine; mix all these together with a little sack or cream; put them in puff-paste and fry them; serve them hot.

To make Custards.

TAKE two quarts of thick sweet cream, boil it with some bits of cinnamon, and a quartered nutmeg, keep it stirring all the while, and when it has boil'd a little time, pour it into a pan to cool, and stir it till it is cool, to keep it from creaming; then beat the yolks of sixteen eggs, the whites of but six, and mix your eggs with the cream when it is cool, and sweeten it with fine sugar to your taste, put in a very little salt, and some rose or orange-flower water; then strain all thro' a hair sieve, and fill your cups or crust; it must be a pretty quick oven; when they boil up they are enough.

To make Cheesecakes.

TAKE a pint of cream and warm it, and put to it five quarts of milk warm from the cow, then put runnet to it, and when it is come, put the curd in a linen bag or cloth, and let it drain well from the whey, but do not squeeze it much; then put it in a mortar, and break the curd as fine as butter; then put to your curd half a pound of almonds blanched, and beaten exceeding fine (or half a pound of dry mackaroons beat very fine) if you have almonds, grate in a *Naples* biſket: but if you uſe mackaroons, you need not; then add to it the yolks of nine eggs beaten, a whole nutmeg grated, two perfumed plumbs diſſolved in roſe or orange-flower water, half a pound of fine ſugar, mix all well together; then melt a pound and a quarter of butter, and ſtir it well in, and half a pound of currants plump'd; let it ſtand to cool till you uſe it. Then make your puff-paſte thus: take a pound of fine flour, and wet it with cold water, roll it out, and put into it by degrees a pound of freſh butter; uſe it juſt as it is made.

Another Way to make Cheeſecakes.

TAKE a gallon of new milk, ſet it as for a cheeſe, and gently whey it; then break it in a mortar, ſweeten it to your taſte; put in a grated nutmeg, ſome roſe-water and ſack; mix theſe together, and ſet it over the fire, a quart of cream and make it into a haſty pudding, mix that with it very well, and fill your pattipans juſt as they are going into the oven; your oven muſt be ready, that you may not ſtay for that; when they riſe well up they are enough. Make your paſte thus: take about a pound of flour, and ſtrew into it three ſpoonfuls of loaf ſugar beaten and ſifted, and rub into it a pound of butter, one egg, and a ſpoonful of roſe-water, the reſt cold fair water; make it into a paſte, roll it very thin, and put it into your pans, and fill them almoſt full.

Paſte for Paſties.

RUB ſix pounds of butter into fourteen pounds of flour, put to it eight eggs, whip the whites to ſnow, and make it into a pretty ſtiff paſte with cold water.

To make Cheeſecakes without Runnet.

TAKE a quart of thick cream, and ſet it over a clear fire, with ſome quarter'd nutmeg in it; juſt as it boils up, put in twelve eggs well beaten, and a quarter of a pound of freſh butter; ſtir it a little while on the fire, till it begins to curdle; then take it off, and gather the curd as for cheeſe; put it in a clean cloth, tie it together, and hang it up, that the whey may run from it; when it is pretty dry, put it in a ſtone mortar, with a pound of butter, a quarter of a pint of thick cream, ſome ſack, orange-flower water, and half a pound of fine ſugar; then beat and grind all theſe very well together for an hour or more, till it is very fine; then paſs it thro' a hair ſieve, and fill your pattipans but half full; you may put currants in half the quantity if you pleaſe; a little more than a quarter of an hour will bake them; take the nutmeg out of the cream when it is boiled.

To make Orange or Lemon Tarts.

TAKE ſix large lemons, and rub them very well with ſalt, and put them in water for two days, with a handful of ſalt in it; then change them into freſh water without ſalt every other day for a fortnight; then boil them for two or three hours till they are tender; then cut them in half quarters, and then cut them thus ⟅ as thin as you can; then take pippins pared, cored and quartered, and a pint of fair water, let them boil till the pippins break; put the liquor to your orange or lemon, half the pippins well broken, and a pound of ſugar; boil theſe together a quarter of an hour; then put it in a gallipot, and ſqueeze an orange in it if it be lemon, or a lemon if it is orange; two ſpoonfuls are enough for a tart; your pattipans muſt be ſmall and ſhallow; put fine puff-paſte, and very thin; a little

little while will bake it. Juſt as your tarts are going into the oven, with a feather or bruſh do them over with melted butter, and then ſift double refin'd ſugar on them, and this is a pretty icing on them.

To make Puff-Paſte for Tarts.

RUB a quarter of a pound of butter into a pound of fine flour; then whip the whites of two eggs to ſnow, and with cold water and one yolk make it into a paſte; then roll it abroad, and put in by degrees a pound of butter, flouring it over the butter every time, roll it up, and roll it out again, and put in more butter: ſo do for ſix or ſeven times, till it has taken up all the pound of butter. This paſte is good for tarts, or any ſmall things.

Apple Paſties to fry.

PARE and quarter apples, and boil them in ſugar and water, and a ſtick of cinnamon, and when tender, put in a little white wine, the juice of a lemon, a piece of freſh butter, and a little ambergreaſe or orange-flower water; ſtir all together, and when it is cold put it in puff-paſte, and fry them.

To ſeaſon and bake a Veniſon Paſty.

BONE your haunch or ſide of veniſon, and take out all the ſinews and ſkin; and then proportion t for your paſty, by taking away from one part, and adding to another, till 'tis of an equal thickneſs; then ſeaſon it with pepper and ſalt, about an ounce of pepper; ſave a little of it whole, and beat the reſt; and mix with it twice as much ſalt, and rub it all over your veniſon, letting it lie till your paſte is ready. Make your paſte thus: a peck of fine flour, ſix pounds of butter, a dozen of eggs; rub your butter in your flour, beat your eggs, and with them and cold water make up your paſte pretty ſtiff: then drive it forth for you paſty; let it be the thickneſs of a man's thumb; put under it two or three ſheets of cap-paper well floured: then have

two

two pounds of beef-suet, shred exceeding fine; proportion it on the bottom to the breadth of your venison, and leave a verge round your venison three fingers broad, wash that verge over with a bunch of feathers or brush dipp'd in an egg beaten, and then lay a border of your paste on the place you wash'd, and lay your venison on the suet; put a little of your seasoning on the top, a few corns of whole pepper, and two pounds of very good fresh butter; then turn over your other sheet of paste, so close your pasty. Garnish it on the top as you think fit; vent it in the middle, and set it in the oven. It will ask five or six hours baking. Then break all the bones, wash them, and add to them more bones, or knuckles; season them with pepper and salt, and put them with a quart of water, and half a pound of butter, in a pan or earthen pot; cover it over with coarse paste, and set it in with your pasty; and when your pasty is drawn and dish'd, fill it up with the gravy that came from the bones.

Balls for Lent.

GRATE white bread, nutmeg, salt, shred parsley, a very little thyme, and a little orange or lemon-peel cut small; make them up into balls with beaten eggs, or you may add a spoonful of cream; and roll them up in flour, and fry them.

To keep Venison in Summer.

BEAT pepper very fine, and rub all over it.

Sauce for Roast Venison.

JELLY of currants melted and serv'd hot, with a lemon squeez'd into it.

A fine Potatoe Pye for Lent.

FIRST make your forc'd meat, about two dozen of small oysters just scalded, and when cold chop'd small, a stale roll grated, and six yolks of eggs

eggs boil'd hard, and bruiſed ſmall with the back of a ſpoon; ſeaſon with a little ſalt, pepper, and nutmeg, ſome thyme and parſley, both ſhred ſmall; mix theſe together well, pound them a little, and make it up in a ſtiff paſte, with half a pound of butter and an egg work'd in it; juſt flour it to keep it from ſticking, and lay it by till your pye is fit, and put a very thin paſte in your diſh, bottom and ſides; then put your forc'd meat, of an equal thickneſs, about two fingers broad, about the ſides of your diſh, as you would do a pudding cruſt; duſt a little flour on it, and put it down cloſe; then fill your pye, a dozen of potatoes, about the bigneſs of a ſmall egg, finely pared, juſt boiled a walm or two, a dozen yolks of eggs boiled hard, a quarter of a hundred of large oyſters juſt ſcalded in their own liquor and cold, ſix morels, four or five blades of mace, ſome whole pepper, and a little ſalt butter on the bottom and top; then lid your pye, and bake it an hour: when 'tis drawn, pour in a caudle made with half a pint of your oyſter liquor, three or four ſpoonfuls of white wine, and thickened up with butter and eggs, pour it in hot at the hole on the top, and ſhake it together, and ſerve it.

Artificial Potatoes for Lent: *A Side-Diſh; Second Courſe.*

TAKE a pound of butter, put it into a ſtone mortar, with half a pound of *Naples* biſket grated, and half a pound of *Jordan* almonds beat ſmall after they are blanched, eight yolks of eggs, four whites, a little ſack and orange-flower water; ſweeten to your taſte; pound all together till you don't know what it is, and with a little fine flour make it into ſtiff paſte, lay it on a table, and have ready about two pounds of fine lard in your pan, let it boil very faſt, and cut your paſte the bigneſs of cheſnuts, and throw them into the boiling lard, and let them boil till they are of a yellow brown; when

when they are enough, take them up in a sieve to drain the fat from them; put them in a dish, pour sack and melted butter; strew double refined sugar over the brim of the dish.

Potatoe or Lemon Cheesecake.

TAKE six ounces of potatoes, four ounces of lemon-peel, four ounces of sugar, four ounces of butter; boil the lemon-peel till tender, pare and scrape the potatoes, boil them tender and bruise them; beat the lemon-peel with the sugar, then beat all together very well, and melt the butter in a little thick cream; mix all together very well, and let it lie till cold; put crust in your pattipans, and fill them little more than half full. Bake them in a quick oven half an hour, sift some double refined sugar on them as they go into the oven; this quantity will make a dozen small pattipans.

Sauce for Fish in Lent, *or at any Time.*

TAKE a little thyme, horse-radish, a bit of onion, lemon peel, and whole pepper; boil them in a little fair water; then put in two anchovies, and four spoonfuls of white wine; strain them out, and put the liquor into the same pan again, with a pound of fresh butter; when 'tis melted take it off the fire, and stir in the yolks of two eggs well beaten, with three spoonfuls of white wine; set it on the fire again, and keep it stirring till 'tis the thickness of cream, and pour it hot over your fish. Garnish them with lemon and horse-radish.

To make a savoury Lamb Pye.

SEASON your lamb with pepper, salt, cloves, mace, and nutmeg: so put it into your coffin with a few lamb-stones, and sweet-breads seasoned as your lamb; also some large oysters, and savoury forc'd-meat balls, hard yolks of eggs, and the tops of asparagus two inches long, first boiled green: then put butter all over the pye, lid it, and set it

in

in a quick oven an hour and half; then make the liquor with oyſter liquor, as much gravy, a little claret, with one anchovy in it, a grated nutmeg. Let theſe have a boil, thicken it with yolks of two or three eggs, and when the pye is drawn, pour it in hot.

To make a ſweet Lamb Pye.

CUT your lamb into ſmall pieces, and ſeaſon it with a little ſalt, cloves, mace, and nutmeg; your pye being made, put in your lamb or veal; ſtrew on it ſome ſtoned raiſins and currants, and ſome ſugar; then lay on it ſome forc'd-meat balls made ſweet, and in the ſummer ſome artichoke bottoms boil'd, and ſcalded grapes in the winter, Boil *Spaniſh* potatoes cut in pieces; candied citron, candied orange and lemon-peel, and three or four large blades of mace; put butter on the top; cloſe up your pye and bake it. Make the caudle of white wine, juice of lemon and ſugar: thicken it with the yolks of two or three eggs, and a bit of butter; and when your pye is baked, pour in the caudle as hot as you can, and ſhake it well in the pye, and ſerve it up.

A ſweet Chicken Pye.

TAKE five or ſix ſmall chickens, pick, draw, and truſs them for baking; ſeaſon them with cloves, mace, nutmeg, cinnamon, and a little ſalt; wrap up ſome of the ſeaſoning in butter, and put it in their bellies: and your coffin being made, put them in; put over and between them pieces of marrow, *Spaniſh* potatoes and cheſnuts, both boiled, peeled and cut, a handful of barberries ſtript, a lemon ſliced, ſome butter on the top; ſo cloſe up the pye and bake it, and have in readineſs a caudle made of white wine, ſugar, nutmeg, beat it up with yolks of eggs and butter; have a care it does not curdle; pour the caudle in, ſhake it well together, and ſerve it up hot.

Another

Another Chicken Pye.

SEASON your chickens with pepper, salt, cloves, mace, nutmeg, a little shred parsley, and thyme, mix'd with the other seasoning; wrap up some in butter, put it in the bellies of the chickens, and lay them in your pye; strew over them lemon cut like dice; a handful of scalded grapes, artichoke-bottoms in quarters: put butter on it, and close it up; when 'tis baked, put in a lear of gravy, with a little white wine, a grated nutmeg, thicken it up with butter, and two or three eggs; shake it well together, serve it up hot.

To make an Olio Pye.

MAKE your pye ready; then take the thin collops of the but end of a leg of veal; as many as you think will fill your pye; hack them with the back of a knife, and season them with pepper, salt, cloves, and mace: wash over your collops with a bunch of feathers dipped in eggs, and have in readiness a good handful of sweet herbs shred small; the herbs must be thyme, parsley, and spinach; the yolks of eight hard eggs minced, and a few oysters parboiled and chop'd: some beef-suet shred very fine. Mix these together, and strew them over your collops, and sprinkle a little orange-flower water on them; and roll the collops up very close, and lay them in your pye; strewing the seasoning that is left over them; put butter on the top, and close up your pye; when 'tis drawn, put in gravy, and one anchovy dissolved in it, and pour it in very hot: you may put in artichoke-bottoms and chesnuts, if you please, or sliced lemon, or grapes scalded, or what else is in season: but if you will make it a right savoury pye, leave them out.

To make a Florendine of Veal.

TAKE the kidney of a loin of veal, fat and all, and mince it very fine; then chop a few herbs, and put to it, and add a few currants; seafon it with cloves, mace, nutmeg, and a little falt; and put in fome yolks of eggs, and a handful of grated bread, a pippin or two chop'd, fome candied lemon-peel minced fmall, fome fack, fugar, and orange-flower water. Put a fheet of puff-pafte at the bottom of your difh; put this in, and cover it with another; clofe it up, and when 'tis baked, fcrape fugar on it; and ferve it hot.

Another made Difh.

TAKE half a pound of almonds, blanch and beat them very fine; put to them a little rofe or orange-flower water in the beating; then take a quart of fweet thick cream, and boil it with whole cinnamon, and mace, and quartered dates; fweeten your cream with fugar to your tafte, and mix it with your almonds, and ftir it well together, and ftrain it out through a fieve. Let your cream cool, and thicken it with the yolks of fix eggs; then garnifh a deep difh, lay pafte at the bottom, and then put in fliced artichoke-bottoms, being firft boiled, and upon that a layer of marrow, fliced citron, and candied orange; fo do till your difh is near full; then pour in your cream, and bake it without a lid; when 'tis baked, fcrape fugar on it, and ferve it up hot. Half an hour will bake it.

To make an Artichoke Pye.

BOIL the bottoms of eight or ten artichokes, fcrape and make them clean from the core; cut each of them into fix parts; feafon them with cinnamon, nutmeg, fugar, and a little falt; then lay your artichokes in your pye. Take the marrow of four or five bones, dip your marrow in yolks of eggs and grated bread, and feafon it as you did your arti-

artichokes, and lay it on the top and between your artichokes; then lay on sliced lemon, barberries. and large mace; put butter on the top, and close up your pye; then make your lear of white wine, sack, and sugar; thicken it with yolks of eggs, and a bit of butter; when your pye is drawn, pour it in, shake it together, and serve it hot.

To make a Skirret Pye.

BOIL your biggest skirrets, blanch them, and season them with cinnamon, nutmeg, and a very little ginger and sugar. Your pye being ready, lay in your skirrets; season also the marrow of three or four bones with cinnamon, sugar, a little salt and grated bread, Lay the marrow in your pye, and the yolks of twelve hard eggs cut in halves, a handful of chesnuts boiled and blanched, with some candied orange-peel in slices. Lay butter on the top, and lid your pye. Let your caudle be white wine, verjuice, some sack and sugar; thicken it with the yolks of eggs, and when the pye is baked, pour it in, and serve it hot. Scrape sugar on it.

To make a Turbot Pye.

GUT, wash, and boil your turbot; season it with a little pepper, salt, cloves, mace, nutmeg, and sweet herbs shred fine; then lay it in your pye, or pattipan, with the yolks of six eggs boiled hard; a whole onion, which must be taken out when it is baked. Put two pounds of fresh butter on the top; close it up; when it is drawn, serve it hot or cold: it is good either way.

To make a Chervil or Spinach Tart.

SHRED a gallon of spinach or chervil very small; put to it half a pound of melted butter, the meat of three lemons picked from the skins and seeds; the rind of two lemons grated, a pound of sugar; put this in a dish or pattipan with puff-paste on the bottom and top, and so bake it; when it is bak'd, cut off the lid, and put cream or custard over it, as you do codlin tarts; scrape sugar over it; serve it cold; this is good among other tarts in the winter for variety.

To make Lemon Cheesecakes.

TAKE the peel of two large lemons, boil it very tender, then pound it well in a mortar, with a quarter of a pound or more of loaf sugar, the yolks of six eggs, and half a pound of fresh butter; pound and mix all well together, and fill the pattipans but half full: Orange-cheesecakes are done the same way, only you must boil the peel in two or three waters, to take out the bitterness.

A Fish Pye.

TAKE of soles, or thick flounders, gut and wash them, and just put them in scalding water to get off the black skin; then cut them in scollops, or indented, so that they will join and lie in the pye as if they were whole; have your pattipans in readiness, with puff-paste at the bottom, and a layer of butter on it; then season your fish with a little pepper and salt, cloves, mace, and nutmeg, and lay it in your pattipans, joining the pieces together as if the fish had not been cut; then put in forced balls made with fish, slices of lemon with the rind on, whole oysters, whole yolks of hard eggs, and pickled barberries; then lid your pye and bake it; when it is drawn, make a caudle of oyster liquor and white wine thicken'd up with yolks of eggs and a bit of butter; serve it hot.

To make Marrow Pasties.

MAKE your little pasties the length of a finger, and as broad as two fingers, put in large pieces of marrow dipt in eggs, and seasoned with sugar, cloves, mace, and nutmeg; strew a few currants on the marrow; bake or fry them.

To

To make Mince Pyes of Veal.

FROM a leg of veal cut off four pounds of the fleſhy part in thick pieces, put them in ſcalding water, and let it juſt boil; then cut the meat in ſmall thin pieces, and ſkin it; it muſt be four pounds after it is ſcalded and ſkinned; to this quantity put nine pounds of beef-ſuet well ſkinned; ſhred them very fine with eight pippins pared and cored, and four pounds of raiſins of the ſun ſtoned; when it is ſhred very fine put it in a large pan, or on a table, to mix, and put to it one ounce of nutmegs grated, half an ounce of cloves, as much mace, a large ſpoonful of ſalt, above a pound of ſugar, the peel of a lemon ſhred exceeding fine; when you have ſeaſoned it to your palate, put in ſeven pounds of currants, and two pounds of raiſins ſtoned and ſhred; when you fill your pyes, put into every one ſome ſhred lemon with its juice, ſome candied lemon-peel and citron in ſlices; and juſt as the pyes go into the oven, put into every one a ſpoonful of ſack and a ſpoonful of claret, ſo bake them.

To make butter'd Loaves to eat hot.

TAKE eleven yolks of eggs, beat well, five ſpoonfuls of cream, and a good ſpoonful of ale yeaſt, ſtir all theſe together with flour, till it comes to a little paſte, not too ſtiff; work it well, cover it with a cloth; lay it before the fire to riſe a quarter of an hour; when it is well riſen, make it into a roll, cut it in five pieces, and make them into loaves, flatting them down a little, or they will riſe too much; put them into an oven as hot as for manchet, and when they are taken out of the oven, have at leaſt a pound of butter beaten with roſe-water and ſugar to your taſte; cut all the loaves open at the top, and pour the butter into them, and ſerve them hot to table.

To make Cheesecakes.

TAKE a pound of potatoes when they are boiled and peeled, beat them fine; put to them twelve eggs, six whites; then melt a pound of butter and stir it in; grate half a nutmeg; you must sweeten it to your palate with double refined sugar; then put a piece of puff-paste round the edges of the dish; it must not be overbak'd; when the crust is enough draw it.

Another.

TAKE four quarts of new milk and runnet very cold, and when it is come to a curd and whey take half a pound of butter and rub it with the curd; then boil a pint of cream with a blade of mace and cinnamon, and as much grated *Naples* bisket as will make it of the thickness of pancake batter, and when it is almost cold put it to your curd; then put in a spoonful or two of sack, and as many currants as you like, and put them into a puff-paste.

To make Cheesecakes without Curd.

BEAT two eggs very well, then put as much flour as will make them thick; then beat three eggs more very well, and put to the other, with a pint of cream, and half a pound of butter; set it over the fire, and when it boils put in your two eggs and flour, stir them well, and let them boil till they be pretty thick; then take it off the fire, and season it with sugar, a little salt and nutmeg; put in the currants, and bake them in pattipans, as you do others.

To make a Cabbage-lettuce Pye.

TAKE some of the largest and hardest cabbage-lettuces you can get, boil them in salt and water till they are tender, then lay them in a colander to drain; have your paste laid in your pattipan ready, and lay butter on the bottom; then lay in your

your lettuce, ſome artichoke-bottoms, ſome large pieces of marrow, the yolks of eight hard eggs, and ſome ſcalded ſorrel; bake it, and when it comes out of the oven, cut open the lid, and pour in a caudle made with white wine and ſugar, thickened with eggs; ſo ſerve it hot.

To make the light Wigs.

TAKE a pound and a half of flour, and half a pint of milk made warm, mix theſe together, and cover it up, and let it lie by the fire half an hour; then take half a pound of ſugar and half a pound of butter, then work theſe in the paſte, and make it into wigs, with as little flour as poſſible; let the oven be pretty quick, and they will riſe very much.

To make little Plumb-Cakes.

TAKE two pounds of flour dried in the oven, half a pound of ſugar finely powder'd, four yolks of eggs, two whites, half a pound of butter waſhed with roſe-water, ſix ſpoonfuls of cream warmed, a pound and a half of currants unwaſhed, but pick'd and rubb'd very clean in a cloth; mix all together, make them into cakes, and bake them up in an oven almoſt as hot as for manchet, let them ſtand half an hour till they be coloured on both ſides; then take down the oven lid, and let them ſtand a little to ſoak,

To make Puff-Paſte.

TO a peck of flour you muſt have three quarters the weight in butter; dry your flour well, and lay it on a table; make a hole, and put in it a dozen whites of eggs well beaten, but firſt break into it a third part of your butter; then with water make up your paſte, then roll it out, and by degrees put in the reſt of the butter.

To make a Hare Pye.

SKIN your hare, waſh her, dry her, and bone her; ſeaſon the fleſh with pepper, ſalt, and ſpice, beaten fine in a ſtone mortar; do a young pig at the ſame time in the ſame manner; then make your pye, and lay a layer of pig and a layer of hare till it is full; put butter at the bottom and on the top; bake it three hours: it is good hot or cold.

Another.

BONE your hare as whole as you can, then lard it with the fat of bacon, firſt dipt in vinegar and pepper, then ſeaſon it with pepper, ſalt, a little mace, and a clove or two; put it into a diſh with puff-paſte, and have in readineſs gravy or ſtrong broth made with the bones, and put it in juſt before you ſet it in the oven; when it comes out, pour in ſome melted butter with ſtrong broth and wine; but before you pour it in, taſte how the pye is ſeaſoned, and if it wants, you may ſeaſon the liquor accordingly; if you pleaſe, you may lay ſlices of butter upon the hare before it goes into the oven, which I think beſt, inſtead of the melted butter: after, a glaſs of claret does well, juſt before you ſerve it. To ſeven pounds of lean veniſon without bones, put two ounces and a half of ſalt, and half an ounce of pepper, to ſeaſon this in proportion; ſome chuſe to put in the legs and wings with the bones; divide them at every joint, and take the bones of the body, only cracking the other bones in the limbs.

To ice Tarts.

TAKE a little yolk of egg and melted butter, beat it very well together, and with a feather waſh over your tarts, and ſift ſugar on them juſt as you put them into the oven.

To make an Olio Pye.

TAKE a fillet of veal, cut it in large thin slices, and beat it with a rolling-pin; have ready some forc'd-meat made with veal and suet, grated bread, grated lemon-peel, some nutmeg, the yolks of two or three hard eggs; spread the forc'd-meat all over your collops, and roll them up, and place them in your pye, with yolks of hard eggs, lumps of marrow, and some water; lid it and bake it; when it is done, put in a caudle of strong gravy, white wine and butter.

To make very good Wigs.

TAKE a quarter of a peck of the finest flour, rub into it three quarters of a pound of fresh butter, till it is like grated bread, something more than half a pound of sugar, half a nutmeg, and half a race of grated ginger, three eggs, yolks and whites, beaten very well, and put to them half a pint of thick ale yeast, and three or four spoonfuls of sack; make a hole in your flour, and pour in your yeast and eggs, and as much milk just warm as will make it into a light paste; let it stand before the fire to rise half an hour, then make it into a dozen and half of wigs; wash them over with eggs just as they go into the oven; a quick oven and half an hour will bake them.

To make Almond Cheesecakes.

TAKE a good handful or more of almonds, blanch them in warm water, and throw them in cold; pound them fine, and in the pounding put a little sack, or orange-flower water, to keep them from oiling; then put to your almonds the yolks of two hard eggs, and beat them together; beat the yolks of six eggs, the whites of three, and mix with your almonds, and half a pound of butter melted, and sugar to your taste; mix all well together, and use it as other cheesecake stuff.

To make a Lumber Pye.

PARBOIL the umbles of a deer, clear all the fat from them, and put more than their weight in beef-ſuet, and ſhred it together very ſmall; then put to it half a pound of ſugar, and ſeaſon with cloves, mace, nutmeg, and ſalt, to your taſte; and put in a pint of ſack, half as much claret, and two pounds of currants waſh'd and pick'd; mix all well together, and bake it in puff or other paſte.

To make Lemon Cheeſecakes.

TAKE two large lemons, grate off the peel of both, and ſqueeze out the juice of one; add to it half a pound of fine ſugar, twelve yolks of eggs, eight whites well beaten; then melt half a pound of butter in four or five ſpoonfuls of cream; then ſtir it all together and ſet it over the fire, ſtirring it till it begins to be pretty thick; take it off, and when it is cold fill your pattipans little more than half full: put a fine paſte very thin at the bottom of the pattipans: half an hour with a quick oven will bake them.

To make Cream Cheeſe with old Cheſhire.

TAKE a pound and a half of old cheſhire-cheeſe, ſhave it all very thin, then put it in a mortar and add to it a quarter of an ounce of mace beaten fine and ſifted, half a pound of freſh butter, and a glaſs of ſack; mix and beat all theſe together till they are perfectly incorporated; then put it in a pot what thickneſs you pleaſe, and cut it out in ſlices for cream cheeſe, and ſerve it with the deſert.

All

All Sorts of CAKES.

To make a rich great Cake.

TAKE a peck of flour well dried, an ounce of cloves and mace, half an ounce of nutmegs, as much cinnamon; beat the spice well, and mix them with your flour, and a pound and half of sugar, a little salt, thirteen pounds of currants well wash'd, pick'd and dried, and three pounds of raisins stoned and cut into small pieces, mix all these well together; then make five pints of cream almost scalding hot, and put into it four pounds of fresh butter; then beat the yolks of twenty eggs, three pints of good ale yeast, a pint of sack, a quarter of a pint of orange-flower water, three grains of musk, and six grains of ambergrease; mix these together, and stir them into your cream and butter; then mix all in the cake, and set it an hour before the fire to rise, before you put it into your hoop; mix your sweet-meats in it, two pounds of citron, and one pound of candied orange and lemon-peel, cut in small pieces; you must bake it a deep hoop; butter the sides; put two papers at the bottom, flour it, and put in your cake; it must have a quick oven, four hours will bake it; when it is drawn, ice it over the tops and sides; take two pounds of double refined sugar beat and sifted, and the whites of six eggs beaten to a froth, with three or four spoonfuls of orange-flower water, and three grains of musk and ambergrease together; put all these in a stone mortar, and beat them with a wooden pestle till it is as white as snow, and with a brush or bunch of feathers spread it all over the cake, and put it in the oven to dry, but take care the oven does

does not diſcolour it; when it is cold paper it; it will keep good five or ſix weeks.

A Plumb-Cake.

TAKE ſix pounds of currants, five pounds of flour, an ounce of cloves and mace, a little cinnamon, half an ounce of nutmegs, half a pound of pounded and blanched almonds, half a pound of ſugar, three quarters of a pound of ſliced citron, lemon and orange-peel, half a pint of ſack; a little honey-water, a quart of ale yeaſt, a quart of cream, a pound and half of butter melted and poured into the middle thereof; then ſtrew a little flour thereon, and let it lie to riſe; then work it well together, and lay it before the fire to riſe; work it up till it is very ſmooth; put it in a hoop, with a paper floured at the bottom.

A good Seed-Cake.

TAKE five pounds of fine flour well dried, and four pounds of ſingle refined ſugar beaten and ſifted; mix the ſugar and flour together, and ſift them through a hair ſieve; then waſh four pounds of butter in roſe or orange-flower water; you muſt work the butter with your hand till it is like cream, beat twenty eggs, half the whites, and put to them ſix ſpoonfuls of ſack: then put in your flour, a little at a time; keeping it ſtirring with your hand all the time; you muſt not begin mixing it till the oven is almoſt hot; you muſt let it lie a little while before you put the cake into the hoop; when you are ready to put it into the oven, put into it eight ounces of candied orange-peel ſliced, as much citron, and a pound and half of carraway comfits; mix all well together, and put it in the hoop, which muſt be papered at bottom, and butter'd; the oven muſt be quick; it will take two or three hours baking; you may ice it if you pleaſe.

Another Seed-Cake.

TAKE seven pounds of fine flour well dried, mix with it a pound of sugar beaten and sifted, and three nutmegs grated; rub three pounds of butter into the flour; then beat the yolks of eight eggs, the white of but four, and mix with them a little rose-water, a quart of cream blood warm, a quart of ale yeast, and a little salt; strain all into your flour, and put a pint of sack in with it, and make up your cake; put it into a butter'd cloth, and lay it half an hour before the fire to rise; the mean while fit your paper, and butter your hoop; then take a pound and three quarters of bisket comfits, and a pound and half of citron cut in small pieces, mix these in your cake, and put it into your hoop, run a knife cross down to the bottom; a quick oven, and near three hours will bake it.

Another.

DRY two pounds of flour, then put two pounds of butter into it; beat ten eggs, leave out half the whites; then put to them eight spoonfuls of cream, six of ale yeast, run it through a sieve into the batter, and work them well together, and lay it a quarter of an hour before the fire; then work into it a pound of rough carraways; less than an hour bakes it.

A Plumb-Cake.

TAKE five pounds of fine flour, and put to it half a pound of sugar, of nutmegs, cloves, and mace finely beaten, of each half an ounce, and a little salt, mix these well together; then take a quart of cream, let it boil, take it off, and cut into it three pounds of fresh butter, let it stand till 'tis melted, and when 'tis blood warm, mix with it a quart of ale yeast, a pint of sack, and twenty eggs, ten whites well beaten; put six pounds of currants

rants to your flour, and make a hole in the middle, and pour in the milk and other things, and make up your cake, mixing it well with your hands; cover it warm, and set it before the fire to rise for half an hour; then put it in the hoop; if the oven be hot, two hours will bake it: the oven must be quick; you may perfume it with ambergrease, or put sweet-meats in it if you please. Ice it when cold, and paper it.

An ordinary Cake to eat with Butter.

TAKE two pounds of flour, and rub into it half a pound of butter; then put to it some spice, a little salt, a quarter and half of sugar, half a pound of raisins stoned, and half a pound of currants; make these into a cake, with half a pint of ale yeast, four eggs and as much warm milk as you see convenient; mix it well together; an hour and half will bake it. This cake is good to eat with butter for breakfast.

A French *Cake to eat hot.*

TAKE a dozen of eggs, a quart of cream and as much flour as will make it into a thick batter; put to it a pound of melted butter, half a pint of sack, and one nutmeg grated; mix it well, and let it stand three or four hours; then bake it in a quick oven, and when you take it out, slit it in two, and pour a pound of butter on it melted with rose-water; cover it with the other half, and serve it up hot.

To make Portugal *Cakes.*

TAKE a pound and quarter of fine flour well dried, and break a pound of butter into the flour, and rub it in, adding a pound of loaf-sugar beaten and sifted, a nutmeg grated, four perfumed plumbs, or some ambergrease, mix these well together, and beat seven eggs, but four whites, with three spoonfuls of orange-flower water; mix all these

these together, and beat them up an hour; butter your little pans, and just as they are going into the oven, fill them half full,. and searce some fine sugar over them; little more than a quarter of an hour will bake them. You may put a handful of currants into some of them; take them out of the pans as soon as they are drawn, keep them dry; they will keep good three months.

To make Jumbals.

TAKE the whites of three eggs, beat them well, and take off the froth; then take a little milk, and a little flour, near a pound, as much sugar sifted, and a few carraway seeds beaten very fine; work all these in a very stiff paste, and make them into what form you please: bake them on white paper.

To make March-pane.

TAKE a pound of *Jordan* almonds, blanch and beat them in a marble mortar very fine; then put to them three quarters of a pound of double refined sugar, and beat them with a few drops of orange-flower water; beat all together till 'tis a very good paste, then roll it into what shape you please; dust a little fine sugar under it as you roll it, to keep it from sticking. To ice it, searce double refined sugar as fine as flour, wet it with rose-water, and mix it well together, and with a brush or bunch of feathers spread it over your march-pane: bake them in an oven that it not too hot; put wafer paper at the bottom, and white paper under that, so keep them for use.

To make Almond Puffs.

TAKE half a pound of *Jordan* almonds, blanch and beat them very fine with three or four spoonfuls of rose water; then take half an ounce of the finest gum dragant steeped in rose-water three or four days before you use, it, then put it to the almonds,

monds, and beat it together; then take three quarters of a pound of double refined sugar beaten and sifted, and a little fine flour, and put to it; roll it into what shape you please; lay them on white paper, and put them in an oven gently hot, and when they are baked enough, take them off the papers and put them on a sieve to dry in the oven when 'tis almost cold.

To make Biskets.

TAKE a pound of loaf-sugar beaten and sifted, and half a pound of almonds blanch'd and beat in a mortar, with the whites of five or six eggs; put your sugar in a bason, with the yolks of five eggs, when they are both mingled, strew in your almonds; then put in a quarter of a pound of flour, and fill your pans fast; butter them and put them into the oven; strew sugar over them, bake them quick, and then turn them on a paper, and put them again into the oven to harden.

To make little hollow Biskets.

BEAT six eggs very well with a spoonful of rose-water, then put in a pound and two ounces of loaf-sugar beaten and sifted; stir it together till 'tis well mixed in the eggs, then put in as much flour as will make it thick enough to lay out in drops upon sheets of white paper; stir it well together till you are ready to drop it on your paper; then beat a little very fine sugar and put it into a lawn sieve, and sift some on them, the oven must not be too hot, and as soon as they are baked, whilst they are hot, pull off the papers from them, and put them in a sieve, and set them in an oven to dry; keep them in boxes with papers between.

To make Wigs.

TAKE two pounds of flour, and a quarter of a pound of butter, as much sugar, a nutmeg grated,

grated, a little cloves and mace, and a quarter of an ounce of carraway-seeds, cream and yeast as much as will make it up into a pretty light paste; make 'em up, and set them by the fire to rise till the oven be ready, they will quickly be baked.

To make Gingerbread.

TAKE a pound and half of treacle, two eggs beaten, half a pound of brown sugar, one ounce of ginger beaten and sifted; of cloves, mace and nutmegs all together half an ounce, beaten very fine, coriander-seeds and carraway-seeds of each half an ounce, two pounds of butter melted; mix all these together, with as much flour as will knead it into a pretty stiff paste; then roll it out, and cut it into what form you please; bake it in a quick oven on tin-plates; a little time will bake it.

Another Sort of Gingerbread.

TAKE half a pound of almonds, blanch and beat them till they have done shining; beat them with a spoonful or two of orange-flower water, put in half an ounce of beaten ginger, and a quarter of an ounce of cinnamon powder'd; work it to a paste with double refined sugar beaten and sifted; then roll it out, and lay it on papers to dry in an oven after pyes are drawn.

Another.

TO one pound of flour, three quarters of a pound of sugar, and an ounce of nutmegs; ginger and cinnamon together beaten and sifted; a quarter of a pound of candied orange-peels or fresh peel cut in small stripes; two ounces of sweet butter rubb'd in the flour; take the yolks of two eggs, beat with eight spoonfuls of sack, and six of yeast, make it up in a stiff paste; roll it thin, and cut it with a glass; bake them and keep them dry.

To make Dutch *Gingerbread.*

TAKE four pounds of flour, and mix with it two ounces and half of beaten ginger, then rub in a quarter of a pound of butter, and add to it two ounces of carraway-ſeeds, as much orange-peel dried and rubb'd to powder, a few coriander-ſeeds bruiſed, and two eggs; mix all up into a ſtiff paſte with two pounds and a quarter of treacle; beat it very well with a rolling pin, and make it up into thirty cakes; put in a candied citron; prick them with a fork; butter papers, three double, one white, and two brown; waſh them over with the white of an egg; put 'em into an oven not too hot, for three quarters of an hour.

To make Buns.

TAKE two pounds of fine flour, a pint of ale yeaſt, put a little ſack in the yeaſt and three eggs beaten, knead all theſe together with a little warm milk, a little nutmeg, and a little ſalt; then lay it before the fire till it riſe very light; then knead in a pound of freſh butter, and a pound of round carraway comfits, and bake them in a quick oven on floured papers in what ſhape you pleaſe.

To make French *Bread.*

TAKE half a peck of fine flour, put to it ſix yolks of eggs, and four whites, a little ſalt, a pint of good ale yeaſt, and as much new milk, made a little warm, as will make it a thin light paſte; ſtir it about with your hand, but by no means knead it: then have ready ſix wooden quart diſhes, and fill them with dough; let them ſtand a quarter of an hour to heave, and then turn them out into the oven; and when they are baked, raſp them: the oven muſt be quick.

To make Wigs.

TAKE three pounds and a half of flour, and three quarters of a pound of butter, and rub it into the flour till none of it be seen; then take a pint or more of new milk, and make it very warm, and half a pint of new ale yeast, then make it into a light paste; put in carraway-seeds, and what spice you please; then make it up, and lay it before the fire to rise; then work in three quarters of a pound of sugar, and then roll them into what form you please, pretty thin, and put them on tin plates, and hold them before the oven to rise again, before you set them in; your oven must be pretty quick.

To make Gingerbread.

TAKE three pounds of fine flour, and the rind of a lemon dried and beaten to powder, half a pound of sugar or more, as you like it, and an ounce and half of beaten ginger: mix all these well together, and wet it pretty stiff with nothing but treacle; make it into long rolls or cakes, as you please; you may put candied orange-peel and citron in it: butter you paper you bake it on, and let it be bak'd hard.

To make Shrewsbury *Cakes.*

TAKE to one pound of sugar three pounds of the finest flour, a nutmeg grated, some beaten cinnamon; the sugar and spice must be sifted into the flour, and wet it with three eggs, and as much melted butter as will make it of a good thickness to roll into a paste; mould it well and roll it; cut it into what shape you please perfume them, and prick them before they go into the oven.

To make Almond Cakes.

TAKE a pound of almonds, blanch and beat them exceeding fine with a little rose or orange-flower water; then beat three eggs, but two whites, and put to them a pound of sugar sifted; then put in your almonds, and beat all together very well; put sheets of white paper, and lay the cakes in what form you please, and bake them; you may perfume them if you like it; bake them in a cool oven.

To make Drop Biskets.

TAKE eight eggs, and one pound of double refined sugar beaten fine, and twelve ounces of fine flour well dried; beat your eggs very well, then put in your sugar and beat it, and then your flour by degrees, beating it all very well together for an hour without ceasing: your oven must be as hot as for half-penny bread; then flour some sheets of tin, and drop your biskets what bigness you please, and put them into the oven as fast as you can; and when you see them rise, watch them; and if they begin to colour, take them out again, and put in more; and if the first are not enough, put them in again; if they are right done, they will have a white ice on them; you may put in carraway-seeds if you please; when they are all bak'd, put them all in the oven again till they are very dry, and keep them in your stove.

To make little Cracknels.

TAKE three pounds of flour finely dried, three ounces of lemon and orange-peel dried, and beaten to a powder, an ounce of coriander-seeds beaten and searced, and three pounds of double refined sugar beaten fine and searced; mix these together with fifteen eggs, half of the whites taken out, a quarter of a pint of rose-water, as much orange-flower water; beat the eggs and water well together, then put in your orange-peel and coriander-seeds, and beat it again very well with two spoons, one in each hand; then beat your sugar in by little and little, then your flour by a little at a time, so beat with both ſpoons an hour longer; then ſtrew ſugar on papers, and drop them the bigneſs of a walnut, and ſet them in the oven; the oven muſt be hotter than when pies are drawn; do not touch them with your finger before they are bak'd; let the oven be ready for them againſt they are done; be careful the oven does not colour them.

To make the thin Dutch *Biſket.*

TAKE five pounds of flour, two ounces of carraway-ſeeds, half a pound of ſugar, and ſomething more than a pint of milk; warm the milk, and put into it three quarters of a pound of butter; then make a hole in the middle of your flour, and put in a full pint of good ale yeaſt; then pour in the butter and milk, and make theſe into a paſte, letting it ſtand a quarter of an hour by the fire to riſe; then mould it, and roll it into cakes pretty thin; prick them all over pretty much, or they will bliſter; bake them a quarter of an hour.

To make an ordinary Seed-Cake.

TAKE ſix pounds of fine flour, rub it into a thimble-full of carraway-ſeeds finely beaten, and two nutmegs grated, and mace beaten; then heat a quart of cream hot enough to melt a pound of butter in it, and when it is no more than blood-warm, mix your cream and butter with a pint of good ale yeaſt, and then wet your flour with it; make it pretty thin; juſt before it goes into the oven, put in a pound of rough carraways, and ſome citron ſliced thin; three quarters of an hour in a quick oven will bake it.

To make the Marlborough *Cake.*

TAKE eight eggs, yolks and whites, beat and ſtrain them, and put to them a pound of ſugar beaten and sifted; beat it three quarters of an hour together, then put three quarters of a pound of flour well dried, and two ounces of carraway-seeds; beat it all well together, and bake it in a quick oven in broad tin pans.

Another Sort of little Cakes.

TAKE a pound of flour and a pound of butter, rub the butter into the flour, two spoonfuls of yeast and two eggs, make it up into a paste; slick white paper, roll your paste out the thickness of a crown, cut them out with the top of a tin canister, sift fine sugar over them, and lay them on the slick'd paper; bake them after tarts an hour.

To make the white Cake.

TAKE three quarts of the finest flour, a pound and half of butter, a pint of thick cream, half a pint of ale yeast, half a quarter of a pint of rose-water and sack together, a quarter of an ounce of mace, nine eggs, abating four whites, beat them well, five ounces of double refined sugar, mix the sugar and spice and a very little salt with your dry flour, and keep out half a pint of the flour to strew over the cake; when it is all mix'd, melt the butter in the cream; when 'tis a little cool, strain the eggs into it, yeast, *&c.* make a hole in the midst of the flour, and pour all the wetting in, stirring it round with your hand all one way till well mix'd; strew on the flour that was saved out, and set it before the fire to rise, cover'd over with a cloth; let it stand so a quarter of an hour; you must have in readiness three pounds and half of currants, wash'd and pick'd, and well dried in a cloth; mingle them in the paste without kneading; put it in a tin hoop; set it in a quick oven, or it will not rise; it must stand an hour and half in the oven.

To

To make another Sort of Gingerbread.

TAKE a pound and a half of treacle, two eggs beaten, a pound of butter melted, half a pound of brown sugar, an ounce of beaten ginger, and of cloves, mace, corriander-seeds and carraway-seeds, of each half an ounce; mix all these together with as much flour as will knead it into a paste; roll it out, and cut it into what form you please; bake it in a quick oven on tin plates; a little time will bake it.

To make Biskets.

TO a quart of flour take a quarter of a pound of butter, and a quarter of a pound of sugar, one egg, and what carraway-seeds you please, wet it with milk as stiff as you can, then roll them out very thin, cut them with a small glass, bake them on tin plates; your oven must be slack; prick them very well just as you set them in, and keep them dry when bak'd.

To make brown French *Loaves.*

TAKE a peck of coarse flour, and as much of the raspings of bread beaten and sifted as will make it look brown, then wet it with a pint of good yeast, and as much milk and warm water as will wet it pretty stiff; mix it well, and set it before the fire to rise; make it into six loaves; make it up as light as you can, and bake it well in a quick oven.

To make the hard Bisket.

TAKE half a pound of fine flour, one ounce of carraway-seeds, the whites of two eggs, a quarter of a pint of ale yeast, and as much warm water as will make it into a stiff paste; then make it into long rolls, bake it an hour; the next day pare it round, then ſlice it in thin ſlices, about half an inch thick; dry it in the oven; then draw it, turn it, and dry the other ſide; they will keep the whole year.

To make Whetſtone *Cakes.*

TAKE half a pound of fine flour, and half a pound of loaf ſugar ſearced, a ſpoonful of carraway-ſeeds dried, the yolk of one egg, the whites of three, a little roſe-water, with ambergreaſe diſſolved in it; mix it together, and roll it out as thin as a wafer, cut them with a glaſs, lay them on floured paper, and bake them in a ſlow oven.

To make a good Plumb Cake.

TAKE four pounds of flour, put to it half a pound of loaf ſugar beaten and ſifted, of mace and nutmegs half an ounce beaten fine, a little ſalt; beat the yolks of thirty eggs, the whites of fifteen, a pint and a half of ale yeaſt, three quarters of a pint of ſack, with two grains of ambergreaſe and two of muſk ſteep'd in it five or ſix hours; then take a large pint of thick cream, ſet it on the fire, and put in two pounds of butter to melt, but not boil; then put your flour in a bowl, make a hole in the midſt, and pour in your yeaſt, ſack, cream, and eggs; mix it well with your hands, make it up, not too ſtiff, ſet it to the fire a quarter of an hour to riſe; then put in ſeven pounds of currants pick'd and waſh'd in warm water, then dried in a coarſe cloth, and kept warm till you put them into your cake, which mix in as faſt as you can, and put candied lemon, orange and citron in it; put it in your hoop, which muſt be ready butter'd and fixed; ſet it in a quick oven, bake it two hours or more; when it is near cold, ice it.

Another

Another Plumb Cake.

TAKE four pounds of flour, four pounds of currants, and twelve eggs, half the whites taken out, near a pint of yeaſt, a pound and half of butter, a good half pint of cream, three quarters of a pound of loaf-ſugar, beaten mace, nutmegs and cinnamon, half an ounce, beaten fine; mingle the ſpices and ſugar with the flour; beat the eggs well and put to them a quarter of a pint of roſe-water, that had a little muſk and ambergreaſe diſſolved in it; put the butter and cream into a jug, and put it in a pot of boiling water to melt; when you have mixed the cake, ſtrew a little flour over it; cover it with a very hot napkin, and ſet it before the fire to riſe; butter and flour your hoop, and juſt as your oven is ready, put your currants into boiling water to plump; dry them in a hot cloth, and mix them in your cake; you may put in half a pound of candied orange, lemon, and citron; let not your oven be too hot, two hours will bake it, three if it is double the quantity; mix it with a broad pudding-ſtick, not with your hands; when your cake is juſt drawn, pour all over it a gill of brandy or ſack; then ice it.

Another Plumb Cake with Almonds.

TAKE four pounds of fine flour dried well, five pounds of currants well pick'd and rubb'd, but not waſh'd, five pounds of butter waſh'd and beaten in orange-flower water and ſack, two pounds of almonds beaten very fine, four pounds of eggs weighed, half the whites taken out, three pounds of double refined ſugar, three nutmegs grated, a little ginger, a quarter of an ounce of mace, as much cloves finely beaten; a quarter of a pint of the beſt brandy; the butter muſt be beaten to cream, then put in your flour and all the reſt of the things, beating it till you put it in the oven; four hours will bake it, the oven must be very quick; put in orange, lemon-peel candied, and citron, as you like.

A rich Seed Cake, call'd the Nun's Cake.

TAKE four pounds of your finest flour, and three pounds of double refined sugar beaten and sifted, mix them together, and dry them by the fire till you prepare your other materials. Take four pounds of butter, beat it in your hands till it is very soft like cream, then beat thirty five eggs, leave out sixteen whites, and strain out the treddles of the rest, and beat them and the butter together till all appears like butter; put in four or five spoonfuls of rose or orange-flower water, and beat it again; then take your flour and sugar, with six ounces of carraway-seeds, and strew it in by degrees, beating it up all the time for two hours together; you may put in as much tincture of cinnamon or ambergrease as you please; butter your hoop, and let it stand three hours in a moderate oven.

To ice a great Cake.

TAKE two pounds of double refined sugar, beat and sift it very fine, and likewise beat and sift a little starch and mix with it; then beat six whites of eggs to a froth, and put to it some gum-water; the gum must be steeped in orange-flower water; then mix and beat all these together two hours, and put it on your cake; when it is baked, set it in the oven a quarter of an hour.

Another Seed Cake.

TAKE a pound of flour, dry it by the fire, add to it a pound of fine sugar beaten and sifted; then take a pound and a quarter of butter, and work it it in your hand till it is like cream; beat the yolks of ten eggs, the whites of ſix; mix all theſe together with an ounce and half of carraway-ſeeds, and a quarter of a pint of brandy; it muſt not ſtand to riſe.

****

CREAMS *and* JELLIES.

Lemon Cream.

TAKE five large lemons, and ſqueeze out the juice, and the whites of ſix eggs well beaten, ten ounces of double refined ſugar beaten very fine, and twenty ſpoonfuls of ſpring water; mix all together and ſtrain it through a jelly-bag; ſet it over a gentle fire, ſkim it very well; when it is as hot as you can bear your finger in it, take it off, and pour it into glaſſes; put ſhreds of lemon-peel into ſome of the glaſſes.

Another Lemon Cream.

TAKE the juice of four large lemons, half a pint of water, a pound of double refined ſugar, beaten fine, the whites of ſeven eggs, and the yolk of one beaten very well; mix all together, ſtrain it, ſet it on a gentle fire, ſtirring it all the while, and ſkim it clean; put into it the peel of one lemon when it is very hot, but not boil; take out the lemon-peel, and pour it into *China* diſhes.

To make Orange Cream.

TAKE a pint of the juice of *Seville* oranges, put to it the yolks of ſix eggs, the whites of four;

four; beat the eggs very well, and ſtrain them and the juice together; add to it a pound of double refined ſugar beaten and ſifted; ſet all theſe together on a ſoft fire, and put the peel of half an orange into it, keep it ſtirring all the while, and when it is almoſt ready to boil, take out the orange-peel, and pour out the cream into glaſſes or *China* diſhes.

To make Gooſeberry Cream.

TAKE two quarts of gooſeberries, put to them as much water as will cover them; let them boil all to maſh, and run them through a ſieve with a ſpoon; to a quart of the pulp, you muſt have ſix eggs well beaten, and when the pulp is hot, put in an ounce of freſh butter, ſweeten it to your taſte, put in your eggs, and ſtir them over a gentle fire till they grow thick; then ſet it by, and when it is almoſt cold, put into it two ſpoonfuls of juice of ſpinach, and a ſpoonful of orange-flower water or ſack, ſtir it well together, and put it in your baſons; when it is cold ſerve it to the table.

Some love the gooſeberries only maſhed, not pulped through a ſieve, and put the butter, and eggs, and ſugar as the other, but no juice of ſpinach.

To make Barley Cream.

TAKE a ſmall quantity of pearl barley, and boil it in milk and water till it is tender: then ſtrain the liquor from it, and put your barley into a quart of cream, and let it boil a little; then take the whites of five eggs, and the yolk of one beaten with a ſpoonful of fine flour, and two ſpoonfuls of orange-flower water, then take the cream off the fire, and mix the eggs in by degrees, and ſet it over the fire again to thicken; ſweeten it to your taſte; pour it into baſons, and when it is cold ſerve it up.

To make Steeple Cream.

TAKE five ounces of hart's-horn, and two ounces of ivory; put them into a ſtone-bottle, fill it up with fair water to the neck, and put in a ſmall quantity of gum-arabick, and gum-dragant; then tie up the bottle very cloſe, and ſet it into a pot of water with hay at the bottom, let it boil ſix hours; then take it out, and let it ſtand an hour before you open it, leſt it fly in your face; then ſtrain it in, and it will be a ſtrong jelly; then take a pound of blanched almonds, beat them very fine, and mix it with a pint of thick cream, letting it ſtand a little; then ſtrain it out and mix it with a pound of jelly; ſet it over the fire till it is ſcalding hot, ſweeten it to your taſte with double refined ſugar; then take it off, and put in a little amber, and pour it out into ſmall high gallipots like a ſugar loaf at top; when it is cold turn it out, and lay whipt cream about them in heaps.

To make Blanch'd Cream.

TAKE a quart of the thickeſt ſweet cream you can get, ſeaſon with fine ſugar and orange-flower water; then boil it; then beat the whites of twenty eggs with a little cold cream, take out the treddles, and when the cream is on the fire and boils, pour in your eggs, ſtirring it very well till it comes to a thick curd; then take it up and paſs it through a hair ſieve; then beat it very well with a ſpoon till it is cold, and put it in diſhes for uſe.

To make Quince Cream.

TAKE quinces, ſcald them till they are ſoft; pare them, maſh the clear part of them, and pulp it through a ſieve; take an equal weight of quince, and double refined ſugar beaten and ſifted, and

and the whites of eggs, and beat it till it is as white as ſnow, then put it in diſhes.

To make Almond Cream.

TAKE a quart of cream, boil it with nutmeg, mace, and a bit of lemon-peel, and ſweeten it to your taſte; then blanch ſome almonds, and beat them very fine; then take nine whites of eggs well beaten, and ſtrain them to your almonds, and rub them very well through a thin ſtrainer; ſo thicken your cream; juſt give it one boil; and pour it into *China* diſhes; and when it is cold ſerve it up.

To make Ratafia Cream.

TAKE ſix large laurel leaves, and boil them in a quart of thick cream; when it is boiled, throw away the leaves, and beat the yolks of five eggs with a little cold cream, and ſugar to your taſte; then thicken your cream with your eggs, and ſet it over the fire again, but let it not boil; keeping it ſtirring all the while, and pouring it into *China* diſhes; when it is cold it is fit for uſe.

To make Sack Cream.

TAKE the yolks of two eggs, three ſpoonfuls of fine ſugar, and a quarter of a pint of ſack; mix them together, and ſtir them into a pint of cream; then ſet them over the fire till it is ſcalding hot, but let it not boil. You may toaſt ſome thin ſlices of white bread, and dip them in ſack or orange-flower water, and pour your cream over them.

To make Rice Cream.

TAKE three ſpoonfuls of the flour of rice, as much ſugar, the yolks of two eggs, two ſpoonfuls of ſack, or roſe or orange-flower water; mix all theſe, and put them to a pint of cream, ſtir it over the fire till it is thick, then pour it into *China* diſhes.

To

To make Hart's-horn Jelly.

TAKE a large gallipot, and fill it with hart's-horn, and then fill it full with ſpring water, and tie a double paper over the gallipot, and ſet it in a baker's oven with houſhold bread; in the morning take it out, run it through a jelly-bag, ſeaſon with juice of lemons, double refin'd ſugar, and the whites of eight eggs well beaten; let it have a boil, and run it through the jelly bag again into your jelly glaſſes; put a bit of lemon-peel in the bag.

To make Calves-foot Jelly.

TO four calves feet take a gallon of fair water, cut them in pieces, put them in a pipkin cloſe covered, and boil them ſoftly till almoſt half be conſumed; and run it through a ſieve, and let it ſtand till it is cold; then with a knife take off the fat, and top and bottom, and the fine part of the jelly melt in a preſerving pan or ſkillet, and put in a pint of rheniſh wine, the juice of four or five lemons, double refin'd ſugar to your taſte, the whites of eight eggs beaten to a froth; ſtir and boil all theſe together near half an hour; then ſtrain it through a ſieve into a jelly bag; put into your jelly bag a ſprig of roſemary, and a piece of lemon-peel; paſs it through the bag till 'tis as clear as water. You may cut ſome lemon-peel like threads, and put in half the glaſſes.

To make whipt Cream.

TAKE a quart of thick cream, and the whites of eight eggs beaten with half a pint of ſack; mix it together, and ſweeten it to your taſte with double refined ſugar; you may perfume it if you pleaſe with ſome muſk or ambergreaſe tied in a rag, and ſteeped a little in the cream; whip it up with a whiſk, and a bit of lemon-peel tied in the middle of the

the whisk; take the froth with a spoon, and lay it in your glasses or basons.

To make whipt Syllabubs.

TAKE a quart of cream, not too thick, a pint of sack, and the juice of two lemons; sweeten it to your palate, put it into a broad earthen pan, and with a whisk whip it; as the froth rises, take it off with a spoon, and lay it in your syllabub-glasses; but first you must sweeten some claret, sack, or white wine, and strain it, and put seven or eight spoonfuls of the wine into your glasses, and then gently lay in your froth. Set them by. Do not make them long before you use them.

To make a fresh Cheese.

TAKE a quart of cream, and set it over the fire till it is ready to boil, then beat nine eggs, yolks and whites, very well; when you are beating them, put to them as much salt as will lie on a small knife's point; put them to the cream, with some nutmeg quartered, and tied up in a rag; let them boil till the whey is clear; then take it off the fire, put it in a pan, and gather it as you do cheese; then put it in a cloth, and drain it between two; then put it in a stone mortar, grind it, and season it with a little sack, orange-flower water and sugar; then put it in a little earthen colander, and let it stand two hours to drain out the whey, then put it in the middle of a *China* dish and pour thick cream about it. So serve it to the table.

To make Almond Butter.

TAKE a pound of the best *Jordan* almonds, blanched in cold water, and as you blanch them throw them into fair water; then beat them in a marble mortar very fine, with some rose or orange-flower water, to keep them from oiling; then take a pound of butter out of the churn before

'tis

'tis ſalted, but it muſt be very well waſhed; and mix it with your almonds, with near a pound of double refin'd ſugar beaten and ſifted; when 'tis very well mix'd, ſet it up to cool; when you are going to uſe it, put into a colander, and paſs it through with the back of a ſpoon into the diſh you ſerve it in. Hold your hand high and let it be heaped up.

To make Ribbon Jelly.

TAKE out the great bones of four calf's-feet, and put the feet into a pot with ten quarts of water, three ounces of hart's-horn, three ounces of iſing-glaſs, a nutmeg quarter'd, four blades of mace; then boil this till it comes to two quarts, and ſtrain it through a fine flannel bag; let it ſtand twenty-four hours; then ſcrape off all the fat from the top very clean; then heat it, and put it to the whites of ſix eggs beaten to a froth; boil it a little, and ſtrain it again through a flannel bag; then run the jelly into little high glaſſes; run every colour as thick as your finger; one colour muſt be thorough cold before you put another on, and that you run on muſt not be blood-warm for fear it mixes together; you muſt colour red with cochineal, green with ſpinach, yellow with ſaffron, blue with ſyrup of violets, white with thick cream, and ſometimes the jelly by itſelf.

To make Orange Cream.

TAKE the juice of ſix oranges, ſet it on the fire, let it be ſcalding hot, but not boil; beat three yolks of eggs with as much ſugar as will make it ſweet enough to your taſte; beat them up together, and let them have one boil up, keep it ſtirring, ſcum it, and put it into glaſſes, and ſerve it up cold.

To make Cream of any preſerv'd Fruit.

TAKE half a pound of the pulp of any preſerv'd fruit, put it in a large pan, put to it the whites of two or three eggs; beat them together

ther exceeding well for an hour; then with a spoon take it off, and lay it heaped up high on the dish or salver with other creams, or put it in the middle bason: raspberries will not do this way.

To make a Snow Posset.

TAKE a quart of new milk, and boil it with a stick of cinnamon and quarter'd nutmeg; when the milk is boiled, take out the spice, and beat the yolks of sixteen eggs very well, and by degrees mix them in the milk till it is thick; then beat the whites of the sixteen eggs with a little sack and sugar into a snow; then take the bason you design to serve it up in, and put in it a pint of sack; sweeten it to your taste; set it over the fire, and let one take the milk, and another the whites of eggs, and so pour them together into the sack in the bason; keep it stirring all the while it is over the fire; when it is thorough warm take it off, cover it up, and let it stand a little before you use it.

To make a Jelly Posset.

TAKE twenty eggs, leave out half the whites, and beat them very well; put them into the bason you serve it in, with near a pint of sack, and a little strong ale; sweeten it to your taste, and set it over a charcoal fire, keep it stirring all the while; then have in readiness a quart of milk or cream boiled with a little nutmeg and cinnamon, and when your sack and eggs are hot enough to scald your lips, put the milk to it boiling hot; then take it off the fire, and cover it up half an hour; strew sugar on the brim of the dish, and serve it to the table.

To make Flummery Caudle.

TAKE a pint of oatmeal, and put it to two quarts of fair water; let it stand all night, in the morning stir it, and strain it into a skillet, with three or four blades of mace, and a nutmeg quartered; set it on the fire, and keep it stirring, and let it boil a quarter of an hour; if it is too thick, put in more water, and let it boil longer; then add a pint of rhenish white wine, three spoonfuls of orange-flower water, the juice of two lemons, and one orange, a bit of butter, and as much fine sugar as will sweeten it; let a l these have a walm, and thicken it with the yolks of two or three eggs. Drink it hot for a breakfast.

To make Tea Caudle.

MAKE a quart of strong green tea, pour it out into a skillet, and set it over the fire; then beat the yolks of four eggs, and mix them with a pint of white wine, a grated nutmeg, sugar to your taste, and put all together; stir it over the fire till it is very hot, then drink it in *China* dishes as caudle.

A fine Caudle.

TAKE a pint of milk, and turn it with sack; then strain it, and when it is cold, put it in a skillet with mace, nutmeg, and some white bread sliced; let all these boil, and then beat the yolks of four or five eggs, the whites of two, and thicken your caudle, stirring it all one way, for fear it curdles; let it warm together, then take it off and sweeten it to your taste.

To make Harts-horn or Calves-foot Jelly without Lemons.

TAKE a pair of calves feet, boil them with six quarts of fair water to mash; it will make three quarts of jelly; then strain it off, and let it stand still till 'tis cold, take off the top, and save the middle, and melt it again and scum it; then take six whites of eggs beaten to a froth, half a pint of rhenish wine, and one lemon juiced, and half a pound of fine powdered sugar; stir all together, and let it boil, then take it off, and put to it as much spirit of vitriol as will sharpen it to your palate, about one pennyworth will do; let it not boil after the vitriol is in; let your jelly-bag be made of thick flannel, then run it through till it is very clear; you may put the whites of the eggs that ſwim at the top into the bag firſt, and that will thicken the bag.

To make Oatmeal Caudle.

TAKE two quarts of ale, one of ſtale beer, and two quarts of water; mix them all together, and add to it two ſpoonfuls of pot-oatmeal, twelve cloves, five or ſix blades of mace, and a nutmeg quartered or bruiſed; ſet it over the fire, and let it boil half an hour, ſtirring it all the while; then ſtrain it out thro' a ſieve, and put in near a pound of fine ſugar, and a bit of lemon-peel; pour it into a pan, and cover it cloſe, that it may not ſcum; warm it as you uſe it.

To make Salop.

TAKE a quart of water, and let it boil a quarter of an hour, then put in a quarter of an ounce of ſalop finely powdered, and let it boil half an hour longer, ſtirring it all the while; then ſeaſon it with white wine and juice of lemons, and ſweeten it to your taſte; drink it in *China* cups, as chocolate; it is a great ſweetener of the blood.

Boil ſago till it is tender and jellies, a ſpoonful and half to a quart of water, then ſeaſon it as you do ſalop, and drink it in chocolate diſhes; or if you pleaſe leave out the wine and lemon, and put in a pint of thick cream and a ſtick of cinnamon, and thicken it up with two or three eggs.

To make Lemon Syllabubs.

TAKE a quart of cream, half a pound of ſugar, a pint of white wine, the juice of two or three lemons, the peel of one grated; mix all theſe, and put them in an earthen pot, and milk it up as faſt as you can till it is thick, then pour it into your

5 glaſſes,

glaſſes, and let them ſtand five or ſix hours; you may make them over night.

To make white Leach.

TAKE half a pound of almonds, blanch and beat them with roſe-water, and a little milk; then ſtrain it out, and put to it a piece of iſinglaſs, and let it boil on a chafing-diſh of coals half an hour; then ſtrain it into a baſon, ſweeten it, and put a grain of muſk into it, let it boil a little longer, and put to it two or three drops of oil of mace or cinnamon, and keep it till it is cold; eat it with wine or cream.

To make white Wine Cream.

TAKE a quart of cream, ſet it on the fire, and ſtir it till it is blood-warm; then boil a pint of white wine with ſugar till it is ſyrup, ſo mingle the wine and cream together; put it in a *China* baſon, and when it is cold ſerve it up.

To make Strawberry or Raſpberry Fool.

TAKE a pint of raſpberries, ſqueeze and ſtrain the juice with orange-flower water; put to the juice five ounces of fine ſugar; then ſet a pint of cream over the fire, and let it boil up; then put in the juice; give it one ſtir round, and then put it into your baſon; ſtir it a little in the baſon, and when it is cold uſe it,

To make Sack Cream.

TAKE a quart of thick cream and ſet it over the fire, and when it boils take it off; put a piece of lemon-peel in it, and ſweeten it very well; then take the *China* baſon you ſerve it in, and put into the baſon the juice of half a lemon, and nine ſpoonfuls of ſack; then ſtir in the cream into the baſon by a ſpoonful at a time, till all the cream is in; when it is little more than blood-warm, ſet it by till next day; ſerve it with wafers round it.

To make Ratafia Biſket.

TAKE four ounces of bitter almonds, blanch and beat them as fine as you can; in beating them put in the whites of four eggs, one at a time; then mix it up with ſifted ſugar to a light paſte; roll them and lay them on wafer paper, and on tin plates; make the paſte ſo light that you may take it up with a ſpoon; bake them in a quick oven.

To make Piſtachia Cream.

PEEL your piſtachias, beat them very fine, and boil them in cream; if it is not green enough, add a little juice of ſpinach; thicken it with eggs, and ſweeten to your taſte; pour it in baſons, and ſet it by till it is cold.

To make Harts-horn Flummery.

TAKE three ounces of harts-horn, and boil it with two quarts of ſpring-water; let it ſimmer over the fire ſix or ſeven hours, till half the water is conſumed; or elſe put it in a jug, and ſet it in the oven with houſhold bread; then ſtrain it through a ſieve, and beat half a pound of almonds very fine, with ſome orange-flower water in the beating; when they are beat mix a little of your jelly with it, and ſome fine ſugar; ſtrain it out and mix it with your other jelly; ſtir it together till it is little more than blood-warm, then pour it into half-pint baſons, fill them about half full; when you uſe them, turn them out of the diſh as you do flummery; if it does not come out clean, hold the baſon a minute or two in warm water; eat it with wine and ſugar.

Put ſix ounces of harts-horn in a glaz'd jug with a long neck, and put in three pints of ſoft water; cover the top of the jug cloſe, and put a weight on it to keep it ſteady; ſet it in a pot or kettle of water twenty four hours; let it not boil, but be ſcalding hot; then ſtrain it out, and make your jelly.

A Sack Posset without Eggs.

TAKE a quart of cream, or new milk, and grate three *Naples* biskets in it, and let them boil in the cream; grate some nutmeg in it, and sweeten it to your taste; let it stand a little to cool, and then put half a pint of sack a little warm in your bason, and pour your cream to it, holding it up high in the pouring; let it stand a little, and serve it.

A Sack Posset without Cream or Eggs.

TAKE half a pound of *Jordan* almonds, lay them all night in water, blanch, and beat them in a stone mortar very fine, with a pint of orange-flower water, or fair water a quart, and half a pound of sugar, a two-penny loaf of bread grated, let it boil till it is thick, continually stirring it; then warm half a pint of sack, and put to it; stir it well together, and put a little nutmeg and cinnamon in it.

To make a Posset with Ale.
King William's *Posset.*

TAKE a quart of cream, and mix it with a pint of ale, then beat the yolks of ten eggs, and the whites of four; when they are well beaten, put them to the cream and ale; sweeten it to your taste, and slice some nutmeg in it; set it over the fire, and keep it stirring all the while;. when it is thick, and before it boils, take it off, and pour it into the bason you serve it in to the table.

To make the Pope's *Posset.*

BLANCH and beat three quarters of a pound of almonds so fine, that they will spread between your fingers like butter; put in water as you beat them, to keep them from oiling; then take a pint of sack or sherry, and sweeten it very well with double refined sugar; make it boiling hot, and at the same time put half a pint of water to your almonds, and make them boil; then take both off the fire, and mix them very well together with a spoon; serve it in a *China* dish.

To make very fine Syllabubs.

TAKE a quart and half a pint of cream, a pint of rhenish, half a pint of sack, three lemons, and near a pound of double refined sugar; beat and sift the sugar, and put it to your cream; grate off the yellow rind of your three lemons, and put that in; squeeze the juice of the three lemons into your wine, and put that to your cream, then beat all together with a whisk just half an hour; then take it up all together with a spoon, and fill your glasses; it will keep good nine or ten days, and is best three or four days old; these are call'd *the everlasting Syllabubs.*

To make an Oatmeal Sack Posset.

TAKE a pint of milk, and mix in it two spoonfuls of flour of oatmeal, and one of sugar; put in a blade of mace, and let it boil till the rawness of the oatmeal is gone off; in the mean time have in readiness three spoonfuls of sack, three of ale, and two of sugar; set them over the fire till scalding hot, then put them to your milk; give one stir, and let it stand on the fire a minute or two, and pour it in your bason; cover your bason with a pye-plate, and let it stand a little to settle.

Preserves, Conserves, *and* Syrups.

To preserve Oranges whole.

TAKE the best *Bermudas* oranges, pare them with a penknife very thin, and lay your oranges in water three or four days shifting them every day; then put them in a kettle with fair water, put-

putting a board on them, to keep them down in the water; have a ſkillet on the fire with water, that may be in readineſs to ſupply the kettle with boiling water; as it waſtes it muſt be fill'd up three or four times while the oranges are doing, for they will take up ſeven or eight hours in boiling, for they muſt be ſo tender that a wheat-ſtraw may be thruſt through them; then take them up, and ſcoop the ſeeds out of them, making a little hole on the top; then weigh them, and to every pound of orange take a pound and three quarters of double refined ſugar finely beaten and ſifted; fill up your oranges with ſugar, and ſtrew ſome on them, and let them lie a little; then make your jelly for them thus: take two dozen of pippins and ſlice them into water, and when they are boiled tender ſtrain the liquor from the pulp, and to every pound of orange you muſt have a pint and half of this liquor, and put to it three quarters of the ſugar you left in filling the oranges; ſet it on the fire, and let it boil, and ſcum it well, and put it in a clean earthen pan till it is cold; then put it in your ſkillet, and put in your oranges, and with a ſmall bodkin jobb the oranges as they are boiling, to let the ſyrup into them; ſtrew on the reſt of your ſugar while they are boiling; and when they look clear, take them up and put them in your glaſſes, but one in a glaſs juſt fit for them, and boil the ſyrup till it is almoſt a jelly; then fill up your oranges and glaſſes, and when they are cold paper them up, and put them in your ſtove.

To preſerve whole Quinces white.

TAKE the largeſt quinces of the greeneſt colour, and ſcald them till they are pretty ſoft, then pare them, and core them with a ſcoop; then weigh your quinces againſt ſo much double refined ſugar, and make a ſyrup of one half, and put in your quinces and boil them as faſt as you can; then you muſt have in readineſs pippin liquor, let it be very ſtrong of the pippins; and when it is ſtrained out, put in the other half of your ſugar, and make it a jelly; and when your quinces are clear put them into the jelly, and let them ſimmer a little, they will be very white: ſo glaſs them up, and when they are cold paper them, and keep them in a ſtove.

To preſerve Gooſeberries.

TAKE of the beſt *Dutch* gooſeberries before they are too ripe, ſtone them, and put them in a ſkillet with ſo much fair water as will cover them; ſet them on a fire to ſcald, and when they are tender take them out of the liquor, and peel off the outer ſkin as you do codlins, and throw them into ſome double refin'd ſugar, powdered and ſifted; put a handful more of gooſeberries into that water, and let them boil a little, then run the liquor thro' a ſieve; take the weight of your peel'd gooſeberries in double refin'd ſugar, break the ſugar in lumps, and wet the lumps in the liquor that the gooſeberries were ſcalded in, and put your ſugar in a preſerving pan over a clear fire, let it boil up, and ſcum it well; then put in your gooſeberries, and let them boil till they look clear; then place them in your glaſſes, and boil the liquor a little longer, and pour it on your gooſeberries in the glaſſes; when they are cold paper them.

To preſerve Raſpberries in Jelly.

TAKE of the largeſt and beſt raſpberries, and to a pound take a pound and a quarter of ſugar made into a ſyrup, and boiled candy high; then put in the raſpberries, ſet them over a gentle fire, and as they boil ſhake them; when the ſugar boils over them, take them off the fire, ſkim them, and ſet them by a little; then ſet them on again, and have half a pint of juice of currants by you, and at ſeveral times put in a little as it boils; ſhake them often as they grow nearer to be enough, which you may know by ſetting ſome in

a ſpoon

a spoon to try if it will jelly, for when they jelly they are enough; then lay them in your glasses and keep the jelly to cover them; but before you put it to them pick out all the seeds, and let the jelly cover them well.

To preserve Apricocks.

TAKE your apricocks, stone and pare them; take their weight in double refined sugar beaten and sifted, and put your apricocks in a silver cup or tankard, and cover them over with the sugar, letting them stand so all night; the next day put them in a preserving pan, set them on a gentle fire, and let them simmer up a little while; then let them boil till they are tender and clear, taking them off sometimes to turn and skim; keep them under the liquor as they are doing, and with a small clean bodkin or great needle job them sometimes, that the syrup may penetrate into them; when they are enough take them and put them in glasses, boil and skim the syrup, and when it is cold put it on your apricocks.

To preserve white Pear Plumbs.

TAKE pear-plumbs when they are yellow, before they are too ripe, give them a slit in the seam, and prick them behind; make your water almost scalding hot, and put a little sugar to it to sweeten it; and put in your plumbs, and cover them close; set them on the fire to coddle, and take them off sometimes a little, and set them on again; take care they do not break; have in readiness as much double refined sugar boil'd to a height as will cover them, and when they are coddled pretty tender, take them out of the liquor, and put them into your preserving pan to your syrup, which must be but blood-warm when your plumbs go in; let them boil till they are clear, skim them, take them off, and let them stand two hours; then set them on again, and boil them, and when they are thoroughly preserved

ſerved, take them up and lay them in glaſſes; boil your ſyrup till it is thick, and when 'tis cold put in your plumbs; a month after, if your ſyrup grows thin, you muſt boil it again, or make a fine jelly of pippins, and put on them, This way you may do the pimordian plumb, or any white plumb; and when they are cold paper them up.

To preſerve Damſons whole.

TAKE ſome damſons, cut them in pieces, and put them in a ſkillet over the fire, with as much water as will cover them; when they are boiled, and the liquor pretty ſtrong, ſtrain it out; and for every pound of your whole damſons wiped clean, a pound of ſingle refined ſugar, put the third part of the ſugar in the liquor, and ſet it over the fire, and when it ſimmers put in your damſons; let them have one good boil, and take them off for half an hour, cover'd up cloſe; then ſet them on again, and let them ſimmer over the fire, often turning them; then take them out, put them into a baſon, and ſtrew all the ſugar that was left on them, and pour the hot liquor over them, cover them up, and let them ſtand till the next day; then boil them up again till they are enough; take them up, and put them in pots; boil the liquor till it jellies, and pour it on them when it is almoſt cold, ſo paper them up.

To parch Almonds.

TAKE a pound of ſugar, make it into a ſyrup, and boil it candy-high, then put in three quarters of a pound of *Jordan* almonds blanched; keep them ſtirring all the while till they are dry and criſp, then put them in a box, and keep them dry.

To dry Apricocks.

TAKE to a pound of apricocks, a pound of double refined ſugar; ſtone them, pare them, and put them into cold water; when they are all ready,

ready, put them into a skillet of hot water, and scald them till they are tender; then drain them very well from the water, and put them into a silver bason; have in readiness your sugar boil'd to sugar again, and pour that sugar over your apricocks; cover them with a silver plate, and let them stand all night; the next day set them over a gentle fire, and let them be scalding hot, turning them often; you must do them twice a-day, till you see them begin to candy; then take them out, and set them in your stove or glasses to dry, heating your stove every day till they are dry.

To preserve green Plumbs.

TAKE green plumbs grown to their full bigness, but before they begin to ripen; let them be carefully gathered with their stalks and leaves, put them in to cold spring water over a fire, and let them boil very gently; when they will peel, take off the skins; then put the plumbs into other cold water, and let them stand over a very gentle fire till they are soft; put two pounds of double refin'd sugar to every pound of plumbs, and make the sugar with some water into a thick syrup before the plumbs are put in; the stones of the plumbs are not to be grown so hard, but that you may thrust a pin thro' them. After the same manner do green apricocks.

To make Sugar Plates.

TAKE a pound of double refined sugar beaten and fearced; blanch and beat some almonds and mix with it, and beat them together in a mortar, with gum dragant dissolved in rose-water, till it is a paste; roll it out, and strew sugar on the papers or plate, and bake it after manchet; gild it if you please, and serve sweetmeats on it.

To clear Sugar.

TAKE two or three whites of eggs, and put 'em into a bason of water, and with a very clean hand

hand lather that as you do ſoap; take nothing but the froth, and when your ſyrup boils, with a ladle cover it with it; do this till your ſyrup is clear, making ſtill more froth, and covering the ſyrup with it; it will make the worſt ſugar as clear as any, and fit to preſerve any fruit.

To preſerve Plumbs green.

THE plumbs that will be greeneſt are the white plumbs that are ripe in wheat harveſt; gather them about the middle of *July* whilſt they are green; when gathered, lay them in water twelve hours; then ſcald them in two ſeveral waters, let not the firſt be too hot, but the ſecond muſt boil before you put the plumbs in; when they begin to ſhrivel, peel off the ſkin as you do codlins, keep them whole, and let a third water be made hot, and when it boils, put in your plumbs, and give them two or three walms; then take them off the fire, and cover them cloſe for half a quarter of an hour, till you perceive them to look greeniſh and tender; then take them out and weigh them with double refin'd ſugar, equal weight; wet a quarter of a pound of your ſugar in four ſpoonfuls of water, ſet it on the fire, and when it begins to boil, take it off, and put in your plumbs one by one, and ſtrew the reſt of your ſugar upon them, only ſaving a little to put in with your perfume, muſk or ambergreaſe, which muſt be put in a little before they are done: let them boil ſoftly on a moderate fire half an hour or more, till they are green and the ſyrup thickiſh, put your plumbs in a pot or glaſſes; let the ſyrup have two or three walms more, and put it to them; when they are cold paper them up.

To preſerve black Pear Plumbs, or any black Plumb.

TAKE a pound of plumbs, give them a little ſlit in the ſeam; then take ſome of your worſt plumbs, and put them in a gallipot cloſe cover'd, and

and ſet them in a pot of boiling water, and as they yield liquor ſtill pour it out. To a pint of this liquor, take a pound and a quarter of ſugar; put them together, and give them a boil and a ſkim, after which take it off to cool a little; then take your pound of plumbs, and as you put them in, give every one of them a prick or two with a needle, ſo ſet them again on a ſoft fire a pretty while; then take them off, and let them ſtand till the next day, that they may drink up the ſyrup without breaking the ſkin; the next day warm them again once or twice, till you ſee the ſyrup grows thick, and the plumbs look of the right black, ſtill ſkimming them, and when they will endure a boil, give them two or three walms, and ſkim them well, and put them in your glaſſes. Be ſure you keep ſome of the ſyrup in a glaſs, that when your plumbs are ſettled and cold, you may cover them with it. The next day paper them up, and keep them for uſe.

To make white Jelly of Quinces.

PARE your quinces, and cut them in halves; then core and parboil them; when they are ſoft, take them up and cruſh them through a ſtrainer, but not too hard, only the clear juice. Take the weight of the juice in fine ſugar; boil the ſugar candy high, and put in your juice and let it ſcald a while, but not boil; if any froth ariſe, ſkim it off, and when you take it up, have ready a white preſerved quince cut in ſmall ſlices, laying them in the bottom of your glaſſes, and pour your jelly to them; it will candy on the top and keep moiſt on the bottom a long time.

To make clear Cakes of the Jelly of any Fruit.

TO half a pound of jelly, take ſix ounces of ſugar; wet your ſugar with a little water, and boil it candy high; then put in your jelly; let it boil very faſt till it jelly; then put it into glaſſes, and when it is dried enough on one ſide, turn it into glaſs plates. Set them in a ſtove to dry leiſurely; let your ſtove be hot againſt your cakes be turned.

To make clear Cakes of any Sort.

TAKE your gooſeberries, or other fruit, and put them in an earthen pot ſtopt very cloſe, and put them in a kettle of water, and let them boil till they break; then take them out, and run them through a cloth; take the weight of the liquor in ſugar; boil the ſugar candy high; then put in your juice, and let it ſtand over a few embers to dry till it is thick like a jelly; if you fear it will change colour, put in three or four drops of juice of lemon; pour it out into clear cake glaſſes, and dry them with a little fire.

To make brown Sugar.

TAKE gum arabick, and diſſolve it in water till it is pretty thick; then take as much double refined ſugar finely ſifted and perfumed as will make the gum into a ſtiff paſte; roll it out like jumballs, and ſet it in an oven exactly heated, that it may raiſe them and not boil; for if it boils it is ſpoiled; you may colour ſome of them.

To make Paſtils.

TAKE double refined ſugar beaten and ſifted as fine as flour; perfume it with muſk and ambergreaſe; then have ready ſteeped ſome gum arabick in orange-flower water, and with that make the ſugar into a ſtiff paſte; drop into ſome of it three or four drops of oil of mint, oil of cloves, oil of cinnamon, or what oil you like, and let ſome only have the perfume; then roll them up in your hand like little pellets, and ſqueeze them flat with a ſeal. Dry them in the ſun.

To

To fricasee Almonds.

TAKE a pound of *Jordan* almonds, do not blanch them, or but one half of them: beat the white of an egg very well, and pour it on your almonds, and wet them all over; then take half a pound of double refined sugar, and boil it to sugar again; put your almonds in, and stir them till as much sugar hangs on them as will; then set them on plates, and put them into the oven to dry after bread is drawn, and let them stay in all night. They will keep the year round if you keep them dry, and are a pretty sweetmeat.

To make Almond Cakes.

BOIL a pound of double refined sugar up to a thin candy; then have in readiness half a pound of almonds blanched, and finely beaten with some rose or orange-flower water, the juice of one lemon, the peels of two grated into the juice; put all these together, stir them over a gentle fire till all the sugar is well melted, but be sure it does not boil after the lemon is in; then put it into your clear cake glasses: perfume them, and when they are a little dry, cut them into what shape you please.

To make Orange Cakes.

PARE your oranges very thin, and take off the white rinds in quarters; boil the white rinds very tender, and when they are enough, take them up, scrape the black off, and squeeze them between two trenchers; beat them in a stone mortar to a fine pulp with a little sugar; pick the meat out of the oranges from the skins and seeds, and mix the pulp and meat together, and take the weight and half of sugar; boil the sugar to a candy height, and put in the oranges, stir them well together, and when it is cold drop them on a pye-plate, and set them in a stove. You may perfume them. To the rinds of six oranges put the meat of nine lemons. Cakes are made the same way, only as many rinds as meat, and twice the weight of sugar.

To make March-pane unboiled.

TAKE a pound of almonds, blanch them and beat them in rose-water; when they are finely beaten, put to them half a pound of sugar, beat and searced, and work it to a paste; spread some on wafers, and dry it in an oven; when it is cold, have ready the white of an egg beaten with rose-water, and double refined sugar. Let it be as thick as butter, then draw your march-pane thro' it, and put it in the oven: it will ice in a little time, then keep them for use.

If you have a mind to have your march-pane large, cut it when it is rolled out by a pewter-plate, and edge it about the top like a tart, and bottom with wafer-paper, and set it in the oven, and ice it as aforesaid: when the icing rises, take it out, and strew coloured comfits on it, or serve sweetmeats on it.

To preserve Cherries.

PICK and stone your cherries; weigh them, and take their weight of single refined sugar beaten fine; mix three parts of the sugar with juice of currants, put it in your preserving-pan, giving it a boil and a skim, and then put in your cherries; let them boil very fast, now and then strewing in some of the sugar that was left till all is in; skim it well, and when they are enough, which you may know by trying some in a spoon, and when it jellies, take it off, and fill your glasses, and when they are cold, paper them up.

To preserve Currants in Jelly.

TAKE your currants, strip them, and put them in an earthen pot; tie them close down, set them in a kettle of boiling water, and let them stand three hours, keeping the water boiling; then

then take a clean flaxen cloth, and ſtrain out the juice; when it has ſettled, take a pound of double refined ſugar, beaten and ſifted, and put to a pint of the clear juice; have in readineſs ſome whole currants ſtoned, and when the juice boils, put in your currants, and boil them till your ſyrup jellies, which you may know by taking up ſome in a ſpoon; then put it in your glaſſes. This way make jelly of currants, only leaving out the whole currants; when cold, paper them up.

To preſerve Barberries.

TAKE the largeſt barberries you can get, and ſtone them; to every pound of barberries take three pounds of ſugar, and boil it till is candy high; then put in the barberries, and let them boil till the ſugar boils over them all; then take them off, ſkim them, ſet them on again, and give them another boil, and put them in an earthen pan, cover them with paper, and ſet them by till the next day; then put them in pots, and pour the ſyrup over them; cover them with paper, and keep them in a ſtove. If the ſyrup grows thin you may make a little jelly of pippins, and put them in when it is ready, and give them one walm, and pour them again into glaſſes.

To preſerve whole Pippins.

TAKE *Kentiſh* pippins or apple-johns, pare them, and ſlice them into fair water; ſet them on a clear fire, and when they are boiled to maſh, let the liquor run through a hair ſieve. Boil as many apples thus, till you have the quantity of liquor you would have. To a pint of this liquor you muſt have a pound of double refined ſugar in great lumps, wet the lumps of ſugar with the pippin liquor, ſet it over a gentle fire, let it boil, and ſkim it well, and while you are making the jelly, you muſt have your whole pippins boiling at the ſame time; they muſt be the faireſt and beſt pippins you can get; ſcoop out the cores, and pare them neatly, and put them into fair water as you do them; you muſt likewiſe make a ſyrup ready to put them into, the quantity as you think will boil them in clear; you muſt make that ſyrup with double refined ſugar and water; tie up your whole pippins in a piece of fine muſlin ſeverally, and when your ſugar and water boils put them in; let them boil very faſt, ſo faſt that the ſyrup always boils over them; ſometimes take them off, and then ſet them on again, and let them boil till they are clear and tender; then take off the tiffany or muſlin they were tied up in, and put them into glaſſes that will hold but one in a glaſs; then ſee if your jelly of apple-johns be boiled to jelly enough; if it be, ſqueeze in the juice of two lemons, and put muſk and ambergreaſe in a rag, and let it have a boil; then ſtrain it through a jelly-bag into the glaſſes your pippins were in; you muſt be ſure to drain your pippins well from the ſyrup they were boiled in; before you put them in you glaſſes, you may if you pleaſe boil lemon-peel in little pieces in water till they are tender, and then boil them in the ſyrup your pippins were boiled in; then take them out, and lay them about the pippins before the jelly is put in; when they are cold, paper them up.

To make Pippin Jelly.

TAKE fifteen pippins pared, cored and ſliced, and put them into a pint and half of water, let them boil till they are tender, then put them ir a ſtrainer, and let the thin run from them as much as it will; to a pint of liquor take a pound of double refined ſugar; wet your ſugar, and boil it to ſugar again; then cut ſome chips of candied orange or lemon-peel, cut it as fine as threads, and put it into your ſugar, and then your liquor, and let it boil till it is a jelly, which will be quickly; you may perfume it with ambergreaſe if you pleaſe; pour the jelly into shallow glasses; when it is cold paper it up, and keep it in your stove.

To candy Angelica.

TAKE angelica that is young, cut it in fit lengths, and boil it till it is pretty tender, keeping it close covered; then take it up and peel off the strings, then put it in again, and let it simmer and scald till it is very green; then take it up, dry it in a cloth, and weigh it, putting to every pound of angelica a pound of double refined sugar beaten and sifted; put your angelica in an earthen pan, strew the sugar over it, and let it stand two days, then boil it till it looks very clear; put it in a colander to dry the syrup from it, and take a little double refined sugar and boil it to sugar again; then throw in your angelica, and take it out in a little time, and put it on glass plates; it will dry in your stove, or in an oven after pies are drawn.

To make Jelly of white Currants.

TAKE your largest currants, strip them into a bason; bruise and strain them, and to every pint of juice a pound of double refined sugar; just wet your sugar with a little fair water, and set it on a slow fire till it melts; then make it boil, and at the same time let your juice boil in another thing; skim them both very well, and when they have boiled a pretty while, take off your sugar, and strain the juice into it through a muslin; then set it on the fire and let it boil; if you please you may stone some white currants and put them in, and let them boil till they are clear; have a care you do not boil them too high; let them stand a while, then put them in glasses.

If you would make clear cakes of white currants, boil the juice just as this is; but this observe, that when you put your juice and sugar together, they must stand but so long on the fire till they are warm and well mixed, they must boil together; and when it is cold put it in flat glasses, and into your stove to dry them; turn them often.

To make white Marmalade.

TAKE your quinces, scald them, pare them, and scrape the pulp clean from the cores, adding to every pound of pulp a pound of double refined sugar; put a little water to your sugar to dissolve it, and boil it candy high; then put in the quince-pulp, and set it on the fire till it comes to a body; let it boil very fast; when it is enough put it in gallipots.

To make red Quince Marmalade.

PARE, core, and quarter your quinces, then weigh them, and to a pound of quince allow a pound of single refined sugar beaten small, and to every pound of quince a pint of liquor; make your liquor thus; put your parings and cores, and three or four quinces cut in pieces, into a large skillet, with water proportionable to the quantity of quinces you do; cover it and set it over the fire, and let it boil two or three hours; then put in a quart of barberries, and let them boil an hour, and strain all out; then put your quince, and liquor, and a quarter of your sugar, into a skillet or large preserving-pan, and let them boil together over a gentle fire; cover it close, and take care it does not burn; strew in the rest of your sugar by degrees, and stir it often from the bottom, but do not break the quince till it is near enough; then break it in lumps as small as you like it; when it is of a good colour and very tender, try some in a spoon; if it jellies it is enough, then take it off, and put it in gallipots; when it is cold paper it up.

To make Marmalade of Cherries.

TAKE four pounds of cherries, stone them and put them in a preserving-pan, with a quart of juice of currants; set them on a charcoal fire, and

let

let the fire draw away most of the juice; break or mash them, and boil three pounds of sugar candy high, and put the cherries to it, and set it on the fire again, and boil it till it comes to a body; so put it in glasses, and when it is cold paper it up.

To make a Paste of green Pippins.

TAKE pippins, scald them, and peel them till they are green; when you have peeled them, have fresh warm water ready to put them into, and cover them close, and keep them warm till they are very green; then take the pulp of them, but none of the core, and beat it in a mortar, and pass it through a colander, and to a pound of the pulp put a pound and an ounce of double refined sugar, boil your sugar till it will ball between your fingers, put in your pulp, and take it off the fire to mix it well together; set it on the fire again, and boil it till it is enough, which you may know by dropping a little on a plate, and then put it in what form you please; dust it with sugar, and set in the stove to dry; turn it, and dust the other side.

To make white Quince Paste.

SCALD the quinces tender to the core, pare them, and scrape the pulp clean from the core; beat it in a mortar, and pulp it through a colander; take to a pound of pulp a pound and two ounces of sugar; boil the sugar till it is candy high, then put in your pulp; stir it about constantly till you see it come clear from the bottom of the preserving-pan, then take it off and lay it on plates pretty thin; you may cut it in what shape you please, or make quince chips of it; you must dust it with sugar when you put it into the stove, and turn it on papers in a sieve, and dust the other side; when they are dry put them in boxes, with papers between; you may make red quince paste the same way as this, only colour the quince with cochineal.

To dry Pears or Apples.

TAKE poppering pears, and thrust a picked stick into the head of them beyond the core; then scald them, but not too tender, and pare them the long way; put them in water, and take the weight of them in sugar; clarify it with water, a pint of water to a pound of sugar; strain the syrup, and put in the pears; set them on the fire and boil them pretty fast for half an hour; cover them with paper and set them by till the next day; then boil them again, and set them by till the next day; then take them out of the syrup, and boil it till it is thick and ropy; then put the syrup to them; if it will not cover them, add some sugar to them; set them over the fire and let them boil up, then cover them with paper and set them in a stove twenty four hours; then lay them on plates, dust them with sugar, and set them in your stove to dry; when one side is dry, lay them on papers, turn them, and dust the other side with sugar; squeeze the pears flat by degrees; if it is apples, squeeze the eye to the stalk; when they are quite dry put them in boxes, with papers between.

To dry Pears or Pippins without Sugar.

TAKE your pears or apples, wipe them clean, and take a bodkin and run it in at the head and out at the stalk; put them in a flat earthen pot and bake them, but not too much; you must put a quart of strong new ale to half a peck of pears, tie white paper over the pot, that they may not be scorched in baking; and when they are bak'd let them stand to be cold, and take them out to drain; squeeze the pears flat, and the apples the eye to the stalk; lay them on sieves with wide holes to dry, either in a stove or an oven that is not too hot.

To

To candy any Sort of Flowers.

TAKE your flowers, and pick them from the white part; then take fine ſugar and boil it candy high, boil as much as you think will receive the quantity of flowers you do, then put in the flowers, and ſtir them about till you perceive the ſugar to candy well about them; then take them off from the fire, and keep them ſtirring till they are cold in the pan you candied them in; then ſift the looſe ſugar from them, and keep them in boxes very dry.

To candy Orange Flowers.

TAKE half a pound of double refined ſugar, finely beaten, wet it with orange-flower water, and boil it candy high; then put in a handful of orange-flowers, keeping it ſtirring, but let it not boil; when the ſugar candies about them, take it off the fire; drop it on a plate, and ſet it by till it is cold.

To make Syrup of any Flowers.

CLIP your flowers, and take their weight in ſugar; then take a gallipot, and put a row of flowers and a ſtrewing of ſugar, till the pot is full; then put in two or three ſpoonfuls of the ſame ſyrup or ſtill'd water; tie a cloth on the top of the pot, put a tile on that, ſet your gallipot in a kettle of water over a gentle fire, and let it infuſe till the ſtrength is out of the flowers, which will be in four or five hours; then ſtrain it through a flannel, and when it is cold bottle it up.

To candy any ſort of Fruit.

AFTER you have preſerved your fruit, dip them ſuddenly into warm water, to take off the ſyrup; then ſift on them double refined ſugar till they look white; then ſet them on a ſieve in a warm oven, taking them out to turn two or three times; let them not be cold till they be dry, and they will look clear as diamonds; ſo keep them dry.

Another Way to preserve Oranges.

TAKE right *Seville* oranges, the thickest rind you can get, lay them in water, changing the water twice a day for two days, then rub them well with salt, wash them well afterwards, and put them in water, changing the water twice a-day for two days more; then put them in a large pot of water to boil, having another pot of boiling water ready to throw them into, as the other grows bitter; change them often till they are tender; then take them up in a linen cloth, and a woollen over it, to keep them hot; take out one at a time, and make a little hole at the top, and pick out the seeds, but do not break the meat; pare them as thin as you can with a sharp penknife; take to a pound of oranges before they are open'd, a pound of double refined sugar and a pint of fair water, boil it and skim it, and let it be ready when you pare them, to throw them into; when they are all pared, set them on the fire, cover them close, and keep them boiling as fast as they can boil, till they look clear; then take them up into a deep gallipot, with the holes upward, fill them with syrup, and when they are almost cold, pour the rest of the syrup over them; let them stand a fortnight or three weeks in that syrup; then make a jelly of pippins, and when it is almost ready, take your oranges out of the gallipot, pour all the syrup out of them, put them into the jelly, and let them have a boil or two; then put them into your glasses, and when they are near cold fill them with jelly; the next day paper them.

To preserve Gooseberries in Hops.

TAKE the largest *Dutch* gooseberries, and with a knife cut them a-cross at the head and half way down, picking out the seeds clean with a bodkin, but do not break them; then take fine long thorns, scrape them, and put them on your gooseberries, putting the leaf of the one to the cut of the other, and so so till your thorn is full; then put them into a new pipkin with a close lid, cover them with water, and let them stand scalding till they are green; then take them up, and lay them upon a sieve to drain from the water, be sure they boil not in the greening, for if they have but one walm they are spoiled; and while they are greening make a syrup for them. Take whole green gooseberries and boil them in water till they all break, then strain the water through a sieve, and weigh your hops, and to a pound of hops put a pound and half of double refined sugar, put the sugar and hops into the liquor, and boil them open till they are clear and green, then take them up and lay them upon pye-plates, and boil your syrup longer; lay your hops in a pretty deep gallipot, and when the syrup is cold pour it on them; cover them with paper, and keep them in a stove.

To preserve Gooseberries whole without stoning.

TAKE the largest preserving gooseberries, and pick off the black eye, but not the stalk, then set them over the fire in a pot of water to scald, cover them very close, and let them scald, but not boil or break, and when they are tender take them up into cold water; then take a pound and a half of double refined sugar to a pound of gooseberries, clarify the sugar with water, a pint to a pound of sugar; when the syrup is cold, put your gooseberries single into your preserving-pan, put the syrup to them, set them on a gentle fire, and let them boil, but not too fast, lest they break; when they are boiled, and you perceive the sugar has entered them, take them off, cover them with white paper, and set them by till the next day; then take them out of the syrup, and boil the syrup till it begins to be ropy, skim it, and put it to them again, and set them on a gentle fire, and let them preserve gently,

till

till you perceive the syrup will rope; then take them off, and set them by till they are cold, covering them with paper; then boil some gooseberries in fair water, and when the liquor is strong enough strain it out, let it stand to settle, and to every pint take a pound of double refined sugar, make a jelly of it, and put the gooseberries in glasses; when they are cold cover them with the jelly; the next day paper them; wet, and then half dry the paper that goes in the inside, it closes down better; and then put on the other papers, and put them in your stove.

To make Conserve of red Roses, or any other Flowers.

TAKE rose-buds, pick them, and cut off the white part from the red; put the red flowers into a sieve and sift them to take out the seeds; then weigh them, and to every pound of flowers take two pounds and a half of loaf sugar; beat the flowers pretty fine in a stone mortar, then by degrees put the sugar to them, and beat it very well till it is well incorporated together; then put it into gallipots, and tie it over with paper, and over that leather; it will keep for seven years.

To stew Apples.

TAKE to a quart of water a pound of double refined sugar beaten fine, boil and skim it, and put into it a pound of the largest and clearest pippins, pared, cut in halves, and cored; let them boil, cover'd with a continual froth, till they be as tender and clear as you would have them; then put in the juice of two lemons, and a little peel cut like threads; let them have five or six walms after the lemon is in, then put them in a *China* dish or salver you serve them in; they should be done two hours before used.

To

To dry Plumbs or Apricocks.

TAKE your plumbs or apricocks and weigh them, and to every pound of fruit allow a pound of double refin'd ſugar; then ſcald your plumbs, ſtone them, and take off the ſkins, laying your plumbs on a dry cloth; then juſt wet your ſugar, ſet it over the fire, and keep it ſtirring all one way till it boils to ſugar again; take that ſugar, laying ſome in the bottom of your preſerving pan, and your plumbs on it; ſtrew the reſt of the ſugar on the plumbs, and let it ſtand till it is melted; then heat it ſcalding hot twice a-day, but let it not boil; when the ſyrup is very thick, and candies about the pan, then take them out of the ſyrup, lay them on glaſſes to dry, and keep them continually warm, ſifting a little ſugar over them till they are almoſt dry; wet the ſtones in the ſyrup, and dry them with ſugar, and put them at one end of the plumb, and when they are thorough dry, keep them in boxes, with papers between.

To make Sugar of Roſes.

CLIP off all the whites from the red roſe-buds, and dry the red in the ſun; to an ounce of that finely powder'd, you muſt have one pound of loaf ſugar; wet the ſugar with roſe-water (but if in the ſeaſon, juice of roſes) boil it to a candy height; then put in your powder of roſes, and the juice of a lemon; mix it well together; then pour it on a pye-plate, and cut it into lozenges, or what form you pleaſe.

To preſerve ſmall Cucumbers green.

TAKE ſmall cucumbers, boil them, but not very tender; when you take them out of the water, make a hole through every one with a large needle; then pare and weigh them, and to every pound allow a pound of ſugar, which make into ſyrup, with a pint of water to every pound of ſugar; you muſt green

green them before you put them into the ſugar; then let them boil, keeping them cloſe cover'd; then put them by, and for three or four days boil them a little every day; put into the ſyrup the peel of a freſh lemon; then make a freſh ſyrup with double refin'd ſugar, you muſt have three quarters of a pound to a pound of cucumbers, and a quarter of a pint of fair water, the juice of a lemon, and a little ambergreaſe boil'd in it; ſo do them for uſe; paper them when cold.

To preſerve Mulberries whole.

SET ſome mulberries over the fire in a ſkillet, and draw from them a pint of juice, when it is ſtrained; then take three pounds of ſugar beaten very fine, wet the ſugar with the pint of juice; boil up your ſugar and ſkim it, and put in two pounds of ripe mulberries, letting them ſtand in the ſyrup till they are thoroughly warm; then ſet them on the fire, and let them boil very gently; do them but half enough, ſo put them by in the ſyrup till next day; then boil them gently again, and when the ſyrup is pretty thick, and will ſtand in a round drop when it is cold, they are enough; put all together in a gallipot for uſe.

To make Roſe Drops.

THE roſes and ſugar muſt be beat ſeparately into a very fine powder, and both ſifted; to a pound of ſugar an ounce of red roſes; they muſt be mixed together, and then wet with as much juice of lemon as will make it into a ſtiff paſte; ſet it on a ſlow fire in a ſilver porringer, and ſtir it well, and when is is ſcalding hot quite through, take it off and drop it on a paper; ſet them near the fire, the next day they will come off.

To candy Flowers.

GAther your flowers when dry, cut off the leaves as far as the colour is good; according to your

 quantity,

quantity, take of double refined ſugar, and wet it with fair water, and boil it to a candy height; then put in your flowers, of what ſort you pleaſe, as primroſes, violets, cowſlips, or borage with a ſpoon; take them out as quick as you can, with as little of the ſyrup as may be, and lay them in a diſh over a gentle fire, and with a knife ſpread them, that the ſyrup may run from them; then change them upon another warm diſh, and when they are dry from the ſyrup, have ready ſome double refined ſugar beaten and ſifted, and ſtrew ſome on your flowers; then take the flowers in your hand, and rub them gently in the hollow of your hand, and that will open the leaves, a ſtander-by ſtrewing more ſugar into your hand as you ſee convenient; ſo do till they are thoroughly open'd and dry; then put your flowers into a dry ſieve, and ſift all the ſugar clean from them; they muſt be kept in a dry place; roſemary flowers muſt be put whole into your ſyrup; young mint-leaves you muſt open with your fingers, but all bloſſoms rub with your hand as directed.

To make Cakes of Flowers.

BOIL double refin'd ſugar candy high, and then ſtrew in your flowers, and let them boil once up, then with your hand lightly ſtrew in a little double refined ſugar ſifted, and then as quick as may be put it into your little pans, made of card, and prick'd full of holes at bottom; you muſt ſet the pans on a pillow, or cuſhion; when they are cold, take them out.

To make Wormwood Cakes.

TAKE one pound of double refined ſugar ſifted, mix it with the whites of three or four eggs well beat, into this drop as much chymical oil of wormwood as you pleaſe, ſo drop them on paper; you may have ſome white and ſome marble, with ſpecks of colours with the point of a pin; keep your colours ſeverally in little gallipots; for red, take a drachm

drachm of cochineal, a little cream of tartar, as much of allum, tie them up ſeverally in little bits of fine cloth, and put them to ſteep in one glaſs of water two or three hours: when you uſe the colour, preſs the bags in the water, and mix ſome of it with a little of the white of egg and ſugar. Saffron colours yellow, and muſt be tied in a cloth, as the red, and put in water. Powder blue mixed with the ſaffron-water, makes a green: for blue, mix ſome dry powder blue with ſome water.

To candy Orange-Flowers.

TAKE orange-flowers that are ſtiff and freſh pick'd, boil them in a good quantity of ſpring water in a preſerving pan; when they are tender, take them out, drain them in a ſieve, and lay them between two napkins till they be very dry; take the weight of your flowers in double refined ſugar, if you have a pound, take half a pint of water and boil with the ſugar, till it will ſtand in a drop, then take it off the fire, and when it is almoſt cold put it to the flowers, which muſt be in a ſilver baſon; ſhake them very well together, and ſet them in a ſtove or in the ſun, and as they begin to candy, take them out, and put them on glaſſes to dry, keeping them turning till they are dry.

A fine way to preſerve Raſpberries.

TAKE the juice of red and white raſpberries and codlin jelly; to a pint and half, two pounds of double refined ſugar; boil it, and ſcum, and then put in three quarters of a pound of large pick'd raſpberries; let them boil very faſt, till they jelly and are clear; don't take them off the fire, that will make them hard; a quarter of an hour will do them when they begin to boil; then put your raſpberries in the glaſs firſt, and ſtrain the ſeeds from the jelly, and put it to them; and when they begin to cool, ſtir them gently, that they may not all lie on the top

top of the glass; and when cold, lay papers close on them; first wet the papers, and dry them in a cloth.

To make a strong Apple-Jelly.

LET your water boil in the pan you make it in, and when the apples are par'd and quarter'd, put them into your boiling water; let there be no more water than will just cover them, and let it boil as fast as possible; and when the apples are all to pieces, put in about a quart of water more, and let it boil half an hour longer, then run it thro' a jelly-bag, and use it as occasion for any sort of sweet-meat; in the summer codlins are best, in the winter golden runnets or winter pippins.

To preserve Raspberries whole.

TAKE the full weight of your raspberries in double refined sugar, beaten and sifted; lay your raspberries single in the bottom of your preserving-pan, and put all your sugar over them; set them on a slow fire, till there is some syrup in the bottom of the pan; then set them on a quick fire, till all the sugar be thoroughly melted; give them two or three walms, scum them, take them up, and put them in glasses.

To make Biskets.

TAKE the whites of four eggs, the yolks of ten, beat them a quarter of an hour with four spoonfuls of orange-flower water; add to it one pound of loaf sugar beaten and sifted; then beat them together an hour longer; then stir in half a pound of dry flour, and the peel of a lemon grated; mix it well together, then butter the pans and fill them, searce some sugar over them as you put them into the oven; when they are risen in the oven, take them out and lay them on a clean cloth; and when the oven is pretty cool, put them in again on sieves, and let them stand till they are dry, and will snap in breaking.

To

To make Chocolate Almonds.

TAKE a pound of chocolate finely grated, and a pound and half of the best sugar finely sifted; then soak gum dragant in orange-flower water, and work them into what form you please; the past must be stiff; dry them in a stove.

To make Lemon Puffs.

TAKE a pound and a quarter of double refin'd sugar beaten and sifted, and grate the rinds of two lemons, and mix well with the sugar; then beat the whites of three new-laid eggs very well, and mix it well with your sugar and lemon peel; beat them together an hour and a quarter, then make it up in what form you please; be quick to set them in a moderate oven; don't take them off the papers till cold.

To preserve Oranges whole.

TAKE the best and largest *Seville* oranges, water them three days, shifting them twice a day, boiling them in a copper with a great deal of water till they are tender; they must be tied in a cloth and kept under water, the water must boil before you put them in; then take to every pound of orange, a pound and half of double refin'd sugar, beaten and sifted; then have in readiness apple-water made of John-apples; take to every pint of that water a pound of sugar; then take a third part of the sugar and put to the water; boil it a while, and set it by to cool; then cut a little hole in the bottom of your orange, pick out all the seeds, and fill them up with what sugar is left; prick your oranges all over with a bodkin, then put them into your syrup, boiling them so fast that the syrup may cover them, then put in your sugar that is left: when the syrup will jelly, and the oranges look clear, they are enough; then glass them with the holes uppermost, and pour the syrup upon them.

To make Almond Loaves.

BLanch your almonds in hot water, and throw them into cold; then take their weight in double refined sugar finely searced, beat them together until they come to a paste; make them up into little loaves, and ice them over with some white of egg and sugar; bake them on paper; if you please you may throw your almonds into orange-flower water instead of cold water.

To make Lemon Bisket.

TAKE six yellow rinds well beat, with a pound of double refin'd sugar, and whites of four eggs, till come to a paste; lay them on wafer-paper, so bake them on tins.

To make Orange Chips crisp.

PARE your oranges very thin, leaving as little white on the peel as possible; throw the rinds into fair water as you pare them off, then boil them therein very fast till they are tender, still filling up the pan with boiling water as it wastes away; then make a thin syrup with part of the water they were boil'd in, and put the rinds therein, and just let 'em boil; then take them off, and let them lie in the syrup three or four days; then boil them again, till you find the syrup begins to draw between your fingers; then take them off, from the fire, and let them drain through a colander; take out but a few at a time, because, if they cool too fast, it will be difficult to get the syrup from them, which must be done by passing every piece of peel through your fingers, and laying them single on a sieve, with the rind uppermost; the sieves may be set in a stove, or before the fire; but in summer the sun is hot enough to dry them; three pounds of sugar will make syrup to do the peels of twenty-five oranges.

To make Syrup of Orange Peel.

TO every pint of the water, in which the orange-peels were steep'd, put a pound of sugar, boil it, and when it has boiled a little squeeze in some juice of lemon, making it more or less sharp to your taste; filter the lemon-juice thro' cap-paper; as it boils skim it clear; when boiled enough to keep, take it off the fire, and when cold bottle it; when your orange-peels are dried on one side, turn the other, and do so till they are crisp; brush the sugar from them, then take a cloth dipt in warm water and wipe off all that remains of sugar on the rind side; then lay them on the sieve again, and in an hour they will be dry enough to put into your boxes to keep.

To make Orange Marmalade.

TAKE a pound of the best *Seville* oranges, pare off all the yellow rind very thin, quarter the peel, put them in water, cover them down close, and shift the water six or seven times as it boils, to take the bitterness out, and that they may look clear and be tender; then take them out, dry them in a cloth, take out all the strings, and cut them thin as palates; then take a pound of double refin'd sugar beaten, and boil it with a little water to a candy height; skim it clean and put in your peels, let them boil near half an hour; have in readiness your orange-meat all pick'd from the skins and seeds, and the juice of two large lemons, and put it into the peels, boiling all together a quarter of an hour longer; so glass it up, and paper it when cold.

To make Orange Cakes.

CUT your oranges, pick out all their meat and juice free from the strings and seeds, and set it by; then boil it, and shift the water till your peels are tender; dry them in a cloth, mince them small,

ſmall, and put them to the juice; to a pound of that weigh a pound and a half of double refined ſugar; dip your lumps of ſugar in water, and boil it to a candy height; take it off the fire, and put in your juice and peel, ſtir it well, and when it is almoſt cold put it in a baſon, and ſet it in a ſtove; then lay it thin on earthen plates to dry, and as it candies faſhion it with your knife; and as they dry lay them on glaſs; when your plate is empty, put more out of your baſon.

To make Lemon Cakes.

GRATE off the yellow rind of your lemon, and ſqueeze your juice to that peel; take two apples to every lemon, pare and core them, and boil them clear, then put them to your lemon; to a pound of this put two pounds of double refined ſugar, then order it as the orange.

To candy Orange Flowers.

TAKE orange-flowers that are ſtiff and freſh, boil them in a good quantity of ſpring-water in a preſerving-pan, and when they are tender take them up, drain them through a ſieve, and dry them between napkins every day; take their weight in double refined ſugar, and to a pound put half a pint of water, boil it till it ſtands in a thick drop, and when it is almoſt cold put it to your flowers in a ſilver or *China* baſon; ſhake them well together, and ſet them in a ſtove, or in the ſun, and when they begin to candy take them out, and lay them on glaſſes to dry; ſift ſugar on them, and turn them every day till they are criſp.

To make clear Candy.

TAKE ſix ounces of water, and four ounces of fine ſugar ſearced, ſet it on a ſlow fire to melt without ſtirring, let it boil till it comes to a ſtrong candy; then have ready your peel or fruit ſcalded hot in the ſyrup they were kept in, drain them very well from it, and put them into your candy, which you muſt rub on the ſides of your baſon with the back of your ſpoon till you ſee the candy pretty white; take out the fruit with a fork, touch it not with your fingers; if right, the candy will ſhine on your fruit, and dry in three or four hours in an indifferent hot ſtove; lay your fruit on ſieves.

To keep Fruit in Syrup to candy.

IF you candy orange or lemon-peels, you muſt firſt rub them with ſalt, then cut in what faſhion you pleaſe, and keep them in water two days, then boil them tender, ſhifting the water you boil them in two or three times; you muſt have a ſyrup ready, a pint of water to a pound of ſugar, ſcald your peels in it till they look clear. Fruit is done the ſame way, but not boil'd till you put them in your ſyrup; you muſt heat your ſyrup once a week, taking out your fruit, and put them in again while the ſyrup is hot; the ſyrup will keep all the year.

To dry Apricocks like Prunello's.

TAKE a pound of apricocks, being cut in halves or quarters, let them boil till they be very tender in a thin ſyrup; let them ſtand a day or two in the ſtove; then take them out of the ſyrup, and lay them drying till they be as dry as prunello's, then box them; you may make your ſyrup red with the juice of red plumbs; if you pleaſe you may pare them.

To preſerve green Cucumbers.

TAKE gerkins, rub them clean, and green them in hot water; then take their weight in double refin'd ſugar, boil it to a thick ſyrup with a quarter of a pint of ſpring-water to every pound of ſugar; then put in your cucumbers and ſet them over the fire, but not to boil faſt, ſo do two or three days; the laſt day boil them till they are tender and clear, ſo glaſs them up. 5

To

To make clear Cakes of Gooseberries.

TAKE your white *Dutch* gooseberries when they are thorough ripe, break them with your fingers, and squeeze out all the pulp into a fine piece of cambrick or thick muslin, to run thro' clear; then weigh the juice and sugar one against the other; then boil the juice a little while; then put in your sugar and let it dissolve, but not boil; skim it and put it into glasses, and stove it in a warm stove.

Another Way to make Orange Marmalade.

RASP your oranges, cut out all the meat, boil the rinds very tender, and cut them very fine; then take three pounds of double refined sugar, and a pint of water, boil and skim it, and then put in a pound of rind; boil very fast till the sugar is very thick, then put in the meat of your oranges, the seeds and skins being pick'd out, and a pint of very strong pippin jelly; boil all together very fast half an hour, then put it in flat pots or glasses; when it is cold paper it up.

To preserve Cherries.

GATHER your cherries of a bright red, not too ripe, weigh them, and to every pound of cherries put three quarters of a pound of double refin'd sugar beaten fine; stone them, and strew some sugar on them as you stone them; to keep their colour, wet your sugar with fair water, near half a pint, and boil and skim it, then put in three small spoonfuls of the juice of currants that was infused with a little water; give it another boil and skim, and put in your cherries; boil them till they are tender, then pour them into a *China* bason; cover them with paper, and set them by twenty-four hours; then put them in your preserving pan and boil them till they look clear; put them in your glass clear from the syrup, and put the syrup on them strain'd thro' muslin.

To preserve green Apricocks.

BEFORE the stones are hard, wet them and lay them in a coarse cloth, and put to them two or three handfuls of salt, rubbing them till the roughness is off; then put them in scalding water, and set them over the fire till almost boiled; then set them off till almost cold; do this two or three times; after this let them be close covered, and when they look green, let them boil till they begin to be tender; weigh them, and take their weight in double refined sugar, to a pound of sugar half a pint of water; make the syrup, and when almost cold put in your apricocks, boil them well till clear; warm the syrup two or three times till thick, or put them in cold jelly, or dry them as you use them.

To preserve Apricocks that are ripe.

GATHER your apricocks about half ripe, before they look too yellow; weigh them, and to every pound put three quarters of a pound of treble refined sugar finely beaten and sifted; then pare them, and cut them in the parting to take out the stone; then make a fine syrup of the sugar, keeping a little out to strew on them whilst they are boiling; and after they are boiled a little, take them out of the pan and put them in a bason; cover them close with paper, and let them stand twenty-four hours; be careful not to break them in taking them out; the next day boil them up for good; put them into your glasses with care; strain your syrup over them through muslin.

To candy Orange Chips.

PARE your oranges, and soak the peelings in water two days, shifting the water twice; but if you love them bitter, soak them not; tie your peels up in a cloth, and when your water boils put them in, and let them boil till they are tender; then take what double refined sugar will do, break it

small

ſmall, wet it with a little water, and let it boil till it is near candy high; then cut your peels of what lengths you pleaſe, and put them into the ſyrup; ſet them on the fire, and let them heat well through; then let them ſtand a while; heat them twice a day, but not boil; let them be ſo done till they begin to candy, then take them out and put them on plates to dry, and when dry keep them near the fire.

To candy Orange Flowers.

FIRST pick your orange-flowers, and boil them quick in fair water till they are very tender; then drain them through a hair ſieve very clean from the water; to a pound of double refined ſugar take half a pint of fair water, and as much orange-flower water, and boil it up to a thick ſyrup; then pour it out into broad flat glaſſes, and let the ſyrup ſtand in the glaſſes about an inch thick; when it is near cold, drop in your flowers, as many as you think convenient, and ſet your glaſſes in a ſtove with a moderate heat, for the ſlower they candy, the finer the rock will be; when you ſee it is well candied top and bottom, and that it glitters, break the candy at top in as great flakes as you can, and lay the biggeſt piece at the bottom on glaſs-plates, and pick out the reſt, piling it up with the flowers to what ſize you pleaſe; after that it will preſently be dry in a ſtove.

To ſcald Fruit for preſent Uſe.

PUT your fruit into boiling water, as much as will almoſt cover them, ſet them over a ſlow fire, keep it in a ſcald till tender, turning the fruit where the water does not cover; when tender, lay paper cloſe on it, let it ſtand till cold; to a pound of fruit put half a pound of ſugar; let it boil, but not faſt, till it looks clear; all fruit are done whole but pippins, and they in halves, with orange or lemon-peel, and juice of lemon; cut your peel very thin, like threads, and strew them on your pippins.

To make Marmalade of Apricocks.

GATHER your apricocks just turn'd from the green, of a very pale yellow, pare them thin and weigh them, three quarters of a pound of double refined sugar to a pound of apricocks; then cut them in halves, take out the stones, and slice them thin; beat your sugar, and put it in your preserving pan with your sliced apricocks, and three or four spoonfuls of water; boil and skim them, and when they are tender put them in glasses.

To make a Gooseberry Gam.

GATHER your gooseberries full ripe, but green, top and tail them, and weigh them, a pound of fruit to three quarters of a pound of double refined sugar, and half a pint of water; boil them till clear and tender, then put it in pots.

To keep Orange Flowers in Syrup.

PICK off the leaves, and throw them in water boiling on the fire, and squeeze into it the juice of two or three lemons; let them boil half a quarter of an hour, and then throw them into cold water; then lay them on cloths to drain well; then beat and sift some double refined sugar, lay some on the bottom of a gallipot, and then a layer of flowers, and then more sugar, till all is in; when the sugar melts put in more, till there is a pretty deal of syrup, so paper them up for use; you may put them in jelly, or what you please.

To make white Quince Marmalade.

SCALD your quinces tender, take off the skin, aud pulp them from the core very fine, and to every pound of quince have a pound and a half of double refined sugar in lumps, and half a pint of water; dip your sugar in the water, and boil and skim

ſkim it till it is a thick ſyrup; then put in your quince, boil and ſkim it on a quick fire a quarter of an hour, ſo put it in your pots.

To make red Quince Marmalade.

PARE and core a pound of quince, beat the parings and cores and ſome of your worſt quinces, and ſtrain out the juice; to every pound of quince take ten or twelve ſpoonfuls of that juice and three quarters of a pound of loaf ſugar; put all into your preſerving-pan, cover it cloſe, and let it ſtew over a gentle fire two hours; when it is of an orange-red, uncover, and boil it up as faſt as you can; when of a good colour, break it as you like it; give it a boil and pot it up.

To preſerve Apricocks ripe.

GATHER your apricocks of a fine colour, but not too ripe; weigh them, and to every pound of apricocks put a pound of double refin'd ſugar beaten and ſifted; ſtone and pare your apricocks; as you pare them put them into the pan you do them in, with ſugar ſtrew'd over and under them; let them not touch one another, but put ſugar between; cover them up and let them lie till the next day, then ſtir them gently till the ſugar is melted; then put them on a quick fire and let them boil half an hour, ſkimming exceeding well all the while; then take it off and cover it till it is quite cold, or till the next day; then boil it again, ſkimming it very well till it is enough; ſo put it in pots.

To preſerve green Apricocks.

TAKE green apricocks, about the middle of *June*, or when the ſtone is hard, put them on the fire in cold water three or four hours, cover them cloſe, but firſt take their weight in double refined ſugar; then pare them nicely; dip your

ſugar

ſugar in water, and boil the water and ſugar very well; then put in your apricocks, and let them boil till they begin to open; then take out the ſtone, and cloſe it up again, and put them in the ſyrup, and let them boil till they are enough, ſkimming all the while; then put them in pots.

To preſerve the great white Plumb.

TO a pound of plumbs take three quarters of a pound of double refined ſugar in lumps; dip your ſugar in water, and boil and ſkim very well; ſlit your plumbs down the ſeam, and put them into the ſyrup with the ſlit downward; let them ſtew over the fire a quarter of an hour; ſkim very well and take them off; and when cold turn them, and cover them up, and turn them in the ſyrup, every day, two or three times a day for five days; then put them in pots.

To make Jelly of Currants.

STRIP your currants, put them in a jug, and infuſe in water; ſtrain out the juice upon ſugar, ſweeten to your taſte, boil it a great while till it jellies, ſkimming all the while, and then put it in your glaſſes.

To make Apricock Chips.

PARE your apricocks, and part them in the middle; take out the ſtone, and cut them croſsways pretty thin; as you cut them ſtrew a very little ſugar over them beaten and ſifted, then ſet them on the fire, and let them ſtew gently a quarter of an hour; then take them off, cover them up, and ſet them by till the next day; then ſet them on the fire as long as before; take them out one by one and lay them on a ſieve; ſtrew ſugar on the ſieve, and over

over them; dry them in the fun or cool oven, turn them often; when dry put them in boxes.

To make a fweet Bag for Linen.

TAKE of orrice roots, fweet calamus, cyprefs roots, of dried lemon-peel, and dried orange-peel; of each a pound; a peck of dried rofes; make all thefe into a grofs powder; coriander feed four ounces, nutmegs an ounce and a half, an ounce of cloves; make all thefe into fine powder and mix with the other; add mufk and ambergreafe; then take four large handfuls of lavender-flowers dried and rubb'd; of fweet-marjoram, orange-leaves, and young walnut-leaves, of each a handful, all dried and rubb'd; mix all together, with fome bits of cotton perfumed with effences, and put it up into filk bags to lay with your linen.

To make the burning Perfume.

TAKE a quarter of a pound of damafk rofe-leaves, beat them by themfelves, an ounce of orrice root fliced very thin and fteeped in rofe-water, beat them well together, and put to it two grains of mufk, as much civet, two ounces of benjamin finely powder'd; mix all together, and add a little powder'd fugar, and make them up in little round cakes, and lay them fingly on papers to dry; fet them in a window where the fun comes, they will dry in two or three days. Make them in *June.*

All

All Sorts of Made Wines.

To make Apricock Wine.

TAKE three pounds of sugar and three quarts of water, let them boil together, and skim it well; then put in six pounds of apricocks pared and stoned, and let them boil till they are tender; then take them up, and when the liquor is cold bottle it up; you may if you please, after you have taken out the apricocks, let the liquor have one boil with a sprig of flower'd clary in it: the apricocks make marmalade, and are very good for present spending.

To make Damsin Wine.

GATHER your damsins dry, weigh them, and bruise them with your hand; put them into an earthen stein that has a faucet, put a wreath of straw before the faucet; to every eight pounds of fruit a gallon of water; boil the water, skim it, and put it to your fruit scalding hot; let it stand two whole days; then draw it off, and put it into a vessel fit for it, and to every gallon of liquor put two pounds and a half of fine sugar; let the vessel be full, and stop it close; the longer it stands the better; it will keep a year in the vessel; bottle it out; the small damsin is the best: you may put a very small lump of double refined sugar in every bottle.

To make Gooseberry Wine.

TAKE to every four pounds of gooseberries a pound and a quarter of sugar, and a quart of fair

fair water; bruise the berries, and steep them twenty-four hours in the water, stirring them often; then press the liquor from them, and put your sugar to the liquor; then put it in a vessel fit for it, and when it has done working stop it up, and let it stand a month; then rack it off into another vessel, and let it stand five or six weeks longer; then bottle it out, putting a small lump of sugar into every bottle; cork your bottles well, and at three months end it will be fit to drink. In the same manner is currant and raspberry wine made; but cherry wine differs, for the cherries are not to be bruised, but stoned, and put the sugar and water together, and give it a boil and a skim, and then put in your fruit, letting it stew with a gentle fire a quarter of an hour; then let it run through a sieve without pressing, and when it is cold put it in a vessel, and order it as your gooseberry or currant wine. The only cherries for wine are, the great bearers, murrey cherries, morelloes, black *Flanders*, or the *John Treduskin* cherries.

Pearl Gooseberry Wine.

TAKE as many as you please of the best pearl gooseberries, bruise them, and let them stand all night; the next morning press or squeeze them out, and let the liquor stand to settle seven or eight hours; then pour off the clear from the settling, and measure it as you put it into your vessel, adding to every three pints of liquor a pound of double refined sugar; break your sugar in small lumps, and put it in the vessel, with a bit of ising-glass, stop it up, and at three months end bottle it out, putting into every bottle a lump of double refined sugar. This is the fine gooseberry wine.

To make Cherry Brandy.

TAKE six dozen pounds of cherries, half red and half black, mash or squeeze them with

you

your hands to pieces, and put to them three gallons of brandy, letting them ſtand ſteeping twenty-four hours; then put the maſhed cherries, and liquor a little at a time, into a canvas bag, and preſs it as long as any juice will run; ſweeten it to your taſte, put it into a veſſel fit for it, let it ſtand a month, and bottle it out; put a lump of loaf ſugar into every bottle.

To make Cherry Wine.

PULL the ſtalks of the cherries, and maſh them without breaking the ſtones; then preſs them hard thro' a hair bag, and to every gallon of liquor put a pound and a half of ſix-penny ſugar; the veſſel muſt be full, and let it work as long as it makes a noiſe in the veſſel; then ſtop it up cloſe for a month or ſix weeks; when it is fine, draw it into bottles, put a lump of loaf ſugar into each bottle, and if any of them fly, open them all for a moment, and cork them well again; it will not be fit to drink in leſs than a quarter of a year.

To make Currant Wine.

TAKE four gallons of currants, not too ripe, and ſtrip them into an earthen ſtein that has a cover to it; then take two gallons and a half of water, and five pounds and a half of double refined ſugar; boil the ſugar, and water together, ſkim it, and pour it boiling hot on the currants, letting it ſtand forty-eight hours; then ſtrain it through a flannel bag into the ſtein again, let it ſtand a fortnight to ſettle, and bottle it out.

To make ſtrong Mead.

TAKE of ſpring-water what quantity you pleaſe, make it more than blood-warm, and diſſolve honey in it till it is ſtrong enough to bear an egg,

egg, the breadth of a shilling, then boil it gently, near an hour, taking off the scum as it rises; then put to about nine or ten gallons, seven or eight large blades of mace, three nutmegs quartered, twenty cloves, three or four sticks of cinnamon, two or three roots of ginger, and a quarter of an ounce of *Jamaica* pepper; put these spices into the kettle to the honey and water, a whole lemon, with a sprig of sweet-briar, and a sprig of rosemary; tie the briar and rosemary together, and when they have boiled a little while, take them out, and throw them away; but let your liquor stand on the spice in a clean earthen pot, till the next day; then strain it into a vessel that is fit for it, put the spice in a bag, hang it in the vessel, stop it, and at three months draw it into bottles: be sure that it is fine when it is bottled; after it is bottled six weeks, it is fit to drink.

To make small white Mead.

TAKE three gallons of spring-water, make it hot, and dissolve in it three quarts of honey, and a pound of loaf sugar; let it boil about half an hour, and skim it as long as any rises; then pour it out into a tub, and squeeze in the juice of four lemons, put in the rinds but of two, twenty cloves, two races of ginger, a top of sweet-briar, and a top of rosemary; let it stand in a tub till it is but blood-warm; then make a brown toast, and spread it with two or three spoonfuls of ale yeast; put it into a vessel fit for it; let it stand four or five days, then bottle it out.

To make Raisin Wine.

TAKE two gallons of spring-water, and let it boil half an hour; then put into a stein-pot two pound of raisins stoned, two pounds of sugar, the rind of two lemons, and the juice of four; then pour

pour the boiling water on the things in the ftein, and let it ftand cover'd four or five days; ftrain it out and bottle it up: in fifteen or fixteen days it will be fit to drink; it is a very cool and pleafant drink in hot weather.

To make Shrub.

TAKE two quarts of brandy, and put it in a large bottle, adding to it the juice of five lemons, the peels of two, and half a nutmeg; ftop it up and let it ftand three days, and add to it three pints of white wine, a pound and half of fugar; mix it, ftrain it twice through a flannel, and bottle it up; it is a pretty wine, and a cordial.

To make Orange Wine.

PUT twelve pounds of fine fugar and the whites of eight eggs well beaten into fix gallons of fpring-water; let it boil an hour, fkimming it all the time; take it off, and when it is pretty cool put in the juice and rind of fifty *Seville* oranges, and fix fpoonfuls of good ale yeaft, and let it ftand two days; then put it into your veffel, with two quarts of rhenifh wine, and the juice of twelve lemons; you muft let the juice of lemons and wine, and two pounds of double refined fugar, ftand clofe cover'd ten or twelve hours before you put it in the veffel to your orange wine, and fkim off the feeds before you put it in; the lemon-peels muft be put in with the oranges, half the rinds muft be put into the veffel; it muft ftand ten or twelve days before it is fit to bottle.

To make Birch Wine.

IN *March* bore a hole in a birch tree, and put in a faucet, and it will run two or three days together without hurting the tree; then put in a pin to ftop it, and

and the next year you may draw as much from the ſame hole; put to every gallon of the liquor a quart of good honey, and ſtir it well together; boil it an hour, ſkim it well, and put in a few cloves and a piece of lemon-peel; when it is almoſt cold put to it ſo much ale yeaſt as will make it work like new ale; and when the yeaſt begins to ſettle, put it in a runlet that will juſt hold it; ſo let it ſtand ſix weeks, or longer if you pleaſe; then bottle it, and in a month you may drink it; it will keep a year or two; you may make it with ſugar, two pounds to a gallon, or ſomething more, if you keep it long; this is admirably wholeſome as well as pleaſant, an opener of obſtructions, good againſt the phthiſic, the ſpleen and ſcurvy, a remedy for the ſtone; it will abate heat in a fever or thruſh, and has been given with good ſucceſs.

To make Sugar Wine.

BOIL twenty-ſix quarts of ſpring-water a quarter of an hour, and when it is blood-warm put twenty-five pounds of *Malaga* raiſins pick'd, rub'd, and ſhred into it, with half a buſhel of red ſage ſhred, and a porringer of ale yeaſt; ſtir all well together, and let it ſtand in a tub covered warm ſix or ſeven days, ſtirring it once a day; then ſtrain it out and put it in a runlet; let it work three or four days, and ſtop it up; when it has ſtood ſix or ſeven days put in a quart or two of *Malaga* ſack, and when it is fine bottle it.

To make Cowſlip Wine.

TO ſix gallons of water put fourteen pounds of ſugar, ſtir it well together, and beat the whites of twenty eggs very well, and mix it with the liquor, and make it boil as faſt as poſſible; ſkim it well, and let it continue boiling two hours; then ſtrain it thro' a hair ſieve, and ſet it a cooling; and when it is as cold as wort ſhould be, put a ſmall quantity of yeaſt to it on a toaſt, or in a diſh; let it ſtand all night working; then bruiſe a peck of cowſlips, put them into your veſſel, and your liquor upon them, adding ſix ounces of ſyrup of lemons; cut a turf of graſs and lay on the bung; let it ſtand a fortnight, and then bottle it; put your tap into your veſſel before you put your wine in, that you may not ſhake it.

To make Raſpberry Wine.

TAKE your quantity of raſpberries and bruiſe them, put them in an open pot twenty-four hours, then ſqueeze out the juice, and to every gallon put three pounds of fine ſugar and two quarts of canary; put it into a ſtein or veſſel, and when it hath done working ſtop it cloſe; when it is fine bottle it: it muſt ſtand two months before you drink it.

To make Raſpberry Wine another way.

POUND your fruit and ſtrain them through a cloth, then boil as much water as juice of raſpberries, and when it is cold put it to your ſqueezings; let it ſtand together five hours, then ſtrain it and mix it with the juice, adding to every gallon of this liquor two pounds and a half of fine ſugar; let it ſtand in an earthen veſſel cloſe cover'd a week, then put it in a veſſel fit for it, and let it ſtand a month, or till it is fine: bottle it off.

To make Morella Cherry Wine.

LET your cherries be very ripe, pick off the ſtalks, and bruiſe your fruit without breaking the ſtones; put them in an open veſſel together; let them ſtand twenty-four hours; then preſs them, and to every gallon put two pounds of fine ſugar; then put it up in your caſk, and when it has done working ſtop it cloſe; let it ſtand three or four months and bottle it; it will be fit to drink in two months.

To make Quince Wine.

TAKE your quinces when they are thorough ripe, wipe off the fur very clean; then take out the cores, bruise them as you do apples for cyder, and press them, adding to every gallon of juice two pounds and a half of fine sugar; stir it together till it is dissolved; then put it in your cask, and when it has done working, stop it close; let it stand till *March* before you bottle it. You may keep it two or three years, it will be the better.

Another sort of Raspberry Wine.

TAKE four gallons of raspberries, and put them in an earthen pot; then take four gallons of water, boil it two hours, let it stand till it is blood-warm, put it to the raspberries, and stir them well together; let it stand twelve hours; then strain it off, and to every gallon of liquor put three pounds of loaf sugar, set it over a clear fire, and let it boil till all the scum is taken off; when it is cold, put it into bottles, and open the corks every day for a fortnight, and then stop them close.

To make Lemon Wine.

TAKE six large lemons, pare off the rind, cut them, and squeeze out the juice; steep the rind in the juice, and put to it a quart of brandy; let it stand in an earthen pot close stopt three days; then squeeze six more, and mix with two quarts of spring-water, and as much sugar as will sweeten the whole; boil the water, lemons, and sugar together, letting it stand till it is cool; then add a quart of white wine, and the other lemon and brandy, and mix them together, and run it thro' a flannel bag into some vessel; let it stand three months and bottle it off; cork your bottles very well, and keep it cool; it will be fit to drink in a month or six weeks.

To make Elder Wine.

TAKE twenty-five pounds of *Malaga* raiſins, rub them and ſhred them ſmall; then take five gallons of fair water; boil it an hour, and let it ſtand till it is but blood-warm; then put it in an earthen crock or tub, with your raiſins; let them ſteep ten days, ſtirring them once or twice a day; then paſs the liquor thro' a hair ſieve, and have in readineſs five pints of the juice of elder-berries drawn off as you do for jelly of currants; then mix it cold with the liquor, ſtir it well together, put it into a veſſel, and let it ſtand in a warm place; when it has done working ſtop it cloſe: bottle it about *Candlemas.*

To make Barley Water.

TAKE of pearl barley four ounces, put it in a large pipkin and cover it with water; when the barley is thick and tender, put in more water and boil it up again, and ſo do till it is of a good thickneſs to drink; then put in a blade or two of mace, or a ſtick of cinnamon; let it have a walm or two and ſtrain it out; ſqueeze in the juice of two or three lemons, and a bit of the peel, and ſweeten it to your taſte with fine ſugar; let it ſtand till it is cold, and then run it through a bag, and bottle it up; it will keep three or four days.

To make Barley Wine.

TAKE half a pound of *French* barley and boil it in three waters, and ſave three pints of the laſt water, and mix it with a quart of white wine, half a pint of borage-water, as much clary-water, a little red roſe-water, the juice of five or ſix lemons, three quarters of a pound of fine ſugar, and the thin yellow rind of a lemon; brew all theſe quick together, run it through a ſtrainer and bottle it up; it is pleaſant in hot weather, and very good in fevers.

To

To make Plumb Wine.

TAKE twenty pounds of *Malaga* raisins, pick, rub, and shred them, and put them into a tub; then take four gallons of fair water, boil it an hour, and let it stand till is blood-warm; then put it to your raisins; let it stand nine or ten days, stirring it once or twice a day; strain out your liquor, and mix with it two quarts of damsin-juice; put it in a vessel, and when it has done working stop it close; at four or five months bottle it.

To make Ebulum.

TO a hogshead of strong ale take a heap'd bushel of elder-berries, and half a pound of juniper-berries beaten; put in all the berries when you put in the hops, and let them boil together till the berries break in pieces, then work it up as you do ale; when it has done working, add to it half a pound of ginger, half an ounce of cloves, as much mace, an ounce of nutmegs, as much cinnamon, grosly beaten, half a pound of citron, as much eryngo root, and likewise of candied orange-peel; let the sweet-meats be cut in pieces very thin, and put with the spice into a bag, and hang it in the vessel when you stop it up; so let it stand till it is fine, then bottle it up, and drink it with lumps of double refined sugar in the glass.

To make Cock Ale.

TAKE ten gallons of ale and a large cock, the older the better; parboil the cock, flay him and stamp him in a stone mortar till his bones are broken (you must craw and gut him when you flay him) then put the cock into two quarts of sack, and put to it three pounds of raisins of the sun stoned, some blades of mace, and a few cloves; put all these into a canvas bag, and a little before you find the ale has done working, put the ale and bag together into a vessel; in a week or nine days time bottle it up; fill the bottle but juſt above the neck, and give it the ſame time to ripen as other ale.

To make Elder Wine at Chriſtmas.

TAKE twenty pounds of *Malaga* or *Lipara* raiſins, rub them clean, and ſhred them ſmall; then take five gallons of water, boil it an hour, and when it is near cold put it in a tub with the raiſins; let them ſteep ten days, and ſtir them once or twice a day; then ſtrain it thro' a hair ſieve, and by infuſion draw three pints of elder-juice, and one pint of damſin-juice; make the juice into a thin ſyrup, a pound of ſugar to a pint of juice, and not boil it much, but juſt enough to keep; when you have ſtrained out the raiſin-liquor, put that and the ſyrup into a veſſel fit for it, and two pounds of ſugar; ſtop the bung with a cork till it gathers to a head, then open it, and let it ſtand till it has done working; then put the cork in again, and ſtop it very cloſe, and let it ſtand in a warm place two or three months, and then bottle it; make the elder and damſin-juice into ſyrup in its ſeaſon, and keep it in a cool cellar till you have convenience to make the wine.

To make fine Milk Punch.

TAKE two quarts of water, one quart of milk, half a pint of lemon-juice, and one quart of brandy, ſugar to your taſte; put the milk and water together a little warm, then the ſugar, then the lemon-juice, ſtir it well together, then the brandy; ſtir it again, and run it through a flannel bag till it is very fine, then bottle it; it will keep a fortnight, or more.

To make Mead.

TO thirteen gallons of water put thirty-two pounds of honey, boil and ſkim it well, then take roſemary, thyme, bay-leaves and ſweet-briar, one handful all together; boil it an hour, then put it into a tub

tub with two or three good handfuls of the flour of malt; stir it till it is but blood-warm, then strain it through a cloth and put it into a tub again; then cut a toast round a quartern loaf, spread it over with good ale yeast, and put it into your tub; when the liquor has done fermenting put it up in your vessel; then take cloves, mace, nutmegs, an ounce and a half, ginger an ounce, sliced; bruise the spice, and tie all up in a rag, and hang it in the vessel; stop it up close for use.

Sage Wine another way.

TAKE thirty pounds of *Malaga* raisins picked clean and shred small, and one bushel of green sage shred small; then boil five gallons of water, let the water stand till it is lukewarm, then put it in a tub to your sage and raisins; let it stand five or six days, stirring it twice or thrice a day; then strain and press the liquor from the ingredients, put it in a cask, and let it stand six months, then draw it clean off into another vessel; bottle it in two days; in a month or six weeks it will be fit to drink, but best when it is a year old.

To make Palermo *Wine.*

TAKE to every quart of water a pound of *Malaga* raisins, rub and cut the raisins small, and put them to the water, and let them stand ten days, stirring once or twice a day; you may boil the water an hour before you put it to the raisins, and let it stand to cool; at ten days end strain out your liquor, and put a little yeast to it; and at three days end put it in the vessel, with one sprig of dried wormwood; let it be close stopt, and at three months end bottle it off.

To make Clary Wine.

TAKE twenty-four pounds of *Malaga* raisins, pick them and chop them very small, put them in a tub, and to each pound a quart of water; let them

them ſteep ten or eleven days, ſtirring it twice every day; you muſt keep it covered cloſe all the while; then ſtrain it off, and put it into a veſſel, and about half a peck of the tops of clary, when it is in bloſſom; ſtop it cloſe for ſix weeks, and then bottle it off; in two or three months it is fit to drink. It is apt to have a great ſettlement at bottom; therefore it is beſt to draw it off by plugs, or tap it pretty high.

To recover Wine that is turned ſharp.

RACK off your wine into another veſſel, and to ten gallons put the following powder; take oyſter-ſhells, ſcrape and waſh off the brown dirty outſide of the ſhell; then dry them in an oven till they will powder; a pound of this powder to every nine or ten gallons of your wine: ſtir it well together, and ſtop it up, and let it ſtand to ſettle two or three days, or till it is fine; as ſoon as it is fine, bottle it off, and cork it well.

To fine Wine the Liſbon *way.*

TO every twenty gallons of wine, take the whites of ten eggs, and a ſmall handful of ſalt; beat it together to a froth, and mix it well with a quart or more of the wine; then pour it into the veſſel, and in a few days it will be fine.

To clear Wine.

TAKE half a pound of hartſhorn, and diſſolve it in cyder, if it be for cyder, or rheniſh wine for any liquor. This is enough for a hogſhead.

To make Raiſin Wine.

TAKE the beſt *Malaga* raiſins, and pick the large ſtalks out, and have your water ready boil'd and cold; meaſure as many gallons as you deſign to make, and put it into a great tub, that it may have room to ſtir: to every gallon of water put ſix pounds of raiſins, and let it ſtand fourteen days, ſtirring

ſtirring it twice a day; when you ſtrain it off, or preſs it, you muſt do nothing to it, but leave enough to fill up your caſk, which you muſt do as it waſtes: it will be two months or more before it has done working: you muſt not ſtop it while you hear it hiſs.

To make Orange Wine with Raiſins.

TAKE thirty pounds of new *Malaga* raiſins, pick them clean, and chop them ſmall; you muſt have twenty large *Seville* oranges, ten of them you muſt pare as thin as for preſerving. Boil about eight gallons of ſoft water, till a third part be conſumed; let it cool a little; then put five gallons of it hot upon your raiſins and orange-peel; ſtir it well together, cover it up, and when it is cold, let it ſtand five days, ſtirring it up once or twice a day; then paſs it through a hair ſieve, and with a ſpoon preſs it as dry as you can, and put it in a runlet fit for it, and put to it the rinds of the other ten oranges, cut as thin as the firſt; then make a ſyrup of the juice of twenty oranges with a pound of white ſugar. It muſt be made the day before you tun it up; ſtir it well together, and ſtop it cloſe; let it ſtand two months to clear, then bottle it up; it will keep three years, and is better for keeping.

To make Cherry Wine.

PULL off the ſtalks of the cherries, and maſh them without breaking the ſtones; then preſs them hard through a hair bag, and to every gallon of liquor put two pounds of eight-penny ſugar. The veſſel muſt be full, and let it work as long as it makes a noiſe in the veſſel, then ſtop it up cloſe for a month or more, and when it is fine, draw it into dry bottles, and put a lump of ſugar into every bottle. If it makes them fly, open them all for a moment, and ſtop them up again; it will be fit to drink in a quarter of a year.

To make Gooseberry Wine.

BOIL eight gallons of water, and one pound of sugar an hour; skim it well, and let it stand till it is cold; then to every quart of that water allow three pounds of gooseberries, first beaten or bruised very well; let it stand twenty four hours; then strain it out, and to every gallon of this liquor put three pounds of seven-penny sugar; let it stand in the vat twelve hours; then take the thick scum off, and put the clear into a vessel fit for it, and let it stand a month; then draw it off, and rinse the vessel with some of the liquor; put it in again, and let it stand four months, and bottle it.

To make Frontiniac Wine.

TAKE six gallons of water, twelve pounds of white sugar, and six pounds of raisins of the sun cut small; boil these together an hour; then take of the flowers of elder, when they are falling, and will shake off, the quantity of half a peck; put them in the liquor when it is almost cold; the next day put in six spoonfuls of syrup of lemons, and four spoonfuls of ale yeast, and two days after put it in a vessel that is fit for it; and when it has stood two months, bottle it off.

To make English Champaign, or the fine Currant Wine.

TAKE to three gallons of water nine pounds of *Lisbon* sugar; boil the water and sugar half an hour, skim it clean, then have one gallon of currants pick'd, but not bruised; pour the liquor boiling-hot over them; and when cold, work it with half a pint of balm two days; then pour it through a flannel or sieve; then put it into a barrel fit for it, with half an ounce of ising-glass well bruised; when it has done working, stop it close for a month; then bottle it, and in every bottle put a very small lump of of double refined sugar; this is excellent wine, and has a beautiful colour.

To make Saragosa *Wine or* English *Sack.*

TO every quart of water put a sprig of rue, and to every gallon a handful of fennel-roots; boil these half an hour, then strain it out, and to every gallon of this liquor put three pounds of honey, boil it two hours, and skim it well; when it is cold, pour it off, and turn it into the vessel, or such cask as is fit for it; keep it a year in the vessel, and then bottle it; it is a very good sack.

To make Cyder.

PULL your fruit before it is too ripe, and let it lie but one or two days, to have one good sweat; your apples must be pippins, pearmains or harveys (if you mix winter and summer fruit together, it is never good;) grind your apples, and press it; when your fruit is all press'd, put it immediately into a hogshead, where it may have some room to work, but no vent, but a little hole between the hoops, but close bung'd; put three or four pounds of raisins into a hogshead, and two pounds of sugar, it will make it work better; often racking it off is the best way to fine it, and always rack it into small vessels, keeping them close bung'd, and only a small vent hole; if it should work after racking, put into your vessel some raisins for it to feed on; and bottle it in *March*.

To make the fine Clary Wine.

TO ten gallons of water put twenty-five pounds of sugar, and the whites of twelve eggs well beaten; set it over the fire, and let it boil gently near an hour; skim it clean, and put it in a tub; and when it is near cold, then put into the vessel you keep it in, about half a strike of clary in the bossom, stript from the stalks, flowers and little leaves together, and a pint of new ale-yeast; then put in the liquor, and stir it two or three times a day for three days; when it it has done working, ſtop it up; and bottle it at three or four months old, if it is clear.

To make Currant Wine.

GATHER your currants full ripe, ſtrip them and bruiſe them in a mortar, and to every gallon of the pulp put two quarts of water, firſt boiled, and cold; you may put in ſome raſps, if you pleaſe; let it ſtand in a tub twenty four hours to ferment, then let it run through a hair ſieve; let no hand touch it; let it take its time to run; and to every gallon of this liquor put two pounds and a half of white ſugar; ſtir it well, and put it in your veſſel, and to every ſix gallons put in a quart of the beſt rectified ſpirit of wine; let it ſtand ſix weeks, and bottle it; if it is not very fine, empty it into other bottles, or at firſt draw it into large bottles; and then, after it has ſtood a fortnight, rack it off into ſmaller.

To make Elder-flower Water.

TAKE two large handfuls of dried elder-flowers, and ten gallons of ſpring-water; boil the water, and pour it ſcalding hot upon the flowers; the next day put to every gallon of water five pounds of *Malaga* raiſins, the ſtalks being firſt pick'd off, but not waſh'd; chop them groſly with a chopping-knife, then put them into your boiled water, and ſtir the water, raiſins and flowers well together; and ſo do twice a day for twelve days; then preſs out the juice clear, as long as you can get any liquor out; then put it in your barrel fit for it, and ſtop it up two or three days till it works; and in a few days ſtop it up cloſe, and let it ſtand two or three months, till it is clear; then bottle it.

To make Elder Wine.

TAKE ſpring water, and let it boil half an hour; then meaſure five gallons, and let it ſtand to cool; then have in readineſs twenty pounds of raiſins of the ſun well picked and rubbed in a cloth, and

and hack them ſo as to cut them, but not too ſmall; then put them in, the water being cold, and let them ſtand nine days, ſtirring them two or three times a day; then have ready ſix pints of the juice of elder-berries full ripe, which muſt be infuſed in boiling water, or baked three hours; then ſtrain out the raiſins, and when the elder liquor is cold, mix that with it; but it is beſt to boil up the juice to a ſyrup, a pound of ſugar to every pint of juice; boil and ſkim it, and when cold mix it with your raiſin liquor, and three or four ſpoonfuls of good ale yeaſt; ſtir it well together; then put it into a veſſel fit for it; let it ſtand in a warm place to work, and in your cellar five or ſix months.

To make Gooſeberry Wine.

TAKE twenty four quarts of gooſeberries full ripe, and twelve quarts of water, after it has boiled two hours; pick and bruiſe your gooſeberries one by one in a platter with a rolling-pin, as little as you can, ſo they be all bruiſed; then put the water, when it is cold, on your maſh'd gooſeberries and let them ſtand together twelve hours; when you drain it off, be ſure to take none but the clear; then meaſure the liquor, and to every quart of that liquor put three quarters of a pound of fine ſugar, the one half loaf-ſugar; let it ſtand to diſſolve ſix or eight hours, ſtirring it two or three times; then put it in your veſſels, with two or three ſpoonfuls of the beſt new yeaſt; ſtop it eaſy at firſt, that it may work if it will; when you ſee it has done working, or will not work, ſtop it cloſe, and bottle it in froſty weather.

Mountain Wine.

PICK out the big ſtalks of your *Malaga* raiſins; then chop them very ſmall, five pounds to every gallon of cold ſpring-water; let them ſteep a fortnight or more, ſqueeze out the liquor, and barrel it in a veſſel fit for it; firſt fume the veſſel with brimſtone; don't ſtop it up till the hiſſing is over.

Lemon

Lemon Wine; or what may pass for Citron Water.

TAKE two quarts of brandy, one quart of spring-water, half a pound of double refined sugar, and the rinds of sixteen lemon; put them together in an earthen pot; pour into it twelve spoonfuls of milk boiling hot; stir it together, and let it stand three days; then take off the top, and pass the other two or three times through a jelly-bag; bottle it; it is fit to drink, or will keep a year or two.

To make strong Beer.

TO a barrel of beer take two bushels of malt, and half a bushel of wheat, just crack'd in the mill, and some of the flour sifted out of it; when your water is scalding hot, put it into your mashing vat; there let it stand till you can see your face in it; then put your malt upon it; then put your wheat upon that, and do not stir it; let it stand two hours and a half; then let it run into a tub that has two pounds of hops in it, and a handful of rosemary-flowers; when it is all run, put it in your copper, and boil it two hours; then strain it off, setting it a cooling very thin, and set it a working very cool; clear it very well before you put it a working; put a little yeast to it, when the yeast begins to fall, put it into your vessel; and when it has done working in the vessel, put in a pint of whole wheat, and six eggs; then stop it up; let it stand a year, and then bottle it; then mash again; stir the malt very well in, and let it stand two hours, and let that run and mash again, and stir it as before; be sure you cover your mashing vat well up; mix the first and second running together, it will make good houshold beer.

To make Elder Ale.

TAKE ten bushels of malt to a hogshead; then put two bushels of elder-berries, pick'd from the

the stalks, into a pot or earthen pan, and set it in a pot of boiling water till the berries swell; then strain it out, and put the juice into the guile-vat, and beat it often in; and so order it as the common way of brewing.

All Sorts of Cordial Waters.

The great Palsey Water.

TAKE of sage, rosemary, and betony-flowers, of each a handful; borage, and bugloss-flowers, of each a handful; of lilly of the valley and cowslip flowers, of each four or five handfuls; steep these in the best sack; then put to them balm, spike-flowers, mother-wort, bay-leaves, leaves of orange-tree, with the flowers, of each one ounce; citron peel, piony-seeds, and cinnamon, of each half an ounce; nutmegs, cardamums, mace, cubebs, yellow sanders, of each half an ounce; lignum aloes, one dram; make all these into powder; then add jujubes, the stones taken out, and cut in pieces, half a pound; pearl prepared, smaragdes, musk and saffron, of each ten grains; ambergrease one scruple, red roses dried one ounce; as many lavender flowers as will fill a gallon glass; steep all these a month, and distil them in an alembick very carefully; then take pearl prepared, smaragdes, musk and saffron, of each ten grains; ambergrease, one scruple; red roses dried, red and yellow sanders, of each one ounce; hang these in a white sarcenet bag in the water; stop it close. This water is of excellent use in all swoonings, in weakness of heart and decay of spirits; it restores speech in apoplexies

plexies and palsies; it helps all pains in the joints from cold or bruises, bathing the place outwardly, and dipping cloths and laying on it; it strengthens and comforts the vital spirits, and helps the memory; restoreth lost appetite, helpeth all weakness of the stomach: taken inwardly, or bathed outwardly, it taketh away giddiness of the head, and helpeth hearing; it makes a pleasant breath, it is good in the beginning of dropsies; none can sufficiently express the virtues of this water: when it is taken inwardly, drop ten or twelve drops on a lump of sugar, a bit of bread, or in a dish of tea; but in a fit of the palsey give so much every hour to restore speech. Add to the rest of the flowers single wall-flowers, and the roots and flowers of single pionies, and missletoe of the oak, of each a good handful.

The Lady Hewet's *Water.*

TAKE red sage, betony, spearmint, unset hyssop, thyme, balm, pennyroyal, celandine, water-cresses, hearts-ease, lavender, angelica, germander, calamint, tamarisk, coltsfoot, avens, valerian, saxifrage, pimpernel, vervain, parsley, rosemary, savory, scabious, agrimony, mother-thyme, wild marjoram, roman wormwood, carduus benedictus, pellitory of the wall, field daisies, flowers and leaves, of each a handful, after they are pick'd and wash'd; of rue, yarrow, comfry, plantane, camomile, maidenhair, sweet marjoram, and dragons, of each a handful, before they are wash'd or pick'd; red rose leaves and cowslip flowers, of each half a peck, rosemary flowers a quarter of a peck, hartshorn two ounces, juniper-berries one drachm, china roots an ounce, comfry-roots slic'd, aniseeds, fennel-seeds, carraway-seeds, nutmegs, ginger, cinnamon, pepper, spikenard, parsley-seeds, cloves and mace, of each three drachms, sassafras slic'd half an ounce, elecampane roots, melilot-flowers, cala-

mus

mus-aromaticus, cardamums, lignum-aloes, rhubarb ſliced thin, galingal, veronica, and cubebs, of each two drachms, muſk twenty-four grains, ambergreaſe twenty grains, powder of coral two drachms, powder of amber one drachm, powder of pearl two drachms, white ſugar-candy one pound; waſh the herbs, and ſwing them in a cloth till they are dry, then cut them and bruiſe the drugs, putting them into an earthen pot; then put thereto ſuch a quantity of ſherry ſack as will cover them, let them ſteep twenty-four hours; then diſtil it at twice in an alembick, drawing from each three pints of water; mix it all together, put it into quart bottles, and divide the cordials into three parts, putting into each bottle of water a like quantity; ſhake it often together at the firſt; the longer you keep it the better it will be; there never was a better cordial in caſes of the greateſt illneſs, two or three ſpoonfuls almoſt revive from death.

The Lady Allen's *Water.*

TAKE of balm, roſemary, ſage, carduus, wormwood, dragons, ſcordium, mugwort, ſcabious, tormentil-roots and leaves, angelica-roots and leaves, marigold-flowers and leaves, betony-flowers and leaves, centaury-tops, pimpernel, wood-ſorrel, rue, agrimony, roſa ſolis, of each half a pound, liquorice four ounces, elecampane-roots, two ounces; waſh the herbs, ſhake and dry them in a cloth, then ſhred them, ſlice the roots, put all into three gallons of the beſt white wine, and let them ſtand cloſe covered two days and two nights, ſtirring them morning and evening; then take out ſome of the herbs, lightly ſqueezing them with your hands, and fill a ſtill full; let them ſtill twelve hours in a cold ſtill with a reaſonable quick fire; then put the reſt of the herbs and the wine in an alembick,

bick, and diſtill them till all the ſtrength is out of the herbs and wine: mix all the water in both ſtills together, ſweeten ſome, but not all; for caſes of great illneſs, warm ſome of that unſweeten'd, blood-warm, and put in it a little ſyrup of gilliflowers, and go to bed, covering warm: it is a very excellent water.

Plague Water.

TAKE roſa ſolis, agrimony, betony, ſcabious, centaury tops, ſcordium, baum, rue, wormwood, mugwort, celandine, roſemary, marigold leaves, brown ſage, burnet, carduus, and dragons, of each a large handful, angelica roots, piony roots, tormentil roots, elecampane roots and liquorice, of each an ounce; cut the herbs, ſlice the roots, put them all into an earthen pot, adding to them a gallon of white wine, and a quart of brandy, and let them ſteep two days cloſe cover'd, then diſtil it in an ordinary ſtill with a gentle fire; you may ſweeten it, but not much.

Dr. Stevens's *Water.*

TAKE a gallon of the beſt *Gaſcoigne* wine or ſack, then take of ginger, galingal, cinnamon, nutmegs, cloves, mace, aniſeeds, carraway ſeeds, coriander ſeeds, of every of theſe a drachm; then take ſage, mint, camomile, thyme, pellitory of the wall, pot marjoram, roſemary-flowers, penny-royal, wild thyme, common lavender, of each of theſe a handful; bruiſe the ſpice and ſeeds, ſtamp the herbs, put them all into the wine, and let it ſtand cloſe cover'd twelve hours, ſtirring it often; then diſtil it in an alembick, and mix it as you pleaſe.

To make Aqua Mirabilis.

TAKE cubebs, cardamums, galingal, cloves, mace, nutmegs, cinnamon, of each two drachms, bruiſed ſmall; then take of the juice of celandine a pint

pint, the juice of ſpearmint half a pint, the juice of balm half a pint; the flowers of melilot, cowſlip, roſemary, borage, bugloſs, and marigolds, of each three drachms; ſeeds of fennel, coriander and carraway, of each two drachms; two quarts of the beſt ſack, a quart of white wine, of brandy, the ſtrongeſt angelica-water, and red roſe-water of each one pint; bruiſe the ſpices and ſeeds, and ſteep them with the herbs, and flowers in the juices, waters, ſack, white wine and brandy all night; in the morning diſtil it in a common ſtill paſted up; from this quantity draw off a gallon at leaſt; ſweeten it to your taſte with ſugar candy; bottle it up and keep it in ſand, or very cool.

A Tincture of Ambergreaſe.

TAKE ambergreaſe and muſk, of each an ounce, and put to them a quarter of a pint of ſpirit of wine; ſtop it cloſe, tie it down with leather, and ſet it in horſe dung ten or twelve days.

To make Orange or Lemon Water.

TO the outer rind of an hundred oranges or lemons, put three gallons of brandy and two quarts of ſack; and let them ſteep in it one night; the next day diſtil them in a cold ſtill; a gallon, with the proportion of peels, is enough for one ſtill, and of that you may draw off between three and four quarts; draw it off till you taſte it begins to be ſouriſh; ſweeten it to your taſte with double refin'd ſugar; mix the firſt, ſecond and third running together; if it is lemon-water, it ſhould be perfumed; put two grains of ambergreaſe, and one of muſk, ground fine, tie it in a rag, and let it hang five or ſix days in a bottle, and then put it in another, and ſo for a great many if you pleaſe, or elſe you may put three or four drops of tincture of ambreaſe in it; cork it very well: the orange is an excellent water for the ſtomach, and the lemon is a fine entertaining water.

King Charles II'*s Surfeit Water.*

TAKE a gallon of the beſt aqua-vitæ, a quart of brandy, a quart of aniſeed-water, a pint of poppy-water, and a pint of damaſk roſe-water: put theſe in a large glaſs jar, adding to it a pound of fine powder'd ſugar, a pound and a half of raiſins ſtoned, a quarter of a pound of dates ſtoned and ſliced, one ounce of cinnamon bruiſed, cloves one ounce, four nutmegs bruiſed, one ſtick of liquorice ſcrap'd and ſlic'd; let all theſe ſtand nine days cloſe cover'd, ſtirring it three or four times a day; then add to it three pounds of freſh poppies, or three handfuls of dry'd poppies, a ſprig of angelica, two or three of balm; ſo let it ſtand a week longer, then ſtrain it out and bottle it.

The Walnut Water.

TAKE a peck of walnuts in *July*, and beat them pretty ſmall, adding to them of clove-gilliflowers, poppy-flowers, cowſlip-flowers dried, marigold-flowers, ſage-flowers, and borage-flowers of each two quarts; then put to them two ounces of mace beaten, two ounces of nutmegs bruiſed, and one ounce of cinnamon bruiſed; ſteep all theſe in a pot with a gallon of brandy, and two gallons of the ſtrongeſt beer; let it ſtand twenty-four hours, and ſtill it off.

To make Orange-flower Brandy.

TAKE a gallon of *French* brandy, and boil a pound of orange-flowers a little while, and put them to it; ſave the water, and with that make a ſyrup to ſweeten it.

A Cordial Water that may be made in Winter.

TAKE three quarts of brandy or ſack, put two handfuls of roſemary and two handfuls of baum

to

to it chopt pretty ſmall, one ounce of cloves, two ounces of nutmegs, three ounces of cinnamon; beat all the ſpices groſly, and ſteep them with the herbs in the wine; then put it in a ſtill paſted up cloſe; ſave near a quart of the firſt running, and ſo of the ſecond, and of the third; when it is diſtilled mix it all together, and diſſolve about a pound of double refin'd ſugar in it, and when it is ſettled bottle it up.

The Golden Cordial.

TAKE two gallons of brandy, two drachms and a half of alkermes, a quarter of a drachm of oil of cloves, an ounce of the ſpirit of ſaffron, three pounds of double refin'd ſugar powder'd, and a book of leaf gold. Firſt put your brandy into a large bottle, then put three or four ſpoonfuls of brandy in a *China* cup, mix your alkermes in it; then put in your oil of cloves, and mix that, and do the like to the ſpirit of ſaffron; pour all into your bottle of brandy; then put in your ſugar, cork your bottle, and tie it down cloſe; ſhake it well together for two or three days, and let it ſtand about a fortnight; you muſt ſet the bottle ſo, that when it is rack'd off into other bottles it muſt only be gently tilted; put into every bottle two leaves of gold cut ſmall; you may put one or two quarts to the dregs and it will be good, though not ſo good as the firſt.

The Fever Water.

TAKE of *Virginia* ſnake-root ſix ounces, carduus-ſeeds and marigold-flowers, of each four ounces, twenty green walnuts, carduus-water, poppy-water, of each two quarts, two ounces of hartſhorn; ſlice the walnuts, and ſteep all in the waters a fortnight; then add to it an ounce of *London* treacle, and diſtil it all in an alembick paſted up; three drops of ſpirit of amber in three ſpoonfuls of this water will deliver a woman of a dead child.

To make the firft Liquid Laudanum.

TAKE a quart of fack, half a pint of fpirit of wine, four ounces of opium, and two ounces of faffron; flice the opium, pull the faffron, and put it in a bottle with the fack and fpirit of wine; adding to it cinnamon, cloves and mace, of each a drachm; cork and tie down the bottle, and fet it in the fun or by the fire twenty days; pour it off the dregs and it is fit to ufe; ten, fifteen, twenty, or twenty-five drops.

A fine Cordial Water.

BEAT two pounds of double refined fugar very well, and put to it a gallon of the beft brandy, ftirring it a good while; then add confection of alkermes and oil of cloves of each one drachm, fpirit of faffron an ounce; ftir it a quarter of an hour; then add three fheets of leaf gold, and bottle it up; it will keep as long as you pleafe.

To make Spirit of Carraways.

TAKE of carraway comfits two pounds, put them into a glafs bottle with a wide mouth, put upon the carraways fpirit of wine as much as will cover them, one drachm of ambergreafe rub'd to powder, with as much fine fugar, and tied up in a rag; let this ftand three months clofe ftopt, then pour off the fpirit clear from the feeds; take a little of this dropt in beer or ale for wind or pain in the bowels.

To cure the Spleen or Vapours.

TAKE an ounce of the filings of fteel, two drachms of gentian fliced, half an ounce of carduus feeds bruifed, half a handful of centaury tops; infufe all thefe in a quart of white wine four days; drink

drink four ſpoonfuls of the clear every morning, faſting two hours after it, and walking about; if it binds too much, take once or twice a week ſome little purging thing to carry it off.

Hyſteric Water.

TAKE zedoary, roots of lovage, ſeeds of wild parſneps, of each two ounces, roots of ſingle piony four ounces, of miſſletoe of the oak three ounces, myrrh a quarter of an ounce, caſtor half an ounce; beat all theſe together, and add to them a quarter of a pound of dried millepedes; pour on theſe three quarts of mugwort-water, and two quarts of brandy; let them ſtand in a cloſe veſſel eight days, then diſtil it in a cold ſtill paſted up; you may draw off nine pints of water; ſweeten it to your taſte, and mix all together. This is an excellent water to prevent fits, or to be taken in faintings.

A Stone Water.

TAKE beans in pod, and cut them in ſmall pieces, fill good part of an ordinary ſtill with them, and put to them two good handfuls of yarrow, and diſtil them together in a cold ſtill; let the party drink a glaſs when in pain, and at the changes of the moon.

To make Poppy Brandy.

TAKE ſix quarts of the beſt and freſheſt poppies, cut off the black ends of them, put them in a glaſs jar that will hold two gallons, and preſs them in it, then pour over it a gallon of brandy, ſtop the glaſs very well, and ſet it in the ſun for a week or more, then ſqueeze out the poppies with your hand, and ſweeten it to your taſte with double refined ſugar, adding to it an ounce and half of alkermes: mix it well together and bottle it up. This is in imitation of roſa ſolis.

To make Cherry Brandy.

TO every four quarts of brandy put four pounds of red cherries, two pounds of black, and one quart of raſpberries, a few cloves, a ſtick of cinnamon, and a bit of orange-peel; let theſe ſtand a month cloſe ſtopt, then bottle it off; adding a lump of ſugar in every bottle.

To make Citron Water.

TO a gallon of brandy take ten citrons, pare the outſide rinds of the citrons, dry the rinds very well, then beat the remaining part of the citrons all to maſh in a mortar, and put it into the brandy; ſtop it cloſe and let it ſtand nine days, then diſtil it; take rinds that are dry and beat them to powder, infuſe them nine days in the ſpirit, and diſtil it over again; ſweeten it to your taſte with double refined ſugar; let it ſtand in a large jug for three weeks, then rack it off into bottles. This is the true *Barbadoes* receipt for citron water.

Stitch Water.

TAKE a gallon of new ale wort, and put to as much ſtone-horſe dung as will make it pretty thick; add to this a pound of *London* treacle, two pennyworth of ginger ſliced, and ſix pennyworth of ſaffron, mix theſe together, and diſtil off in a cold ſtill: take three or four ſpoonfuls at a time.

To make Carraway Brandy.

STEEP an ounce of carraway-ſeeds and ſix ounces of ſugar in a quart of brandy for nine days, and clear it off; it is a good cordial.

The

The Saffron Cordial.

FILL a large still with marigold-flowers, adding to them of nutmegs, mace, and *English* saffron, of each an ounce; then take three pints of muscadine, or tent, or *Malaga* sack, and with a sprig of rosemary dash it on the flowers; then distil it off with a slow fire, and let it drop on white sugar-candy; draw it off till it begins to be sour; save a pint of the first running to mix with other waters on an extraordinary occasion, mix the rest together to drink it by itself. This cordial is excellent in fainting, and for the small pox or ague; take five or six spoonfuls at a time.

The fine Clary Water.

TAKE a quart of borage-water, put it in an earthen jug, and fill it with two or three quarts of clary-flowers fresh gather'd; let it infuse an hour over the fire in a kettle of water, then take out the flowers and put in as many fresh flowers, and so do for six or seven times together; then add to that water two quarts of the best sack, a gallon of fresh flowers, and two pounds of white sugar-candy beaten small, and distil it all off in a cold still; mix all the water together, and sweeten it to your taste with the finest sugar. This is a very wholesome, and fine entertaining water. Cork the bottles well and keep it cool.

To make Spirit of Saffron.

TAKE four drachms of the best saffron, put it in a quart bottle, pour on it a pint of the ordinary spirit of wine, and add to it half a pound of white sugar-candy beaten small; stop it close with a cork, and a bladder tied over it; set it in the sun, shake it twice a day, till the candy is dissolv'd, and the spirit of a deep orange colour; let it stand two days

days longer to settle, clear it off in another bottle, and keep it for use; give a small spoonful to a child, and a large one to a man or woman; it is excellent in any pestilential disease; it is good against colds, or the consumptive cough.

Black Cherry Water for Children.

TAKE six pounds of black cherries and bruise them small, then put to them the tops of rosemary, sweet-marjoram, spearmint, angelica, baum, marigold flowers, of each a handful, dried violets an ounce, aniseeds and sweet fennel seeds, of each half an ounce bruised; cut the herbs small, mix them together, and distil them off in a cold still. This water is excellent for children, giving them two or three spoonfuls at a time.

To make Gripe Water.

TAKE of penny-royal ten handfuls, coriander seeds, aniseeds, sweet fennel seeds, caraway seeds, of each one ounce; bruise them and put them to the herbs in an earthen pot; sprinkle on them a pint of brandy; let them stand all night, the next day distil it off, and take six, seven, or eight spoonfuls of this water, sweetened with syrup of gilliflowers warm, and go to bed; cover very warm to sweat if you can, and drink some of it as long as the gripes continue.

To make the Dropsy Water.

TAKE a bushel of picked elder berries, put them in a large tub, with as much water or strong beer as will cover them, a quart of ale yeast, and a piece of leaven as big as a penny loaf; break it to pieces, and stir it together once or twice a day for eight days together; then put them in a pot, and distil off a gallon in an alembick: It must

be

be drank three times a day, in the morning faſting, before dinner, and laſt at night, till you have drank up the quantity.

Lily of the Valley Water.

TAKE the flowers of lily of the valley, diſtil them in ſack, and drink a ſpoonful or two as there is occaſion; it reſtores ſpeech to thoſe who have the dumb palſy or apoplexy, it is good againſt the gout, it comforts the heart, and ſtrengthens the memory; it helps the inflammation of the eyes, being dropt into them. Take the flowers, put them into a glaſs cloſe ſtopt, and ſet it into a hill of ants for a month; then take it out, and you will find a liquor that comes from the flowers, which keep in a phial; it eaſeth the pains of the gout, the place affected being anointed therewith.

To make Vertigo Water.

TAKE the leaves of red ſage, cinquefoil, and wood betony, of each a good handful, boil them in a gallon of ſpring water till it comes to a quart; when it is cold put into it a pennyworth of roach-alum, and bottle it up; when you uſe it put a little of it in a ſpoon, or in the palm of your hand, and ſnuff it up; go not into the air preſently.

Dr. Burgeſs's *Antidote againſt the Plague.*

TAKE three pints of muſcadine, and boil therein one handful of ſage, as much rue, angelica-roots one ounce, zedoary-roots one ounce, *Virginia* ſnake-root half an ounce, ſaffron twenty grains; let all theſe boil till a pint be conſumed, then ſtrain it and ſet it over the fire again, and put therein two pennyworth of long pepper, half an ounce of ginger, as much nutmegs; beat all the ſpice, and let

them

them boil together a little, and put thereto a quarter of an ounce of mithridate, as much *Venice* treacle, and a quarter of a pint of the best angelica water; take it warm both morning and evening, two spoonfuls if already infected; if not infected, one spoonful is enough for a day, half a spoonful in the morning, and as much at night. This had great success, under God, in the plague; it is good likewise against the small-pox, or any other pestilential disease.

The Lady Onslow'*s Water for the Stone.*

TAKE as much saxifrage, as, being distill'd, will yield two quarts of water, add to this a peck of hogs haws bruised, filipendula and parsley, of each three handfuls; parsley of break-stone and mother-thyme, of each two handfuls; marshmallow-roots, parsley-roots, of each one handful; four large horse-radish roots, red nettle-seed and burdock-seed, of each an ounce; bruise the seeds, cut the herbs, and slice the roots; mix them well together with three quarts of white wine, and as much new milk from the cow; distil them and the saxifrage water together in a cold still, and draw it off as long as any water will come; the saxifrage must be distill'd in *May*, and the other water the latter end of *September* or *October*, when the haws are ripe. Let the person, when the fit of the stone cometh, take three or four spoonfuls of white wine, and as much of this water mixed together. If the distemper abate not, take six spoonfuls of this water once in six hours, till it is removed. You may sweeten it with syrup of marshmallows,

Centaury Water.

TAKE one pound of gentian and six pounds of green centaury, beat the gentian, shred the centaury, and put them into an earthen pot, with as much white wine as will cover them; let it stand five

five days, and diſtil it in an ordinary ſtill. This is an excellent water; take three or four ſpoonfuls at a time in a morning, and faſt two hours after it, and uſe exerciſe; likewiſe take it at night, an hour or two before you go to bed.

To make Tincture of Hiera-picra.

TAKE a drachm of hiera-picra, a drachm of cochineal, and two drachms of aniſeeds, and put them into a bottle, with a pint of the beſt ſack and a pint of brandy; ſhake them well together five or ſix days, then let it ſtand to ſettle twelve hours, ſo pour it off into another bottle clear from the dregs, and keep it for uſe; it is very good againſt the cholick or ſtomach-ach, and removes any thing that offends the ſtomach; take four ſpoonfuls of it faſting, and faſt two hours after it; you muſt take it conſtantly three weeks or a month, and it is well to drink the following drink after it.

Take new laid eggs and break them, ſave the ſhells, and pull off the ſkin that is in the inſide; dry the ſhells, and beat them to powder; ſift them, and put ſix ſpoonfuls of this powder into a quart of the following waters: take of fennel-water, parſley-water, mint-water, and black cherry-water, of each half a pint; take a quarter of a pint at a time, ſhaking the glaſs when you pour it out, three times a day, at eleven in the morning, at three in the afternoon, and eight at night; and you ſhould take it as long as you take the hiera-picra.

To make Lime Water.

TAKE a pound of unſlack'd lime, put it into an earthen jug well glaz'd, adding to it a gallon of ſpring water boiling hot; cover it cloſe till it is cold, then ſkim it clean, let it ſtand two days, pour it clear off into glaſs bottles, and keep it for uſe; the older the better. The virtues are as follow.

For a ſore, warm ſome of the water and waſh the ſore well with it for half an hour, then lay a plaiſter on the ſore of ſome gentle thing, and lay a cloth over the plaiſter four or five double, wet with this water, and as it dries wet it again, and it will heal it.

For a flux or looſeneſs, take two ſpoonfuls of it cold in the morning, and two at night as you go to bed; do this ſeven or eight days together for a man or woman; but if for a child, one ſpoonful at a time is enough; and if very young, half a ſpoonful at a time; it will keep twenty years, and no one who has not experienced it knows the virtues of it.

A Milk Water for a cancerous Breaſt.

TAKE ſix quarts of new milk, four handfuls of cranes-bill, and four hundred of wood-lice; diſtil this in a cold ſtill with a gentle fire; then take an ounce of crabs-eyes, and half an ounce of white ſugar-candy, both in fine powder; mix them together, and take a drachm of the powder in a quarter of a pint of the milk water in the morning, at twelve at noon, and at night; continue taking this three or four months, it is an excellent medicine.

Cock Water for a Conſumption.

TAKE an old cock, kill him and quarter him, and with clean cloths wipe the blood from him; then put the quarters into a cold ſtill, part of a leg of veal, two quarts of old *Malaga* ſack, a handful of thyme, as much ſweet marjoram and roſemary, two handfuls of pimpernel, four dates ſtoned and ſliced, a pound of currants, as many raiſins of the ſun ſtoned, a pound of ſugar-candy finely beaten; when all is in, paſte up the ſtill, let it ſtand all night, the next morning diſtil it, mix the water together, and ſweeten it to your taſte with white ſugar-candy; drink three or four ſpoonfuls an hour before dinner and ſupper.

Another

Another Water againſt a Conſumption.

TAKE a pound of currants, and of harts-tongue, liverwort and ſpeedwell, of each a large handful; then take a peck of ſnails, lay them all night in hyſſop, the next morning rub and bruiſe them, and diſtil all in a gallon of new milk; ſweeten it with white ſugar-candy, and drink of this water two or three times a day, a quarter of a pint at a time; it has done great good.

Another Water againſt a Conſumption.

TAKE three pints of the beſt canary and a pint of mint-water, of candied eryngo roots, dates, *China* roots, and raiſins ſtoned, of each three ounces; of mace a quarter of an ounce; infuſe theſe twelve hours in an earthen pot cloſe cover'd over a gentle fire; when it is cold ſtrain it out, and keep it in a clean pan or glaſs jar for uſe; then make about a quart of plain jelly of harts-horn, and drink a quarter of a pint of this liquor with a large ſpoonful of jelly night and morning for two or three months together.

A Water to ſtrengthen the Sight.

TAKE roſemary-flowers, ſage, betony, rue, and ſuccory, of each a handful; infuſe theſe in two quarts of ſack, and diſtil them in an alembick: the doſe is a ſpoonful in the morning faſting till the water is done.

Rue Water good for Fits of the Mother.

TAKE of rue, and green walnuts, of each a pound, figs a pound and a half; bruiſe the rue and walnuts, ſlice the figs, lay them between the rue and walnuts, and diſtil it off; bottle it up and keep it for uſe: take a ſpoonful or two when there is any appearance of a fit.

An opening Drink.

TAKE penny-royal, red sage, liverwort, hore-hound, maidenhair, hyssop, of each two hand-fuls, figs and raisins stoned, of each a pound, blue cur-rants half a pound, liquorice, aniseeds, coriander-seeds, of each two ounces; put all these in two gal-lons of spring-water, and let it boil away two or three quarts; then strain it, and when it is cold put it in bottles: drink half a pint in the morning, and as much in the afternoon; keep warm and eat little.

For a Distemper got by an ill Husband.

TAKE two pennyworth of gum dragant, pick and clean it, and put it in an earthen pot; put to it as much red rose-water as it will drink up, stir it two or three times a day, till it is all dissolv'd into a jelly: then put in three grated nutmegs, a little double-refin'd sugar, finely powder'd, and a little cinnamon-water, no more than will leave it in a jelly: take the quantity of a nutmeg in the morning fast-ing, and last at night; but first prepare the body for it, by taking six pennyworth of *pulvis sanctus* in posset-drink, and drink broth in the working.

For a Cough settled on the Stomach.

TAKE half a pound of figs, as many raisins of the sun stoned, a stick of liquorice scrap'd and sliced, a few aniseeds, and sweet fennel-seeds, with some hyssop wash'd; boil all these in a quart of spring-water till it comes to a pint; strain it, and sweeten it very well with white sugar-candy: take two or three spoonfuls of it morning and night, or when you please.

To make Hungary Water.

TAKE four ounces of rosemary-flowers, and a pint of spirits of wine, infuse it twelve hours, and draw it off in a glass still.

A Drink

A Drink to preſerve the Lungs.

TAKE three pints of ſpring-water, put it to an ounce of flour of ſulphur, and let it boil on a ſlow fire till half is conſumed; let it ſtand to ſettle and ſtrain it out; then pour it on one ounce of liquorice ſcrap'd, and a drachm of coriander-ſeeds, and as many aniſeeds bruiſed; let it ſtand to ſettle, and drink a quarter of a pint morning and night.

An excellent Snail Water.

TAKE of comfry and ſuccory-roots, of each four ounces, liquorice three ounces, the leaves of harts-tongue, plantain, ground-ivy, red nettle, yarrow, brooklime, water-creſſes, dandelion, and agrimony, of each two large handfuls; gather theſe herbs in dry weather, and do not waſh them, but wipe them clean with a cloth; then take five hundred of ſnails, cleanſed from their ſhells, but not ſcoured, and of whites of eggs beaten up to a water, a pint, four nutmegs groſly beaten, the yellow rind of one lemon and one orange; bruiſe all the roots and herbs, and put them together with the other ingredients in a gallon of new milk and a pint of canary; let them ſtand cloſe covered forty eight hours, and then diſtil them in a common ſtill with a gentle fire; this quantity will fill your ſtill twice; it will keep good a year, and is beſt when made ſpring or fall, but it is the beſt when new; you muſt not cork up the bottles in three months, but cover them with paper; it is immediately fit for uſe; and when you uſe it take a quarter of a pint of this water, and put to it as much milk warm from the cow, and drink it in the morning, and at four o'clock in the afternoon, and faſt two hours after it; to take powder of crabs-eyes with it, as much as will lie on a ſixpence, mightily aſſiſts to ſweeten the blood. When you drink this water, be very regular in your diet, and eat nothing ſalt or ſour.

Eye Water.

TAKE orrice-root flic'd two ounces, white copperas finely beaten an ounce, put them in three pints of running water, shake it well together three or four days, and then use it; if a watery eye, you may add a bit of bole-armoniac.

To make Briony Water.

TAKE twelve pounds of briony-root, pound it to mash, then take a quart of the juice of rue, a quart of the juice of mugwort leaves, of savin three handfuls, sweet basil two handfuls, mother of thyme, nepp, and pennyroyal, of each three handfuls; dittany of *Crete* and dry orange-peel of each four handfuls; myrrh two ounces, castor an ounce, both powder'd, and likewise the orange-peel; distil this off in an alembick; first cut your herbs, and put them in the bottom of your still, then put in your briony-root, then mix your powders in a *China* dish with some sack, then pour in six quarts of sack; close up your still and draw it off.

A Water to take after taking Balsam of Tolu.

TAKE a pint of whites of eggs beaten to a froth, five nutmegs bruised, two handfuls of dried spearmint, two handfuls of unset hyssop; add to these a gallon of new milk, and distil it off in a cold still; you may draw off about three pints: take six spoonfuls of this water at a time, with sugar-candy in it.

To make the true Daffy's *Elixir.*

TAKE five ounces of aniseeds, three ounces of fennel-seeds, four ounces of parsley-seeds, six ounces of *Spanish* liquorice, five ounces of sena, one ounce of rhubarb, three ounces of elecampane, seven ounces of jalap, twenty one drachms of saffron, six ounces of manna, two pounds of raiſins, a quarter of an ounce of cochineal, two gallons of brandy; ſtone the raiſins, ſlice the roots, bruiſe the jalap; put them all together, keep them cloſe cover'd fifteen days; then ſtrain it out.

Milk Water.

TAKE two good handfuls of wormwood, as much carduus, as much rue, four handfuls of mint, as much baum, half as much angelica; cut theſe a little, put them in a cold ſtill, with three quarts of milk; let your fire be quick till your ſtill drops, then a little ſlower; you may draw off two quarts; the firſt quart will keep all the year: this is extraordinary good in fevers, ſweetened with ſugar or ſyrup of cloves.

A Powder to cure a Rupture.

TAKE half a pound of knots of ſcurvy-graſs before they are quite blown, one pound of comfry-roots, half a pound of fern-roots, one ounce of juniper berries, one ounce of dragons-blood, half a pound of the roots of ſolomon-ſeal, a quarter of an ounce of nutmegs, a quarter of an ounce of mace; ſcrape your roots very clean, ſlice them thin, and put every ſort by themſelves in a clean paper bag; lay them on a clean earthen diſh, and let them be put in a ſlow oven till they are dry enough to powder; you muſt do the like to your ſcurvy-graſs, that they may be all finely powder'd and mix'd together, and kept cloſe in a glaſs with paper round it: You may in any liquor give as much of this powder to a young child as will lie on a ſixpence, morning and night; to one of ſeven years more; to a man or woman as much as will lie on a ſhilling: put the powder in a ſpoon, and wet it to mix, and take it three weeks.

Tincture of Hiera-Picra.

PUT an ounce of hiera-picra into a quart of brandy; let your bottle hold more than a quart, that you may have room to shake it; let it stand five days near the fire, shaking it often, and stop it close. This is a good purge, take half a quarter of a pint going to bed, drink a draught of warm ale or broth a little while after it; you may take it nine or ten days together; it opens the stomach, causes digestion, prevents green sickness, and kills worms in children.

A good Remedy for a hollow aching Tooth.

TAKE of camphire and crude opium, of each four grains, make them into three pills with as much oil of cloves as is convenient, roll them in cotton, apply one of them to the aching tooth, and repeat it if there is occasion.

A successful Method to cure the Jaundice.

IN the first place give the patient a vomit of the infusion of crocus-metallorum, or oxymel of squills, according to his constitution; then take of aloes and rhubarb, of each two scruples, of prepar'd steel a drachm, tartar vitriolated a scruple; make pills with syrup of horehound, of which give four every night.

Take of the roots of turmerick half an ounce, tops of centaury the lesser, roman wormwood and horehound, of each a handful, roots of the greater nettle two ounces; boil them in three pints of water to the consumption of half; when it is almost boiled enough, add to it juniper-berries an ounce, yellow-sanders and goose-dung made into a nodulus, of each three drachms, saffron two scruples, rhenish wine a pint; when it is boil'd enough strain it, and add to it compound water of snails and earth-worms,

worms, of each two ounces; take three ounces of it after each time of taking the following electuary.

Take of the conserve of sea wormwood, and outward rind of orange-peels, of each two ounces; of species of diacurcumæ and prepared steel, of each three drachms; of prepared earth-worms and rhubarb, of each two drachms; flowers of sal-armoniac and salt of amber, of each two scruples; of saffron powder'd one scruple, with a sufficient quantity of syrup of horehound, make an electuary: of which take the quantity of a large nutmeg twice a day, drinking three ounces of the bitter tincture after it.

For a Rheumatism, or Pain in the Bones.

TAKE a quart of milk, boil it, and turn it with three pints of small-beer; then strain the posset on seven or nine globules of stone-horse dung tied up in a cloth, and boil it a quarter of an hour in the posset-drink; when it is taken off the fire press the cloth hard, and drink half a pint of this morning and night hot in bed; if you please you may add white wine to it. This medicine is not good if troubled with the stone.

To make Treacle Water.

TAKE juice of green walnuts four pounds, of rue, carduus, marigolds, and baum, of each three pounds, roots of butter-bur half a pound, roots of burdock a pound, angelica and master-wort, of each half a pound, leaves of scordium six handfuls, *Venice* treacle and mithridate, of each half a pound, old canary wine a pound, white wine vinegar six pounds, juice of lemon six pounds; distil this in an alembick, and on any illness take four spoonfuls going to bed.

To make Usquebaugh.

TO three gallons of brandy put four ounces of aniseeds bruised, the next day distil it in a cold still pasted up, then scrape four ounces of liquorice and pound it in a mortar, dry it in an iron-pan, do not burn it, put it in the bottle to your diſtill'd water, and let it ſtand ten days, then take out the liquorice, and to every ſix quarts of the ſpirits put in cloves, mace, nutmegs, cinnamon and ginger, of each a quarter of an ounce, dates ſton'd and ſlic'd four ounces, raiſins ſtoned half a pound; let theſe infuſe ten days, then ſtrain it out, tincture it with ſaffron, and bottle it and cork it well.

Mr. Denzil Onſlow'*s Surfeit Water.*

TAKE a gallon and a half of the beſt brandy, half a buſhel of poppies, half a handful of rue, and as much wormwood; of ſage, baum, hyſſop, mint, and ſweet-marjoram, of each one handful; half a pound of roſa ſolis; waſh, pick, and dry theſe herbs in a coarſe cloth; then ſhred them very fine. Take half a pound of liquorice ſcraped; of coriander-ſeeds, and aniſeeds, of each an ounce; a few cloves all bruiſed; a pound of raiſins ſtoned, a pound of loaf ſugar; put all theſe in an earthen jar, cover'd very cloſe, and ſet it in a cool cellar, ſtirring them twice a day, till the poppies look pale; put a little ſaffron in with the other ingredients, ſtrain it off into another jar, and in a fortnight, when it is ſettled, bottle it: mix the herbs that are ſtrained from it with milk; it is a cordial milk-water.

An excellent Medicine for the Dropſy.

TAKE of the leaves that grow upon the ſtem or ſtalk of the artichoke, bruiſe them in a ſtone mortar, then ſtrain them thro' a fine cloth, and put to each pint of the juice a pint of *Madeira* wine; take four or five ſpoonfuls the firſt thing in the morning, and the ſame quantity going to bed, ſhaking the bottle well every time you uſe it.

Another Medicine for the Dropſy.

TAKE about three ſpoonfuls of the beſt muſtard-ſeed, and about half a handful of bay-berries, the like quantity of juniper-berries, an ounce of horſe-

horſe-radiſh, and about half a handful of ſage of vertue, as much wormwood-ſage, half a handful of ſcurvy-graſs, a quarter of a handful of ſtinking orach, a little ſprig of wormwood, a ſprig of green broom, and half an ounce of gentian root; ſcrape, wipe, and cut all theſe, and put them into a bottle that will hold a gallon; then fill the bottle with the beſt ſtrong beer you can get, ſtop it cloſe, let it ſtand three or four days, and drink every morning faſting half a pint.

A Remedy for rheumatic Pains.

TAKE of ſena, hermodactils, turpethum, and ſcammony, of each two drachms; of zedoary, ginger, and cubebs, of each one drachm, mix them and let them be powdered; the doſe is from one drachm to two in any convenient vehicle. Let the parts affected be anointed with this liniment: Take palm oil two ounces, oil of turpentine one ounce, volatile ſalt of hartſhorn two drachms; afterwards lay on a mucilaginous plaiſter. Some that have been very much troubled with rheumatic pains, have by taking of hartſhorn in compound water of earthworms, found mighty benefit.

An excellent Medicine for the ſpotted, and all other malignant Fevers.

TAKE of the beſt *Virginia* ſnakeweed, root of contrayerva finely powdered and *Goa* ſtone, of each half a ſcruple, caſtor and camphire, of each five grains, make them into a bolus with a ſcruple of *Venice* treacle and as much ſyrup of piony as is ſufficient; repeat the bolus every ſix hours, drinking a draught of the following julep after it.

Take ſcorzonera roots two ounces, butter-bur-roots half an ounce, of baum and ſcordium, of each a handful, of coriander-ſeeds three drachms, of liquorice, figs, and raiſins, of each an ounce; let them boil in three pints of ſpring-water to a quart, then ſtrain it, and add to it compound piony-water three ounces, ſyrup of raſpberries an ounce and a half: let the patients drink of it plentifully.

A ſpecific Cure for ſtopping Blood.

TAKE two ounces of clarified roch-alum, finely powdered, and melt it in a ladle, adding to it half an ounce of dragons-blood in powder, and mix them well together; then take it off the fire, keeping it ſtirring till it comes to the conſiſtence of a ſoft paſte, fit for making up into pills; make your pills of the bigneſs of a large pea, and as the paſte cools, warm it again to ſuch a degree as the whole quantity may be made into pills; this medicine is proper in all caſes of violent bleedings, without exception; the ordinary or uſual doſe is half a grain, to be taken once in four hours till the bleeding ſtops, taking a glaſs of water or ptiſan after it, and after every doſe, and another of the ſame liquor a quarter of an hour after; in violent caſes give half a drachm for a doſe.

To make Stoughton's *Elixir.*

PARE off the rinds of ſix *Seville* oranges very thin, and put them in a quart bottle, with an ounce of gentian ſcraped and ſliced, and ſix pennyworth of cochineal; put to it a pint of the beſt brandy; ſhake it together two or three times the firſt day, and then let it ſtand to ſettle two days, and clear it off into bottles for uſe; take a large tea ſpoonful in a glaſs of wine in a morning, and at four in the afternoon; or you may take it in a diſh of tea.

An excellent Medicine for a Pain in the Stomach.

TAKE of *tinctura sacra* (or tincture of hiera-picra) one ounce in the morning, fasting an hour; then drink a little warm ale; do this two or three times a week, till you find relief.

For a Pain in the Stomach.

TAKE a quarter of a pound of blue currants, wipe them clean, and pound them in a mortar, with an ounce of aniseeds bruised; before you put them to the currants, make this into a bolus with a little syrup of clove-gilliflowers; take every morning the quantity of a walnut, and drink rosemary-tea, instead of other tea, for your breakfast; if the pain returns, repeat it.

For a Stitch in the Side.

TAKE rosin, pound and sift it, and with treacle mix it into an electuary, and lick it up often in the day or night.

To cure an intermitting Ague and Fever, without returning.

TAKE jesuits bark in fine powder one ounce, salt of steel and *Jamaica* pepper, of each a quarter of an ounce; treacle or melasses, four ounces; mix these together, and take the quantity of a nutmeg three times a day when the fit is off, and a draught of warm ale, or white wine after it.

Dr.

Dr. Hall's *Plaister for an Ague.*

TAKE a pennyworth of black soap, one pennyworth of gunpowder, one ounce of tobacco-snuff, and a glass of brandy; mix these in a mortar very well together; spread plaisters on leather for the wrists, and lay them on an hour before you expect the fit.

Excellent for a Burn or Scald.

TAKE of oil-olive three ounces, white wax two ounces, sheep suet an ounce and half, minium and *Castile* soap, of each half an ounce; dragon's-blood and camphire, of each three drachms; make them into a salve by melting them together: anoint with oil to take out the fire; then put the plaister on; dress it every day.

Water in a Consumption, or in Weakness after Sickness.

TAKE a calf's-pluck fresh killed, but do not wash it; cut it in pieces, and put it in a cold still; but first put at the bottom of your still a sheet of white paper well butter'd; then put in your pluck, with mint, baum, borage, hyssop, and oak lungs, of each about two handfuls; wipe and cut the herbs, but do not wash them; put in a gallon of new milk warm from the cow, paste up the still, and let it drop on white sugar-candy; it will draw off about seven pints; mix it together, and bottle it for use: drink a quarter of a pint in the morning, and as much at four in the afternoon.

A Stay to prevent a sore Throat in the Small Pox.

TAKE rue, shred it very fine, and give it a bruise; mix it with honey and *album Græcum*, and work it together; put it over the fire to heat; sew

ſew it up in a linen ſtay, and apply it to the throat pretty warm; as it dries repeat it.

To prevent Pitting, and to take off Redneſs.

TAKE rue, and chop it, boil it in hogs-lard till it is green; ſtrain it out, and keep it for uſe; warm a little in a ſpoon, and with a feather anoint the face as they begin to ſhell off; do it as often as convenient.

An admirable Serecloth.

TAKE a pound of frankincenſe beaten fine, and a pound of roſin beaten, a pound of black pitch, and four ounces of cummin-ſeeds powder'd, of ſaffron dried and powder'd, mace beaten and ſifted, and cloves beaten fine, of each four penny-worth; an ounce of liquid laudanum, and a pound of deer-ſuet.

Seaſon a new pipkin; firſt lay it in cold water; then boil water in it, and ſet it by till it is cold; then dry it, and put in your deer-ſuet, and let it melt, ſhaking it about as you do for melting butter; then put in your other ingredients, and ſet over the fire to boil; then take it off, and ſprinkle in your liquid laudanum; let it ſimmer a little; take it off, and when it is fit to ſpread, ſpread it on the thickeſt brown paper, and uſe it on occaſion: it is good for bruiſes, aches, pains, burns, ſcalds, and ſore breaſts; wipe the plaiſter every day, and put it on again: one or two plaiſters will do.

For the Cholic.

TAKE of camomile-flowers and mallow-leaves, of each a handful; juniper-berries and fenu-greek-ſeeds, of each half an ounce: let the ſeeds and berries be bruiſed; boil them in a pint of water; add to it ſtrained, of turpentine diſſolved, with the yolk

yolk of an egg, and oil of camomile, of each an ounce; diacatholicon ſix drachms, hiera-picra two drachms; mix, and give it. After the operation of the clyſter, give the patient the following mixture: take of rue and camomile-water, of each an ounce; cinnamon-water an ounce, liquid laudanum twenty drops, ſyrup of white poppies an ounce.

How to make the Lime Drink, famous for curing the Stone.

TAKE half a peck of lime-ſtones new burnt, and put them into four gallons of water; ſtir it well at the firſt putting in; then let it ſtand, and ſtir it again; as ſoon as it is very well ſettled, ſtrain off the clear into a large pot, and put to it four ounces of ſaxifrage, and four ounces of liquorice, ſliced thin, raiſins of the ſun ſtoned one pound, half a pound of blue currants, mallows, and mercury, of each a handful; coriander, fennel, and aniſeeds, of each an ounce; let the pot ſtand cloſe covered for nine days; then ſtrain it; and, being ſettled, pour the cleareſt of it into bottles; you may drink half a pint of it at a time, as often as you pleaſe: in your morning's draught, put a drachm of winter cherries powder'd. This has cured ſome who have been ſo tormented with the ſtone in the bladder, that they could not make water, after they had in vain tried abundance of other remedies.

A Receipt for the Cure of the Stone and Gravel, whether in the Kidneys, Ureters, or Bladder.

TAKE marſhmallow-leaves, the herb mercury, ſaxifrage, and pellitory of the wall, of each, freſh gathered, three handfuls; cut them ſmall, mix them together, and pound them in a clean ſtone mortar, with a wooden peſtle, till they come to a maſh; then take them out, ſpread them thin in a broad

broad glazed earthen pan, and let them lie, ſtirring them about once a day, till they are thoroughly dry (but not in the ſun) and then they are ready, and will keep good all the year. Of ſome of theſe ingredients ſo dried, make tea, as you do common tea with boiling water, as ſtrong as you pleaſe, but the ſtronger the better; and drink three, four, or more tea-cups full of it blood-warm, ſweetened with coarſe ſugar, every morning and afternoon, putting into each cup of it half a ſpoonful, or more, of the expreſſed oil of beach nuts, freſh drawn (which in this caſe has been experienced to be vaſtly preferable to oil of almonds, or any other oil) ſtirring them about together, as long as you ſee occaſion.

This medicine, how ſimple ſoever it may ſeem to ſome, is yet a fine emollient remedy, is perfectly agreeable to the ſtomach (unleſs the beach oil be ſtale or rancid) and will ſheath and ſoften the aſperity of the humours in general, particularly thoſe that generate the gravel and ſtone, relaxing and ſuppling the ſolids at the ſame time: and it is well known by all phyſicians, that emollient medicines lubricate, widen, and moiſten the fibres, ſo as to relax them into their proper dimenſions, without forcing the parts; whereupon obſtructions of the reins and urinary paſſages are opened, and cleared of all lodgments of ſandy concretions, gravel and paſſable ſtones, and made to yield better to the expulſion of whatever may ſtop them up; and likewiſe takes away, as this does, all heat and difficulty of urine and ſtranguries; and withal, by its ſoft mucilaginous nature, cools and heals the reins, kidneys, and bladder, giving preſent eaſe in the ſtone-cholic; breaks away wind, and prevents its returns, as it always keeps the bowels laxative.

An

An excellent Vomit.

TAKE a quarter of a pound of clear alum, beaten and sifted as fine as flour, divide it into three parts, the first the biggest: put a quarter of a pint of water in a sauce-pan, and put in your biggest paper of alum, and let it simmer over the fire, but not boil; take it off, cool it to blood-warm; drink it off, but take nothing after it; sit still till it has worked once; keep very warm, and take nothing in the working; but you may walk about after it has worked once; take it three mornings together, or more, if there be occasion, till the stomach is clear. There is no case where a vomit is proper, but this is good.

A fine Purge.

TAKE an ounce of liquorice, scrape it and slice it thin, and a spoonful of coriander-seeds bruised; put these into a pint of water, and boil it a little; and strain this water into an ounce of sena; let it stand six hours; strain it from the sena, and drink it fasting.

A purging Diet-drink in the Spring.

TAKE six gallons of ale, three ounces of rhubarb, sena, madder-roots, and dock-roots, of each twelve ounces; twelve handfuls of scabious, and as much agrimony, three ounces of aniseeds; slice and cut these, put them in a bag, and let it work in the ale; drink of it three or four times a day.

For a sore Mouth in Children.

TAKE half a pint of verjuice, strain into it four spoonfuls of the juice of sage; boil this with fine sugar to a syrup, and with a feather anoint the mouth often; touch it not with a cloth, or rub it; the child may lick it down, it will not hurt it.

To

To create a good Appetite and ſtrengthen the Stomach.

TAKE of the ſtomachic pill with gums, extractum rudii, of each a drachm, reſin of jalap half a ſcruple, tartar vitriolated one ſcruple, oil of aniſeeds four drops; mix with ſyrup of violets, and make into pills, of which take four or five over night; they are of excellent uſe in the megrims and vertigo, by reaſon they carry the humour off from the ſtomach, which fumes up into the head.

A very good Medicine for the Bloody-flux.

TAKE of the beſt rhubarb, finely powder'd, half an ounce, of red ſaunders two drachms, cinnamon one drachm, crocus martis aſtringent three drachms, of *Lucatellus*'s balſam what ſuffices; make a maſs of pills, of which take three every night and morning for a fortnight. This has cured ſome who have loſt a vaſt quantity of blood, after other remedies have proved ineffectual.

For red or ſore Eyes.

TAKE a quarter of an ounce of white copperas, and an ounce of bole-armoniac; beat them to a fine powder, adding an ounce of camphire; ſet two quarts of ſpring-water on the fire; when it boils, take it off, and let it ſtand till it is lukewarm; then put in your ingredients ſtirring till cold: drop the clear into the eye.

For a Pain in the Stomach, or Heavineſs of Heart.

TAKE a pint of roſe-water, put to it ſome double refined ſugar, and a pennyworth of ſaffron tied up in a piece of lawn: let it ſtand two or three days, and then at any time take three ſpoonfuls.

For Fits from Wind or Cold.

TAKE three drops of oil of amber in ſome burnt wine, or mace ale. If it is given in black cherry water, it is good to forward labour in child-bed.

To make the red Balls.

TAKE rue, dragon, roſemary, ſage, baum, betony, plantane, pimpernel, dandelion, ſcabious, wormwood, mugwort, ſaxifrage, red brambletops, tormentil, ſhepherds-purſe, lovage, carduus, centaury, angelica, agrimony, fumitory, ſcordium, of each a handful; gather theſe in dry weather, pick and chop them, put them in a broad pan, pour on them a pint of white wine, and let it ſtand nine or ten days in the ſun, ſtirring it ſometimes; then ſtrain it out, ſqueezing it with your hand; wipe your pan clean, and put in your juice, with half an ounce of powder of pearl prepared, half an ounce of *Venice*-treacle, half an ounce of powder of coral, powder of crabs claws two ounces, one ounce of confection of alkermes, and of bole-armoniac powder'd, as much as will make it the thickneſs of a ſyrup; let it ſtand in the ſun to dry two or three days, or till it will roll up into balls, what ſize you pleaſe; if it is too thin, uſe more bole-armoniac; dry them well, and keep them for uſe: ſcrape as much as will lie on a ſixpence, and take it in a glaſs of ſack, or ſmall cordial, going to bed.

To make Elixir Proprietatis.

TAKE of myrrh, aloes, and ſaffron, of each four drachms, infuſe them in a pint of the beſt brandy; firſt put in the myrrh, and let it ſtand twelve hours; then the ſaffron and aloes; ſet it by the fire three or four days, ſhaking it very often; then ſtrain it off. Take ſixty or ſeventy drops, more or leſs, in a little white wine, in a morning fasting, for a week or ten days together; it is good for any illness in the stomach, or in the bowels: it is the best of physic for children.

To cure a pimpled Face.

TAKE an ounce of live brimstone, as much roch-alum, as much common salt; white sugar-candy, and spermaceti, of each two drachms; pound and sift all these into a fine powder, and put it in a quart bottle; then put to it half a pint of brandy, three ounces of white lily water, and three ounces of spring-water; shake all these well together, and keep it for use. When you use it, shake the bottle, and bathe the face well; and when you go to bed, dip rags in it, and lay it all over the face; in ten or twelve days it will be perfectly cured.

A Purge for Hoarseness, or any Illness on the Lungs.

TAKE four ounces of the roots of sorrel, of hyssop and maidenhair, of each half a handful; raisins stoned a quarter of a pound, sena half an ounce, barley-water two quarts; put all these in a jug, and infuse them in a kettle of water two hours; strain it out, and take a quarter of a pint morning and night.

An Electuary for a cold or windy Stomach.

TAKE gum-guaiacum one ounce, cubebs and cardamums of each a quarter of an ounce; beat and sift all these, and mix it with syrup of gilliflowers into an electuary. Take night and morning the quantity of a a nutmeg; drink a little warm ale after it.

An Electuary for a Pain in the Stomach.

TAKE conserve of wood-sorrel and mithridate an equal quantity; mix it well together, and take night and morning the quantity of a nutmeg; so do for fifteen days together.

To keep Artichokes all the Year.

IN the latter end of the season boil them till they be half enough, and then dry them on a hair-cloth upon a kiln the space of fifty hours, till they are very dry; lay them in a dry place; when you use them, soak them a night in water, and boil them till they are tender.

To keep Walnuts all the Year.

ALmost in the latter end of the season, take off the green shell of your nuts, and dry them on a hair cloth on the kiln forty hours; when they are dry, keep them for use; when you would use them, soak them three days in water, shifting them three times a day.

To make Ink.

GET one pound of the best galls, half a pound of copperas, a quarter of a pound of gum arabick, a quarter of a pound of white sugar-candy; bruise the galls, and beat your other ingredients fine, and infuse them all in three quarts of white wine or rain-water, and let them stand hot by the fire three or four days; then put all into a new pipkin; set it on a slow fire, so as not to boil; keep it frequently stirring, and let it stand five or six hours, till one quarter is consumed; and when cold, strain it through a clean coarse piece of linen; bottle it, and keep it for use.

To waſh Gloves.

TAKE the yolk of an egg, and beat it, and egg the gloves all over, and lay them on a table, and with a hard bruſh and water rub them clean; then rinſe them clean, and ſcrape white lead in water pretty thick, and dip the gloves in; let them dry, and as they begin to dry, ſtretch and rub them till they be limber, dry, and ſmooth; then gum them with gum-dragant ſteeped in ſweet water, and let them dry on a marble ſtone. If you colour them, ſcrape ſome of the following colours amongſt the white lead; the dark colour is umber; for brick colour red lead; for a jeſſamy yellow oaker; for copper colour red oaker; for lemon colour turmerick.

To make Paſte for the Hand.

TAKE a pound of bitter almonds blanched, and two handfuls of ſtoned raiſins, beat them together till they are very fine; then take three or four ſpoonfuls of ſack or brandy, as much ox-gall, three or four ſpoonfuls of brown ſugar, and the yolks of three eggs; beat it well together, ſet it over the fire, and give it two or three boils: when it is almoſt cold, mix it with the almonds; put it in gallipots; the next day cover it cloſe, and keep it cool, and it will be good five or ſix months.

To make Syrup of Marſhmallows.

TAKE marſhmallow roots four ounces, graſs root, aſparagus roots, liquorice, ſton'd raiſins, of each half an ounce; the tops of marſhmallows, pellitory, pimpernel, ſaxifrage, plantane, maiden-hair white and black, of each a handful, red chickes an ounce; the four greater and four leſſer cold ſeeds, of each three drachms; bruiſe all theſe, and boil them in three quarts of water till it comes to two; then put to it four pounds of white ſugar, till it comes to a ſyrup.

To make Syrup of Saffron.

TAKE a pint of the beſt canary, as much baum-water, and two ounces of *Engliſh* ſaffron; open and pull the ſaffron very well, and put it into the liquor to infuſe; let it ſtand cloſe cover'd (ſo as to be hot, but not boil) twelve hours; then ſtrain it out as hot as you can, and add to it two pounds of double refined ſugar; boil it till it is well incorporated, and when it is cold bottle it, and take one ſpoonful in a little ſack or ſmall cordial, as occaſion ſerves.

A Syrup for a Cough, or Aſthma.

TAKE of hyſſop and pennyroyal-water, of each a quarter of a pint, ſlice into it a ſmall ſtick of liquorice, and a few raiſins of the ſun ſtoned: let it ſimmer together a quarter of an hour, and then make it into a ſyrup with brown ſugar-candy; boil it a little, and then put in four or five ſpoonfuls of ſnail-water; give it a walm, and when it is cold, bottle it; take one ſpoonful morning and night, with three drops of balſam of ſulphur in it; you may take a little of the ſyrup without the drops once or twice a day; if the party is ſhort-breath'd, a bliſter is very good.

To make Syrup of Balſam for a Cough.

TAKE one ounce of balſam of *Tolu*, and put to it a quart of ſpring-water, let them boil together two hours; then put in a pound of white ſugar-candy finely beaten, and let it boil half an hour longer; take out the balſam, and ſtrain the ſyrup thro' a flannel bag twice; when it is cold, put it in a bottle. This ſyrup is excellent for a cough; take a ſpoonful of it as you lie down in your bed, and a little at any time when your cough troubles you; you

may

may add to it two ounces of syrup of red poppies, and as much of raspberry syrup.

A Syrup for a Cough.

TAKE of oak-lungs, *French* moss, and maidenhair, of each a handful; boil all these in three pints of spring-water, till it comes to a quart; then strain it out, and put to it six-pennyworth of saffron tied up in a rag, and two pounds of brown sugar-candy; boil it up to a syrup, and when it is cold bottle it; take a spoonful of it as often as your cough troubles you.

Another.

TAKE of unset hyssop, coltsfoot-flowers, and black maidenhair, of each an handful; of white horehound two handfuls; boil these herbs together in three quarts of water till it come to three pints; then take it off, and let the herbs stand in it till it is cold; then squeeze them out very dry, and strain the liquor, and let it boil a quarter of an hour, skim it well; to every pint put in half a pound of white sugar, and let it boil, and skim it, till it comes to a syrup; when it is cold bottle it; take two spoonfuls night and morning, and at any time when the cough is troublesome take one spoonful; don't cork the bottles, but tie them down with a paper.

For a Cough.

TAKE three quarts of spring-water, and put it in a large pipkin, with a calf's-foot, and four spoonfuls of barley, and a handful of dried poppies; boil it together till one quart be consumed; then strain it out, and add a little cinnamon, and a pint of milk, and sweeten it to your taste with loaf sugar; warm it a little, and drink half a pint as often as you please.

Another.

TAKE two ounces of raisins of the sun stoned, one ounce of brown sugar-candy, one ounce of conserve of roses, add to these a little flour of brimstone, mix all well together in a mortar, and take the quantity of a nutmeg night and morning.

To make Conserve of Hips.

GATHER the hips before they grow soft, cut off the heads and stalks, slit them in halves, and take out all the seed and white that is in them very clean; then put them in an earthen pan, and stir them every day, else they will grow mouldy; let them stand till they are soft enough to rub thro' a coarse hair sieve; as the pulp comes, take it off the sieve; then add its weight in sugar, and mix it well together without boiling, keeping it in deep gallipots for use.

****

MEDICINES *and* SALVES.

To cure the Rickets.

OPEN a vein in both ears between the junctures, mix a little aqua-vitæ with the blood, and with it anoint the breast, sides, and neck; then take three ounces of the green ointment, warm a little of it in a spoon, and anoint the wrists and ancles as hot as it may be endured; do this for nine nights just before bed-time; shift not the shirt all the time. If the veins do not appear, rub it with a little lint dipt in aqua-vitæ, or else cause the child to cry, and that will make the veins more visible, and bleed the better.

To

To make the Drink.

TAKE a quart of ſpring-water, of liverwort one handful, liquorice, aniſeeds, coriander-ſeeds, ſweet fennel-ſeeds, and harſhorn, of each an equal quantity; forty raiſins of the ſun ſtoned; fourteen figs: boil all theſe together till one half is conſumed; then put in three ſpoonfuls of honey, and boil it a little more; let it ſtand till it is cold, ſtrain it out, put in two ſpoonfuls of ſyrup of gilliflowers, and bottle it up; take two or three ſpoonfuls morning and evening.

The green Ointment.

TAKE rue, camomile, hyſſop, hogs-fennel, red fennel, roſemary, bays, ladies-mantle, Paul's betony, water-betony, balm, nepp, valerian, mallows, nightſhade, plantane, comfry, adders-tongue, *Roman* wormwood, common wormwood, vervain, clary, agrimony, red ſage, ground-ivy, feverfew, ſelf-heal, melilot, bramble-tops, marſhmallows, ſanicle, ribwort, may-weed, of each two large handfuls; pick and chop them; then take four pounds of butter unwaſh'd, and three pounds of boars-greaſe; melt them together, put in the herbs, and let it boil two hours; then ſtrain it out; let it ſtand a little, and put it into pots for uſe.

Another way to cure the Rickets.

MAKE the drink thus: Take polypodium of the oak, three ounces, of liverwort, and harts-tongue, of each a good handful; betony twenty leaves; white horehound and nepp, of each four tops: boil theſe all together in three quarts of ſweet-wort; till it come to two; then ſtrain it, and when it is cold, put to it two quarts of middling-wort; let it work together; then put it in a little veſſel; and when it has done working take half a quarter

quarter of an ounce of rhubarb sliced very thin; put it in a little linen bag, with a stone in it to keep it from swimming, and hang it in the vessel; when it is three days old, let the child drink of it a quarter of a pint in the morning, and as much in the afternoon at four o'clock, or when the child will take it. You must likewise anoint the child morning and night with this following ointment: take butter in the month of *May*, as soon as it is taken out of the churn, and wash it with the dew of wheat, to a pound of butter take a handful of red sage, as much of rue, camomile, and hyssop; boil all these in the butter, and skim it till it is boiled clear; then strain it out, and keep it in a gallipot for use; you must anoint the reins of the back and the ribs, stroaking it downwards, and upon the small of the belly, and swing the child often with the heels upwards.

To make Charity Oil.

TAKE poplar buds in the beginning of *May* one handful, and put them into a pint and half of oil, and half a pint of *Aqua-vitæ*, cover them close, and let them stand till the following herbs are in season; then add to your buds, betony, charity sanicle, the tops of St. *John*'s wort when blown, adders-tongue, comfry, self-heal, beam, southernwood, pennyroyal, flowers of red sage, parsley, clowns all-heal, balsam, knotgrass, sweet-marjoram, lavender-cotton, red rose-buds, camomile, lavender-tops when blown, of each a small handful; but of poplar-buds, red rose-buds, and adders-tongue double the quantity; gather the herbs in dry weather, and wipe them clean with a cloth; shred them pretty grosly before you put them in; let them steep in a stone pot cover'd very close; then set them on the fire in a skillet; let them simmer with a slow fire five or six hours, then strain it out. This oil is good for any green wound, bruise, burn, or ach; and for inward bruises,

bruises, taking a spoonful in a little warm sack; and for any outward swelling, warm it and anoint the part affected.

An excellent Plaister for any Pain occasioned by a Cold or Bruise.

TAKE of the plaister of red lead and oxycroceum, of each equal parts; of the best *Thebian* opium one scruple; spread it on leather, and lay it to the part affected, after you have well anointed it with this ointment: take of ointment of marshmallows one ounce, oil of *Exeter* half an ounce, oil of spike, and spirit of hartshorn, of each a drachm.

For a Dropsy.

TAKE of horse-radish roots sliced thin, and sweet fennel-seeds bruised, of each two ounces; smallage and fennel-roots sliced, of each an ounce; of the tops of thyme, winter-savory, sweet marjoram, water-cresses, and nettles, of each a handful; bruise the herbs, and boil them in three pints of sack, and three of water, to the consumption of half; let it stand close covered for three hours; then strain it, and drink a draught of it twice a day sweetened with syrup of fennel, fasting two hours after it.

For the Gripes.

TAKE a glass of sack warmed, and dissolve in it one drachm of *Venice* treacle, or *Diascordium*; drink it off going to bed; cover warm.

To stay a Looseness.

TAKE a very good nutmeg, prick it full of holes, and toast it on the point of a knife; then boil it in milk till half be consumed; then eat the milk with the nutmeg powdered in it: in a few times it will stop.

For the Strangury.

TAKE half a pint of plantane-water, one ounce of white sugar-candy finely powder'd, two spoonfuls of sallad-oil, and the juice of a lemon; beat all these together very well, and drink it off.

For a Drought in a Fever.

TAKE of sal-prunella one ounce, dissolve it in spring-water, and put as much sugar to it as will sweeten it; simmer it over the fire till it is a syrup; put some into posset-drink, and take it two or three times a day, or when very thirsty.

A Plaister for an Ague.

TAKE *Venice* turpentine, and mix with it the powder of white hellebore-roots, till it is stiff enough to spread on leather. It must be laid all over the wrist, and over the ball of the thumb, six hours before the fit comes.

For a Chin-cough.

TAKE a spoonful of woodlice, bruise them, mix them with breast-milk, and take them three or four mornings according as you find benefit. It will cure; but some must take it longer than others.

An admirable Tincture for green Wounds.

TAKE balsam of *Peru* one ounce, storax calamita two ounces, benjamin three ounces, succotrine aloes, myrrh, and frankincense, of each half an ounce; angelica-roots and flowers of St. *John*'s wort, of each half an ounce, spirit of wine one pint; beat the drugs, scrape and slice the roots, and put it into a bottle; stop it well, and let it stand in the sun *July*, *August*, and *September*; then strain

I it

it through a fine linen cloth, put it in a bottle, ſtop it cloſe, and keep it for uſe. Apply it to a green wound by anointing it with a feather; then dip lint in it, and put it on, binding it up with a cloth; but let no plaiſter touch it; twice a day wet the lint with a feather; but do not take it off till it is well.

To take off Blackneſs by a Fall.

RUB it well with a cold tallow candle, as ſoon as it is bruiſed; and this will take off the blackneſs.

To break a Bile.

TAKE the yolk of a new-laid egg, ſome honey and wheat-flour; mix them well together, ſpread it on a rag, and lay it on cold.

A Poultice for a hard Swelling.

BOIL the fineſt wheat-flour in cream, till it is pretty thick; then take it off, and put in mallows chopt; ſtir it, and apply it as hot as can be endured; dreſs it twice a day, and make freſh every time.

To ſtay Vomiting.

TAKE aſh-leaves, boil them in vinegar and water, and apply them hot to the ſtomach; do this often.

A Poultice for a ſore Breaſt, Leg, or Arm.

BOIL wheat-flour in ſtrong ale very well, and pretty thick; then take it off the fire, and ſcrape in ſome boars-greaſe, ſtir it well and apply it hot.

A Salve for a Blaſt, Burn, or Scald.

TAKE *May* butter freſh out of the churn, neither waſhed nor ſalted, put into it a good quantity

quantity of the green inner rind of elder, put it in a pipkin, and ſet that in a pot of boiling water; let it infuſe a day or two; then ſtrain it out and keep it in a pot for uſe.

An excellent Remedy for Agues, which has been often tried with very great Succeſs.

TAKE of black ſoap, gunpowder, tobacco and brandy, of each an equal quantity; mix them well together, and three hours before the fit comes, apply to the patient's wriſt; let this be kept on for a fortnight.

To cure the Bite of a mad Dog.

TAKE two quarts of ſtrong ale, two pennyworth of treacle, two garlick-heads, a handful of cinquefoil, ſage and rue; boil them all together to a quart; ſtrain it, and give the patient three or four ſpoonfuls twice a day: take dittany, agrimony, and ruſty bacon, beaten well together, and apply to the ſore, to keep it from feſtering.

For ſpitting Blood.

TAKE of cinnabar of antimony one ounce, and mix it with two ounces of conſerve of red roſes; take as much as a nutmeg night and morning.

To know if a Child has Worms or not.

TAKE a piece of white leather, prick it full of holes with your knife, rub it with wormwood, ſpread honey on it, and ſtrew the powder of ſuccotrine aloes on it; lay it on the child's navel when it goes to bed; and if it has worms, the plaiſter will ſtick faſt; and if it has not, it will fall off.

To

To ſtop Vomiting.

TAKE half a pint of mint-water, an ounce of ſyrup of violets, a quarter of an ounce of mithridate, and half an ounce of ſyrup of roſes; mix all theſe well together, and let the party take two ſpoonfuls firſt, and then one ſpoonful after every vomiting, till it is ſtayed.

To cure the Tooth-ach.

LET the party that is troubled with the tooth-ach lie on the contrary ſide, drop three drops of the juice of rue into the ear on that ſide the tooth acheth, let it remain an hour or two, and it will remove the pain.

A rare Mouth Water.

TAKE roſemary, rue, celandine, plantane, bramble-leaves, woodbine-leaves, and ſage, of each a handful; beat them, and ſteep them in a quart of the beſt white wine vinegar two days and nights; then preſs it well, ſtrain it, put to it ſix ounces of alum, and as much honey, boil them a little together ſoftly, till the alum is diſſolved: when it is cold, keep it for uſe.

To make Lozenges for the Heart-burn.

TAKE of white ſugar-candy a pound, chalk three ounces, bole-armoniac five ſcruples, crabs-eyes one ounce, red coral four ſcruples, nutmegs one ſcruple, pearl two ſcruples; let all theſe be beaten and ſifted, and made all into a paſte with a little ſpring-water; roll it out, and cut your lozenges out with a thimble; lay them to dry; eat four or five at a time, as often as you pleaſe.

To make Syrup of Garlick.

TAKE two heads of garlick, peel it clean, and boil it in a pint of water a pretty while; then change

change your water and boil it till the garlick is tender.; then ſtraining it off, add a pound of double refined ſugar to it, and boil it till it is a thick ſyrup; ſkim it well, and keep it for uſe; take a ſpoonful in a morning faſting, another laſt at night, for a ſhort breath.

To prevent After-pains.

TAKE nine ſingle piony-ſeeds powdered, the ſame quantity of powder of borax, and a little nutmeg; mix all theſe with a little white aniſeed-water in a ſpoon, and give it the woman; and a little aniſeed-water after it, as ſoon as poſſible after ſhe is laid in bed.

To cure the Tooth-ach.

TAKE half an ounce of conſerve of roſemary over night, and half a drachm of extract of rudium in the morning; do this three times together; keep warm.

To ſtop Bleeding at Mouth, Noſe or Ears.

IN the month of *May* take a clean cloth, and wet it in the ſpawn of frogs, nine days, drying it every day in the wind; lay up that cloth, and when you have need, hold it to the place where the blood runs, and it will ſtop.

Another to ſtop Bleeding.

TAKE two handfuls of the tops of bramble-wood and boil it in a quart of old claret till it comes to a pint; give ſix ſpoonfuls once in half an hour: in the winter the roots will do.

To cure the Dropſy.

TAKE ſix gallons of ale pretty ſtrong, but little hopt; alexander, red ſage, ſcurvy-graſs, ground-ivy, and the long green leaves of flower-deluce,

deluce, of each two handfuls; bruiſe theſe well, and boil them well in ale; then ſtrain it out, and when it is cool, work it as other ale; put it in your veſſel, and when it is clear, drink of it in a morning faſting; uſe no other drink except white wine; ſometimes drink good draughts of it at a time.

An excellent Medicine for Shortneſs of Breath.

TAKE half an ounce of flour of brimſtone, a quarter of an ounce of beaten ginger, and three quarters of an ounce of beaten ſena; mix all together in four ounces of honey; take the bigneſs of a nutmeg night and morning for five days together; then once a week for ſome time; then once a fortnight.

For Shortneſs of Breath.

TAKE two quarts of elder-berry juice when very ripe, put one quart in a pipkin to boil, and as it conſumes, put in the reſt by a little at a time; boil it to a balſam; it will take five or ſix hours in boiling. Take a little of it night and morning, or any time.

To cure a pimpled Face, and ſweeten the Blood.

TAKE ſena one ounce, put it in a ſmall ſtone pot, and pour a quart or more of boiling water on it, then fill it up with prunes; cover with paper, and ſet it in the oven with houſhold-bread; take every day, one, two, three, or more, of the prunes and liquor, according as it operates; continue this always, or at leaſt half a year.

To cure the Dropſy, Rheumatiſm, Scurvy, and Cough of the Lungs.

TAKE *Engliſh* orrice-roots, ſquills, and elecampane-roots, each one ounce, hyſſop and horehound-leaves, each one handful, the inner rind of green elder and dwarf-elder, of each one handful, ſena one ounce and half, agarick two drachms, ginger one drachm; cut the roots thin, bruiſe the leaves, and put them into two quarts of the beſt *Liſbon* wine; let theſe boil an hour and half on a gentle fire in an earthen mug, very cloſe ſtopt with a cork, and tied down with a bladder, that no air come to it, and ſet it in a large pot of boiling water; ſet it ſo that no water get into the mug, which muſt hold three quarts, that all the ingredients may have room to go in; when it is almoſt cold, ſtrain it out very hard; take this for a week together if you can, and then miſs a day; and if that does not do, go on with your other bottle of the ſame; take it in a morning faſting, ten ſpoonfuls at a time, without any poſſet-drink; it will both vomit and purge you; it is of an unpleaſant taſte; therefore take a lump of ſugar after it: when it is quite cold, after it is ſtrain'd off, let it ſtand in a flagon to ſettle a night and a day; then bottle it up clear and fine for uſe: it is an admirable medicine.

To ſtop Bleeding.

TAKE a pint of plantane-water, put to it two ounces of iſing-glaſs, and let it ſtand twenty-four hours to diſſolve; pour it from the dregs, and put in a pint of red port wine, and add to it three or four ſticks of cinnamon, and two ounces of double refined ſugar; give it a boil or two, and pour it off: let the party take two or three ſpoonfuls two or three times a day.

To

To cure a Cancer.

TAKE a drachm of the powder of crabs claws finely ſearced, and made into a paſte with damaſk roſe-water, and dried in pellets of lozenges; powder the lozenges as you uſe them, and drink the powder in whey every morning faſting: if there be a ſore, and it is raw, anoint it with a ſalve made of dock-roots and freſh butter; make a ſeaton or iſſue in the neck; keep a low diet, and abſtain from any thing that is ſalt, ſour or ſtrong.

To cure the Joint Evil.

TAKE good ſtore of elder leaves, and diſtil them in a cold ſtill; let the perſon drink every morning and evening half a pint of this water, and waſh the ſores with it morning and evening, firſt warming it a little; lay freſh elder leaves on the ſores, and in a little time you will find they will dry up; but be ſure to follow it exactly. It has cured, when all other remedies have failed.

For the Green Sickneſs.

TAKE centaury the leſs, wormwood, and roſemary flowers, of each a handful, gentian root a drachm, coriander ſeeds two drachms; boil theſe in a quart of water; ſweeten it with ſyrup of ſteel; take four or five ſpoonfuls in the morning, and as much in the afternoon.

To take off Freckles.

TAKE either-bean flower water, elder-flower water, or May-dew gathered from corn, four ſpoonfuls, and add to it one ſpoonful of oil of tartar *per deliquium*; mix it well together, and often waſh the face with it; let it dry on.

To make Pomatum.

TAKE a drachm of white wax, two drachms of *sperma ceti*, an ounce of oil of bitter almonds; slice your wax very thin, and put it in a gallipot, and put the pot in a skillet of boiling water; when the wax is melted, put in your *sperma ceti*, and just stir it together; then put in the oil of almonds; after that take it off the fire, and out of the skillet, and stir it till cold with a bone-knife; then beat it up in rose-water till it is white; keep it in water, and change the water once a day.

A Salve for a Sprain.

TAKE a quarter of a pound of virgin-wax, a quarter of a pound of frankincense, half a pound of *Burgundy* pitch; melt them well together, stirring them all the while till they are melted; then give them a good boil, and strain them into water; work it well into rolls, and keep it for use; the more it is worked, the better it is; spread it on leather.

A rare green Oil for Achs and Bruises.

TAKE a pot of oil of olives, and put it into a stone pot of a gallon, with a narrow mouth; then take southernwood, wormwood, sage, and camomile, of each four handfuls; a quarter of a peck of red rose-buds, the white cut from them; shred them together grossly, and put them into the oil; and once a day, for nine or ten days, stir them well; and when the lavender spike is ripe, put four handfuls of the tops in, and let it stand three or four days longer, covered very close; then boil them an hour upon a slow fire, stirring it often; then put to it a quarter of a pint of the strongest *aqua vitæ*, and let it boil an hour more; then strain it through a coarse cloth, let it stand till it is cold, and keep it in glasses

for

for uſe; warm a little in a ſpoon or ſaucer and bathe the part affected.

To take out Spots of the Small-pox.

TAKE half an ounce of oil of tartar, and as much oil of bitter almonds; mix it together, and with a fine rag daub it often on the face and hands, before the air has penetrated into the ſkin or fleſh.

For the Cholic.

TAKE a drachm and a half of Dr. *Holland*'s powder, mix it with a little ſack, and take it, drinking a glaſs of ſack after it; it gives preſent eaſe.

An approved Remedy againſt ſpitting of Blood.

TAKE of the tops of ſtinging-nettles, and plantane leaves, of each a like quantity; bruiſe them, ſtrain the juice out, and keep it cloſe ſtopt in a bottle; take three or four ſpoonfuls every morning and evening, ſweetened with ſugar of roſes; the juice of comfry-roots drank with wine is alſo very good; let the patient be blooded at firſt, and ſometimes gently purged; but if there happens to be any inward ſoreneſs, occaſioned by ſtraining, this electuary will be very convenient; *viz.* Take an ounce of *Lucatellus*'s balſam, of conſerve of roſes two ounces, twelve drops of ſpirit of ſulphur, to be made into a ſoft electuary with ſyrup of white poppies; the doſe is the quantity of a nutmeg every morning and evening.

A Receipt that cured a Gentleman, who had a long time spit Blood in a great Quantity, and was wasted with a Consumption.

TAKE of hyssop water, and of the purest honey, of each a pint; of agrimony and colts-foot of each a handful; a sprig of rue, brown sugar-candy, liquorice sliced, shavings of hartshorn, of each two ounces; aniseeds bruised one ounce; of figs sliced, and raisins of the sun stoned, of each four ounces: put them all into a pipkin with a gallon of water, and boil it gently over a moderate fire, till half is consumed; then strain it, and when it is cold, put it into bottles, keep it close stopt, and take four or five spoonfuls every morning, at four in the afternoon, and at night the last thing: if you add fresh water to the ingredients, after the first liquor is strained off, you will have a pleasant drink, to be used at any time when you are dry.

An infallible Cure for the galloping Consumption.

TAKE half a pound of raisins of the sun stoned, of figs and honey, of each a quarter of a pound; of *Lucatellus*'s balsam, powder of steel, and flour of elecampane, of each half an ounce; a grated nutmeg, one pound of double refined sugar pounded: shred and pound all these together in a stone mortar pour on it a pint of sallad-oil by degrees; eat a bit of it four times a day the bigness of a nutmeg; every morning drink a glass of old *Malaga* sack, with the yolk of a new laid egg, and as much flour of brimstone as will lie upon a sixpence; the next morning as much flour of elecampane, altertemately.

For

For the Scurvy.

TAKE a pound of guaiacum bark, half a pound of ſaſſafras, and a quarter of a pound of liquorice; boil all theſe in three quarts of water, till it comes to three pints; and when it is cold, put it in a veſſel with two gallons of ale: in three or four days it is fit to drink; uſe no other drink for ſix or twelve months, according to the violence of the diſtemper: it will certainly cure.

For the Jaundice.

TAKE ſome tares, dry them in an oven, and beat them to powder; ſift them, and take a ſpoonful of that powder in a morning faſting, and drink half a pint of white wine after it; do this for three mornings together, and it will cure though very far gone.

For Corns on the Feet.

TAKE the yeaſt of beer (not of ale) and ſpread it on a linen rag, and apply it to the part affected; renew it once a day for three or four weeks; it will cure.

For Chilblains.

ROAST a turnep ſoft; beat it to maſh, and apply it as hot as can be endured to the part affected; let it lie on two or three days, and repeat it two or three times.

To ſtop Bleeding inwardly.

TAKE two drachms of henbane-ſeed, and the like of white poppy-ſeed; beat them up with conſerve of roſes, and give the quantity of a nutmeg at a time; or take twelve handfuls of plantane-leaves, and ſix ounces of freſh comfry-roots; beat theſe, and ſtrain out the juice, adding to it ſome fine ſugar, and drink it off.

To stop Vomiting.

TAKE a large nutmeg, grate away half of it and toast the flat side till the oil ouze out; then clap it to the pit of the stomach; let it lie so long as it is warm; repeat it often till cured.

To kill a Tetter.

TAKE flour of brimstone, ginger, and burnt alum, a like quantity; mix it with unsalted butter, anoint, as hot as can be endured, at bed-time: in the morning wash it off with celandine-water heated; while this is continued, the party must sometimes take cordials, to keep the humour from going inward.

An Ointment for a Blast.

TAKE velvet-leaves, wipe them clean, chop them small, put them to unsalted butter out of the churn, and boil them gently, till they are crisp; then strain it into a gallipot, and keep it for use; lay velvet-leaves over the part, after it is anointed.

A Poultice to ripen Tumours.

TAKE half a pound of figs, white lily-roots, and bean-flour or meal, of each two ounces; boil these in water till it comes to a poultice; spread it thick on a cloth, apply it warm, and shift it as often as it grows dry.

For the Teeth.

TAKE a pint of spring-water, put to it six spoonfuls of the best brandy; wash the mouth often with it, and in the morning roll a bit of alum a little while in the mouth.

For a Drought in a Fever.

MAKE barley-water, sweeten it with syrup of violets, and tincture it with spirit of vitriol; let

let them drink ſometimes of this; put *ſal prunella* in beer or poſſet-drink, and ſometimes drink of that; and if they are ſick and faint, give a ſpoonful of cordial in a diſh of tea.

A Powder that has reſtored Sight when almoſt loſt.

TAKE of betony, celandine, ſaxifrage, eye-bright, penny-royal, and leviſticum, of each a handful; of aniſeeds and cinnamon, of each half an ounce; grains of paradiſe, ginger, hyſſop, parſley, origany, oſier of the mountain, of each a drachm; galangal and ſugar, of each an ounce; make all into a fine powder, and eat of it every day with your meat ſuch a quantity as you uſed to eat of ſalt, and inſtead of it: the oſier you muſt have at the phyſic-garden.

For a Cough ſettled on the Stomach.

TAKE half a pound of figs ſliced, raiſins of the ſun ſtoned as many, and a ſtick of liquorice ſcraped and ſliced, a few aniſeeds, and ſome hyſſop waſhed clean; put all theſe into a quart of ſpring-water; boil it till it comes to a pint; then ſtrain it, and ſweeten it with white ſugar-candy; take two or three ſpoonfuls morning and night, and when the cough troubles you.

To cure a Dropſy.

TAKE of horſe-radiſh roots ſlic'd two ounces; ſweet fennel-roots ſliced two ounces, ſweet fennel-ſeeds beaten two ounces, the tops of thyme, winter-ſavory, ſweet-marjoram, water-creſſes and nettle-tops, of each one handful, wiped and ſhred ſmall; boil theſe in three pints of ſpring-water, a quart of ſack, and a pint of white wine; cover it cloſe, and let it boil till half be conſumed; then take it off the fire, and let it ſtand to ſettle three hours; then ſtrain it it out, and to every draught put in an ounce of the syrup of the five opening roots. Take this in the morning fasting, and at three o'clock in the afternoon, fasting three hours after it. If the party have the scurvy (which usually goes with the dropsy) then add a spoonful of the juice of scurvy-grass to each draught.

An excellent Method to cure the Dropsy.

TAKE a good quantity of black snails, stamp them well with bay-salt, and lay to the hollow of the feet, putting fresh twice a day; take likewise a handful of spearmint and wormwood, bruise them, and put them in a quart of cream, which boil till it comes to an oil; then strain and anoint those parts which are swelled. Take of the tops of green broom, which, after you have dried in an oven, burn upon a clean hearth to ashes, which mingle very well with a quart of white wine, let it stand all night to settle, and in a morning drink half a pint of the clearest; at four in the afternoon, and at night going to bed, do the same. Continue laying the poultice to your feet, and drinking the white wine for three weeks together: this method has been often used with success.

An experienced Eye-water to strengthen the Sight, and prevent Cataracts.

TAKE of eye-bright tops, two handfuls, of celandine, vervain, betony, dill, ground-pine, clary, avens, pimpernel, and rosemary-flowers, of each a handful; of capons gall and aloes bruised, of each half an ounce; of long pepper, a drachm; infuse twenty-four hours in two quarts of white wine: then draw it off in a glass still: drop the water with a feather into the eye often.

For

For Stuffing in the Lungs.

TAKE white sugar-candy powdered and sifted, two ounces; *China* roots powdered and sifted, one ounce; flour of brimstone one ounce: mix these with conserve of roses, or the pap of an apple; and take the bigness of a walnut in the morning, fasting an hour after it; and the last at night, an hour after you have eaten or drank.

To cure Spitting of Blood, if a Vein is broken.

TAKE mice-dung beaten to powder, as much as will lie on a sixpence; and put in a quarter of a pint of the juice of plantane, with a little sugar; give it in the morning fasting, and at night going to bed. Continue this some time, and it will make whole, and cure.

To give Ease in a violent Fit of the Stone.

TAKE a quart of milk, and two handfuls of dried sage, a pennyworth of hemp-seed, and one ounce of white sugar-candy; boil all these together a quarter of an hour, and then put in half a pint of rhenish wine. When the curd is taken off, put the ingredients in a bag, and apply it to the grieved part; and of the liquor drink a good glass full. Let both be as hot as can be endured. If there is not ease the first time, warm it again, and use it. It seldom fails.

For the Strangury.

TAKE three spoonfuls of the juice of camomile, in a small glass of white wine, thrice a day, for three days together.

To procure easy Labour.

TAKE of figs, and raisins of the sun stoned, of each half a pound, four ounces of liquorice scraped and sliced; one spoonful of aniseeds bruised; boil all these in two quarts of spring-water, till one pint is wasted; then strain it out, and drink a quarter of a pint of it morning and evening six weeks before the time.

To procure speedy Delivery when the Throws are great.

TAKE half a drachm of borax powder'd, and mixed with a glass of white wine, some sugar, and a little cinnamon-water; if it does no good the first time, try it again two hours after; so likewise the third time.

To bring away the After-birth.

GIVE thirty or thirty-five drops of oil of juniper in a good glass of sack.

To prevent After-pains.

TAKE half an ounce of large nutmegs and toast them before the fire, and one ounce of the best cinnamon, and beat them together; then mix it with the whites of two eggs, beating it together in a porringer; take every morning in bed as much as will lie on the point of a knife, and so at night, drinking after it the following caudle.

Take of *Alicant* wine or tent, red rose-water, and plantane-water, of each a quarter of a pint; mingle them together, and beat three new-laid eggs, yolks and whites, making a caudle of them; put into it two ounces of double refined sugar, and a quarter of an ounce of cinnamon; you must boil the cinnamon in the wine and water before the eggs are in; and after all is mixed, put to it half a drachm of the powder of knot-

knot-grass; take of this six spoonfuls morning and evening after the electuary.

Another for the same.

TAKE a small quantity of bole-armoniac, and boil it in new milk. Let the party drink of it morning and evening, if it be either a woman with child, or in child-bed.

Take also some hog's dung, and wrap it in a fine linen-rag; warm it well, and put it to the lower part of the belly, and it will stop immediately.

To stop Floodings.

TAKE the white of an egg, and beat it well with four or five spoonfuls of red rose-water, and drink it off morning and night nine mornings together: it has cured, when all other things have failed.

Let the party often take ising-glass boil'd or dissolved in warm new milk, a pint at a time.

A Plaister for a Weakness in the Back.

TAKE plantane, comfry, knot-grass, and shepherds-purse, of each a handful; stamp them small; and boil them in a pound of oil of roses, and a little vinegar; when it is well boiled, strain it, and set it on the fire again, adding to it of wax four ounces, chalk, bole-armoniac and terra-sigillata, of each one ounce, boil all well, keeping it constantly stirring; then cool it, make it into rolls, and keep it for use; spread it on leather when you lay it to the back.

A Drink for the same.

TAKE four roots of comfry, and of knot-grass and clary one handful, a sprig of rosemary, a little galangal, a good quantity of cinnamon and nutmeg sliced, and the pith of the chine of

an

an ox. Stamp and boil all these in a quart of muscadine; then strain it, and put in six yolks of eggs; sweeten the caudle to your taste with double refined sugar, and drink a good draught morning and evening. Take of crocus martis, and conserve of red roses mixed together, three or four times in a day.

For the Dysentery or bloody Flux.

TAKE an iron ladle; anoint it with fine wax; put into it glass of antimony, what you please; set it on a slow fire without flame half an hour, still stirring it with a spatula; then pour it on a clean linen cloth, and rub off all the wax. Grind it to powder.

This is the receipt as I had it; but I kept it three quarters of an hour on the fire, and could not rub off any wax. The dose of a boy of seven or eight years is three grains; for a weak adult five grains; for a strong woman twelve or fourteen grains; for a very strong man eighteen or twenty grains.

N. B. I never gave above fourteen grains; and in the making of it put about a drachm of wax to an ounce of the glass. It sometimes vomits, always purges, and seldom fails of success. I always intermit one day at least betwixt every dose.

For a Flux.

TAKE a pint of new milk, and dissolve in it half a quarter of a pound of loaf sugar, and two drachms of mithridate; give this for a clyster moderately warm; repeat it once or twice, if there be occasion.

For the falling down of the Fundament.

TAKE ginger, slice it, and put it in a little pan; heat it by clear well-kindled coals, and put it in a close-stool. Let the party sit over it, and receive

ceive the fume; cast in the ginger by little and little, and keep warm.

To increase Milk in Nurses.

MAKE gruel with lentils, and let the party drink freely of it; or else boil them in posset-drink, which they like best.

A good Purge.

INfuse an ounce of sena in a pint of water, till half be consumed; when it is cold, add to it one ounce of syrup of roses, and one ounce of syrup of buckthorn; mix them well together. This quantity makes two strong purges for either man or woman, and four for a child.

To prevent Miscarrying.

TAKE of dragons-blood the weight of a silver two-pence, and a drachm of red coral, the weight of two barley-corns of ambergrease; make all these into a very fine powder, mix them well together, and keep them close in a box; if you are frighted, or need it, take as much at a time as will lie on a penny, and keep very still and quiet. Take it in a caudle made with muscadine or tent, and the husks of almonds dried and beaten to powder, and thicken it with the yolks of eggs. Take it in the morning fasting, and at night going to bed; this do till you are out of danger, and lay the following plaister to the back.

Take *Venice* turpentine, and mix it with bole-armoniac, and spread it on black-brown paper, the length and breadth of a hand, and lay it to the small of the back, keeping bed.

For the Green-sickness.

TAKE an ounce of the filings of steel, or rusty iron beaten to powder, and mix it with two ounces of flour of brimstone; then mix it up into an electuary with treacle; the party must take the quantity of a nutmeg in the morning fasting, and at four in the afternoon, continuing it till cured.

To procure a good Colour.

TAKE germander, rue, fumitory, of each a good handful, one pennyworth of saffron tied up in a rag, half a pound of blue currants bruised; stamp the herbs, and infuse all the ingredients in three pints of sack over a gentle fire till half be consumed; drink a quarter of a pint morning and evening, and walk after it; repeat this quantity once or twice.

You may add a spoonful of the following syrup to every draught: Take three ounces of the filings of steel, and put it in a glass bottle with a drachm of mace, and as much cinnamon; pour on them a quart of the best white wine; stop it up close, and let it stand fourteen days, shaking the bottle every day; then strain it out into another bottle, and put two pounds of fine loaf sugar to it finely beaten; let it stand till the sugar is dissolved, without stirring it; then clear it into another bottle, and keep it for use.

A Receipt for the Gout.

THE following prescription of the celebrated Mess. *Boerhave* and *Osterdyke*, for the cure of the gout, has been tried with so much success by a gentleman who was afflicted with that distemper from the age of fifteen to upwards of forty, and is now, as he hopes, perfectly cured of it, and is returning (with all proper caution) to his usual (temperate) manner of living; and it has besides done so much good to several others to whom the salutary regimen has been communicated, that he thinks he cannot do a more acceptable survice to the publick, nor make a better acknowledgment for the benefit he has received by it, than to publish the same for the general good of his fellow-creatures; and though he cannot anſwer for it, that it may have the ſame happy effects on every conſtitution that it has had with him; yet he doubts not that the innocence of the method preſcribed, and the diſintereſted manner in which he offers it to the publick, will be a ſufficient juſtification of his good intentions, and a better recommendation of its genuineneſs and efficacy, than any thing he can ſay further on this ſubject.

Profeſſors BOERHAAVE *and* OSTDERDYKE'*s* *Regimen preſcribed for the Gout.*

THEY are of opinion, that the gout is not to be cured by any other means but by milk, a diet which will in twelve months time alter the whole maſs of blood; and in order thereto, the following directions muſt be ſtrictly obſerved and followed:

I. You muſt not taſte any liquor, only a mixture of one third milk, and two thirds water, your milk as new as you can get it, and to drink it as often as you have occaſion, without adding any other to it. A little tea and coffee is likewiſe permitted, with milk.

II. In the morning as ſoon as awake, and the ſtomach has made a digeſtion, you muſt drink eight ounces of ſpring-water, and faſt two hours after; eat milk and bread, milk-pottage, or tea with milk, with a little bread, and freſh butter.

III. At dinner you muſt not eat any thing but what is made of barley, oats, rice, or millet-ſeed, carrots, potatoes, turneps, ſpinage, beans, peaſe, *&c.* You may likewiſe eat fruit when full ripe, baked pears or apples, apple-dumplins; but above all, milk and biſket is very good, but nothing ſalt or ſour, not even a *Seville* orange.

IV. At ſupper you muſt eat nothing but milk and bread.

V. It is necessary to go to bed betimes, even before nine o' clock, to accustom yourself to sleep much, and use yourself to it.

VI. Every morning before you rise, to have your feet, legs, arms, and hands, well rubbed with pieces of woolen cloth for half an hour, and the same going to bed. This article must be strictly observed; for by this means the humours, knobs, and bunches will be dissipated, and prevent their fixing in the joints, by which they become useless.

VII. You must accustom yourself to exercise, as riding on horseback, which is best, or in any coach, chaise, *&c.* the more the better; but take care of the cold weather, winds and rain.

Lastly, In case a fit of the gout should return, and be violent, which they are of opinion will not, then a little dose of opium, or laudanum, may be taken to compose you; but no oftner than necessity requires. They are of opinion that your father or mother having the gout, is of no consequence, if you will resolve to follow the foregoing directions strictly.

For the Gout.

TAKE a pound of bees-wax, and half a pound of rosin, of olibanum four ounces, of litharge of gold finely powdered, and white lead, of each twelve ounces; of neats-foot oil a pint. Set the oil, together with the bees-wax and rosin, over the fire, as soon as they are melted, put in the powders, keeping it continually stirring with a stick; as soon as it is boiled enough, take it off the fire, and pour it on a board anointed with neats-foot oil, and make it into rolls; apply this plaister, spread on sheeps-leather, to the part affected; once a week take of caryocostinum four drachms dissolved in white wine, keeping yourself warm after it; by applying this plaister, and taking the caryocostinum, there are many which have found very great benefit.

Another for the ſame.

TAKE as much *Venice* treacle as a hazel-nut, mixed up with a ſcruple of *Gaſcoign*'s powder, three or four nights together, when the fit is either on you, or coming on.

For the Piles.

TAKE of the tops of parſley, of mullet, and of elder-buds, of each one handful; boil in a ſufficient quantity of freſh butter till it looks green, and has extracted the ſmell of the herbs; ſtrain, and anoint the place with it three or four times a day.

A bitter Draught.

TAKE of the leaves of *Roman* wormwood, tops of centaury, and St. *John*'s wort, of each a ſmall handful, roots of gentian ſliced two drachms, carraway-ſeeds half an ounce; infuſe theſe in half a pint of rheniſh, and three pints of white wine, for four or five days; take a quarter of a pint in the morning, filling up the bottle, and it will ſerve two or three months.

For the Piles.

MIX calcined oyſter-ſhells with honey, and anoint the part tenderly night and morning.

Another for the ſame.

TAKE a ſheet of lead, and have a piece of lead made like a ſlick-ſtone; then between them grind white lead and ſallad-oil till it is very fine; put it in a gallipot for uſe. If the piles are inward, cut a piece of old tallow-candle, and dip it in this ointment, and put it up; if outward, put ſome on a fine rag, and put it to them.

For the Hemorrhoids inflamed.

LET the party dip their finger in balſam of ſulphur, made with oil of turpentine, and anoint the place two or three times a day.

For Costiveness.

TAKE virgin-honey a quarter of a pound, and mix it with as much cream of tartar as will bring it to a pretty thick electuary, of which take the bigness of a walnut when you please; and for your breakfast eat water-gruel with common mallows boiled in it, and a good piece of butter; the mallows must be chopt small, and eaten with the gruel.

To raise a Blister.

THE seeds of *Clematitis peregrina*, being bound hard on any place, will in an hour or two raise a blister, which you must cut and dress with melilot plaister, or colewort leaves, as other blisters.

Likewise leaven mixed with a little verjuice, and about half a pennyworth of *Cantharides*, and spread on leather the bigness you please, will in nine or ten hours raise a blister; which dress as usual.

A Plaister for the Feet in a Fever.

TAKE of briony-roots one pound, tops of rue a handful, black soap four ounces, and bay-salt two ounces; beat all this in a mash, and out of this spread on a cloth for both feet; apply it warm, and sew cloths over them, and let them lie twelve hours; if there be occasion, renew them three times.

A Drink for a Fever.

TAKE a quart of spring-water, an ounce of burnt hartshorn, a nutmeg quartered, and a stick of cinnamon; let it boil a quarter of an hour; when it is cold sweeten it to your taste with syrup of lemons, or fine sugar, with as many drops of spirit of vitriol as will just sharpen it. Drink of this when you please.

A Vomit.

TAKE seven or eight daffodil-roots, and boil them in a pint of posset-drink, and in the working drink

drink carduus-water a gallon or more; your poſſet muſt be cold when you drink it, and your carduus-tea muſt be blood-warm; if it works too much, put ſome ſalt in a diſh of poſſet, and drink it off.

For the Hiccup.

TAKE three or four preſerved damſons in your mouth at a time, and ſwallow them by degrees.

For the Cramp.

TAKE of roſemary-leaves, chop them very ſmall, ſew them in fine linen, make them into garters, and wear them night and day; lay a down pillow on your legs in the night.

For Weakneſs in the Hands after a Palſey.

TAKE of the tops of roſemary, bruiſe it, and make it up into a ball as big as a great walnut, and let the party roll it up and down in their hand very often, and graſp it in the hand till it is hot; do this very often.

For an old Ach or Strain.

TAKE an ounce of *Lucatellus*'s balſam, and mix it with two drachms of oil of turpentine; gently heat it; anoint the place, and put new flannel on it.

A new Method for curing the Venereal Diſeaſe.

IT need not be ſaid what direful accidents daily happen to people by ſalivations, as the loſs of teeth, of hearing, of a healthful conſtitution, and often even of life itſelf; and what makes this caſe ſtill more deplorable is, that it hath been generally thought, that nothing but an high ſalivation is the proper and adequate cure for this diſtemper; but the learned Dr. *Chicoyneau* has happily diſcovered and proved the contrary. His method, which is ſometimes called, *The* Montpelier *method*, and ſometimes, *The new*

new French *method*, and which is attended with very little pain, and no danger at all, is as follows:

The doctor, according as he finds the patient's case to be, sometimes orders a little blood to be taken away, sometimes a gentle purge or two to be taken; but always makes him bathe five or six times, and always an hour at each time; after which the whole operation consists in nothing more than rubbing his feet, legs, and arms, four, five, or six times, as the case requires, with a mercurial ointment, in such quantities, and at such proper intervals of time, that no high salivation may be raised thereby; sometimes indeed, but not always, a gentle, moderate spitting will ensue, nor is it possible, in some constitutions, to prevent it; but then it is never carried high nor encouraged, it is neither troublesome nor dangerous; the patient during this time keeps his chamber, and observes a regular diet; and all he suffers is only a little feverish heat and restlessness, sometimes for a day or two, when the operation is at the height.

After this manner only, without any further trouble or danger, does Dr. *Chicoyneau* cure the most inveterate pox, with all its symptoms and attendants; it is therefore greatly to be wished, that all our surgeons, and others who undertake the cure of this disease, could be prevailed on, out of regard to the ease and safety of mankind, wholly to lay aside the old pernicious way of salivation, and embrace this new and safe method.

There are some hundreds of gentlemen in *England*, that can, from their own experience, bear witness to the excellency and efficacy of it: three have lately been cured by it, two by Dr. *Chicoyneau* himself, in *France*, and the other here in *London*.

If any person is desirous to be further informed as to this practice, he may consult a book written by Dr. *Chicoyneau*, and translated into *English* by Dr. *Willoughby*.

loughby, intituled, *The practice of ſalivation ſhewn to be of no uſe or efficacy in the cure of the venereal diſeaſe, but greatly prejudicial to it*, &c. or elſe a treatiſe publiſhed by Dr. *Didier*, one of the profeſſors at *Montpelier*; or laſtly, a pamphlet lately publiſhed here, intituled, *A Letter from a phyſician in* London, *to his friend in the country*, giving an account of the *Montpelier* practice in curing the venereal diſeaſe, *&c.*

For the Jaundice.

TAKE half an ounce of rhubarb powdered, and beat it well, with two handfuls of good currants well cleanſed; and of this electuary take every morning a piece as big as a nutmeg, for fourteen or fifteen mornings together, or longer, if need require.

For the Cholic.

TAKE half a pint of Dr. *Stephens*'s water, as much plague-water, as much juniper-berry-water, and an ounce of powder of rhubarb; ſhake the bottle, and take four or five ſpoonfuls at a time when the fit is on you, or likely to come.

For a Burn.

MIX lime-water with linſeed-oil; beat it together, and with a feather anoint the place, and put on a plaiſter to defend it.

To cure a Place that is ſcalded.

TAKE linſeed-oil, and put to it as much thick cream; beat them together very well, and keep it for uſe; anoint the place that is ſcalded twice a day, and it will cure it; put on it ſoft rags, and let nothing preſs it.

The bitter Draught.

TAKE of gentian-root three drachms, of camomile-flowers one ounce, of roſemary-flowers one ounce, tops of centaury, tops of *Roman* wormwood, tops of carduus, of each one handful; boil all theſe in two quarts of ſpring-water till it comes to a quart; you may add a pint of white wine to it; ſtrain it out, and when it is cold, bottle it; drink a quarter of a pint in the morning, and as much at four o'clock in the afternoon.

To draw out a Thorn.

TAKE the roots of comfry, and bruiſe them in a mortar with a little boars-greaſe, and uſe this as a plaiſter.

For a ſcald Head.

TAKE three ſpoonfuls of juice of comfry, two pennyworth of verdigreaſe, and half a pound of hogs-lard; melt it together, but let it not boil: cut off the hair, and anoint the place: it will cure it.

For the Falling-ſickneſs.

TAKE the after-birth of a woman, and dry it to powder, and drink half an ounce thereof in a glaſs of white wine for ſix mornings together: If the patient be a man, it muſt be the after-birth of a female child; if a woman, the contrary.

For the Trembling at the Heart.

MAKE a ſyrup of damaſk roſes, and add thereto a ſmall quantity of red coral, pearl, and ambergreaſe, all finely beaten and powdered; take this ſo long as your pains continue, about a ſpoonful at a time.

For a Pleuriſy, if the Perſon cannot be blooded.

TAKE of carduus, the ſeeds or leaves, a large handful; boil them in a pint of beer till half is conſumed; then ſtrain it, and give it the party warm; they muſt be faſting when they take it, and faſt ſix hours after it, or it will do them harm.

To

To draw a Rheum from the Eyes.

ROAST an egg hard: then cut out the yolk, and take a spoonful of cummin-seed, and a handful of bears-foot; bruise them, and put them into the white of the egg; lay it on the nape of the neck, bind it on with a cloth, and let it lie twenty-four hours, and then renew it: it will cure in a little time.

To clear the Eyes.

TAKE the white of hens-dung, dry it very well, and beat it to powder; sift, and blow it into the eyes when the party goes to bed.

For a Pin or Web in the Eye.

TAKE the gall of a hare, and honey, of each a like quantity; mix them together, take a feather, and put a little into the eye; it will cure in two or three days.

If a hair or fish-bone stick in the throat, immediately swallow the yolk of a raw egg: it is a very good thing.

An extraordinary Ointment for Burns and Scalds.

TAKE of red dock-leaves and mallow-leaves, of each a large handful, two heads of houseleek, of green elder, the bark being scraped from it, a small handful; wash the herbs, and the elder; which being cut small, boil in it a pint and half of cream; boil till it comes to an oil, which, as it rises up, take off with a spoon; afterwards strain, and put to it three drachms of white lead powdered fine.

A very good Drink to be used in all Sorts of Fevers.

TAKE two ounces of burnt hartshorn; boil it with a crust of bread in three pints of water to a quart; strain, and put to it of barley, cinnamon-water,

water, two ounces, cochineal half a drachm; sweeten it with fine sugar, and let the patient, as often as he is thirsty, drink plentifully of it; rub the cochineal in a mortar together with the sugar.

To cure the Yellow or Black Jaundice.

TAKE a quart of white wine, a large red dock-root, a bur-root, that which bears the small bur, two pennyworth of turmerick, a little saffron, a little of the white goose-dung; boil all these together a little while; then let it run through a strainer; drink it morning and evening three days.

A Plaister for the Sciatica.

TAKE of yellow wax a pound, the juice of marjoram and red sage, of each six spoonfuls, juice of onions two spoonfuls: let all these boil together till the juice is consumed; and when it is cold, put in two ounces of turpentine, and of nutmegs, cloves, mace, aniseeds, and frankincense, of each a pennyworth finely powdered; stir it well together, and make a plaister.

A Salve for the King's Evil.

TAKE a burdock-root, and a white lily-root, wash, dry, and scrape them; wrap them in brown paper, and roast them in the embers; when they are soft, take them out, and cut off the burn or hard, and beat them in a mortar with boars-grease and bean-flour; when it is almost enough, put in as much of the best turpentine as will make it smell of it; then put it in a pot for use.

The party must take inwardly two spoonfuls of lime-water in the morning, and fast two hours after it, and do the same at four o'clock in the afternoon; if there be any swelling of the evil, they must bathe it with this water a quarter of an hour together, a little warmed, and wet a cloth, and bind it on the lace; but if the skin be broken, only wash it in the

water,

water, and spread a thin plaister of the salve, and lay on it; shift it once a day; if very bad, you must dress it twice a day.

To make the lime-water: Take a lime-stone as big as a man's head, it must be well burnt; put it into six quarts of boiling water, cover it close, but sometimes stir it; the next day, when it is settled, pour off the clear water, and keep it in bottles for use.

To cure Burstenness.

TAKE hemlock, and bruise it a little; heat it pretty well, and apply it twice a day, without any truss, and keep the party as still as may be; this has cured, when many other things have failed.

A Powder for Burstenness.

TAKE a good quantity of wild musk, roots and all; pick, wash, and dry them; then take of currant-leaves, vine-leaves, and strings, an equal quantity; then take a quart of hemp-seed; you must lay the seed at the bottom of a pot, and the leaves and roots on the top; then put it into an oven, dry them, rub them to powder, and sift them together; the party must take as much of this powder, as will lie on a sixpence in a little ale in the morning, and at four in the afternoon, and continue it five or six weeks. The powder should be made in *May*, if possible.

For the Chin-cough.

TAKE a spoonful of the juice of pennyroyal, mixed with sugar candy beaten to powder; take this for nine mornings together.

To cure the Itch without Sulphur.

TAKE a handful of elecampane-root, and as much sharp-pointed dock, shred them small, and boil them in two quarts of spring-water till it comes to a pint; strain the liquor, and with it let the party wash his hands and face two or three times a day.

For

For the Itch.

TAKE of camomile and velvet-leaves, scurvy-grass and capons feathers, of each one handful; boil these in half a pound of butter out of the churn, till it is an ointment; then strain it out, and mix it with half an ounce of black pepper beaten fine; stir it in till it is cold, and anoint the party with it all over; keep on the same linen for a week; then wash with warm water and sweet herbs, and put on clean linen: before you begin to use this, you must take brimstone and milk for three mornings; keep warm, and purge well after it is over.

For the Scurvy or Dropsy.

STAMP the leaves of elder, and strain the juice, and to a quarter of a pint of juice put so much white wine; warm it a little, and drink it off; do this four or five mornings together; if it purge you, it will certainly do good: take this in the spring.

For a Looseness.

BOIL a good handful of bramble-leaves in milk, sweetened with loaf sugar; drink it night and morning.

For an Ague.

GIVE as much *Virginia* snake-root, dried and powdered, as will lie upon a shilling, in a glass of sherry or sack, just before the cold fit begins; use this two or three times till the ague is gone.

Another.

TAKE an ounce and half of the best refined aloes, and steep it in a quart of brandy; infuse it forty-eight hours, and take four spoonfuls just before the fit comes.

Another.

Another.

TAKE a pint of red rose-water, and put to it an ounce of white sugar-candy, and the juice of three *Seville* oranges; mix all together, and drink it off an hour before you expect the fit; it cures at once or twice taking.

An Ointment for a Burn or Scald.

TAKE a pound of hogs-lard, two good handfuls of sheeps-dung, and a good handful of the green bark of the elder, the brown bark being first taken off; boil all these to an ointment: you must first take out the fire with sallad-oil, a bit of an onion, and the white of an egg, beaten well together; then anoint with the ointment, and in less than a week it will be well.

A Cerecloth.

TAKE three pounds of oil-olive, of red lead, and white lead, of each half a pound, both powdered and sifted; then take three ounces of virgin-wax, two ounces of *Spanish* soap, and as much deers-suet; put all these into a brass kettle, setting it over the fire, stirring it continually till it comes to the height of a salve, which you may know by dropping a little on a trencher; and if it neither hangs to the trencher, nor your fingers, it is enough; then dip your cloths in, and when you take them out, throw them into a pail of water; as they cool, take them out, lay them on a table, and clap them; when you have done, roll them up with papers between, and keep them for use; they must be kept pretty cool. This cerecloth is good for any pain, swelling, or bruise.

The yellow Balsam.

TAKE eight ounces of burgundy-pitch, three ounces and half of yellow bees-wax sliced, one pound of deer-suet, one ounce of *Venice* turpentine beaten

beaten up in plantane-water, half a pint of red roses, a quarter of a pint of vinegar of red roses, twenty-four cloves of garlick, and of salt-petre dried before the fire half the quantity of a nutmeg: bruise the garlick in a stone mortar, and set the oil, vinegar, and garlick, in an earthen pipkin over the fire; let it boil gently half an hour; then put in the pitch and wax, and when that is melted, put in the suet, and one ounce of palm-oil; let it boil a quarter of an hour longer; then take it off the fire, and put in the turpentine and salt-petre; set it over the fire again for a little while; then take it off, and let it stand to cool; then pour it gently into your gallipots; be sure you put in no dregs; the vinegar will fall to the bottom; tie the gallipots down with leather: it is an excellent salve for sore legs, biles, whitloes, sore breasts, and may be safely used to draw corruption out of any sore; put a little of it on lint, and put a plaister of the following black salve over it:

The Black Salve.

TAKE a pint of oil-olive, three quarters of a pound of yellow wax, of frankincense finely beaten and searced, the best mastich, olibanum and myrrh, of each two ounces; half a pound of white lead finely ground, and two drachms of camphire, boil these till they are black; then let it stand a little; oil a board, and pour it on; oil your hand, and make it up in rolls for use.

For the Falling Sickness.

TAKE of the powder of man's skull, of cinnabar, and antimony, of each a drachm; of the root of male-piony, and frogs liver dried, of each two drachms; of the salt of amber half a drachm, conserve of rosemary two ounces, syrup of pionies enough to make it into a soft electuary, of which give the quantity of a large nutmeg every morning and evening, drinking after it three ounces of the water of the lilies

lilies of the valley; take it three days before the new-moon, and three days before the full-moon: to bring the patient quickly out of the fit, let the noſtrils and temples be rubbed with the oil of amber.

For an Ague.

TAKE a quart of ſtrong beer, and a good quantity of the youngeſt artichoke-leaves; ſhred them, and boil them very well together; when you think it almoſt enough, put a ſpoonful of muſtard-ſeed bruiſed, and give it one boil; then ſtrain it, and bottle it; take half a pint as hot as you can, half an hour before the fit comes.

A calcined Water to dry up Ulcers, and old Sores.

TAKE of the beſt *Roman* vitriol three ounces, camphire one ounce; beat them into fine powder, put them into the bottom of a crucible, and fix it in hot embers; cover it with white paper, and put a little tile on it; let it be well calcined, but not too much; when it is cold beat it into fine powder, and ſift it; then add to it three ounces of bole-armoniac, beaten and ſifted; mix all together, and to half an ounce of this powder put a quart of ſpring or plantane-water; boil the water, and when it is blood-warm, put in your half ounce of powder, and ſtir it together in a pewter baſon till it is quite cold; then put it in a bottle for uſe; when you uſe it, ſhake the bottle, and pour ſome out, and uſe it as hot as can be endured, either by ſyringe or waſhing the place twice or thrice a day; and uſe the following plaiſter or ſalve.

The Leaden Plaiſter.

TAKE of white lead three ounces, of red lead ſeven ounces, of bole-armoniac nine ounces; beat all into fine powder, and put to them a pint of the beſt oil-olive; incorporate them over the fire,

and

and let them boil gently half an hour, putting in one ounce of oil of *Exeter*; stir it continually, and when it is enough, make it up in rolls. This is a drying plaister.

A Salve for a Burn or Scald.

TAKE a pound of mutton-suet shred small, melt it, and put into it thyme, sweet-marjoram, melilot, pennyroyal, and hyssop, of each a good handful chopt small; let it stand together four days; then heat it, and strain it out, and put in the same quantity of herbs again, and let it stand four days longer; then heat it, and strain it out, and to that liquor put five pounds of white rosin, and two pounds of bees-wax sliced, and boil it up to a salve; when it is cold enough, oil a board, pour it on it, and make it up in rolls. This is an admirable salve, when the fire is taken out; you must take out the fire with oil, then lay on the plaister: it is good for a small cut, or issue inflamed.

A green Salve.

TAKE five handfuls of clowns all-heal, stamp it, and put it in a pot, adding to it four ounces of boars-grease, half a pint of oil-olive, and wax three ounces sliced; boil it till the juice is consumed, which is known when the stuff doth not bubble at all; then strain it, and put on the fire again, adding two ounces of *Venice* turpentine; let it boil a little, and put it in gallipots for use; melt a little in a spoon, and if the cut or wound be deep, dip your tents in it; if not, dip lint, and put on it, defending the place with a leaden plaister; dress it once a day.

For a sore Breast, when it is broken.

TAKE a quarter of a pound of raisins of the sun stoned, and beat them very small; then add to it near as much honey, and beat it together into a salve;

ſalve; ſpread it on a cloth, and make tents, if occaſion; dreſs it once a day; when it is well drawn, uſe the yellow balſam, and black or leaden plaiſter.

A Poultice for a ſore Breaſt, before it is broken.

BOIL white bread and milk to a poultice; then put to it oil of lilies, and the yolk of an egg; ſet it over the fire again to heat, and apply it as hot as can be endured; dreſs it morning and night till it is broke: then dreſs it with the poultice of raiſins.

To diſperſe Tumours.

TAKE of yellow wax, frankincenſe, and roſin, of each four ounces; melt them together, ſtrain it out, and when it is cold, make it into a roll, and keep it for uſe.

To keep a Cancer in the Breaſt from increaſing.

TAKE of lapis calaminaris four ounces, all in one piece; and having made it red hot in a crucible nine times, quench it every time in a pint of white wine; then take two ounces of lapis tutty, and having burnt that red hot in a crucible three times, quench that every time in a pint of red roſe-water; then beat the tutty and the calaminaris ſtone together in a mortar very fine, and put in a glaſs bottle, with the roſe-water and white wine; ſhake it three or four times a day for nine days, before you begin to uſe it: you muſt keep the wine and the roſe-water cloſe covered when you quench the ſtone, that the ſteam does not go out; when you uſe it, ſhake it well, dip rags in it, and lay them to the breaſt; let the rags remain on till it is dreſſed again; it muſt be dreſſed twice a day, night and morning: the clear water is excellent for weak or ſore eyes.

For a Swelling in the Face.

TAKE a handful of damask rose leaves; boil them in running water till they are tender; stamp them to a pulp, and boil white bread and milk till it is soft; then put in your pulp, with a little hogs-lard, and thicken it with the yolk of an egg, and apply it warm.

For a sore Throat.

MAKE a plaister of *Paracelsus* four inches broad, and so long as to come frome ear to ear, and apply it warm to the throat; then bruise housleek, and press out the juice; add an equal quantity of honey, and a little burnt alum; mix all together, and let the party often take some on a liquorice stick.

A Purging Diet-drink.

TAKE of garden scurvygrass six handfuls, water-cresses, brooklime, and peach-blossoms, of each four handfuls, nettle-tops and fumitory of each three handfuls, monks-rhubarb, and sena of each four ounces, china two ounces, sarsaparilla three ounces, rhubarb one ounce; coriander and sweet fennel-seed, of each half an ounce; cut the herbs, slice the roots, bruise the seeds; put them in a thin bag, and hang them in four gallons of small ale; after three days drink a pint of it every morning; be regular in diet, eat nothing salt or sour.

Pills to purge the Head.

TAKE of the extract of rudium two drachms, and pill fœtida one drachm; mix these well together, and make into twelve pills; take two, or, if the constitution be strong, three of them, at six o'clock in the morning: drink warm gruel, thin broth, or posset-drink, when they work.

For a Canker in the Mouth.

TAKE celandine, columbine, ſage and fennel, of each one handful; ſtamp and ſtrain them, and to the juice put a ſpoonful of honey, half a ſpoonful of burnt alum, and as much bole-armoniac beaten fine; mix and beat all theſe together very well, and wrap a little flax about a ſtick, and rub the canker with it; if it bleeds, it is the better.

A Water for ſore or weak Eyes.

TAKE ground-ivy, celandine and daiſies, of each a like quantity, ſtampt and ſtrained; add to the juice a little ſugar and white roſe water, ſhake this together, and with a feather drop it into the eyes; this takes away all manner of inflammations, ſpots, itching, ſmarting, or webb, and is an excellent thing for the eyes.

An excellent Preſcription for the Cure of Worms.

THE following receipt is an extraordinary remedy for the worms which breed in human bodies, and with which vaſt numbers of people of all ages and both ſexes are afflicted, and ſome of them very ſeverely, eſpecially children, and other young perſons, of whom abundance are carried off yearly by being thrown thereby into convulſions, epileptic fits, vomitings, looſeneſſes, white or green ſickneſs, and other diſorders, which had been judged to have proceeded from other cauſes, when the occaſion thereof was worms. But as there is ſuch a variety of diſorders proceeding from thoſe inteſtine animals, repreſenting other diſeaſes, I ſhall, for the information of ſuch as may little imagine their malady to be occaſioned by worms, when it appears ſo plain to themſelves and their phyſicians, that it is this or that other diſeaſe, firſt ſet down ſome of the many ſigns and ſymptoms of worms, and then preſcribe the remedy to deſtroy, expel, and rid the patient's body of them; and this is a medicine so effectually adapted, and so innocent withal, that if it be pursued as directed, they that take it may depend it will not fail utterly and safely to do it, be the worm of any kind, or situated in any part of the body.

It is to be noted, that there are divers sorts of worms that breed in the body, and take up their residence therein, either in the stomach or bowels, and sometimes near the *sphincter ani*, or fundament, and often knit themselves together, and appear like a bag of worms, and are supposed to be bred from the *ova* or eggs of those animals swallowed down with the food, and encouraged and fed by viscidities in the passages; and according as they reside, or have placed themselves in the body, the symptoms and complaints which such people make are different both in kind and degree; in some to occasion loosenesses, in others costiveness, or frequent desires to go to stool, but cannot; in some to cause a fetid or stinking breath, which is a shrewd sign of worms, as is also a hard or inflamed belly, especially in children, with a voracious appetite, and almost continual thirst, feverishness by fits, and intermitting pulse, and glowing cheeks; in some, a heaviness or pain in the head, startings in sleep, with frightful terrifying dreams; in some, a sleepiness representing a lethargy; in others, a nausea, or loathing of food, with or without motion to vomit, a pain and weight with a gnawing in the stomach, gripings and rumblings in the bowels, like the cholic; in children, a dry cough, and sometimes screaming fits and convulsions, with white lips and white urine; and in both old and young a weakened or lost appetite, giddiness in the head, paleness of countenance, with faintings and cold sweats of a sudden, indigestions, abatement of the strength, and falling away of flesh, as if dropping into a consumption; with many other symptoms, but these are the chief, which ever more or or leſs, ſome or other of them always affect where worms are the cauſe; and for remedy of which the following receipt may be depended on, and very innocent, as well as powerful and effectual, as every one, when they read what it is, will believe, and when they try it, will find.

Take tops of carduus, tops of centaury, *Roman* wormwood, and flowers of camomile (all of them dried, and of the lateſt years growth that you uſe them in) of each a ſmall handful; cut the herbs ſmall, but not the flowers, put them with an ounce of wormſeed bruiſed ſmall into an earthen jar or pickling-pot, and pour upon them a quart of ſpring-water cold; ſtir all about, and then tie the pot over with a double paper, and let it ſtand forty-eight hours, opening and ſtirring it about five or ſix times in that ſpace; at the end of forty eight hours ſtrain it through a cloth, ſqueezing the herbs as dry as you can; which fling away, and of the liquor give to a child from two to four or five years old half a ſpoonful, more or leſs, mixed with a quarter of a ſpoonful of the oil of beech-nuts, every morning upon an empty ſtomach, and to faſt for about an hour after it; and alſo the ſame doſe about four or five in the afternoon every day, for a week or ten days together: by which time, if the caſe be worms, and you make but obſervation, you will find them to come away either dead or alive: older children muſt take more, in proportion to their ages; and grown perſons from three or four to ſix or eight ſpoonfuls, or more, with always half the quantity of the ſaid oil mixed with each doſe, and it will keep the body ſoluble, and ſometimes a little looſe.

This medicine has cured in ſuppoſed incurable caſes, when it has proved at laſt to be from worms, when neither the phyſician or patient have before thought it to be ſo; but if it be not worms, it cannot hurt, but may cure in caſes ſimilar to worms, eſpecially where the ſtomach and bowels are diſordered.

Note, The beech-nut-oil may be had at moft oil-fhops; and the reafon that that oil before any other is advifed, is, that it has a property, as has been often tried, of killing worms of itfelf, when olive-oil and oil of almonds would not do it; and as a confirmation of it, Dr. *Baglivi* fays, in a book of experiments upon live worms from human bodies, That he put worms into divers liquors, which were reputed would kill them, but did not under a great many hours; and that towards night he put others into oil of fweet almonds, and found them alive the next morning; then, after many other experiments, he put one into oil of nuts, where it died prefently: and *Malpighi*, another noted phyfician, fays, That of all common oils, oil of nuts is the beft againft worms; and that at *Milan*, mothers have a cuftom to give their little children once or twice a week toafts dipt in oil of nuts, and to grown people fome fpoonfuls of it fafting: and many other authors fay the fame, particularly Dr. *Nicolas Andry*, of the faculty of phyfic at *Paris*, in his treatife of worms; who alfo fays, if you dip a pencil in oil of nuts, and anoint the bodies of live worms that any one voids, tho' you never touch their heads, they will prefently grow motionlefs, and die beyond recovery; the reafon, he fays, they die fo fuddenly, when anointed, is, becaufe they breathe only by the means of certain little windpipes that run through their bodies: fo that if you ftop up thofe pipes with nut-oil, which hinders the commerce of the air (for that the parts of oil of almonds are more porous than nut-oil, and confequently lefs able to hinder the entrance of the air into the worms) of neceffity the creatures muft die for want of refpiration, though neither the head nor any other part where the pipes are not, be anointed. This is fo true, fays *Malpighi*, that if you put nut-oil upon a worm in any other part but where the pipes are, though the head be not fpared, yet the worm will live, and have its natural motion; and if you put the

oil

oil upon ſome of the pipes only, you ſhall ſee the parts where thoſe pipes are become immoveable; but if you put it, ſays he, upon all the tracheas or pipes, the whole worm becomes motionleſs, and dies in an inſtant: and I do aſſure the public, that the ſame has been many times tried, and found, both by myſelf and others, that no other oil whatever would do what this will. The late Dr. *Radcliffe*, in many of his preſcriptions I have ſeen, ordered that oil preferable to all others, where he had reaſon to ſuſpect the patient had worms; and in one very remarkable caſe of a young lady of thirteen I could name, who was at death's door with the green-ſickneſs, as ſuppoſed, and who, by the uſe of this very oil, and ſuch bitters as he believed the caſe then indicated, once or twice a day repeated, was cured perfectly, upon her voiding cluſters of ſmall worms for ſeveral days together, ſome of which were incloſed in a cyſtis or bag.

This I was willing to obſerve, that people may be ſure to get the oil of nuts, and not any other oil.

A Clyſter for the Worms.

TAKE of rue, wormwood, lavender cotton three or four ſprigs of each; a ſpoonful of aniſeeds bruiſed; boil theſe in a pint of milk, let the third part be conſumed; then ſtrain it out, and add to it as much aloes finely powdered, as will lie on a three-pence; ſweeten it with honey, and give it pretty warm: it ſhould be given three mornings together, and the beſt time is three days before the new or full moon.

Lucatellus's *Balſam.*

TAKE of yellow wax one pound, melt it in a little Canary wine, then add to it oil of olives and *Venice* turpentine of each one pound and a half. Boil them till the wine is evaporated, and when it is almoſt cold, ſtir in of red ſaunders two ounces, and keep it for uſe.

A Salve for a Cerecloth for Bruises or Aches.

TAKE a pint of oil, nine ounces of red lead, two ounces of bees-wax, an ounce of sperma ceti, two ounces of rosin beaten and sifted; set all these on a soft fire in a bell-skillet, stirring till it boils; and then try it on a rag, whether it firmly stick upon it; when it does stick, take it off; and when you have made what cerecloths you please, pour the rest on an oiled board, and make it up in rolls; it is very good for a cut or green wound.

An excellent Recipe to cure a Cold.

TAKE of *Venice* treacle half a drachm, powder of snake-root twelve grains, powder of saffron six grains, volatile salt of hartshorn four grains, syrup of cloves a sufficient quantity to make it into a bolus, to be taken going to rest, drinking a large draught of mountain whey after it; those who cannot afford mountain whey, may drink treacle posset.

To such constitutions as cannot be provoked to sweat, open a vein, or a gentle purge will be of great service.

An Ointment for a Cold on the Stomach.

TAKE an ounce and a half of the oil of *Valentia scabiosa*, oil of sweet almonds a quarter of an ounce, a quarter of an ounce of man's fat, and four scruples of the oil of mace; mix these together, and warm a little in the spoon, and night and morning anoint the stomach; lay a piece of black or lawn-paper on it.

To make Gascoign's *Powder.*

TAKE pearls, crabs-eyes, red coral, white amber, burnt hartshorn, and oriental bezoar, of each half an ounce; the black tips of crabs-claws three

three ounces; make all into a paste, with a jelly of vipers, and roll it into little balls, which dry and keep for use.

A Water to cure red or pimpled Faces.

TAKE a pint of strong white-wine vinegar, and put to it powder of the roots of orrice three drachms, powder of brimstone half an ounce, and camphire two drachms; stamp with a few blanched almonds, four oak apples cut in the middle, and the juice of four lemons, and a handful of bean-flowers; put all these together in a strong double glass bottle, shake them well together, and set it in the sun for ten days; wash the face with this water; let it dry on, and do not wipe it off; this cures red or pimpled faces, spots, heat, morphew, or sun-burn; but you must eat the following diet for three weeks or a month.

Take cucumbers, and cut them as small as herbs to the pot; boil them in a small pipkin with a piece of mutton, and make it into pottage with oatmeal; so eat a mess morning, noon, and night, without intermission, for three weeks or a month: this diet and the water has cured, when nothing else would do.

A good thing to wash the Face in.

TAKE a large piece of camphire, the quantity of a goose-egg, and break it so that it may go into a pint bottle, which fill with water; when it has stood a month, put a spoonful of it in three spoonfuls of milk, and wash in it. Wear a piece of lead beaten exceeding thin, for a forehead-piece, under a forehead-cloth; it keeps the forehead smooth and plump.

For the Worms.

TAKE of wormwood, rue, whitewort, and young leeks of each one handful; chop and strip these herbs very small, and fry them in lard; put

put them on a piece of flannel, and apply them to the ſtomach, as hot as can be borne; and let them lie forty eight hours, changing the herbs when they are dry.

A Plaiſter for Worms in Children.

TAKE two ounces of yellow wax, and as much roſin; boil them half an hour, ſtirring them all the while; ſkim them well, and take it off, and put to it three drachms of aloes, and two ſpoonfuls of treacle, and boil it up again; rub a board with freſh butter, and pour the ſalve thereon; work it well, and make it up in rolls: when you make the plaiſter, ſprinkle it with ſaffron, and cut a hole againſt the navel.

The Stomach Plaiſter.

TAKE of *Burgundy* pitch, frankincenſe, and bees-wax, of each an ounce; melt them together; then put in an ounce of *Venice* turpentine, and an ounce of oil of mace; melt it together, and ſpread your plaiſter on ſheeps-leather; grate on it ſome nutmeg when you lay it on the ſtomach.

To make a Quilt for the Stomach.

TAKE a fine rag four inches ſquare, and ſpread cotton thin over it; take mint and ſweet marjoram dried and rubbed to powder, and ſtrew it over the cotton, pretty thick; then take nutmeg, cloves and mace, of each a quarter of an ounce beaten and ſifted, and ſtrew that over the herbs, and on that ſtrew half an ounce of galangal finely powder'd, then a thin row of cotton, and another fine rag, and quilt it together; when you lay it on the ſtomach, dip it in hot ſack, and lay it on as warm as can be endured: This is very good for a pain in the ſtomach.

For the Pains of the Gout.

MIX *Barbadoes* tar and palm-oil, an equal quantity; juſt melt them together, and gently anoint the part affected.

A preſent Help for the Cholic.

MIX a drachm of mithridate in a ſpoonful of dragon-water, and give it the party to drink in bed, laying a little ſuet on the navel.

A Plaiſter for the Cholic.

SPREAD the whites of four or five eggs well beaten on ſome leather, and over that ſtrew on a ſpoonful of pepper, and as much ginger finely beaten and ſifted; then put this plaiſter on the navel; it often gives ſpeedy eaſe.

For the Ague.

TAKE ſmallage, ribwort, rue, plantane, and olibanum, equal parts; beat all theſe well together with a little bay-ſalt, and put them in a thin bag, and lay it to the wriſt a little before the cold fit comes.

A Powder for Convulſion-fits.

TAKE a drachm and half of ſingle piony-ſeed, of miſletoe of the oak one drachm, pearl, white amber and coral, all finely powdered, of each half a drachm; bezoar two drachms, and five leaves of gold; make all theſe up in a fine powder, and give it in a ſpoonful of black cherry-water, or, if you pleaſe, hyſteric-water: you may give to a child new-born, to prevent fits, as much as will lie on a three-pence, and likewiſe at each change of the moon; and to older people as much as they have ſtrength and occaſion.

To prevent Fits in Children.

TAKE saxifrage, bean pods, black cherry, groundsel and parsley-waters: mix them together with syrup of single piony: give a spoonful very often, especially observe to give it at the change of the moon.

Another.

TAKE a quart of ale, and as much small beer: put into it a handful of southernwood, as much sage, and as much pennyroyal; let it boil half an hour, strain it out, and let the child drink no other drink.

For a Hoarseness with a Cold.

TAKE a quarter of a pint of hyssop-water; make it very sweet with sugar-candy; set it over the fire; and when it is thorough hot, beat the yolk of an egg, brew it in it, and drink it morning and night.

A Remedy for a Cough.

TAKE the yolk of a new-laid egg, and six spoonfuls of red rose-water; beat them well together, and make it very sweet with white-sugar-candy; drink it six nights, going to bed.

An excellent Remedy for Whooping-Coughs.

TAKE dried coltsfoot-leaves a good handful, cut them small, and boil them in a pint of spring-water till half a pint is boil'd away; then take it off the fire, and when it is almost cold, strain it thro' a cloth, squeezing the herb as dry as you can, and then throw it away; dissolve in the liquor an ounce of brown sugar-candy finely powdered, and give the child (if it be about three or four years old,

old, and so in proportion) one spoonful of it, cold or warm, as the season proves, three or four times a day (or oftener, if the fits of coughing come frequently) till well, which will be in two or three days; but it will presently almost abate the fits of coughing.

This herb seems to be a specific for those sorts of coughs, and indeed for all others, in old as well as young; the *Latin* name *Tussilago*, from *Tussis*, the cough, denotes as much; as does also the *Latin* word *Bechium*, from the *Greek* word Βήχιον, a cough; and are the names given it by the ancients, perhaps some thousand years ago; it has wonderfully eased them, when nothing else would do it, and greatly helps in shortness of breath: and in the asthma and phthisic I have not known any thing to exceed it; likewise in wastings or consumptions of the lungs it has been found of excellent use, by its smooth, softning, healing qualities, even where there has been spitting of blood, rawness and soreness of the passages, with hoarseness, *&c.* in blunting the acrimonious humours, which, in such cases, are almost continually dripping upon them; it is to be questioned, whether for those purposes there is to be had, in the whole *Materia Medica*, a medicine so innocent, so safe, and yet so pleasant and effectual, or that can afford relief so soon as this will; grown people may make it stronger than for children. Get the herb of the same year's growth and drying that you use; and the larger the leaves, as being the fuller grown, the better; it is best to be made fresh and fresh, as you want it, and not too much at a time, especially in warm weather.

Pills to purge off a Rheum in the Teeth.

TAKE four drachms of mastich, ten drachms of aloes, three drachms of agarick; beat the mastich and aloes, and grate the agarick: searce them, and make them into pills with syrup of betony: you may

may make but a quarter of this quantity at a time, and take it all out, one pill in the morning, and two at night: you may eat or drink any thing with these pills, and go abroad, keeping yourself warm; and when they work, drink a draught or two of something warm.

To make Daffy's *Elixir.*

TAKE elecampane-roots sliced, and liquorice sliced, aniseeds, coriander-seeds, and carraway-seeds, oriental senna, guaicum bruised, of each two ounces; rhubarb an ounce, saffron a drachm; raisins of the sun stoned a pound; put all these into a glass bottle of a gallon, adding to it three quarts of white aniseed-water; stop the bottle, and let it stand infusing four days, stirring it strongly three or four times a day; then strain it off, and put it into bottles cork'd very well; you must take it morning and night, three spoonfuls going to bed, and as much in the morning, according as you find it work; it requires not much care in diet, nor keeping within; but you must keep warm, and drink something hot in the morning after it has work'd. This elixir is excellent good for the cholic, the gravel in the kidneys, the dropsy, griping of the guts, or any obstructions in the bowels; it purgeth two or three times a day.

An Ointment to cause Hair to grow.

TAKE of boars-grease two ounces, ashes of burnt bees, ashes of southernwood, juice of white lily-root, oil of sweet almonds, of each one drachm; six drachms of pure musk; and according to art make an ointment of these; and the day before the full moon shave the place, anointing it every day with this ointment; it will cause hair to grow where you will have it. Oil of sweet almonds, or spirit of vinegar,

vinegar, is very good to rub the head with, if the hair grows thin.

To preserve and whiten the Teeth.

TAKE a quarter of a pound of honey, and boil it with a little roach alum; skim it well, and then put in a little ginger finely beaten; let it boil a while longer, then take it off; and before it is cold, put to it as much dragons-blood as will make it of a good colour; mix it well together, and keep it in a gallipot for use; take a little on a rag and rub the teeth, you may use it often.

To make Lip Salve.

TAKE a quarter of a pound of alkanet root bruised, and half a quarter of a pound of fresh butter, as much bees-wax, and a pint of claret; boil all these together a pretty while; then strain it, and let it stand till it is cold; then take the wax off the top, and melt it again, and pour it clear from the dregs into your gallipots or boxes: use it when and as often as you please.

To clean and soften the Hands.

SET half a pint of milk over the fire, and put into it half a quartern of almonds blanch'd and beaten very fine; when it boils take it off, and thicken it with the yolk of an egg; then set it on again, stirring it all the while both before and after the egg is in; then take it off, and stir in a small spoonful of sweet oil, and put it in a gallipot; it will keep about five or six days; take a bit as big as a walnut, and rub about your hands, and the dirt or soil will rub off, and it will make them very soft; draw on gloves just as you have used it.

A Re-

A Remedy for Pimples.

TAKE half a quarter of a pound of bitter almonds, blanch, stamp them, and put them into half a pint of spring-water; stir it together, and strain it out; then put to it half a pint of the best brandy, and a pennyworth of the flour of brimstone; shake it well when you use it, which must be often; dab it on with a fine rag.

Another to take away Pimples.

TAKE wheat-flour mingled with honey and vinegar, and lay on the pimples going to bed.

A Water to wash the Face.

BOIL two ounces of *French* barley in three pints of spring-water, shift the water three times; the last water use, adding to it a quartern of bitter almonds blanched, beat, and strained out; then add the juice of two lemons, and a pint of white wine; wash with it at night; put a bit of camphire in the bottle.

To whiten and clean the Hands.

BOIL a quart of new milk, and turn it with a pint of *aqua-vitæ*; and take off the curd; then put into the posset a pint of rhenish wine, and that will raise another curd, which take off; then put in the whites of six eggs well beaten, and that will raise another curd, which you must take off, and mix the three curds together very well, and put them into a gallipot, and put the posset in a bottle; scour your hands with the curd, and wash them with the posset.

A Water for the Scurvy in the Gums.

TAKE two quarts of spring-water, a pound of flower-de-luce root, a quarter of a pound of of roch-alum, two ounces of cloves; of red rose leaves, woodbine leaves, columbine leaves, brown sage, of each two handfuls, and one of rosemary, eight *Seville* oranges, peel and all, only take out the seeds; set these over the fire, and let them boil a quart away; then take it off, strain it, and set it over the fire again, adding to it three quarts of claret, and a pint of honey; let them boil half an hour, skim it well, and when it is cold, bottle it for use; wash and gargle your mouth with it two or three times a day.

To take away Morphew.

TAKE briony roots, and wake-robin; stamp them with brimstone, and make it up in a lump; wrap it in a fine linen rag, dip it in vinegar, and rub the place pretty hard with it; it will take away the morphew spots.

The Italian *Wash for the Neck.*

TAKE a quart of ox-gall, two ounces of roch-alum, and as much white sugar-candy, two drachms of camphire, half an ounce of borax: beat all these in a mortar, and sift them through a fine sieve, then mix them well in the quart of ox-gall; put all together into a three-pint stone bottle well corked; set it to infuse in the sun, or by the fire, six weeks together, stirring it once a day; then strain it from the bottom, and put to every quarter of a pint of this liquor a quart of spring-water, otherwise it will be too thick; set it a little to clarify, and bottle it; put some powder of pearl in the bottle; wash with it.

For a Cold, Dr. Radcliffe's *Receipt.*

MAKE some sack-whey with rosemary boiled in it; mix a little of it in a spoon with twenty grains of *Gascoign*'s powder; then drink half a pint

 of

of your sack-whey, with twelve drops of spirits of hartshorn in it; go to bed, and keep warm; do this two or three nights together.

A Method to cure a Cold.

SHewing, 1. What the catching of cold is, and how dangerous. 2. A present and easy remedy against it. 3. The danger of delaying the cure of it. Taken from the celebrated Dr *George Cheyne*'s book, intituled, *An essay of health and long life*, inscribed to the right honourable Sir *Joseph Jekyll*, master of the rolls; where *p.* 129, 130. the eighth edition, he says, that Dr. *James Keill*, in his *Statica Britannica* had made it out, beyond all possibility of doubting, that catching cold is nothing but sucking in, by the passages of perspiration, large quantities of moist air, and nitrous salts, which by thickening the blood (as is evident from bleeding after catching cold) and thereby obstructing, not only the perspiration, but also all the other finer secretions, raises immediately a small fever, and a tumult in the whole animal œconomy, and, neglected, lays a foundation for consumptions, obstructions of the great viscera, and universal cachexies; the tender, therefore, and valetudinary, ought cautiously to avoid all occasions of catching cold; and if they have been so unfortunate as to get one, to set about its cure immediately, before it has taken too deep root in the habit. From the nature of the disorder thus described, the remedy is obvious; to wit, lying much a-bed, drinking plentifully of small warm sack-whey, with a few drops of spirits of hartshorn, posset-drink, water-gruel, or any other warm small liquors, a scruple of *Gascoign*'s powder morning and night, living low upon spoon-meats, pudding, and chicken, and drinking every thing warm; in a word, treating it at first as a small fever, with gentle diaphoretics; and afterwards, if any cough or spitting should remain, (which this method generally prevents) by softening the breast with a little sugar-candy, and oil of sweet almonds, or a solution of gum-armoniac, an ounce to a quart of barley-water, to make the expectoration easy, and going cautiously and well cloathed into the air afterwards: this is a much more natural, easy, and effectual method, than the practice by balsams, linctuses, pectorals, and the like trumpery in common use, which serve only to spoil the stomach, oppress the spirits, and hurt the constitution.

A Receipt for the Gravel.

PUT two spoonfuls of linseed just bruised into a quart of water, and a little stick of liquorice; boil it a quarter of an hour; then strain it through a sieve, and sweeten it to your taste with syrup of marsh-mallows.

Excellent for Worms in Children.

TAKE fenugreek-seed and wormwood-seed one pennyworth, beat and searced; mix it well in a half-pennyworth of treacle; let the child take a small spoonful in a morning fasting, and fast two hours after it; do this three or four days.

For a Cold.

TAKE rosemary and sliced liquorice, and boil it in small ale, and sweeten it with treacle, and drink it going to bed four or five nights together.

To stop Bleeding in the Stomach.

TAKE oil of spike, natural balsam, bole-armoniac, rhubarb, and turpentine; mix these together, and take as much as a large nutmeg three times a day.

The Tar-pills for a Cough.

TAKE tar, and drop it on powder of liquorice, and make it up into pills; take two every night going to bed, and in a morning drink a glass of water, that liquorice has been three or four days steeped in; do this for nine or ten days together, as you find good.

To cure an Ague.

TAKE small packthread, as much as will go five times about the neck, wrists, and ancles; dip them in oil of amber twice a day for nine days together; keep them on a fortnight after the ague is gone.

For a Looseness.

TAKE sage, and heat it very hot between two dishes; put it in a linen rag and sit on it.

Another.

TAKE frankincense and pitch, and put it on some coals, and sit over it.

For a violent Bleeding at the Nose.

LET the party put their feet in warm water; and if that does not do, let them sit higher in it.

For the Biting of a mad Dog.

PRimrose roots stamped in white wine, and strained; let the patient drink a good draught of it.

For a Purge.

TAKE half an ounce of sena, boil it in a pint of ale till half be consumed; cover it close till the next day; then boil it again till it comes to two spoonfuls; strain it, and add to it two spoonfuls of treacle, and drink it warm; drink gruel, or posset, or or broth after it; keep yourſelf very warm while it is working; or elſe two ounces of ſyrup of roſes, and drink warm ale after it in the working.

For the Itch.

TAKE elecampane-roots, or dock-roots dried, and beaten to powder, and a little beaten ginger, both ſearced very fine; mix it up with freſh butter, and anoint with it in the joints.

For the Dropſy and Scurvy.

TAKE a quart of white wine, ſix ſprigs of wormwood, as much roſemary, half a quarter of an ounce of aloes, the ſame quantity of myrrh, rhubarb, cinnamon, and ſaffron: bruiſe the drugs, pull the ſaffron: and put all into a three-pint ſtone bottle; tie the cork down cloſe, ſet it in a kettle of water and hay, and let it boil three hours; then let it ſtand a day or two to ſettle; let the patient take four ſpoonfuls every morning faſting, and faſt three hours after it, and walk abroad; if it is too long to faſt, and the conſtitution will not bear it, they may drink a draught of water-gruel two hours after it; take this till the quantity is out.

For the Jaundice.

TAKE three bottles of ale, half a pint of the juice of celandine, a quarter of a pint of feverfew, a good handful of the inner rind of barberry-tree, and two pennyworth of ſaffron; divide all into three parts, and put a part into every one of the bottles of ale, and drink a bottle in three mornings: you muſt ſtir after it.

To make Lucatellus's *Balſam, to take inwardly.*

TAKE a quart of the pureſt oil, half a pound of yellow bees-wax, four ounces of *Venice* turpentine, ſix ounces of liquid ſtorax, two ounces of oil-hypericon, two ounces of natural balsam, red rose-water half a pint, and as much plantane-water, red sanders six pennyworth, dragons-blood six pennyworth, mummy six pennyworth, rosemary and bays of each a handful, and sweet-marjoram half a handful; put the herbs and dragons-blood, the wax and mummy, into a pipkin; then put the oil, the turpentine, the oil-hypericon, the storax, the rose-water, and plantane-water, and a quart of spring-water, and if you please some *Irish* slate, some balm of *Gilead*, and some sperma ceti, into another pipkin; set both the pipkins over a soft fire, and let them boil a quarter of an hour; then take it off the fire, and put in the natural balsam and red sanders; give them a boil, and strain all in both pipkins together into an earthen pan; let it stand till it is cold, then pour the water from it, and melt it again; stir it off the fire till it is almost cold; then put it into gallipots, and cover it with paper and leather.

For the Piles.

TAKE galls, such as the dyers use, beat them to powder, and sift them; mix the powder with treacle into an ointment, and dip the rag into it, and apply it to the place affected.

For the Cramp.

TAKE spirit of castor, and oil of worms, of each two drachms; oil of amber one drachm; shake them well together; warm a little in a spoon, and anoint the nape of the neck, chafe it in very well, and cover warm, anoint when in bed.

For a Cough.

TAKE conserve of roses two ounces, diascordium half an ounce, powder of olibanum half a drachm, syrup of jujubes half an ounce; mix these, and take the quantity of a nutmeg three times a day; in the morning, at four, and at night.

For

For a Dropsy.

TAKE three ounces of the outward bark of elm, boiled in three quarts of water till a third part is wasted; drink nothing else; to make it pleasant, you may put in some sugar, or wine, or elder-wine, or syrup made of dwarf elder-berries.

To make Cashew Lozenges.

TAKE half an ounce of balsam of *Tolu*, put it in a silver tankard, and put to it three quarters of a pint of fair water; cover it very close, and let it simmer over a gentle fire twenty four hours; then take ten ounces of loaf-sugar, and half an ounce of *Japan* earth, both finely powdered and sifted; and wet it with two parts of *Tolu* water, and one part orange-flower water, and boil it together, almost to a candy-height; then drop it on pye-plates, but first rub the plates over with an almond, or wash them over with orange-flower water; it is best to do but five ounces at a time, because it will cool before you can drop it; after you have droot them, set the plates a little before the fire; they will slip off the easier; if you would have them perfumed, put in ambergrease.

For Obstructions.

PUT two ounces of steel-filings into a quart bottle of white wine; let it stand three weeks, shaking it once a day; then put in a drachm of mace; let it stand a week longer; then put into another bottle three quarters of a pound of loaf sugar in lumps, and clear off your steel-wine to your sugar, and when it is dissolved, it is fit for use: give a spoonful to a young person, with as much cream of tartar as will lie on a three-pence; to one that is older two spoonfuls, and cream of tartar accordingly.

For a Rheumatism.

LET the party take of the fineſt glazed gun-powder as much as a large thimble may hold; wet it in a ſpoon with milk from the cow, and drink a good half pint of warm milk after it; be covered warm in bed, and ſweat; give it faſting about ſeven in the morning, and take this nine or ten mornings together.

For a Dropſy.

BRUISE a pint of muſtard-ſeed, ſcrape and ſlice a large horſe-radiſh root, ſcrape a handful of the inner rind of elder, and a root of elecampane ſliced; put all theſe into a large bottle, and put to it a quart of good ſtale beer; let it ſteep forty eight hours; drink half a pint every morning faſting, and faſt two hours after it; you may fill it up once or twice.

The Bruiſe Ointment.

TAKE of roſemary, brown ſage, fennel, camomile, hyſſop, baum, woodbine-leaves, ſouthernwood, parſley, wormwood, ſelf-heal, rue, elder-leaves, clowns all-heal, burdock-leaves, of each a handful; put them into a pot with very ſtrong beer, or ſpirits enough to cover them well, and two pounds of freſh butter from the churn; cover it up with paſte, and bake it with bread; and when it is baked, ſtrain it out; when it is cold, ſkim off the butter, melt it, and put it into a gallipot for uſe; the liquor is very good to dip flannels into, and bathe any green bruiſe or ach, as hot as can be borne,

A good Vomit.

TAKE two ounces of the fineſt white alum, beat it ſmall, put it into better than half a pint of new milk, ſet it on a ſlow fire till the milk is turned clear; let it ſtand a quarter of an hour; ſtrain it off, and drink it juſt warm; it will give three or four vomits, and is very ſafe; and an excellent cure for an an ague taken half an hour before the fit; drink good ſtore of carduus-tea after it, or elſe take half a drachm of ipecacuanha, and carduus-tea with it.

Another Vomit.

TAKE rectified butter of antimony, digeſt it with thrice its own weight of alcohol; a ſingle drop or two whereof being taken in ſack, or any convenient vehicle, works well by vomit: it was a ſecret of Mr. *Boyle*'s, and highly valued; and by him communicated to the admiral *Du Queſne:* it is likewiſe recommended by Dr. *Boerhaave.*

An Ointment for a ſcald Head.

TAKE a pound of *May* butter without ſalt out of the churn, a pint of ale, not too ſtale, a good handful of green wormwood; let the ale be hot, and put the butter to melt; ſhred the wormwood, and let them boil together till it turns green; ſtrain it, and when it is cold, take the ointment from the dregs.

To cure the Piles.

TAKE two pennyworth of litharge of gold, an ounce of ſallad-oil, a ſpoonful of white wine vinegar; put all into a new gallipot; beat it together with a knife, till it is as thick as an ointment, ſpread it on a cloth, and apply it to the place; if inward, put it up as far as you can.

An admirable Powder for the Teeth.

TAKE tartar of vitriol two drachms, beſt dragons-blood and myrrh, each half a drachm, gum lac a drachm, of ambergreaſe four grains, and thoſe who like it may add two grains of muſk; mix well, and make a powder, to be kept in a phial cloſe ſtopt. The method of uſing it is thus: put a little of the powder upon a *China* ſaucer, or a piece of white paper; then take a clean linen cloth upon the end of your finger, juſt moiſten it with water, and dip it in the powder, and rub the teeth well once a day, if they be foul;

hut

but if you want to preserve their beauty, only twice a week is sufficient for its use. This powder will preserve the teeth and gums beyond any other, under whatever title dignified or distinguished; and what is commonly called a tainted or stinking breath, mostly proceeds from rotten teeth, or scorbutic gums; which last distemper, so incident and fatal to childrens teeth, this powder will effectually remove. Indeed there is no cure for a rotten tooth, therefore I advise to pull it out; and if this cannot be effected, the above powder will sweeten the breath, and prevent such tooth from any ill savour. The too frequent use of the tooth-brush makes the teeth become long and deformed, altho' it be a good instrument, and the moderate use of it proper enough. After rubbing the teeth with the powder, the mouth may be washed with a little red wine warm, or the like.

To make the Teeth white.

TAKE three spoonfuls of the juice of celandine, nine spoonfuls of honey, half a spoonful of burnt alum; mix these together, and rub the teeth with it.

A Powder for the Teeth.

TAKE half an ounce of cream of tartar, and a quarter of an ounce of powder of myrrh; rub the teeth with it two or three times a week.

To make the right Angel-Salve.

TAKE black and yellow rosin, of each half a pound, virgin-wax and frankincense, of each a quarter of a pound; mastich an ounce, deer suet a quarter of a pound; melt what is to be melted, and powder what is to be powder'd, and sift it fine; then boil them and strain them thro' a canvas bag into a bottle of white wine; then boil the wine with the ingredients an hour with a gentle fire, and let it stand till it is no hotter than blood; then put to it two drachms of camphire, and two ounces of *Venice* turpentine,

pentine, and stir it constantly till it is cold: be sure your stuff be no hotter than blood when you put in your camphire and turpentine, otherwise it is spoiled; make it up in rolls, and keep it for use: it is the best salve made.

To cure an Ague.

TAKE tobacco-dust and soot, an equal quantity, and nine cloves of garlick; beat it well together, and mix it with soap into a pretty stiff paste, and make two cakes something broader than a five shilling piece, and something thicker; lay it on the inside of each wrist, and bind it on with rags; put it on an hour before the fit is expected: if it does not do the first time, in three or four days repeat it with fresh.

To take out the Redness and Scurf after the Small-Pox.

AFTER the first scabs are well off, anoint the face, going to bed, with the following ointment: beat common allum very fine, and sift it thro' a lawn sieve, and mix it with oil like a thick cream, and lay it all over the face with a feather; in the morning have bran boil'd in water till it is slippery; then wash it off as hot as you can bear it; so do for a month or more, as there is occasion.

To make Brimstone Lozenges for a short Breath.

TAKE flour of brimstone and double refined sugar, beaten and sifted, an equal quantity; make it into lozenges with gum dragant steeped in rose water; dry them in the sun, and take three or four a day.

For a Burn.

TAKE common alum, beat and sift it, and beat it up with whites of eggs to a curd; then with a feather anoint the place; it will cure without any other thing.

To

To procure the Menses.

TAKE a quarter of an ounce of pure myrrh made into fine powder; mix it with three quarters of an ounce of conserve of bugloss flowers; two days before your expectation, take this quantity at four times, last at night, and first in the morning; drink after each time a draught of posset-drink made of ale, white wine and milk, and boil in it some pennyroyal, and a few camomile flowers.

To stop Flooding.

DISSOLVE a quarter of an ounce of *Venice* treacle in four spoonfuls of water, and drop in it thirty or forty of *Jones*'s drops; take it when occasion requires, especially in child-bed.

To provoke Urine presently when stopt.

IN a quart of beer boil a handful of the berries of eglantine till it comes to a pint: drink it off luke-warm.

To draw up the Uvula.

TAKE ground-ivy, and heat it well between two tiles, and lay it as warm as can be borne on the top of the head. The blood of a hare dried and drank in red wine, stops the bloody-flux, tho' ever so severe.

For a Thrush in Childrens Mouths.

TAKE a hot sea-coal, and quench it in as much spring-water as will cover the coal; wash it with this five or six times a day.

For the Worms in Children.

TAKE mithridate and honey, of each a pennyworth, oil of mace two pennyworth; melt them together, and spread upon leather cut in the shape of a heart; oil of savin and wormwood, of each six drops; of alum and saffron in powder, of each

each one drachm; rub the oils, and ſtrew the powders, all over the plaiſter; apply it, being warm'd, to the child's ſtomach with the point upwards.

For a Weakneſs in the Back or Reins.

TAKE an ounce of *Venice* turpentine, waſh it in red roſe water, work it in the water till it is white; pour the water from it, and work it up into pills with powder of turmerick and a grated nutmeg; you may put a little rhubarb as you ſee occaſion; take three in the morning, and three in the evening, in a little ſyrup of elder.

For the Yellow Jaundice.

TAKE a handful of burdock-roots, cut them in ſlices to the cores, and dry them; half a handful of the inner rind of barberries, three races of turmerick beat very fine, three or four tabes of the whiteſt gooſe-dung; put all in a quart of ſtrong beer; cover it cloſe, and let it infuſe in the embers all night; in the morning ſtrain it off; add to it a groat's-worth of ſaffron; take half a pint at a time firſt and laſt.

An approved Remedy for a Cancer in the Breaſt.

TAKE off the hard knobs or warts which grow on the legs of a ſtone-horſe; dry them carefully, and powder them; give from a ſcruple to half a drachm every morning and evening in a glaſs of ſack; you muſt continue taking them for a month or ſix weeks, or longer, if the cancer is far gone.

An approved Medicine for the Stone.

TAKE ſix pounds of black cherries, ſtamp them in a mortar till the kernels are bruiſed; then take of the powder of amber, and of coral prepar'd, of each two ounces: put them with the cherries into a ſtill, a ſtill, and with a gentle fire draw off the water; which if you take for the ſtone, mix a drachm of the powder of amber with a ſpoonful of it, drinking three or four ſpoonfuls after it; if for the palſy or convulſions, take four ſpoonfuls, without adding any thing, in the morning faſting.

To give Eaſe in Fits of the Stone, and to cure the Suppreſſion of Urine, which uſually attend them.

TAKE ſnail-ſhells and bees, of each an equal quantity; dry them in an oven with a moderate heat; then beat them to a very fine powder, of which give as much as will lie on a ſixpence, in a quarter of a pint of bean-flower water, every morning, faſting two hours after it: continue this for three days together: this has been often found to break the ſtone, and to force a ſpeedy paſſage for the urine.

****

DIRECTIONS for Painting *Rooms* or *Pales.*

The Price of Materials.

	l.	*s.*	*d.*
One hundred weight of red-lead —	0	18	0
One hundred weight of white-lead —	1	2	0
Linſeed-oil by the gallon — —	0	3	0

A ſmall quantity of oil of turpentine is ſufficient.

THE red-lead muſt be ground with linſeed-oil, and may be uſed very thin, it being the priming or firſt colouring; when it is uſed, ſome drying oil muſt be put to it.

To

To prepare the Drying-oil.

TAKE two quarts of linſeed-oil, put it in a ſkillet or ſauce-pan, and put to it a pound of burnt amber; boil it for two hours gently: prepare this without doors, for fear of endangering the houſe; let it ſettle and it will be fit for uſe; pour the clear off, and uſe that with the white-lead, the lees or dregs being as good to be uſed with red-lead.

For the ſecond Priming.

TAKE a hundred weight of white-lead, with an equal quantity of whiting in bulk, but not in weight; grind them together with linſeed-oil pretty ſtiff; when it is uſed put to it ſome of the drying-oil above-mentioned, with a ſmall quantity of oil of turpentine: this is not to be laid on till the firſt priming is very dry.

To prepare the Putty or Paſte to ſtop all Joints in the Pales or Wood, that no Water may ſoak in.

TAKE a quantity of whiting, and mix it very ſtiff with linſeed-oil and drying-oil, of each an equal quantity; when it is ſo ſtiff it cannot be wrought by the hand, more whiting muſt be added, and beat up with a mallet till it is ſtiffer than dough; when your ſecond priming is dry, ſtop ſuch places as require with this putty; and when the putty is ſkinn'd over, that is, the outſide dry, then proceed and lay on the laſt paint; which is thus ſo be prepared: take of the beſt white-lead, grind it very ſtiff with linſeed-oil, and when it is uſed put to it ſome of the drying-oil, and ſome oil of turpentine; thus will the work be finiſhed to great ſatisfaction, for it will be more clean and more durable that it can be perform'd by a houſe-painter, without you pay conſiderably more than the common rates. Repeat this preparation once in five years, and it will pre-

ſerve

ſerve any outworks that are expoſed to the weather time out of mind. But for rooms or places within doors, proceed thus:

The Wainſcot Colour for Rooms.

WHEN you mix your laſt paint, add to your white lead a ſmall quantity of yellow oker, and uſe it as above directed: it is now the univerſal faſhion to paint all rooms of a plain wainſcot colour; and if it ſhould alter, it is but mixing any other colour with the white lead inſtead of yellow oker: there muſt be bought ſix chamber-pots of earth, and ſix bruſhes, and keep them to what they belong to.

To make yellow Varniſh.

TAKE one quart of ſpirit of wine, ſeven ounces of ſeed-lake, half an ounce of ſandarach, a quarter of an ounce of gum-anime, and one drachm of maſtich; let theſe infuſe for thirty ſix or forty hours: ſtrain it off, and keep it for uſe: it is good for frames of chairs or tables, or any thing black or brown; do it on with a bruſh three or four times, nine times if you poliſh it afterwards, and a day between every doing; lay it very thin the firſt and ſecond time, afterwards ſomething thicker.

To make white Varniſh.

TO a quart of ſpirit of wine, take eight ounces of ſandarach well waſhed in ſpirit of wine; that ſpirit of wine will make the yellow varniſh; then add to it a quarter of an ounce of gum-anime well pick'd, half an ounce of camphire, and a drachm of maſtich; ſteep this as long as the yellow varniſh; then ſtrain it out, and keep it for uſe.

To boil Plate.

TAKE twelve gallons of water, or a quantity according to your plate in largeneſs or quantity; there muſt be water enough to cover it; put the

water

water in a copper, or large kettle; and when it boils put in half a pound of red argol, a pound of common ſalt, an ounce of roch-alum; firſt put your plate into a charcoal-fire, and cover it till it is red hot; then throw it into your copper, and let boil half an hour; then take it out, and waſh it in cold fair water, and ſet it before the charcoal-fire till it is very dry.

Dr. Mead'*s Receipt for the Bite of a mad Dog.*

LET the patient bleed at the arm nine or ten ounces: take of the herb called in *Latin*, *Lichen cinerus terreſtris*, in *Engliſh*, *Aſh-coloured ground liver-wort*, cleaned, dried, and powdered, half an ounce; of black pepper powdered, two drachms: mix theſe well together, and divide the powder into four doſes, one of which muſt be taken every morning faſting, for four mornings ſucceſſively, in half a pint of cows milk warm: after theſe four doſes are taken, the patient muſt go into the cold bath, or a cold ſpring or river, every morning faſting, for a month; he muſt be dipt all over, but not ſtay in (with his head above water) longer than half a minute, if the water be very cold; after this he muſt go in three times a week for a fortnight longer. The *Lichen* is a very common herb, and grows generally in ſandy and barren ſoils all over *England*; the right time to gather it is in the months of *October* and *November*.

Another for the Bite of a mad Dog, which has cured when the Perſon was diſordered, and the ſalt Water failed.

TAKE of tormentil-roots an ounce, aſſa fœtida as much as a bean, caſtor four pennyworth, lignum aloes two pennyworth; ſteep theſe in milk twelve hours; boil the milk, and drink it faſting, before the change or full-moon, or as oft as occaſion.

A Receipt for destroying Bugs.

TAKE of the highest rectified spirit of wine (*viz.* lamp-spirits) half a pint; newly distilled oil, or spirit of turpentine, half a pint; mix them together, adding to it half an ounce of camphire, which will dissolve in it in a few minutes; shake them well together, and with a piece of sponge, or a brush, dip in some of it, wet very well the bed or furniture wherein those vermin harbour or breed, and it will infallibly kill and destroy both them and their nits, although they swarm ever so much; but then the bed or furniture must be well and thoroughly wet with it (the dust upon them being first brushed and shook off) by which means it will neither stain, soil, or in the least hurt, the finest silk or damask bed that is. The quantity here ordered of this curious, neat, white mixture (which costs about a shilling) will rid any one bed whatsoever, though it swarms with bugs; do but touch a live bug with a drop of it, and you will find it to die instantly. If any bug or bugs should happen to appear after once using it, it will only be for want of well wetting the lace, *&c.* of the bed, the foldings of the linings or curtains near the rings, or the joints or holes in and about the bed, head-board, *&c.* wherein the bugs or nits nestle and breed; and then their being well wet again with more of the same mixture, which dries in as fast as you use it, pouring some of it into the joints and holes where the sponge or brush cannot reach, will never fail absolutely to destroy them all. Some beds that have much wood-work, can hardly be thoroughly cleared, without being first taken down; but others that can be drawn out, or that you can get well behind, to be done as it should be, may.

Note, The smell this mixture occasions, will be all gone in two or three days, which yet is very wholeſome, and to many people agreeable ; you muſt remember always to ſhake the mixture together very well whenever you uſe it, which muſt be in the day time, not by candle light, leſt the ſubtilty of the mixture ſhould catch the flame as you are uſing it, and occaſion damage.

An infallible Receipt to deſtroy Bugs.

TO every ounce of quickſilver put the whites of five or ſix eggs ; mix them, and beat them well together in a wooden diſh with a bruſh, till the globules of the quickſilver are but juſt perceptible ; then, after having taken the bedſtead to pieces, and bruſhed it very clean from the duſt and dirt (without waſhing) rub into all the cracks and joints the above mixture, letting it dry on ; nor muſt the bedſtead be waſhed at any time afterwards: by the firſt application they will in moſt places be deſtroy'd ; if not, a ſecond will not fail deſtroying them intirely.

An excellent Way of Waſhing, to ſave Soap, and whiten Cloaths.

TAKE a butter tub, or one of that ſize, and, with a gimblet, bore holes in it about half way ; put into your tub ſome clean ſtraw, and over that about a peck of wood aſhes : fill it with cold water, and ſet it into another veſſel to receive the water as it runs out of the holes of the tub ; if it is too ſtrong a lye, add to it ſome warm water ; waſh your linen in it, ſlightly ſoaping the cloaths before you waſh them ; two pounds of ſoap will go as far as ſix pounds, and make the cloaths whiter and cleaner, when you by experience have got the right way : if it is too ſtrong for the hands, make it weaker with water.

To take Mildew out of Linen.

TAKE soap, and rub it on very well; then scrape chalk very fine, and rub that in well, and lay it on the grass; as it dries, wet it a little; and at once or twice doing it will come out.

An infallible cure for the Bite of a mad Dog.

OF all the diseases incident to mankind, there is none so shocking to our nature as the bite of a mad dog: and yet as terrible as it is, we have known instances, of those who chose rather to hazard the worst effects of it, and to die the worst of deaths, than to follow the advice of their physicians, by making use of the known specific of dipping in the sea, or salt-water. It is for the sake of people of this unhappy temper, who may have the misfortune to be bit, and of those who may have cattle that are so, that we publish the following receipt, which has been frequently made use of in a neighbouring country, and (as the gentleman who communicated it says) was never known to fail.

Take the leaves of rue, picked from the stalks and bruised, six ounces; garlick picked from the stalks and bruised, *Venice* treacle or mithridate, and scrapings of pewter, of each four ounces; boil all these over a slow fire in two quarts of ale, till one pint is consumed; keep it in a bottle close stopped, and give of it nine spoonfuls to the person warm seven mornings successively, and six to a dog, to be given nine days after the bite; apply some of the ingredients to the part bitten.

N.B. This receipt was taken out of *Cathorp* church in *Lincolnshire*, the whole town almost being bitten, and not one person who took this medicine but was cured.

Another

Another for the same.

TAKE the shells of oysters, and calcine the white or inner part of them; when thoroughly calcined, which may be done either in an oven or a crucible, beat them to a fine powder in a mortar: that powder must also be sifted through a fine sieve: when all this is done, put * six gros of the powder into a pint of right neat white wine; and let the patient drink it off, without taking any other thing, of any kind whatever, until at least three hours afterwards; and by all means not to touch butter, or any thing that is oily, during the time of cure. The next day he must take four gros of the same powder in the aforesaid quantity of wine, and the third day two gros, still fasting three hours afterwards; and then the cure is completed.

A Receipt for Colds.

TAKE of *Venice* treacle half a drachm, powder of snake-root twelve grains, powder of saffron six grains, volatile salt of hartshorn four grains, syrup of cloves a sufficient quantity to make it into a bolus; to be taken going to rest, drinking a large draught of warm mountain whey after it.

N. B. Those who cannot afford mountain whey, may drink treacle posset. To such constitutions as cannot be provoked to sweat, opening a vein, or a gentle purge, will be of great service.

* Eight Gros makes a *French* Ounce, which our Apothecaries know how to adjust to their own.

BROTHS, &c. for the SICK.

To make Broth of a Calf's Head.

TAKE half a calf's-head, without the brains and tongue, waſh it clean, cut it to pieces, put it into a gallon of water, ſet it over a ſlow fire. When the ſcum riſes ſkim it clean, and put in one ounce of ivory ſhavings, one drachm of mace, one nutmeg ſliced. Boil it till half is conſumed, and then ſtrain it. Drink three pints a day, either with ſugar or a little ſalt.

To make Broth of a Knuckle or Scrag of Veal.

TAKE any part of a knuckle or ſcrag of veal, put it into a pot with as much water as will cover it, one ounce of hartſhorn ſhavings, half an ounce of vermicelli, two blades of mace, and three cloves; boil it an hour and a half. If the patient be coſtive, boil in it a quarter of a pound of currants, and ſweeten it with *Liſbon* ſugar.

To make a ſtrengthening Drink for very weak Perſons.

TAKE one pound of ſilver-bellied eels; cleanſe them and cut them into ſmall pieces, put them into a pot with five quarts of water, one ounce of ſago, a cruſt of bread, a top of mint, a ſmall handful of pennyroyal, a drachm of mace, as much nutmeg, and a ſmall ſtick of cinnamon; boil it till half is conſumed. Drink of it as often as thirſty.

To make Chicken Broth.

TAKE a chick just killed, bruise it, put it into a sauce-pan with five quarts of water, a blade or two of mace, a small piece of lemon-peel, one spoonful of ground rice; boil it till but two quarts remain.

To make Water Gruel.

TAKE a large spoonful of oatmeal, and a pint of water; mix them together, set it on the fire, and let it boil for some time, stirring it often; then strain it through a sieve, and add to it a good piece of butter, and a little salt, stirring it constantly with a spoon, till the butter is melted.

To make Chicken Water.

TAKE a cock or large fowl, strip off its skin, and bruise it with a rolling-pin. Then put it into a sauce-pan with two quarts of water, a crust of bread, and an ounce of *French* barley. Let it boil till half the water is evaporated, then strain it off, and season it with salt.

To make Barley Water.

TAKE a pound of pearl-barley, and two quarts of water; let it boil half an hour; then strain off the barley, and throw away the water; put the barley into three pints of fresh water, and boil it till it comes to a quart; strain it off, and sweeten it to your palate, adding to it two spoonfuls of white wine, or milk.

To make Seed Water.

TAKE of coriander-seed, carraway-seed, cubebs, sweet fennel-seed, and aniseed, of each half an ounce, bruise them and boil them in a quart of water; strain it, brew it up with the yolk of an egg, and add to it a little sack and double refined sugar.

To make White Caudle.

TAKE four ſpoonfuls of oatmeal, two blades of mace, a piece of lemon-peel, cloves and ginger of each one quarter of an ounce; put theſe into two quarts of water, and let it boil about an hour, ſtirring it often; then ſtrain it out, and add to every quart half a pint of wine, ſome grated nutmeg and ſugar.

To make Brown Caudle.

TAKE ſix ſpoonfuls of oatmeal, a bit of lemon-peel, and two or three blades of mace, put them into two quarts of water, let it boil as before, and ſtrain it. Then add to it a quart of ſtale beer, not bitter, and ſome ſugar; let it boil, and then put to it a pint of white wine.

To make the Pectoral Drink.

TAKE of *China* root one ounce, ſarſaparilla, comfry, and liquorice, of each half an ounce, orrice and elecampane, of each one quarter of an ounce, yellow and red ſaunders, of each two drachms, aniſeeds one drachm, *Malaga* raiſins half a pound; boil theſe in a gallon of ſpring-water, till half is evaporated, and then ſtrain it off, and ſweeten it with ſyrup of maiden-hair.

To make artificial Aſſes Milk.

TAKE of pearl-barley two ounces, of eringo-root, and *China* root, of each one ounce, *Japan* earth one drachm, white maiden-hair and honey of each one ounce, ten ſnails bruiſed; boil theſe in three quarts of water till half be waſted. Drink a quarter of a pint of it, mixed with an equal quantity of warm milk from the cow, and ſweetened with ſyrup of balſam of *Tolu*, morning and night.

To

To make Chicken Broth.

TAKE a chick just killed, bruise it, put it into a sauce-pan with five quarts of water, a blade or two of mace, a small piece of lemon-peel, one spoonful of ground rice; boil it till but two quarts remain.

To make Water Gruel.

TAKE a large spoonful of oatmeal, and a pint of water; mix them together, set it on the fire, and let it boil for some time, stirring it often; then strain it through a sieve, and add to it a good piece of butter, and a little salt, stirring it constantly with a spoon, till the butter is melted.

To make Chicken Water.

TAKE a cock or large fowl, strip off its skin, and bruise it with a rolling-pin. Then put it into a sauce-pan with two quarts of water, a crust of bread, and an ounce of *French* barley. Let it boil till half the water is evaporated, then strain it off, and season it with salt.

To make Barley Water.

TAKE a pound of pearl-barley, and two quarts of water; let it boil half an hour; then strain off the barley, and throw away the water; put the barley into three pints of fresh water, and boil it till it comes to a quart; strain it off, and sweeten it to your palate, adding to it two spoonfuls of white wine, or milk.

To make Seed Water.

TAKE of coriander-seed, carraway-seed, cubebs, sweet fennel-seed, and aniseed, of each half an ounce, bruise them and boil them in a quart of water; strain it, brew it up with the yolk of an egg, and add to it a little sack and double refined sugar.

A SUPPLEMENT TO THE Compleat HOUSEWIFE.

A full Discovery of the Medicines given by me JOANNA STEPHENS, *for the Cure of the* Stone *and* Gravel; *and a particular Account of my Method of preparing and giving the same.*

MY medicines are a powder, a decoction, and pills. The powder consists of egg-shells and snails both calcin'd.

The decoction is made by boiling some herbs (together with a ball which consists of soap, swines-cresses burnt to a blackness, and honey) in water.

The pills consist of snails calcin'd, wild carrot-seeds, burdock-seeds, ashen keys, hips and haws, all burnt to a blackness, soap and honey.

The Powder is thus prepared:

Take hens egg-shells, well drained from the whites, dry and clean; crush them small with the hands, and fill a crucible of the twelfth size (which contains nearly three pints) with them lightly, place it in the fire, and cover it with a tile; then heap coals over it, that it may be in the midst of a very strong

ſtrong clear fire till the egg-ſhells be calcin'd to a grayiſh white, and acquire an acrid ſalt taſte; this will take up eight hours at leaſt. After they are thus calcin'd, put them into a dry clean earthen pan, which muſt not be above three parts full, that there may be room for the ſwelling of the egg-ſhells in ſlacking. Let the pan ſtand uncover'd in a dry room for two months and no longer; in this time the egg-ſhells will become of a milder taſte; and that part which is ſufficiently calcin'd will fall into a powder of ſuch a fineneſs as to paſs through a common hair ſieve, which is to be done accordingly.

In like manner, take garden ſnails with their ſhells, clean'd from the dirt, fill a crucible of the ſame ſize with them whole, cover it, and place it in a fire, as before, till the ſnails have done ſmoaking, which will be in about an hour, taking care that they do not continue in the fire after that. They are then to be taken out of the crucible, and immediately rubb'd in a mortar to a fine powder, which ought to be of a very dark gray colour.

Note, *If pit-coal be made uſe of, it will be proper, in order that the fire may the ſooner burn clear on the top, that large cinders, and not freſh coals, be placed upon the tiles which cover the crucibles.*

Theſe powders being thus prepar'd, take the egg-ſhell powder of ſix crucibles, and the ſnail powder of one, mix them together, rub them in a mortar, and paſs them thro' a cypreſs ſieve. This mixture is immediately to be put up into bottles, which muſt be cloſe ſtopt, and kept in a dry place for uſe. I have generally added a ſmall quantity of ſwines-creſſes burnt to a blackneſs, and rubb'd fine; but this was only with a view to diſguiſe it.

The egg-ſhells may be prepared at any time of the year, but it is beſt to do them in ſummer. The ſnails ought only to be prepared in *May*, *June*, *July*, and

and *August*; and I efteem thofe beft which are done in the firft of thefe months.

The Decoction is thus prepared:

Take four ounces and a half of the beft *Alicant* foap, beat it in a mortar with a large fpoonful of fwines-creffes burnt to a blacknefs, and as much honey as will make the whole of the confiftence of pafte. Let this be form'd into a ball.

Take this ball, and green camomile, or camomile flowers, fweet fennel, parfley, and burdock leaves, of each an ounce; (when there are not greens, take the fame quantity of roots) cut the herbs or roots, flice the ball, and boil them in two quarts of foft water half an hour; then ftrain it off, and fweeten it with honey.

The Pills are thus prepared:

Take equal quantities by meafure, of fnails calcin'd as before, of wild carrot-feeds, burdock-feeds, afhen-keys, hips and haws, all burnt to a blacknefs, or, which is the fame thing, till they have done fmoaking: mix them together, rub them in a mortar, and pafs them thro' a cyprefs fieve. Then take a large fpoonful of this mixture, and four ounces of the beft *Alicant* foap, and beat them in a mortar with as much honey as will make the whole of a proper confiftence for pills; fixty of which are to be made out of every ounce of the compofition.

The Method of giving thefe Medicines is as follows.

When there is a ftone in the bladder or kidneys, the powder is to be taken three times a day, *viz.* in the morning after breakfaft, in the afternoon about five or fix, and going to bed. The dofe is a drachm avoirdupois, or fifty fix grains, which is to be mixt in a large tea cup full of white wine, cyder, or fmall punch; and half a pint of the decoction is to be drank, either cold or milk-warm, after every dofe.

These

These medicines frequently cause much pain at first; in which case it is proper to give an opiate, and repeat it as often as there is occasion.

If the person be costive during the use of them, let him take as much lenitive electuary, or other laxative medicine, as may be sufficient to remove that complaint, but not more: for it must be a principal care, at all times, to prevent a looseness, which would carry off the medicines; and if this does happen, it will be proper to increase the quantity of the powder, which is astringent; or lessen that of the decoction, which is laxative; or take some other suitable means, by the advice of physicians.

During the use of these medicines, the person ought to abstain from salt meats, red wines, and milk, drink few liquids, and use little exercise, that so the urine may be the more strongly impregnated with the medicines, and the longer retained in the bladder.

If the stomach will not bear the decoction, a sixth part of the ball made into pills must be taken after every dose of the powder.

Where the person is aged, of a weak constitution, or much reduced by loss of appetite or pain, the powder must have a greater proportion of the calcin'd snails, than according to the foregoing direction; and this proportion may be increased suitably to the nature of the case, till there be equal parts of the two ingredients. The quantity also of both powder and decoction may be lessened for the same reasons. But as soon as the person can bear it, he should take them in the above mentioned proportion and quantities.

Instead of the herbs and roots before mentioned, I have sometimes used others, as mallows, marshmallows, yarrows red and white, dandelion, water cresses, and horse-radish root, but do not know of any material difference.

This

This is my manner of giving the powder and decoction. As to the pills, their chief ufe is in fits of the gravel, attended with pain in the back and vomiting, and a fuppreffion of urine from a ftoppage in the ureters. In thefe cafes, the perfon is to take five pills every hour, day and night, when awake, till the complaints are removed. They will alfo prevent the formation of gravel and gravel-ftones in conftitutions fubject to breed them, if ten or fifteen be taken every day.

June 16, 1739. J. STEPHENS.

N. B. Mrs. *Stephens* received five thoufand pounds reward on her medicine having been tried and approved, *March* 17, 1739-40. See *London-Gazette*, *March* 23, 1739-40.

A certain Cure for the Dropfy, if taken at the beginning of the Diftemper.

TAKE the ftems that grow from the ftick or root of the artichoke, pluck off the leaves, and bruife only the ftems in a marble mortar; to a quart of juice put a quart of *Madeira* or Mountain wine, ftraining the juice through a piece of muflin: let the patient take a wine glafs of it fafting, and another juft before going to bed, continuing till the cure is compleated. *N. B.* This cured a fon of Dr. *Moore*, late bifhop of *Ely* (who had the advice of feveral phyficians to no effect) and from whom I had the receipt.

For the Rheumatifm.

TAKE one handful of garden fcurvy-grafs pick'd, two fpoonfuls of muftard-feed bruifed, two fmall fticks of horfe-radifh fliced, half an ounce of winter bark fliced, fteep thefe ingredients in a quart of mountain wine three hours before you take it, which muft be three times a day; at eight, eleven, and

and five, if your ſtomach will bear it; if not, then twice only, *viz.* at eight and five, eating and drinking nothing after it for two hours at leaſt; you are to take a quarter of a pint at a time, which you muſt fill up out of another quart of the ſame wine; and ſo continue drinking till both bottles are emptied.

A reſtorative Jelly for any one inclining to a Conſumption.

TAKE four ounces of hartſhorn-ſhavings, two ounces of eringo-root, one ounce of iſinglaſs, two vipers, one pint of ſnails; the ſnails being waſhed and bruiſed, put all theſe into three quarts of pump-water, let them ſimmer till it comes to three pints, then ſtrain it off, and add the juice of two *Seville* oranges, half a pound of white ſugar-candy, and one pint of old rheniſh wine; drink a quarter of a pint faſting, and the ſame quantity an hour before dinner time.

For the Bloody-Flux.

TAKE ſome garlick, preſs out a ſpoonful or two, warm it pretty hot, then dip a double rag in it, lay it upon the navel, let it lie till it is cold; then repeat it two or three times, it cures immediately. By this I cured a gentleman, who had tried ſeveral other things without ſucceſs, *S. C.*

For the Cholick.

LET the patient, when they find any ſymptoms of a fit, take a pint of milk warm, put into it four ſpoonfuls of brandy, and eat it up, and ſo let them take it any other time, if they are ſubject to that diſtemper, it will prevent the fit. This cured Mr. *Blundel* of *Hampſtead*, after he had the advice of ſeveral other phyſician, and had been at the *Bath* without ſucceſs.

For

For an inveterate Looſeneſs.

TAKE a piece of bread of the bigneſs of a crown piece, toaſt it hard on both ſides, then put it into a quarter of a pint of *French* brandy, let it ſoak till it is ſoft, then eat the bread and drink the brandy at night going to bed; this muſt be taken thrice. This cured a near relation of mine who had try'd ſeveral other things before to no purpoſe. *S. C.*

For Dimneſs of Sight and ſore Eyes.

TAKE eyebright, ſweet marjoram and betony dry'd, of each a like quantity, the ſame quantity of tobacco as of all the reſt, take it in a pipe as you do tobacco for ſome time; and take of the right *Portugal* ſnuff, put it into the corner of your eyes morning and night, and take it likewiſe as ſnuff. This cured Judge *Ayres*, Sir *Edward Seymour*, and Sir *John Houblon*, that they could read without ſpectacles, after they had uſed them many years. *S. C.*

For the Piles, a preſent Remedy.

ANOINT the part with ointment of tobacco. This cured an acquaintance of mine, who told it me himſelf. *S. C.*

For a Pleuriſy.

LET the patient bleed pletifully, then drink off a pint of ſpring water, with 30 drops in it of ſpirit of ſal-armoniac; this muſt be done as ſoon as the party is ſeized. Approved by myſelf. *S. C.*

For a Tertian Ague, a never-failing Remedy.

TAKE ſtone brimſtone finely powder'd, as much as will lie upon half a crown, in a glaſs of white wine, about an hour before the fit comes; it cures at twice taking. This I had from one that had cured ſcores with it, and it never failed once.

For a Quinsey or Swelling in the Throat, so that the Patient cannot swallow.

TAKE a toast of houshold bread, as big as will cover the top of the head, well bak'd on both sides, soak it in right *French* brandy; let the top of the head be shav'd, then bind it on with a cloth; if this be done at night going to bed, it will cure before morning, as I myself have had experience of. *S. C.*

For a Rheumatism.

LET the patient take spirit of hartshorn morning and evening, beginning with twenty five drops in a glass of spring water, increasing five every day till they come to fifty, to be continued for a month, if not well sooner. By this I cured a woman that had this distemper to so great a degree, that she was swelled in her head and limbs that she could not lift her hand to her head; but taking this, in three days was much better, and in three weeks time went abroad perfectly well, and has continued so now for above seven years. *S. C.*

To stop Bleeding at the Nose, or elsewhere.

TAKE an ounce-bottle, fill it half full of water, put into it as much *Roman* vitriol as will lie upon the point of a knife; let the part bleed into it, it will stop it in an instant.

For Convulsion Fits in Children.

TAKE assa fœtida and wood-soot, of each one ounce, infuse them in a pint of *French* brandy; give a child in the month three or four drops in breast milk, or black cherry water, soon after it is born, and continue it two or three times a day for a week.

To prevent Convulsions in Children.

TAKE ten grains of coral finely powder'd, give it in breast-milk or black cherry-water, it prevents their having any convulsion fits.

For the Gout in the Stomach, Dr. Lower's *constant Remedy.*

TAKE of *Venice* treacle one drachm, *Gascoign's* powder half a drachm, syrup of poppies as much as is sufficient to make it into a bolus; let the patient take it going to bed.

For an inveterate Head-ach.

TAKE juice of ground-ivy, and snuff it up the nose, it not only easeth the most violent head-ach for the present, but taketh it quite away. This cured one that had been afflicted with it many years, and by the use of it, it immediately cured him, and it never returned.

For the Jaundice.

TAKE the juice of the leaves of artichoke plants, put it into a quart of white wine; take three or four spoonfuls in the morning fasting, and at four in the afternoon.

For the Piles.

TAKE the duck-meat that lies upon ponds and ditches, let it lie till it be dry, then lay it to the part; it cures presently.

For an Asthma.

TAKE of virgins honey one spoonful, mix in it as much rosin as will lie upon a half crown, finely powder'd; let the patient take it in the morning, an hour before breakfast, and again at night, an hour after supper; this must be continued a month.

For an inveterate Cough.

TAKE of *Sperma Ceti* (called by the common people, *Parma citty*) one ſcruple; put it into the yolk of a new-laid egg raw, ſup it up in the morning faſting; it cures at once taking. Approved by ſeveral of my acquaintance, whom I knew it to cure. *S. C.*

To cure Blindneſs, when the Cauſe proceeds from within the Eye.

TAKE a double handful of the top leaves of ſalary, and a ſpoonful of ſalt; pound them together, and when it is pounded make it into a poultice, and put it on the party's contrary hand-wriſt (that is, if the right eye is bad, put it to the left wriſt) and repeat it for about three or four times, but put on freſh once in twenty-four hours.

If the eye is very bad, uſe bay ſalt.

To make Sage Wine.

TAKE four handfuls of red ſage, beat it in a ſtone mortar like green ſauce, put it into a quart of red wine, and let it ſtand three or four days cloſe ſtopt, ſhaking it twice or thrice, then let it ſtand and ſettle, and the next day in the morning take of the ſage wine three ſpoonfuls, and of running water one ſpoonful, faſting after it one hour or better; uſe this from *Michaelmas* to the end of *March*: it will cure any aches or humours in the joints, dry rheums, keep from all diſeaſes to the fourth degree; it helps the dead palſy, and convulſions in the ſinews, ſharpens the memory, and from the beginning of taking it will keep the body mild, ſtrengthen nature, till the fullneſs of your days be finiſhed; nothing will be changed in your ſtrength, except the change of your hair; it will keep your teeth ſound that were not corrupted before; it will keep you from the gout, the dropſy, or any ſwellings of the joints or body.

Receipts, or various Ways of eating Pickled Herrings.

General Directions to be obſerved before the Cutting up a Pickled Herring, *which Way ſoever it is to be eat.*

LAY the fiſh in a pewter plate, or trencher. Beat it on each ſide, with the flat of the knife, to looſen the ſkin. Cut a thin ſtrip off the belly, and ſlit the back, to divide the ſkin; which then muſt be ſtrip'd off, on each ſide (with the knife and fingers) beginning at the neck. Take out the row; and rub the inſide, and the whole herring, with the corner of a towel, dipped in vinegar.

Firſt way.] The fiſh being prepared, as above, cut off the head and tail. Then divide the herring into pieces of about an inch long. Afterwards put the pieces together, as though the fiſh were intire. Then eat it with, or without, oil and vinegar, new bread and butter, *&c.*

Second way.] The herring lying ſkinned, *&c.* in the plate, (as obſerved in the general directions) ſhave it very thin; and, when cut to the bone, turn it, and ſhave it in like manner, on the other ſide. A herring may thus be cut ſo thin, that the pieces of it will quite cover a plate.

Third way.] The herring being prepared (purſuant to the general directions) take it by the tail, in the middle of which cut a ſlit, half an inch long, or more. Pull each tip of the tail, oppoſite ways; by which means the herring will be ſplit into two parts. In one of theſe parts no bone will be left; and the bone left in the other part may eaſily be taken out (from a new pickled herring) by looſening the bone at the neck, and drawing it along The two divided parts of the herring may then be laid together, cut it into ſlices, and eat between bread and butter; or minced and mixed with a ſallad of any kind; or else made into a salmigondi, with chicken, rabbit, or veal. They eat very well with green peas, *Windsor* beans, kidney beans, or potatoes; if, after these are drain'd off, when boiled, a pickled herring, or more, be thrown into the same water; and then taken out, after the water had bubled up a minute or two. Herring-pickle may be used for that of an anchovy; and a little of this pickle thrown into the butter, made as sauce for eels, takes off from their lusciousness.——In many countries, pickled herrings are made to serve all the purposes of ham, or bacon.

N. B. Those who are desirous of being still more conversant with various ways of eating pickled herrings, may consult the ingenious Mr. *Dodd's Essay* (lately printed) *towards a Natural History of the Herring.*

Receipt for making Pickled-Herring Soop.

TAKE a quart of split peas. Put to them five quarts of cold water, a quarter of an ounce of whole *Jamaica* pepper, two large onions, three pickled herrings (wash'd in two or three waters, and the rows out) skinn'd, and cut to pieces.

Boil all together till a quart is diminished. Pour in a pint of boiling water, and let the whole boil a quarter of an hour. Take it off, and strain it thro' a cullender. Throw, into the soop, seven or eight handfuls of celery, three heads of endive, all of them cut very small; (but if on ship-board, where endive is not be had, a larger number of onions may be employ'd in its stead) together with a handful of dried mint, pass'd thro' a lawn-sieve. Set all these on a fire, and boil the whole near three quarters of an hour; stirring the soop perpetually, to prevent burning to, which it will do in a moment, and therefore the pot should stand on a trivet.

Bread, cut into diamonds, and fried criſp in butter, muſt be thrown into the ſoop, which then may be ſerved up.

To ſtuff a Fillet of Veal, or Calf's Heart, with pickled Herrings.

TAKE two herrings: ſkin, bone, and waſh them in ſeveral waters. Chop them very ſmall, with a quarter of a pound of ſuet. Add a handful of bread grated fine; and the like quantity of parſley, cut very ſmall. Throw in a little thyme, nutmeg, and pepper, to your taſte; and mix all together, with two eggs.

Half the quantity of the above ſtuffing is exceedingly good for a calf's heart.

Stuffing, of pickled Herrings, for a roaſt Turkey.

WASH, in ſeveral waters, two pickled herrings; which afterwards ſkin, and take the bone out carefully. Take half a pound of ſuet, and two large handfuls of bread grated. Chop the herrings, ſuet, and bread, (ſeparately) very ſmall. Beat theſe all together in a marble mortar, with the white of an egg; after throwing in a little nutmeg and white pepper.

Pickled-Herring Pudding, for a Hare.

TAKE half a pound of the lean of fine veal, which clear of the ſkin and ſtrings. Two pickled herrings, which waſh in two or three waters; then ſkin, and clear them of the bones. A quarter of a pound of ſuet. Two handfuls of bread grated fine. A handful of parſley. Chop all the above (ſeparately then mix them; throwing in half a nutmeg grated, a little thyme, ſweet-marjoram, and one egg:——Beat the whole together in a marble mortar.

A Receipt

A Receipt to dreſs a Turtle.

CUT his head off; cut it all round, and part the two ſhells, as you would a crab; leave ſome meat to the breaſt-ſhell called the callapee, ſeaſon that with ſome kyon butter, pepper, ſpice, and force meat balls between the fleſh; and bake it with ſome meat in it, and baſte it with ſome *Madeira* wine and butter. Take the deep ſhell call'd the callapaſh, take all the meat out of it, the guts, *&c.* open every gut, and clean it with a penknife, and cut them an inch long, and ſtew them four hours by themſelves; cut the other meat in quarter of a pound pieces; take the fins and clean them as you would good giblets, cut them in pieces like the other; ſtew the fins and meat together, till they are tender, about one hour, and then ſtrain them off; thickening your ſoop; put all your meat and guts into the ſoop as you would ſtewed giblets, ſeaſon it with kyon butter, ſpices, pepper and ſalt, ſhallots, ſweet herbs, and *Madeira* wine, as you like it, and put it all into the deep ſhell, and ſend it to the oven and bake it. Then ſerve it up.

The following Receipts were inſerted in the Carolina Gazette, May 9, 1750; *and it is preſumed that the Introductory Letter will be a ſufficient Authority for adopting them into this Work.*

From the CAROLINA GAZETTE.

To the PRINTER.

SIR,

'I Am commanded by the commons houſe of aſ-
'ſembly to ſend you the incloſed, which you are
'to print in the *Carolina Gazette* as ſoon as poſſible:
'it is the negro *Cæſar*'s cure for poiſon; and like-

'wise his cure for the bite of a rattle-snake: for discovering of which the general assembly hath thought fit to purchase his freedom, and grant him an allowance of 100 *l. per ann.* during life.

May 9, 1749. 'I am, &c.

'JAMES IRVING.'

The Negro Cæsar's *Cure for Poison.*

TAKE the roots of plantane and wild horehound, fresh or dried, three ounces, boil them together in two quarts of water, to one quart, and strain it; of this decoction let the patient take one third part three mornings fasting successively, from which if he finds any relief, it must be continued till he is perfectly recovered: on the contrary, if he finds no alteration after the third dose, it is a sign that the patient has either not been poisoned at all, or that it has been with such poison as *Cæsar*'s antidotes will not remedy, so may leave off the decoction.

During the cure, the patient must live on a spare diet, and abstain from eating mutton, pork, butter, or any other fat or oily food.

N. B. The plantane or hore-hound will either of them cure alone, but they are most efficacious together.

In summer, you may take one handful of the roots and branches of each, in place of three ounces of the roots of each.

For Drink, during the Cure, let them take the following:

Take of the roots of golden-rod six ounces, or in summer two large handfuls, the roots and branches together, and boil them in two quarts of water to one quart (to which also may be added a little horehound and sassafras.) To this decoction, after it is strained, add a glass of rum or brandy, and sweeten it with sugar, for ordinary drink.

Sometimes

Sometimes an inward Fever attends ſuch as are poiſoned, for which he orders the following:

Take a pint of wood-aſhes and three pints of water, ſtir and mix them well together, let them ſtand all night, and ſtrain or decant the lye off in the morning, of which ten ounces may be taken ſix mornings following, warmed or cold, according to the weather.

Theſe medicines have no ſenſible operation, tho' ſometimes they work in the bowels, and give a gentle ſtool.

The Symptoms attending ſuch as are poiſoned, are as follows:

A pain of the breaſt, difficulty of breathing, a load at the pit of the ſtomach, an irregular pulſe, burning and violent pains of the viſcera above and below the navel, very reſtleſs at night, ſometimes wandering pains over the whole body, a reaching and inclination to vomit, profuſe ſweats (which prove always ſerviceable) ſlimy ſtools, both when coſtive and looſe, the face of a pale and yellow colour, ſometimes a pain and inflammation of the throat, the appetite is generally weak, and ſome cannot eat any; thoſe who have been long poiſoned, are generally very feeble, and weak in their limbs, ſometimes ſpit a great deal, the whole ſkin peels, and likewiſe the hair falls off.

Cæſar's *Cure for the Bite of a Rattle-Snake.*

TAKE of the roots of plantane or hore-hound, (in the ſummer, roots and branches together) a ſufficient quantity, bruiſe them in a mortar, and ſqueeze out the juice, of which give, as ſoon as poſſible, one large ſpoonful; if he is ſwelled, you muſt force it down his throat: this generally will cure; but if the patient finds no relief in an hour after, you may give another ſpoonful, which never fails.

If the roots are dried, they muſt be moiſtened with a little water.

To the wound may be applied a leaf of good tobacco moiſtened with rum.

Terms of Art for CARVING.

BArbel, to tuſk
Bittern, to disjoint
Brawn, to leach
Bream, to ſplay
Brew, to untach
Buſtard, to cut up
Capon, to ſouce
Chevin, to fin
Chicken, to fruſh
Coney, to unlace
Crab, to tame
Crane, to diſplay
Curlew, to untach
Deer, to break
Eel, to tranſon
Egg, to tire
Egript, to break
Flounder, to ſauce
Gooſe, to rear
Haddock, to ſide
Hen, to ſpoil
Hern, to diſmember
Lamprey, to ſtring
Lobſter, to barb
Mullard, to unbrace
Partridge, to wing
Paſty, to border
Peacock, to disfigure
Pheaſant, to allay
Pigeon, to thigh
Pike, to ſplat
Plover, to mince
Quail, to wring
Salmon, to chine
Small Birds, to thigh
Sturgeon, to tranch
Swan, to lift
Tench, to ſauce
Trout, to culpon
Turkey, to cut up
Woodcock, to thigh.

Inſtructions for Carving, according to theſe Terms of Art.

To unjoint a Bittern.

RAISE his wings and legs as a hern, and no other ſauce but ſalt.

To cut up a Buſtard.

See *Turkey.*

To ſauce a Capon.

Take a capon, and lift up the right leg, and ſo array forth, and lay in the platter; ſerve your chicken in the ſame manner, and ſauce them with green ſauce, or verjuice.

To unlace a Coney.

Turn the back downward, and cut the flaps or apron from the belly or kidney; then put in your knife between the kidneys, and looſen the fleſh from the bone, on each ſide; then turn the belly downward, and cut the back croſs between the wings, drawing your knife down on each ſide the back-bone, dividing the legs and ſides from the back; pull not the leg too hard, when you open the ſide from the bone; but with your hand and knife neatly lay open both ſides from the ſcut to the ſhoulder; then lay the legs cloſe together,

To

To diſplay a Crane.

Unfold his legs; then cut off his wings, by the joints; after this take up his legs and wings, and ſauce them with vinegar, ſalt, muſtard, and powdered ginger.

To unbrace a Duck.

Raiſe up the pinions and legs, but take them not off, and raiſe the merry-thought from the breaſt; then lace it down each ſide of the breaſt with your knife, wriggling your knife to and fro, that the furrows may lie in and out; after the ſame manner unbrace the mallard.

To rear a Gooſe.

Take off both legs fair, like ſhoulders of lamb; then cut off the belly-piece round cloſe to the end of the breaſt; then lace your gooſe down on both ſides of the breaſt half an inch from the ſharp bone; then take off the pinion on each ſide, and the fleſh you firſt lac'd with your knife; raiſe it up clean from the bone, and take it off with the pinion from the body; then cut up the merry-thought; then cut from the breaſt-bone another ſlice of fleſh quite thro'; then turn up your carcaſe, and cut it aſunder, the back-bone above the loin-bones; then take the rump end of the back-bone and lay it in a diſh, with the ſkinny ſide upwards; [illegible] fore-end of it the r[illegible]t, with the ſkinny [illegible] upwards, and before that the apron of the gooſe; then lay the pinions on each ſide contrary, ſet the legs on each ſide contrary behind them, that the bone ends of the legs may ſtand up croſs in the middle of the diſh, and the wing pinions may come on the outſide of them; put the long ſlice which you cut from the breaſt-bone, under the wing pinions on each ſide, and let the ends meet under the leg-bones, and let the other ends lie cut in the diſh betwixt the leg and the pinion; then pour in your ſauce under the meat; throw on ſalt, and ſerve it to table again.

To diſmember a Hern.

Take off both the legs, and lace it down the breaſt on both ſides with your knife, and open the breaſt-pinion, but take it not off; then raiſe up the merry-thought between the breaſt-bone and the top of it; then raiſe up the brawn; then turn it outward upon both ſides; but break it not, nor cut it off; then cut off the wing-pinions at the joint next the body, and ſtick in each ſide the pinion in the place you turned the brawn out; but cut off the ſharp end of the pinion, and take the middle piece, and that will juſt fit in the place. You may cut up a c[illegible]on or pheaſant the ſame way.

To

To unbrace a Mullard.

This is done the ſame way as to unbrace a duck; which ſee.

To wing a Partridge.

Raiſe his legs and wings, and ſauce him with wine, powdered ginger, and a little ſalt.

To allay a Pheaſant.

Do this as you do a Partridge, but uſe no other ſauce but ſalt.

To wing a Quail.

Do this the ſame way as you do a partridge.

To lift a Swan.

Slit the ſwan down in the middle of the breaſt, and ſo clean through the back, from the neck to the rump; then part it in two halves, but do not break or tear the fleſh; then lay the two halves in a charger, with the ſlit ſides downwards; throw ſalt upon it; ſet it again on the table; let the ſauce be chaldron, and ſerve it in ſaucers.

To break a Teal.

Do this the ſame way as you do a pheaſant.

To cut up a Turkey.

Raiſe up the leg fairly, and open the joint with the point of your knife, but take not off the leg; then with your knife lace down both ſides of the breaſt, and open the breaſt-pinion, but do not take it off; then raiſe the merry-thought betwixt the breaſt-bone and the top of it; then raiſe up the brawn; then turn it outward upon both ſides, but not break it, nor cut it off; then cut off the wing-pinions at the joint next the body, and ſtick each pinion in the place you turned the brawn out, but cut off the ſharp end of the pinion, and take the middle piece, and that will juſt fit in the place. You may cut up a buſtard, a capon, or pheaſant, the ſame way.

To thigh a Woodcock.

Raiſe the wings and legs as you do a hern, only lay the head open for the brains; and as you thigh a hern, ſo you muſt a curlew, plover, or ſnipe, excepting that you have no other ſauce but ſalt.

INDEX.

INDEX.

A.

ACHES *and Bruises*, Page 306 —*an old Ach or Strain*, 323

After-birth, *to bring it away*, 314

After-pains, *how prevented*, 302 314, 315.

Ague, 330. *outward Applications for it*, 282, 300, 331, 345 *inward Remedies*, 330, 333.

Ague tertian, *a never-failing Remedy*, 382.

Almond *Butter*, 190.—— *Cakes*, 176, 177. *Cheesecakes*, 167.— *Cream*, 181. —*Hogs-puddings*, 136. — *Loaves*, 225. — *Pudding*, 125, — *Puffs*, 173. — *to chocolate Almonds*, 224. — *to fricasee them*, 207.—*to parch them whole*, 202.

Amber-gris, *Tincture*, 259.

Angel-Salve, 360

Angelica, *candied*, 211.

Apple-*Fritters*, 140. — *Pasties to fry*, 154.— *Tansey*, 138.— *to dry Apples*, 214. —*without Sugar*, ibid. — *to stew Apples*, 218.

Apricocks; *to dry Apricocks*, 202, 219. — *like Prunelloes*, 228. *to preserve Apricocks*, 201. — *green Apricocks*, 230, 233.—*ripe ones*, ibid. *Marmalade of Apricocks*, 232. *Apricock-wine*, 236.

Aqua Mirabilis, 258.

Artichokes, *to dress*, 16. — *Pye*, 160. *to keep Artichokes all the Year*, 290

Ashen-keys *pickled*, 106.

Asparagus, *to dress*, 15. — *pickled*, 106, 112. — *Soop*, 89.

Asthma, 384

B.

Bacon, *to chuse*, 3. *to salt it*, 76. — *To salt and dry a Ham of Bacon*, 73. *to make Westphalia Bacon*, ibid.

Balls, *savoury*, 28. ——*for* Lent, 155.

Balsam, *of* Lucatellus, 341 *the yellow Balsam*, 331 *a Water to be taken after Balsam of* Tolu, 274.

Barberries, *pickled*, 113, *to preserve them*, 222.

Barley-Cream, 186. — *Water*, 244.—*Wine*, ibid.

Battalia-Pye, *or Bride-Pye*, 35, 148.

Beef *to chuse*, 1. — *collared*, 28, 38. — *potted*, 59, 78. —*alamode*, 46. *fine hung-beef*, 123,

Beer. *To make strong Beer*, 254.

Bile, *to break a Bile*, 299

Birch *Wine*, 240.

Bisk, *of Pigeons*, 89,

Bisket, 174, 181. *the hard Bisket*, ibid. *thin* Dutch *Bisket*, 179. *little hollow Bisket*, 174. *drop Bisket*, 178. *Lemon Bisket*, 225. *Ratafia Bisket*, 196.

Bite *of a mad Dog*, 300, 354, 367.

Bitter *Draught*, 321 *another*, 325.

Black *Cherry Water*, *for Children*, 266.

Blackness,

Blackness *by a Fall*, 299.

Blast, *Ointment for it*, 299.

Bleeding *at Mouth, Nose, or Ears*, 302, 304, 354, 383. *Bleeding inwardly*, 309. —— *in the Stomach*, 353.

Blindness, *to cure it, when from within the Eye*, 385.

Blister; *how to raise one*, 322.

Blood, *to sweeten it*, 303. *Spitting of Blood*, 300.

Bloody *Flux, to stop it, tho' never so severe*, 287, 316, 381.

Boiling, *general Directions for*, 12.

Brandy, *Carraway-Brandy*, 264. *Cherry-Brandy*, 237. *Poppy-Brandy*, 263.

Braun, *to chuse*, 2.

Bread *and Butter Pudding for Fasting Days*, 127. *brown Bread Pudding*, 137. *fine Bread Pudding*, 146. *Rye Bread Pudding*, 140.

Breast *of Veal collar'd*, 58. *to ragoo it*, 61.

Breasts, *sore*, 334, 335.

Breath, *short*, 303.

Briony *Water*, 274.

Broiling, *general Directions for*, 22.

Brochala, *to dress*, 15.

Broom *Buds pickled*, 112.

Broth *strong, to keep for use*, 31.

Broths *for the Sick*, 372

Bruises, 342. *Bruise Ointment*, 358

Buns, 176.

Burns, *various Remedies for them*, 282, 325, 327, 361.

Burstenness, 329.

Bustard, *to chuse*, 7.

Butter, *to chuse*, 5. *how to make it*, 101.

Butter'd *Loaves to eat hot*, 163.

Bugs, *a Receipt for destroying them*, 368

C.

Cabbage *Pudding*, 134. *Cabbage Lettuce Pye*, 164. *to pickle red Cabbage*, 113.

Cakes, 169, *&c.* French *Cake to eat hot*, 172. *ordinary Cake to eat with Butter*, ibid. Portugal *Cakes*, ibid. *a Plumb Cake*, 170. *a good Seed Cake*, ibid. *another*, 171. *a sort of little Cakes*, 180. Whetston *Cakes*, 182. *the white Cake*, 180.

Calf's Head *collared*, 44. *to dress it*, 84. *Hash of it*, 47, 61, 97.

Calf's Foot *Pudding*, 41. *Jelly*, 189. — *without Lemons*, 193. *Calf's-Foot Pudding*, 128.

Cancer, 807.—*in the Breast, to keep it from growing*, 335, 363.

Capon, *to chuse*, 6.

Carraway *Spirits*, 262.—— *Brandy*, 264.

Carp *stewed*, 55. *other ways*, 56, 95.

Carrot *Pudding*, 126. *Carrot or Parsnip Puffs*, 143.

Carrots, *to dress*, 14.

Cashew *Lozenges*, 357.

Caudle

Caudle *of Oatmeal*, 194. *a fine Caudle*, 193. —*Flummery Caudle*, 192. *Tea Caudle*, 193. *for Sweet Pyes*, 29.
Centaury *Water*, 268.
Cerecloth, 331.
Charity Oil, *for outward and inward Bruises, green Wounds*, &c. 296.
Cheese, *to chuse*, 5. *a Summer Cream Cheese*, 99. *a Chedder Cheese*, 101. *the Queen's Cheese*, 102. *New-market Cheese to cut at two years old*, 99. *a thick Cream Cheese*, 102. *ordinary Cream Cheese*, 103. *Slip-coat Cheese*, 102. *to make a fresh Cheese*, 190.
Cheesecakes, 151. —*without Rennet*, 153. *Lemon Cheese-cakes*, 162, 168. *to make them without Curd*, 164. *Cream Cheese with old Cheshire*, 168.
Cherries *preserved*, 208. *Cherry Wine*, 238. *Marmalade of Cherries*, 212. *Morella - Cherry - Wine*, 242.
Chervil *Tart*, 161.
Chesnut *Puddings*, 137.
Chickens, *to chuse*, 7. *fricasied*, 49. *pulled*, ibid. *Chicken-Pye*, 34, 159. *a sweet Chicken-Pye*, 158.
Chilblains, 309.
Chin-cough, 298, 329.
Chips *of Apricocks*, 234. *Orange Chips crisp*, 225.
Chocolate *Almonds*, 224.
Cyder, 251.
Citron *Water*, 264.
Clary *Wine*, 247, *the fine Clary Wine*, 251. *fine Clary Water*, 265.
Clear Cakes *of any Fruit*, 206. —*of the Jelly of any Fruit*, 205.—*of Gooseberries*, 229.
Clear Candy, 227.
Clyster *for Worms*, 341.
Cock, *to chuse*, 6. *Ale*, 245. *Cock Water for Consumption*, 270.
Cockles *pickled*, 122.
Cod *stewed*, 79. *Cod's Head roasted*, 37.
Cold, 351.— *on the Stomach*, 342, 344, 352.
Cholic, 307, 325, *to give present help in a Cholic*, 345, 381.
Collar *of Beef*, 38, 70. *of Calf's Head*, 44. *of Cow heels*, 45. *of a Pig*, 59, 71. *of Salmon*, 56. *of Venison*, 57.
Colliflowers, *to dress*, 16.
Colour, *to procure a good Colour*, 318.
Conserves, 198, &c. *Conserve of red Roses, or any other Flowers*, 218. *of Hips*, 294.
Consumption, 270, 282, 308, 381.
Convulsion *Fits*, 345. *to prevent them*, 383, 384.
Cordial *Water, that may be made in Winter*, 260. *the Golden Cordial*, 261. *the Saffron Cordial*, 265.
Corns *on the Feet*, 309.
Costiveness, *to remove it*, 322.
Cough, 292, 293, 354, 356. *on the Lungs*, 304

304. *on the Stomach*, 272. *Whooping Cough*, 346. *Inveterate Cough*, 385
Courfes, *procured*, 362.
Cow-heel *Pudding*, 131.
Cowflip *Wine*, 241.
Crabs *buttered*, 54.
Cracknels, 178.
Cramp, 323, 356.
Crawfifh *Soop*, 27, 30, 53.
Cream *blanched*, 187. *Whipt Cream*, 189. *Piftachia Cream*, 196. *Cream of any preferved Fruit*, 191. *Steeple Cream*, 187. *White wine Cream*, 195.
Cream *Cheefe*, 99.— *with old Chefhire*, 168.
Cucumbers *fried for Mutton Sauce*, 66. *pickled in Slices*, 105, 110. *pickled another way*, 117. *preferved*, 219, 228. *ftewed*, 81.
Curd *Pudding*, 131.
Currants *preferved in Jelly*, 208. *Jelly of white Currants*, 211. *Currant Wine*, 238, 252.
Cuftards, 151. *Cuftard Pudding*, 141. *Rice Cuftards*, ibid.

D.

Daffy's *Elixir*, 274, 348.
Damfons *preferved whole*, 202.
Delivery *of Women*, 314.
Diftemper *got by an ill Hufband*, 272.
Drink *for a Fever*, 298 — *to preferve the Lungs*, 273. — *for the Rickets*, 295. *an opening Drink*, 272. *a purging Drink*, 336. *Drink for a Rheumatifm, or Pain in the Bones*, 279.
Drop *Bifket*, 178.
Dropfy, 278, 302, 304, 311, 355, 357, 358, 380.
Dropfy *Water*, 266. *Dropfy and Scurvy*, 330
Drought, *to allay a Fever*, 310
Drying Oil, 365.
Ducks, *to chufe*, 7. *to pot*, 71.
Dutch Beef, 75.
Dutch *Gingerbread*, 176.

E.

Ebulum, *or Elder-Ale*, 245.
Eels, *collared*, 36, 57. —— *potted*, 96.—*roafted*, 46.
Eggs, *to chufe*, 5. *fricafied*, 81.—*in another way*, 82.
Egg *Pyes*, 149.
Elder *Flower Water*, 252. *Elder Wine*, 244, 252. *Elder Wine made at Chriftmas*, 246.
Electuary *for a cold or windy Stomach*, 289. *another for a Pain in the Stomach*, 290
Elixir Proprietatis, 289.
Elixir, Daffy's, 348.
Eye *Water*, 274, 312.
Eyes, *red or fore*, 287. *to clear the Eyes*, 327. *fore weak Eyes*, 337. *for Dimnefs of Sight*, 382.

F.

Face, *pimpled*, 289, 303, 350.—*red and pimpled*, 343.
Falling *down of the Fundament*, 316.

Falling-

Falling-*sickness*, 326, 332
Fever *Water*, 261.—*Spotted Fever*, 279. *Plaister for the Feet*, 322. *Drink*, ib.
Fish, *to chuse*, 10.——*Pye*, 162.
Fits *of the Mother*, 271.
Fits *from Wind or Cold*, 288.
Floodings, 315 362.
Florendine *of Veal*, 40, 160.
Flowers *of any sort candied*, 215, 220. *Various ways to candy Orange-Flowers*, 215, 222, 231. *Syrup of any Flowers*, 215.
Flummery *Caudle*, 192.
Flux, 316 *Bloody-flux*, 381.
Fool, *of Strawberries, or Raspberries*, 195.
Forc'd-meat, 31, 82. *to force a Fowl*, 62.
Freckles *taken off*, 305.
French *Barley Pudding*, 129.
French *Beans to dress*, 16. *pickled*, 111.
French *Bread*, 176.
French *Cake*, 172. *brown* French *Loaves*, 181.
Fricasee *of Chickens*, 49.—*of Eggs*, 81. — *of Ox-palates*, 52. — *of great Plaice or Flounders*, ibid. —*of Rabbits*, 51.—*of double Tripe*, ibid. *pale Fricasee*, 46, 65. *brown Fricasee*, 64, 90.
Fritters; *Apple Fritters*, 140. *Curd Fritters*, 139. *fine Fritters*, 144.
Fruits *of any sort, candied*, 215. — *kept in Syrup to candy*, 218.

G.

Gam *of Gooseberries*, 232.
Garlick, *Syrup of it*, 301.
Gascoign's *Powder*, 342.
Gingerbread, *several ways of doing it*, 175, 177, 181. Dutch *Gingerbread*, 176.
Gloves, *how to wash them*, 291.
Golden *Cordial*, 261.
Goose, *to chuse*, 7. *to roast*, 22. *Sauce for*, 25. — *potted*, 81.
Gooseberries, *preserved*, 200. —— *preserved in Hops*, 216. — *without stoning*, 217.
Gooseberry, *Clear-Cakes*, 229. — *Cream*, 186. — *Tansy*, 138. — *Vinegar*, 121. — *Pearl Gooseberry-Wine*, 236.
Gout *Pains*, 318, 319, 345. *in the Stomach*, 384
Green *Ointment for the Rickets*, 295.
Green *Sickness*, 305, 317.
Greens, *to dress*, 13.
Gripes, 297.
Gripe-*Water*, 266.

H.

Hair, *to make it grow*, 348.
Ham, *to boil*, 13. *of Bacon*, *See* Bacon.
Hams *of Pork like Westphalia*, 90. *a Pickle for them*, 92.
Hands, *Paste for them*, 291. *to clean and soften them*, 349. *to make them white*, 350.
Hare, *to chuse*, 9. *roast*, 19. *Sauce for* 25. *dressed*, 72.—*potted*, 79. *to jug a Hare*, 97. *Hare Pye*, 166.

Hartshorn *Flummery*, 196. ——*Jelly*, 189.——*Jelly without Lemons*, 193.
Hash *of roast Mutton*, 66.
Hasty-*pudding*, 133. *little Hasty-puddings to boil in Custard Dishes*, 142.
Head, *to purge it*, 336 *for an inveterate Head-ach*, 384
Heart, *Heaviness*, 287.
Heath-cock, *to chuse*, 8.
Hemorrhoides *inflamed*, 321
Herrings, *how to bake them*, 85.——British, *to dress them*, 386, 387, 388.
Hickup, 323.
Hiera-picra *Tincture*, 269.
Hips, *made into Conserve*, 294.
Hoarseness, 289. — *with a Cold*, 346
Hogs *Puddings with Almonds*, 135. — *with Currants*, ibid.——— *another sort*, ibid. — *black Hogs-Puddings*, 136.
Hung *Beef*, 37.
Hungary-*Water*, 272.
Hysteric *Water*, 263.

I.

Jaundice, *several excellent Medicines for it*, 276. 309, 325, 355 *yellow or black Jaundice*, 328, 363, 384.
Iceing *a great Cake*, 184.
Jelly *Posset*, 192. *Ribbon, Jelly*, 191. *Jelly of any Fruit done into Clear-Cakes*, 205. — *of white Currants*, 211. *of Pippins*, 210.
Ink, *how prepared*, 290.
Joint-*Evil*, 305.
Itch, *cured various ways*, 329, 330, 355
To jug *a Hare*. *See* Hare.
Jumbals, 173.

K.

Katchup, *English*, 116.
King's-*Evil*, 328.

L.

Labour *in Child-birth*, 314.
Lady Onslow's *Water for the Stone*, 268.
Lamb-*pye*, 34. *savoury*, 157. *sweet Lamb-pye*, 158.
Laudanum, *liquid, done the best way*, 262.
Leach, *white*, 195.
Lear *for savoury Pyes*, 29.
Leg *of Lamb, how marinaded*, 62.—*forced*, 63.
Leg *of Mutton à-la-Daube*, 64.
Lemon *Bisket*, 225.——— *Cakes*, 227. —— *Cheese-Cakes*, 162, 168. —— *Cream*, 185. — *pickled*, 119. —— *Pudding*, 144. *Puffs*, 224. —— *Salade*, 125.— *Syllabubs*, 194.— *Tart*, 140. —*Wine*, 243. *another Wine that may pass for Citron Water*, 254.
Leveret, *to chuse*, 9.
Lily *of the Valley Water*, 267.
Lime-*Water*, 269.
Linen, *freed from Mildew*, 272.
Liquor *for colouring Puddings*, 129.
Loaves *made of Almonds*, 225.
Lobsters, *butter'd*, 54. — *potted*, 36. — *made into Soop*, 27. —*pickled*, 108.

Loosness,

Loosenefs, 297, 330, 354, 382.
Lozenges, *for the Heart-burn*, 301. —*for a Cough.*
Lucatellus's *Balsam*, 341, — *to take inwardly*, 355.
Lumber *Pye*, 34, 105. *another*, 168.
Lungs, *a Drink to preserve them*, 273. *a Purge for any Illness of them*, *Stuffing in them*, 313.

M.

Mackrel, *pickled*, 96.
Mangoes, *of Cucumbers*, 107.—*of Melons*, 104.
Marchpane, 173. —— *unboiled*, 208.
Marjoram *Pudding*, 137.
Marketing, *Directions for*, 1—12.
Marlborough *Cake*, 179.
Marmalade, *of Cherries*, 212. — *of Oranges*, 226. —*of Quinces red*, 212. — *of Quinces white*, ibid.
Marrow *Pasties*, 162.—— *Puddings*, 40, 144.
Marsh - mallows; *Syrup thereof*, 291.
Mead, 238, 246. *a small white Mead*, 239.
Mildew, *taken out of Linen*, 370.
Milk-*Water for a cancerous Breast*, 270. *another Milk-Water*, 275.
Milk *in Nurses increased*, 317.
Mince-*Pies of Veal*, 163.
Miscarrying *prevented*, 317
Morphew *removed*, 351.
Mountain *Wine*, 253.
Mouth *sore in Children*, 286. *a rare Mouth-water*, 301
Mulberries, *preserved whole*, 220.
Mullet, *or any other Fish, how boiled*, 54.
Muscles, *or Cockles, pickled*, 122.
Mushroom *Liquor, and Powder*, 86. *another Mushroom Powder*, 121.
Mushrooms *pickled*, 103, 109, 118, 120, 122. — *potted*, 85. — *stew'd*, 44.
Mutton, *to chuse*, 3. *to roast*, 19. *to roast like Venison*, 21, *Pye*, 35.— *Cutlet*, 67. —*dried to cut*, 67. *in Shivers, as* Dutch *Beef*, 75. — *dry'd like Pork*, 76.—*hashed*, 66.— *Leg or Shoulder stuffed with Oysters*, 41. *to force Leg of Mutton*, 63. *Leg of Mutton à-la-Daube*, 64. *Neck of Mutton dressed*, 68.

N.

Nasturtium - *Buds, pickled*, 106.
Neats-*Tongue Pye*, 35. — *potted*, 58.
Neck, Italian *Wash for it*, 351.
Neck *of Mutton dressed*, 68. — *of Veal stew'd*, 95.
Nun's *Cake*, 184.

O.

Oatmeal *Caudle*, 194. — *Pudding*, 129, 145. — *Sack Posset*, 197.
Obstructions *removed*, 357.

Ointment, *for a Burn or Scald*, 327. — *for a Cold on the Stomach*, 342.
Oyster *Soop*, 87.—*Pye*, 148.
Oysters *fried*, 63.—*pickled*, 36, 47, 109, 114.—*stew'd in* French *Rolls*, 39. — *stuffed into a Shoulder or Leg of Mutton*, 41.
Olio *Pye*, 159, 167.
Onions, *small, pickled*, 117.
Orange *Cakes*, 207, 226.—*Chips crisped*, 225.—*candied*, 230.—*Cream*, 186. — *Flowers candied*, 227, 231.—*preserved in Syrup*, 232. *Orange-flower Brandy*, 260. — *Orange Marmalade*, 226, 229. —— *Peel made in Syrup*, 226. —*Wine*, 240.—*with Raisins*, 249.
Oranges *preserv'd whole*, 198, 216, 224.
Ox-*palates in Fricasee*, 52. —*pickled*, 37,

P.

Painting *Rooms or Pales*, 364.
Palermo *Wine*, 247.
Pancakes, 138.—*Rice*, 136.
Parsnips, *to dress*, 14.
Partridge, *to chuse*, 8.
Paste, *of green Pippins*, 213. —*for Hands*, 291. *white Quince Paste*, 213.
Pasties. *See in the different Materials. Little Pasties to fry*, 151.
Pa[illegible]s, *how made*, 206.
Pastry *of all sorts*, 147, &c.
Pears *dry'd*, 114. — *without Sugar*, ibid.
Pear-*Plumbs, white, preserved*, 201. — *black, or any black Plum*, 204.
Pease *Pottage*, 30.
Perfume; *to make the burning Perfume*, 235.
Pheasant, *to chuse*, 8.
Pickle *for Hams*, 91. —*for Tongues*, ibid. —*for either Hams or Tongues*, 92.
Pickles *of all sorts*, 103, &c.
Pies. *See in the different Materials.*
Pigeons, *to chuse*, 9. *to roast*, 21.
Pigeon *Pye*, 35. — *in Jelly*, 80. *pickled*, 115. *stew'd*, 78, 92.—*stew'd with Asparagus*, ibid.
Pigs *Ears ragoo'd*, 38.
Pike *roasted and boiled*, 42, 43.
Piles *cured*, 321, 356, 359, 382 384.
Pills *to purge the Head*, 336. — *to purge off Rheum in the Teeth*, 347.
Pimples *remov'd*, 303, 350.
Pin *or Web in the Eye*, 327.
Pippins; *Jelly of them*, 210. —*preserv'd whole*, 209. *Paste of green Pippins*, 213.
Pistachia *Cream*, 196.
Pith *Pudding*, 131.
Plague, *Dr.* Burgess's *Antidote against it*, 267. *Plague-Water*, 258.
Plain *Pudding very fine*, 146.
Plate, *how to boil it*, 366.
Pleurisy, *cured without bleeding*, 382.
Plumb *Cake*, 170, 171, 183, —— *with Almonds*, ibid. —— *Little Plumb-cakes*, 165.——— *Plum-porridge*, 29. —— *Wine*, 245.

Plumbs *dry'd*, 219. — *preserved green*, 203, 204.
Pockets, *how made*. 98.
Poison, *Negro* Cæsar's *Cure*, 389—391.
Poloe, *how prepared*, 80.
Pomatum, 306.
Poppy *Brandy*, 263.
Pork, *to chuse*, 1. *to boil*, 13. *to roast*, 18. *Hams like* Westphalia, 90.
Portugal *Cakes*, 172.
Posset, *a Jelly Posset*, 192. *a Snow Posset*, ibid. *Sack Posset without Eggs*, 197. *a Posset with Ale, or King* William's *Posset*, ibid. *the Pope's Posset*, ibid.
Potatoes, *to dress*, 14.
Powder *for a Rupture*, 275.
Poultice *for a sore Breast, Leg, or Arm*, 299.—*for a hard Swelling*, 299.
Preserves. *See the respective Materials*.
Pudding *baked*, 141.—*boiled*, 130.—*stewed*, 133.—*for little Dishes*, 142. *Hasty-Pudding*, ibid. *Orange-Pudding*, 125. *New-College-Pudding*, 143. *Oatmeal Pudding*, ibid. *Ratafia Pudding*, 147. *Sweet-meat Pudding*, 142.
Puddings *of divers Sorts*, 125, &c. *a colouring Liquor for Puddings*. *See* Liquor.
Puff-paste, 165.—*for Tarts*, 154.
Puffs, *of Almonds*, 173.—*Carrots, or Parsnips*, 143.—*of Lemons*, 224.
Pulpatoon *of Pigeons*, 14.
Purges, 286, 317
Purslain *Stalks pickled*, 112. *another Way*, 115.
Putty, *or Paste, to stop all Joints in Pales or Wood, that no Water may soak in* 365.

Q.

Quaking *Pudding*. *See* Pudding.
Quilt *for the Stomach*, 344.
Quinces, *kept in Pickle*, 106. *Quince Cream*, 187. *whole Quinces preserv'd*, 199. *White Jelly of Quinces*, 205. *Red Quince Marmalade*, 232, 233.—*white Quince Paste*, 213.—*Quince Wine*, 243.
Quinsey, *or Swelling in the Throat*, 383.

R.

Rabbets, *to chuse*, 9. — *to roast*, 20. — *and Chickens mumbled*, 44.
Radish *Pods pickled*, 110.
Ragoo, *of Oysters*, 43. — *of Pigs Ears*, 38. — *of Sweetbreads*, 43. *for made Dishes*, 29.
Raisin *Wine*, 239.
Raspberry *Fool*, 195. —— *Wine* 242.
Raspberries *preserved in Jelly*, 200. ——— *preserved whole*, 223.
Ratifia *Bisket*, 196. ——— *Cream*, 188. — *Pudding*, 147.
Rattle-Snake, *Negro* Cæsar's *Cure for the Bite thereof*, 391.
Red *Balls*, 288.
Red *Cabbage pickled*, 113.
Rennet, *prepared*, 99.

Rennet *Bag*, 100.
Rheum *in the Eyes*, *in the Teeth*, 347.
Rheumatiſm, *Dropſy, Scurvy, and Cough of the Lungs cured*, 304. *Simple Rheumatiſm*, 358. *Rheumatiſm or Pain in the Bones*, 277, 279, 381, 383.
Ribs *of Beef pickled*, 93.
Rickets *cured*, 294. — *another Way*, 295.
Roaſting, *Rules to be obſerved in*, 17.
Roſes, *Conſerve of red Roſes*, 218. *Sugar of Roſes*, 219. *Roſe-drops*, 220.
Rue-*Water for Fits of the Mother*, 271.
Rump *of Beef baked*, 83.— *ſtewed*, 32, 46.
Rupture, 275.
Rye bread *Pudding*, 140.

S.

Sack-*Cream*, 188, 195.— *Poſſet without Eggs*, 197. *without Cream or Eggs*, ib. *Oatmeal Sack-poſſet*, 198. *Sack Pudding baked.*
Saffron *Cordial*, 265.
Sage *Wine*, 247.
Sagoe *prepared*, 375.
Salmon *potted*, 76.—*pickled*, 114.
Salop, *how made*, 194.
Salve, *for a Blaſt, Burn, or Scald*, 299, 334. *for the King's Evil*, 328.—*for a Sprain*, 306. *Angel Salve*, 360. *The black Salve*, 332. *Green Salve*, 334. *Lip Salve*, 349.
Samphire, *pickled*, 107.
Sauce *for Fiſh, or Fleſh*, 124. *of fry'd Cucumbers for Mutton*, 65. *for a Woodcock*, ibid.
Sauſages, *very fine*, 90.
Scald *Head cured*, 326. *an Ointment for it*, 359.
Sciatica, *Plaiſter for it*, 328.
Scotch *Collops*, 45. *other Ways*, 48, 60, 90.
Scurvy, *ſome excellent Medicines to cure it*, 304, 309, 330.—*in the Gums*, 350.
Seed - *Cake*, 170. *another*, 171. *Ordinary Seed-Cake*, 179. *A good Seed-Cake, call'd Nun's Cake*, 184. *Another Seed-Cake*, ibid.
Shortneſs *of Breath*, 303.
Shrewſbury *Cakes*, 177.
Shrub, *how made*, 240.
Sight; *to ſtrengthen it*, 271. *a Powder that hath reſtored it when almoſt loſt*, 311.
Skirret *Pye*, 161.
Skuets, *how made*, 79.
Small-pox; *to prevent their Pitting, and take off Redneſs*, 283. *to take out their Spots*, 307 —*Redneſs and Scurf after them*, 361. *A Stay to prevent a ſore Throat*, 282.
Smelts, *kept in Jelly*, 89.—*marinated*, 118.
Snail-*Water*, 273.
Snipe, *to chuſe*, 8.
Snow-*Poſſet*, 192.
Soop, 26, 27, 86. *A Gravy-Soop*, 27.—*a Soop or Pottage of Aſparagus*, 89. —*of Craw-fiſh*, 27, 94.—*of green Peas*, 88, 93. *Soop for faſting Days*, 21.
Sparrows, *or Squab Pigeons, pickled*, 105.

Spinage,

Spinage. *to dress*, 14. *Tart*, 161.
Spirit *of Carraways*, 262. *of Saffron*, 265.
Spitting *of Blood, if a Vein is broken*, 300, 307.
Spleen *and Vapours cured*, 262.
Sprain, 306.
Sprats, *pickled for Anchovies*, 105.
Spread-*Eagle Pudding*, 146.
Stakes, *to broil*, 23.
Stew'd *Pudding. See* Pudding.
Stitch *Water*, 264.
Stomach; *Electuary for a Cold, or windy Stomach*, 289. *Some excellent Medicines for Pains in the Stomach*, 281, 290. *Plaister for the Stomach*, 344. *A Quilt for it*, ibid.
Stone; *to make the Lime-drink for the Stone*, 286. *To give Ease in a violent Fit*, 313. *Lady* Onslow's *Water for it*, 268. *Mrs.* Stephen's *Medicines for it*, 378.
Stoughton's *Elixir*, 280.
Strangury, 313.
Strawberry *Fool*, 195.
Strong *Broth*, 94.
Sugar-*Plates*, 203. *Clear Sugar*, ibid. *brown Sugar*, 215. *Sugar of Roses*, 219.
Surfeit-*Water, of King* Charles II. 260.—*of Mr.* Denzil Onslow, 278.
Swan *potted*, 72.
Sweet *Bag for Linen*, 235.
Sweetmeat *Pudding*, 142.
Swelling in the Face, 336.
Syllabubs *whipt*, 190.—*Lemon Syllabubs*, 194. —*other fine Syllabubs*, 198.
Syrups, 198, &c.
Syrup *of any Flower*, 215. —*for a Cough or Asthma*, 292.—*of Marsh-mallows*, 291.—*of Saffron*, 292.

T.

Tansey, *baked*, 45, 138. *Apple Tansey*, 140. *Gooseberry Tansey*, 138.
Tarts, *of Oranges or Lemons*, 153. *Puff-paste for Tarts*, 154. *to ice Tarts*, 166.
Tea-*Caudle*, 193.
Teeth, 310. *to preserve and whiten them*, 349.
Tetter, 310.
Thorn *drawn out*, 326.
Throat, *sore* 336 *to prevent a sore Throat in the Small-pox*, 282
Thrush, *in Childrens Mouths*, 362.
Tincture *of Ambergrease*, 259. *An admirable Tincture for green Wounds*, 298.
Toasts *fried*, 139.
Tongues *to boil*, 13. *to roast*, 20. *potted*, 58. *dried*, 74. *Pickle for them*, 91.
Tooth-*ach cured*, 276, 301, 302.
Treacle *Water*, 277.
Trembling *at the Heart*, 326.
Tumours, *to ripen them*, 310. *to disperse them*, 335.
Turbot *Pye*, 161.
Tureiner, *how made*, 147.
Turneps, *to dress*, 15.
Turkey, *to chuse*, 6. *to roast*, 22. *Pye*, 40. Stew'd 83.
Turtle, *to dress*, 389.

U. Ulcers

U.

Ulcers *and old Sores*, 333.
Urine, *to promote it presently, when stopt*, 362.
Usquebaugh, *how made*, 277.
Uvula, *to draw it up*, 362.
Vapours, *cured*, 262.
Varnish, *white and yellow*, 366.
Veal, *to chuse*, 4. *to roast*, 19. *Pye*, 40. *Cutlets*, 84. *Savoury Dish of Veal*, 67. *Fricasee*, 48
Venison, *to chuse*, 3. *to roast*. 20. *Sauce for*, 25. *artificial*, 60. *to recover it, when it stinks*. 61.
Venereal *Disease*, 323
Venison-*Pasty*. 134. *to season and bake it*. 154. *to stew it*, 33.
Verjuice, *distilled for Pickles*, 123.
Vomits; *some excellent Vomits* 286, 322, 358, 359
Vomiting, *outward Applications to stay it*, 299, 310. *internal Remedy for it*, 301.

W.

Walnut-*water*, 260.
Walnuts, *pickled divers ways*, 104. 107, 117, *preserved all the Year*, 290.
Wash *for the Face*, 343.
Washing, *to save Soap, and whiten Cloaths*, 369.
Water, *for sore or weak Eyes*, 397.—*to wash the Face*, 343.—*to be taken after Balsam of* Tolu, 274.—*against a Consumption*, 270.—*to strengthen the Sight*, 271.—*in a Consumption, or Weakness after Sickness*, 282.—*a fine Cordial - Water*, 262. *Great Palsey Water*, 255. *Lady* Allen's *Water*, 257. *Lady* Hewett's *Water*, 256. *Orange or Lemon-Water*, 259.—*Dr.* Stevens's *Water*, 258. — *a Stone Water*, 263.
Weakness *of the Back*, 315, 363.—*of the Hands, after a Palsy*, 323.
Westphalia *Bacon*, 73.
Whetstone *Cakes*, 182.
White *Leach*, 195.
White-wine *Cream*, ibid.
Wigs, 174. *light Wigs*, 165. *very good Wigs*, 167.
Wine *how to clear it*, 248. *Apricock-wine*, 236. *Barley - wine*, 244. *Birch-wine*, 240. *Cherry-wine*, 238. *Clary-wine*, 247, 251. *Cowslip-wine*, 241. *Currant-wine*, 250, 252. *Damson-wine*, 236. *Elder - wine*, 244, 246. *Frontiniac - wine*, 250. *Gooseberry - wine*, 236, 250. *Lemon - wine*, 243. *Morella Cherry - wine*, 242. *Orange-wine*, 240. — *with Raisins*, 249. *Pearl Gooseberry - wine*, 237. *Plumb - wine*, 245. *Quince-wine*, 243. *Raisin-wine*, 239. *Raspberry-wine*, 242. *Sage - wine*, 247. *To recover Wine*, 248.
Woodcocks, *to chuse*, 8. *to roast*, 21. *Sauce*, 65.
Worms *in Children*; *how to know them*, 300. *Clyster for them*, 341. *Worms cured*, 337. *Plaister for them*, 344.

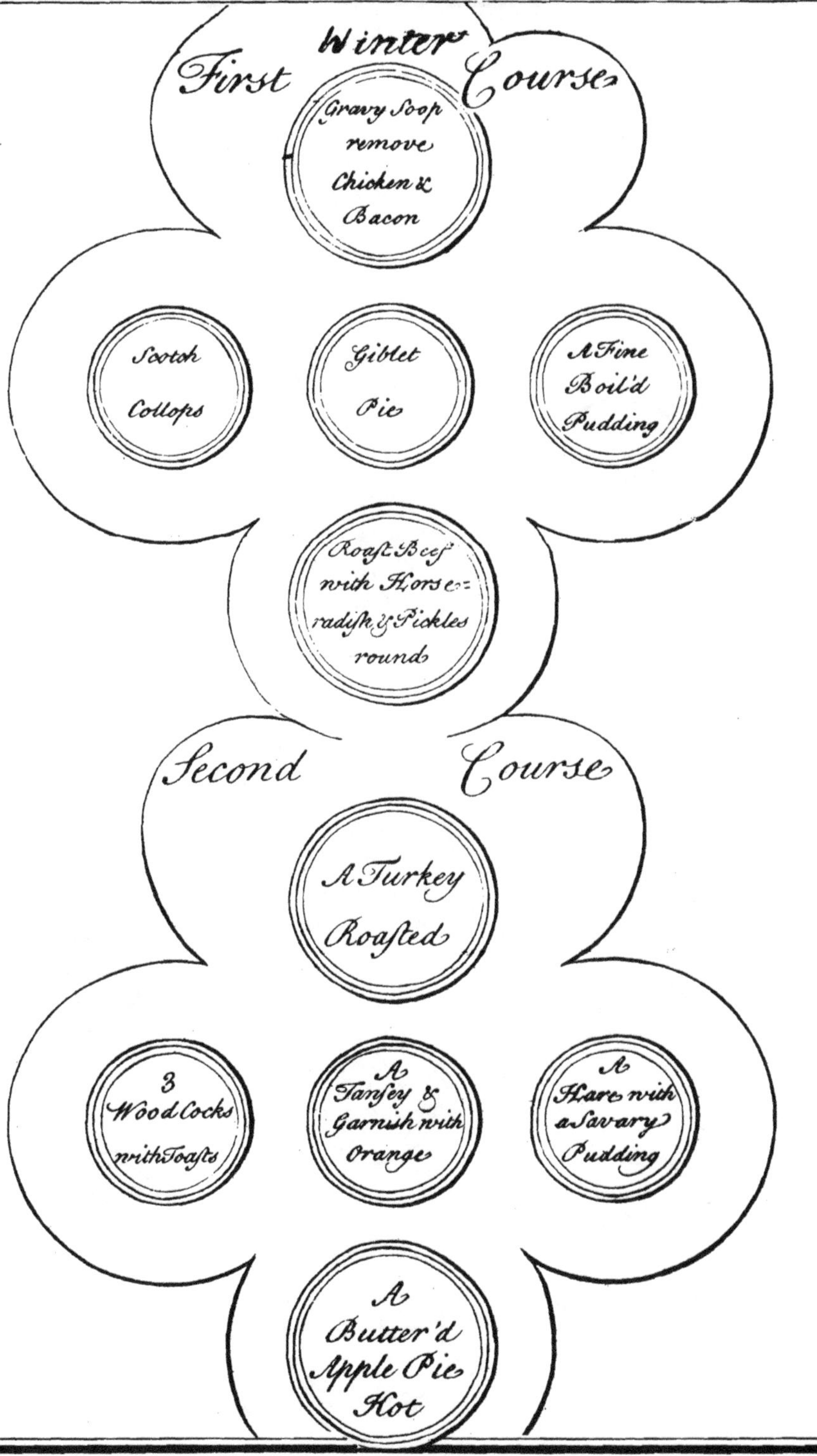
Winter
First Course
Gravy Soop remove Chicken & Bacon
Scotch Collops
Giblet Pie
A Fine Boil'd Pudding
Roast Beef with Horse=radish & Pickles round
Second Course
A Turkey Roasted
3 Wood Cocks with Toasts
A Tansey & Garnish with Orange
A Hare with a Savary Pudding
A Butter'd Apple Pie Hot

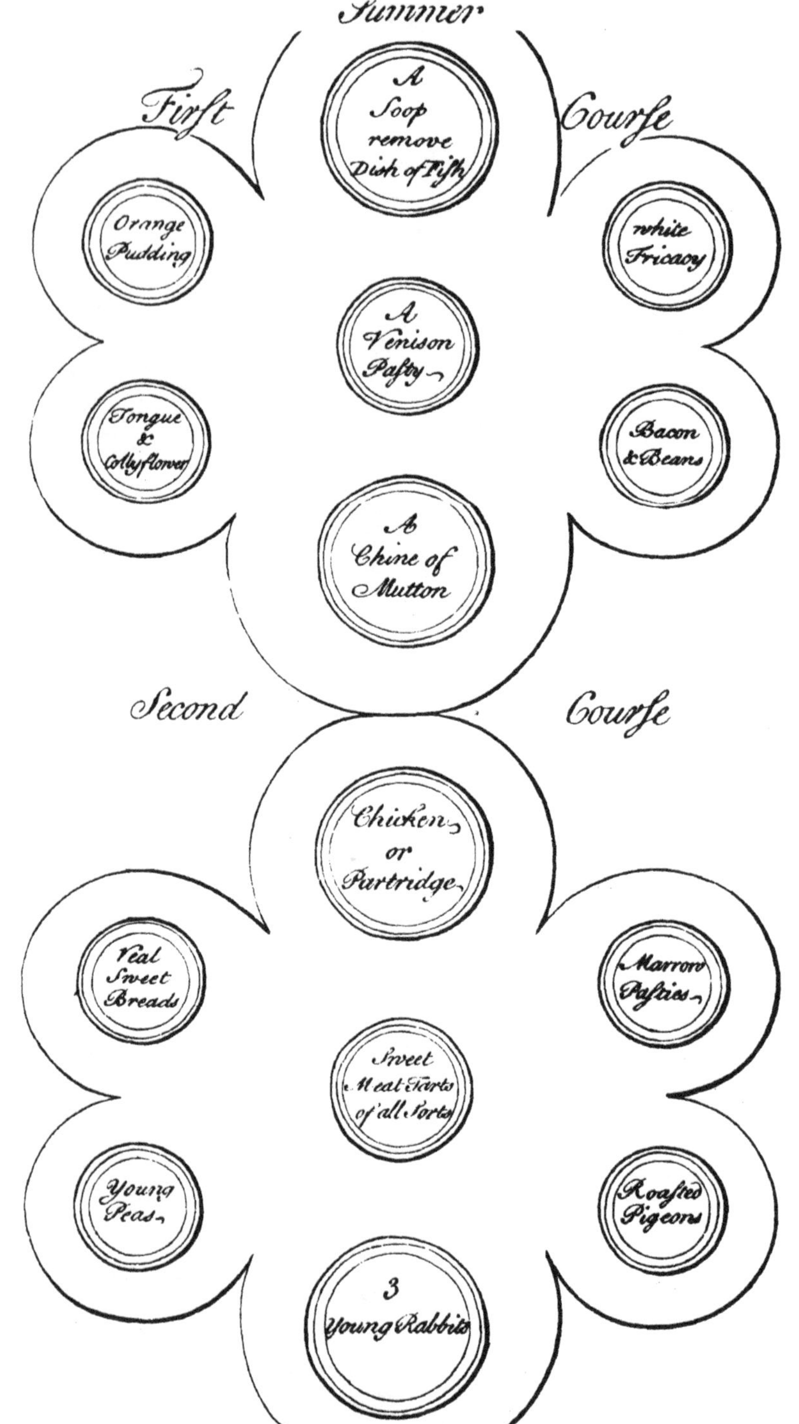
Summer
First
Course
A
Soop
remove
Dish of Fish
Orange
Pudding
white
Fricacy
A
Venison
Pasty
Tongue
&
Collyflower
Bacon
& Beans
A
Chine of
Mutton
Second
Course
Chicken
or
Partridge
Veal
Sweet
Breads
Marrow
Pasties
Sweet
Meat Tarts
of all Sorts
Young
Peas
Roasted
Pigeons
3
Young Rabbits

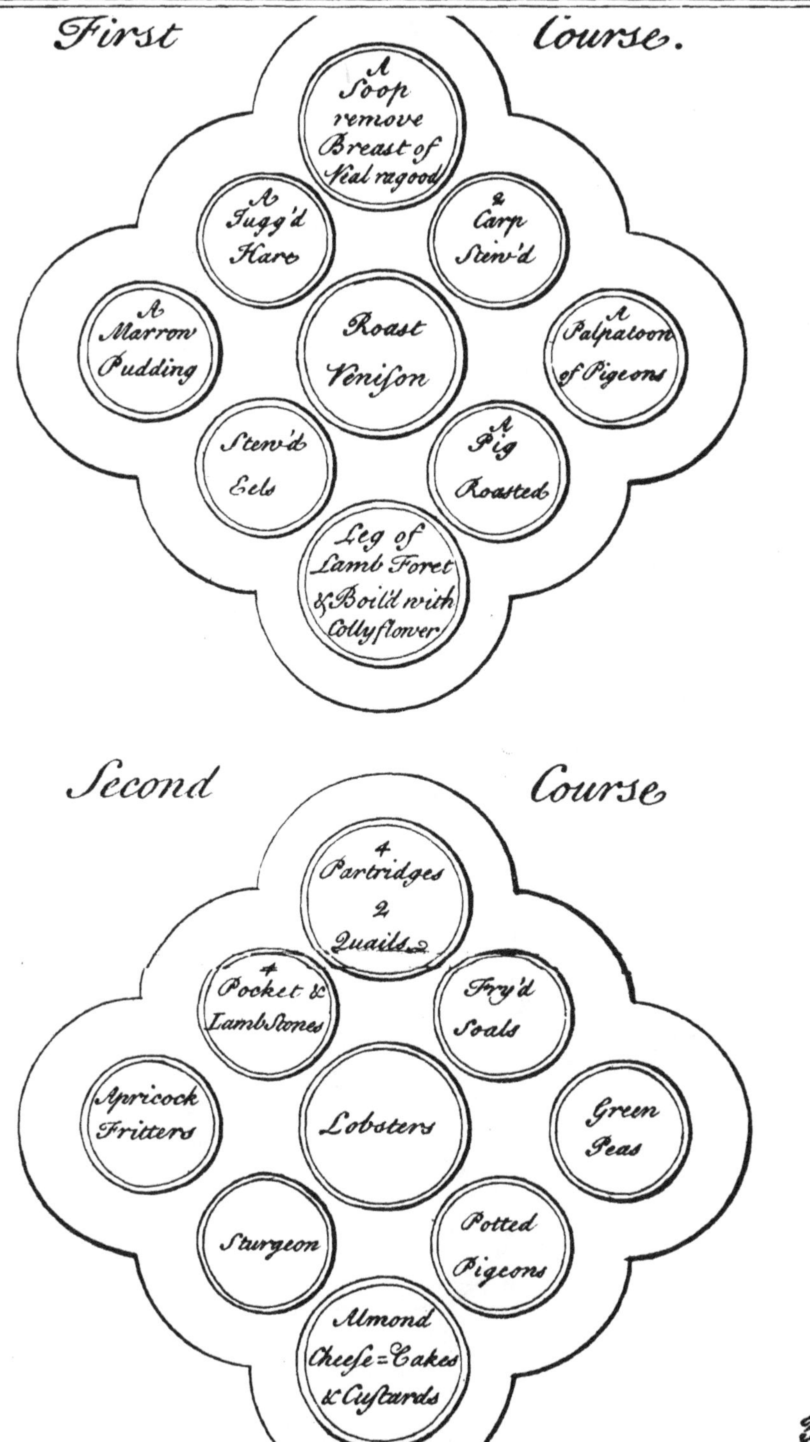
First Course.
A Soop remove Breast of Veal ragood
A Jugg'd Hare
2 Carp Stew'd
A Marrow Pudding
Roast Venison
A Palpatoon of Pigeons
Stew'd Eels
A Pig Roasted
Leg of Lamb Foret & Boil'd with Collyflower
Second Course
4 Partridges 2 Quails
4 Pocket & Lamb Stones
Fry'd Soals
Apricock Fritters
Lobsters
Green Peas
Sturgeon
Potted Pigeons
Almond Cheese=Cakes & Custards

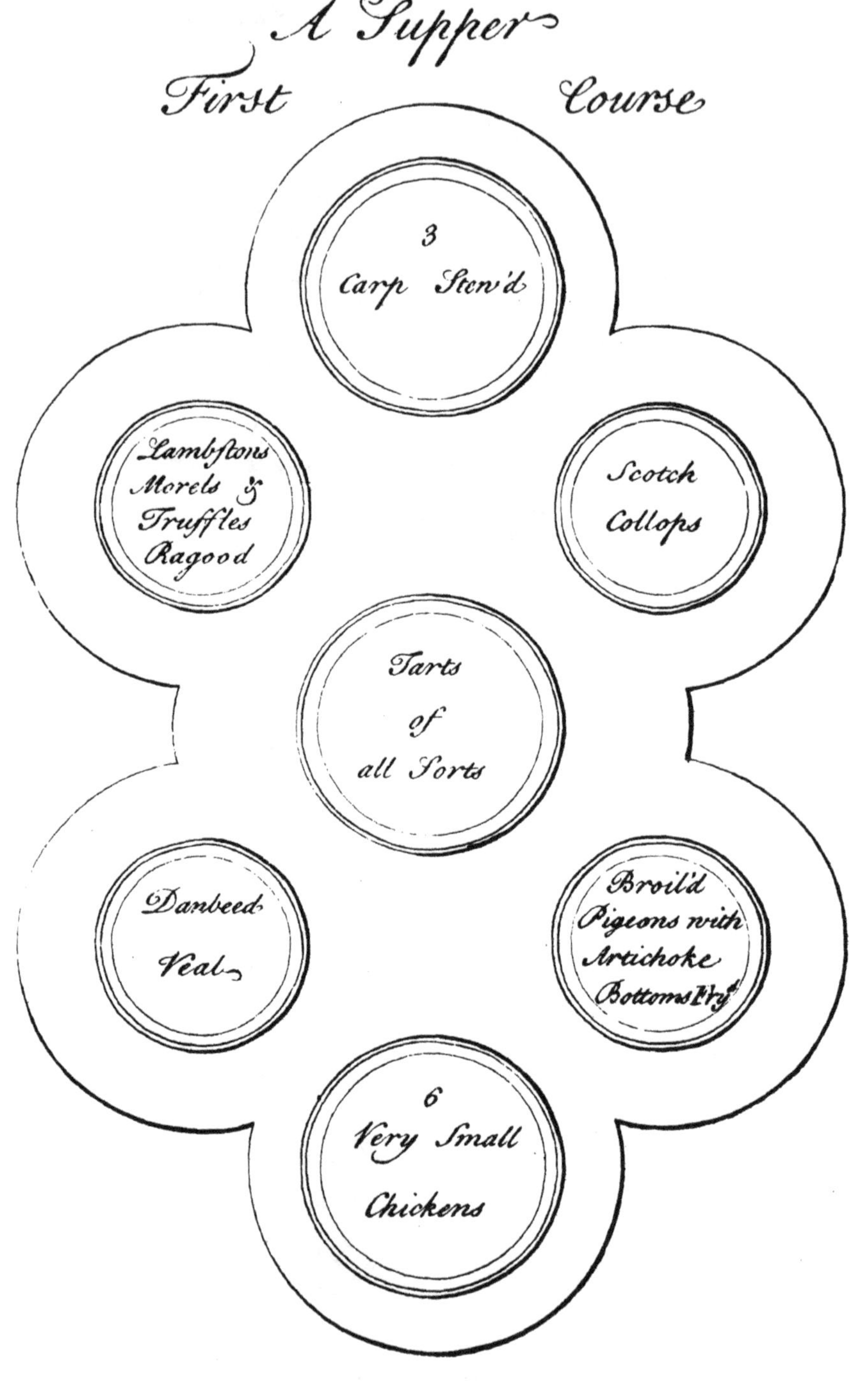
A Supper
First Course
3
Carp Stew'd
Lambstons
Morels &
Truffles
Ragood
Scotch
Collops
Tarts
of
all Sorts
Danbeed
Veal
Broil'd
Pigeons with
Artichoke
Bottoms Fryd
6
Very Small
Chickens

www.ingramcontent.com/pod-product-compliance
Lightning Source LLC
Chambersburg PA
CBHW020351100426
42812CB00001B/22

* 9 7 8 1 4 4 4 6 5 2 3 9 0 *